FIFTY YEARS A
JOURNALIST

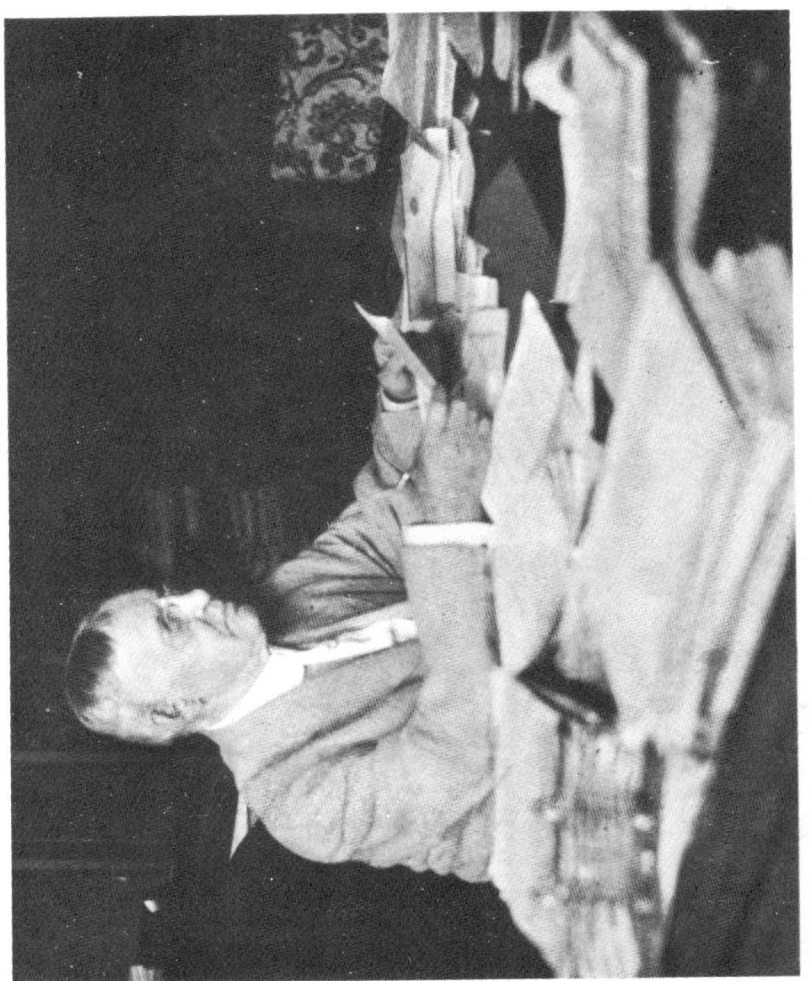

The Author at His Desk

FIFTY YEARS A JOURNALIST

BY
MELVILLE E. STONE

HALF-TONE ILLUSTRATIONS
FROM PHOTOGRAPHS

LINE CUTS BY PAUL BROWN

BOOKS FOR LIBRARIES PRESS
FREEPORT, NEW YORK

First Published 1921
Reprinted 1970

STANDARD BOOK NUMBER:
8369-5447-5

LIBRARY OF CONGRESS CATALOG CARD NUMBER:
76-124259

PRINTED IN THE UNITED STATES OF AMERICA

PRETEXT

It seems to me that no right-minded person can enjoy the business of writing of himself, but the life of a journalist is spent in observing and recording the actions of other men, usually of greater men and perhaps more interesting men than himself, and the journalist who writes of his own life, and of the things that have interested him in that life, necessarily paints a picture of the period of his active days on earth.

De Blowitz, the famous correspondent of the London *Times*, who, in his day, played a greater part in the world's affairs than most statesmen of the time, wrote his memoirs and directed their publication on the ground that "it was unjust that the journalist, unlike other writers, left nothing behind him as a lasting testimonial of his efforts, his work, and his success." The dignity of the editorial office justifies a more prominent record than most editors have left behind them. Bonaparte said of governments that power was founded upon public opinion, and this maxim was never more true than in our own country. I hold the profession of journalism to be one of the highest. In none should the individual feel a greater sense of responsibility to his public, and in no other calling is there a larger field of opportunity for public service.

It would be presuming to say that even as a rule editors are profound, or that they are exceptionally brilliant intellectually. The average and perhaps the best journalistic mind is not consecutive, but rather likely to be discursive. Wherefore, it may not be said that newspaper reading is the best reading, nor that the education derived from the newspaper is the best education, nor, above all, that the newspaper should supplant the school. Newspaper reading tends to superficiality, and the American citizen is superficial. As T. P. O'Connor once said when I asked him for a final judgment upon our people: "They are the best half-educated lot in the world." Newspaper reading is a mania with us.

By reason of his opportunities, an editor is able to pry into the whys and wherefores of many "enterprises of great pith and moment." And in some degree the work has a distinctly permanent value. Out of its abstract and brief chronicle of the day is created a reservoir of fact from which the wise historian might well draw his interpretations and deductions, if he would.

Herbert Spencer, in his work on "The Philosophy of Style," calls attention to a common weakness on the part of those who write our histories. He says: "A modern newspaper statement, though probably true, if quoted as testimony would be laughed at, but the letter of a court gossip written some centuries ago is thought good historical evidence."

And so, having passed man's allotment of three-score and ten, I am to tell a newspaperman's tale.

The fates seem to have set some curious milestones along my pathway at ten-year intervals. For instance, in 1848, the great revolutionary year, I was born. In that year also the first Associated Press was organized. In 1858, I learned to set type. In that year also the first successful Atlantic cable was laid. In 1868, I first began the publication of a newspaper. In 1878, I became a member of the Associated Press, representing the Chicago *Daily News* which I had founded. In 1888, I retired from journalism, as I supposed, permanently. In 1898, having become executive officer of the Associated Press, and having won a contest for supremacy, of four years' duration, I set out on a campaign to extend its foreign service and make it a world-covering institution. In 1908, I entered upon the most eventful ten years of my life. In 1918, having served the Association a quarter of a century, I withdrew from immediate control of its activities.

CONTENTS

FIRST DECADE

	PAGE
THE YEAR OF MY BIRTH	1
THE STATE OF ILLINOIS	3
THE TOWN OF HUDSON	4
MY FAMILY	5
MY CHILDHOOD DAYS	11
AT NAUVOO	14
THE UNDERGROUND RAILWAY	16

SECOND DECADE

THE YEAR 1858	22
MR. LINCOLN'S ELECTION	25
BOYHOOD IN CHICAGO	27

THIRD DECADE

ELECTION OF GENERAL GRANT	31
THE GREAT CHICAGO FIRE	34
IN DAILY JOURNALISM	36
MEETING WITH ITO	37
THE CASE OF BARON DE PALM	39
A TOUR OF THE SOUTH	42
AS A WASHINGTON CORRESPONDENT	44
FOUNDING A DAILY PAPER	50
CREATING 99-CENT STORES	60
ENTER VICTOR F. LAWSON	62
STORY OF "ROSS RAYMOND"	65
DICK LANE, MY BURGLAR FRIEND	71
THE CASE OF JUDGE BLODGETT	74
DETECTIVE JOURNALISM—THE SPENCER CASE	77

CONTENTS

FOURTH DECADE

	PAGE
A Tour in Europe	83
Meeting Gambetta and Clemenceau	90
More Detective Journalism	92
The Campaign of 1880	97
What I Knew About Grant	101
Founding the "Morning News"	107
How to Edit News	109
Origin of a Famous Phrase	116
Acquaintance with Diaz	118
An Invitation from New York	121
Founding the First Mail Train	124
Days with Eugene Field	125
Correcting Some False Ideas	132
The Puritan Strain	133
Practical Jokes	134
Emory Storrs and His Tailor	141
The Campaign of 1884	143
"Not for Forty Nominations!"	149
The Famous Mackin Case	157
The Case of McGarigle	163
Organizing the Linotype Company	165
Convicting the Chicago Anarchists	166
Warfare in Earnest	170
Words Can Kill	171
Hunting Down the Guilty	172
Tense Days	175
Punishing Corrupt Public Officials	177
Retiring from Journalism	179

FIFTH DECADE

A Sentimental Journey	183
Days with Andrew D. White	189
The Diedrichs Affair	190
Banking and Other Activities	194
Visit of W. T. Stead	200
Evolution of News Gathering	204

CONTENTS

	PAGE
THE FIRST ASSOCIATED PRESS	207
A MASTERPIECE OF REPORTING	211
THE CAMPAIGN OF 1896	218
COLLAPSE OF THE UNITED PRESS	223
A PRINCELY OFFER	227
REPORTING THE SPANISH WAR	228
LEONARD WOOD'S PROTÉGÉ	230
A RASCAL NAMED SMITH	232

SIXTH DECADE

FORMING A NEW ASSOCIATED PRESS	235
WIRELESS TELEGRAPHY	239
THE ASSASSINATION OF PRESIDENT MCKINLEY	240
PRINCE HENRY'S VISIT	241
THE MARTINIQUE DISASTER	241
EXTENSION OF THE FOREIGN SERVICE OF THE ASSOCIATED PRESS	243
AUDIENCE OF THE ITALIAN KING	248
AUDIENCE OF POPE LEO XIII	250
DINNER WITH THE KAISER	252
THE DEATH OF POPE LEO XIII	258
THE REMOVAL OF THE RUSSIAN CENSORSHIP ON FOREIGN NEWS	261
THE RUSSO-JAPANESE WAR	278
THE QUALITIES NEEDED IN A WAR CORRESPONDENT	282
THE PORTSMOUTH CONFERENCE	284
THE CASE OF LAGERKRANZ	296

SEVENTH DECADE

GENESIS OF THE WORLD WAR	299
DISCOVERY OF THE NORTH POLE	301
AN ENGLISH PANIC	302
DAYS IN PARIS	303
THE GERMAN SITUATION	304
VISITING ASIA	307
SELECTING AN ASSOCIATE	309
THE WORLD WAR	309
LACK OF PREPAREDNESS	310

CONTENTS

	PAGE
REPORTING THE WAR	317
CASE OF CARDINAL MERCIER	318
CASE OF THE "LUSITANIA"	319
DOCTOR DEPAGE'S HOSPITAL	323
AMERICA IN THE WAR	325
THE MEMORABLE YEAR 1918	329
A FINE FUNERAL	330
CREEL COMMITTEE	342
GREETINGS ABROAD	345
THE ASSOCIATED PRESS OF TO-DAY	361
PRESIDENTIAL YEARS	365
OUR CRITICS	367

LIST OF HALFTONE ILLUSTRATIONS

The Author at His Desk . . . . *Frontispiece*

	FACING PAGE
"Five Oaks," the Cottage in Which I Was Born	4
My Father	20
My Mother	21
A Dedication from Eugene Field	132
President Arthur	133
President McKinley	148
Mr. Kaneko	149
President Roosevelt	276
Prince William of Sweden	277
Lord Northcliffe	292
President Taft	293
President Wilson	324
The Hero of the Battle of the Marne	325
Georges Clemenceau	340
Marshal Foch	341

LIST OF TEXT ILLUSTRATIONS

	PAGE
Rev. James Creighton	7
Rev. William Maine Fox	7
Prof. Ormond Stone	10
Nauvoo Mormon Temple	15
Carthage Jail	16
The Author at Eight Years	17
Facsimile of Letterhead, 1868	32
The Author as an Iron Founder	33
Colonel Forrest	37
Ito in 1872	38
Colonel E. W. Halford	39
"Lola Montez"	40
Henry W. Grady	44
Victor F. Lawson in 1876	62
Melville E. Stone in 1876	62
John J. Flinn	63
"Rose Raymond"	65
Dick Lane	71
William H. Crane	83
Charles Stewart Parnell	85
John Dillon	88
John Ballantyne	108
Joseph Hatton	108
William E. Curtis	108
F. W. Reilly	110
W. S. B. Matthews	111

LIST OF TEXT ILLUSTRATIONS

	PAGE
Colonel Harvey	112
Slason Thompson	112
"Bill" Nye	112
George Ade	112
John T. McCutcheon	113
Senibodi in the *Daily News* Office	114
President Diaz	119
William H. Smith Letter	122
Matthew Arnold's Cable	124
Eugene Field by Himself	127
Mr. Field Reading His Beautiful Poem	131
Eugene Field at Work	133
Inscription in a Book by Eugene Field	135
Field Bursts Into Song	136
A Field Appreciation	138
Casey's of Table d'Hôte Fame	139
Field Invites Himself to My Country Home	139
Appeal for a Small Loan	140
Lord Coleridge	141
Grover Cleveland	155
Joseph C. Mackin	157
Julius S. Grinnell	173
Albert R. Parsons	176
J. J. Knickerbocker	184
Baron Richtofen	190
W. T. Stead	200
D. H. Craig	207
Gerard Hallock	207
Alexander Jones	207
J. W. Simonton	209
William Henry Smith	210
Letter from William McKinley	224

xiv   LIST OF TEXT ILLUSTRATIONS

	PAGE
Letter from William Jennings Bryan	225
Joseph Pulitzer	227
"Major Bellairs"	230
The Rascal Smith	232
Prince Henry	241
Facsimile of Kaiser's Cable	242
"Command" to Audience of the Kaiser	266
Admiral Peary's Telegram	301
Frederick Roy Martin	309
Cardinal Mercier	319
Herbert Stuart Stone	323
Melville E. Stone, Jr.	323
Victor F. Lawson	333
Frank B. Noyes	334
Adolph S. Ochs	340
Dinner of the British Press	345

FIFTY YEARS A
JOURNALIST

FIFTY YEARS A JOURNALIST

FIRST DECADE

The Year of My Birth

I WAS born at Hudson, Illinois, on August 22, 1848.
    The year 1848 was an interesting one. If the period of one's nativity has anything to do with his career, it was a good year for a journalist to be born in. All Europe was ablaze with revolutionary fires. Louis Philippe was dethroned in Paris; another Louis abdicated in Bavaria; Ferdinand of Austria, under compulsion, handed over his sceptre to his son Francis Joseph, whose long reign ended in death at the moment of the complete downfall of his empire in the great World War. There were revolutionary uprisings in all the German states, in Hungary, and in Italy. Great Britain was not free, for while the year saw the close of the Chartist outbreak in England, its principles survived and finally became incorporated into law; and the young Ireland rebellion was on in Ireland. Switzerland ceased her internecine contest and adopted her republican constitution. Garibaldi, Kossuth, Gladstone, Disraeli, were achieving things on the European stage.
    Abraham Lincoln was serving his first term in our Federal Congress, and Stephen A. Douglas his first term in the Senate. The Free-Soil party was organized and the Slavery question became the national political issue in the United States. On February 2nd of the year peace was signed with Mexico, and we took over the Southwest Territory which ultimately developed into the great and prosperous states of California, Oklahoma, New Mexico, and Arizona. The acquisition of this

territory inspired two revolutions in the United States. Whether or not human slavery should be permitted in this new area became a bone of contention, and no settlement of the right of Congress to forbid human bondage in the territories was reached until the Civil War of 1861.

Also the question was revived of the relation of gold and silver in our monetary system. It had been thought to have been arranged by Congress in 1834, when an ounce of gold was declared to be equal to sixteen ounces of silver. This law was ultimately found to be no more effective than King Canute's mandate forbidding the sea to advance. Nine days before the signing of the Mexican peace treaty gold was discovered at Sutter's mill race in Coloma, California. The output of the precious metal was so great that the ratio of sixteen to one could not be maintained. An immutable economic law had been declared three centuries before that no statutory enactment could annul. It had been announced by Sir Thomas Gresham of England, and even before him, by Copernicus and others. It declared that any cheap money circulated in a country would drive a dearer money out of use. This question, the issue over a double monetary standard, called bi-metallism, thus begun in 1848, continued to trouble the nation until the defeat of Mr. Bryan in the Presidential election of 1896.

The lamp of liberty which had been lighted in 1793 and which had flickered out in Europe after Waterloo was relighted.

Inspired by the year, Tennyson wrote Aubrey de Vere that he would publish "In Memoriam." It had grown from time to time after Arthur Hallam's death in 1833. It was the greatest verse of his century, and voiced the spirit of 1848:

> Ring out the old, ring in the new,
>   Ring, happy bells, across the snow;
>   The year is going, let him go;
> Ring out the false, ring in the true.
>
> Ring out the grief that saps the mind,
>   For those that here we see no more;
>   Ring out the feud of rich and poor,
> Ring in redress for all mankind.

> Ring out a slowly dying cause,
>   And ancient forms of party strife;
>   Ring in the nobler modes of life,
> With sweeter manners, purer laws.

The year 1848 was the dawn of a new day.

The State of Illinois

The section of the country in which I first saw the light was what the militarists would call a strategic state. There is a singularly interesting historical note illustrative of this. Back in the days before the formation of the Republic and the adoption of the Federal Constitution, the Colonial Congress adopted what has been well called the "immortal ordinance of 1787" for the governance of the "Northwest Territory," i.e.: the country lying west and north of the Ohio River and east of the Mississippi. The fifth article of this ordinance provided that there should be "formed in the said Territory not less than three, nor more than five states"; that the most western state should have its northern boundary at a line drawn east and west through the "southern bend, or extremity of Lake Michigan," or should extend to the Canadian frontier on Lake Superior. This meant that this "northern line" should divide Illinois from Wisconsin, if the area involved should contain two states and not one.

But thirty years later a very wise man represented this part of the country as a delegate from the Territory of Illinois in the Congress of the United States. It was one Nathaniel Pope, and he had ideas of his own. In January, 1818, he received a petition from the legislature of his territory praying for admission into the Union as a state. This petition he presented to Congress, and he was instructed to prepare and report a bill to deal with the matter. Disregarding wholly the plan of the "immortal ordinance," he fixed the northern boundary of the new State of Illinois at 42° 30′ north latitude, some forty miles north of the "southern bend of Lake Michigan." In explanation of this change he argued that all republics were in danger of dissolution. In that day practically all transportation was by water, and all of the streams and rivers of Illinois below the parallel of the "southern bend of Lake Michigan" flowed south. Therefore, said Judge Pope, if trouble should arise between the North and the South, Illinois would become, by her commercial interest, joined to a southern confederacy of states. But if Congress should go forty miles farther north, as he proposed, for a northern boundary of the new state, they would cross a watershed and join to the state waters which flowed into the Great Lakes and out through the St. Lawrence River. And thus Illinois would have an interest binding her to the northern as well as to the southern portion of the Union, and could never consent to a dissolution of the Republic.

Upon this issue Judge Pope won.

When one remembers that in the hour in which a division of the Union was attempted this state furnished to the contest Mr. Lincoln and General Grant, the prevision of Judge Pope seems dramatic.

The Town of Hudson

Hudson, my birthplace, was and is a village nine miles north of Bloomington, Illinois. The house in which I was born is still standing. It is known as "Five Oaks," and is the home of Thomas Stevenson, brother of the former Vice-President of the United States. It takes its name from five massive trees which have grown from acorns planted many years ago by Mrs. Stevenson's father. The house was built in 1837, and in some ways bears evidence of its age. One section was set apart for my father and his family.

Hudson was also the birthplace of Elbert Hubbard, famed as the editor of the *Philistine*. His father was the village doctor. I met Elbert twice—first at Grand Rapids on the evening of June 11, 1911, when, at a banquet, we were both to speak. The "function" took place in the opera house. The speakers' table was arranged at the back of the footlights on the stage, and the other diners were placed at tables on the floor of the auditorium. As we began I noted the absence of one of the speakers. Two or three courses had been served, when I saw a curiously garbed

"Five Oaks," the Cottage in which I was Born on August 22nd, 1848, at Hudson, Illinois

citizen enter the front door and come stalking through the crowd. There was no mistaking his identity. He wore an ordinary dress coat, a coloured waistcoat, and gray trousers, with tan shoes and a flowing black tie, such as Parisian artists affect. He came on the stage and stopped at the back of my chair, tapped me on the shoulder, and greeted me with: "Hello, Melville, how are you?" And not to be outdone, I replied to the stranger: "Glad to see you, Fra Elbertus." Later in the evening we had an opportunity to become acquainted.

Then on May 1, 1915, as I was leaving the *Lusitania*, which was about to sail on her final, fatal trip, at the foot of the gangplank I encountered Hubbard and his wife. We chatted for a moment. We spoke of the threatening advertisement in the morning papers, cautioning people against taking passage on the ship. "Well, if they sink her," laughed Hubbard, "I will have a chance some day to meet the Kaiser in hell." And with that we parted, at this our second and last meeting. Hubbard and his wife perished when the ship went down.

Another curious character from Hudson was "Buffalo Jones," a quaint Illinois farmer who, accompanied by two cowboys, went out to East Africa and captured with the lasso all sorts of wild animals—such as gave attractiveness to the stories of Winston Churchill and Theodore Roosevelt. On his invitation I heard him lecture in New York one night. He had taken moving pictures of his expedition, and the audience roared with laughter as they saw him seize an untamed lioness, such as challenged the prowess of the great Nimrods, pull her by the tail into focus for the camera, and cuff her about as if she had been a lazy cow. He seemed to have encountered none of the dangers nor to have experienced any of the thrilling episodes of which we had read so much. For him the "desert and the vasty wilds" had no terrors; rhinos, hippos, and even swish-tail lions, were simple playthings. His *sifari* was little more than two cowboys, a few natives, and his ropes.

My Family

My family was of English stock. The first of the name of whom we are acquaint was one Walter atte Stone, who lived at Great Bromley, Essex, England, in 1320, before the days of Chaucer and Wickliffe. The name is supposed to mean Walter at the Stone, indicating the site of his home. Ten generations later, one "Husbandman Symon Stone," aged 50, with his wife Joan, and five children, "imbarqued in ye shippe INCREASE, 15th April, 1635, having taken the oathes of Allegiance," for New England. Ninth in succession from this immigrant was my father.

My father's mother was a Fordyce, one of the family which produced Samuel Fordyce, a well-known railroad builder of St. Louis.

My mother's father was a Creighton, of a lowland Scottish line, well known in Dumfries. In the St. Michael's churchyard, close to the tomb of Robert Burns, lie the bodies of many members of the family. A branch went to Ireland at the time of the Cromwellian Invasion and settled in the County Fermanagh.

My mother's mother was Matilda Fox, of the ancient Fox Sept of Kilcoursey, in the King's County, Ireland.

It thus appears that the blood in my veins is mingled English, Scottish, and Irish. With a somewhat similar ancestry, Baron Speck von Sternberg was appointed German Ambassador to the United States some years ago. I happened to be in Berlin and gave him a dinner. Responding to the personal toast, he rose and said, "My father was German, my mother Scotch, and I was born in England; that makes me an American."

Malvina Stone, the mother of President Chester A. Arthur, and Mary Bryan Stone, wife of Cyrus W. Field, were of our Stone family.

There were many clergymen, physicians, and journalists among my relatives. When John Wesley organized the Methodists, the Irish Creightons were among his followers. In Mr. Wesley's diary he frequently mentions them. On May 28, 1785, he notes that he preached in Mr. (Robert) Creighton's barn at Cavan, Ireland. This Robert Creighton was my great-grandfather. And his brother was the Rev. James Creighton, coadjutor and most intimate friend of Mr. Wesley. James Creighton, with Charles Wesley, was of the hymn writers of the early Methodist connection. In the picture of Wesley's deathbed, often found in Methodist homes,

Rev. James Creighton

he stands holding the hand of the dying founder of the denomination. He ministered at the City Road Wesleyan Chapel, London, for many years after Wesley's death. My grandfather's first cousins were the Rev. Doctor William Creighton Dandy, an eminent Methodist clergyman of Chicago, and Mrs. John Milton Phillips, wife of a well-known Methodist divine of Cincinnati. My father, the Rev. Elijah Stone, was a well-known Methodist minister of Illinois. His uncle was the Rev. Isaac Stone (Methodist) of northern New York, and his brother, the Rev. David Stone (Methodist) of Minnesota. Of the Fox clan, the Rev. William Maine Fox was a pioneer Methodist preacher of Madison, Wisconsin.

Among the journalists was Emily Crawford, the famous Paris correspondent. She and her husband, George Morland Crawford, were people of note in their day. Crawford and the novelist Thackeray had been friends from early manhood. They were both of Trinity College, Cambridge, roommates at 2, Lamb Court, Inner Temple, studying law; members of the same London clubs, and both turned to journalism rather than the profession of law. As the years went on Thackeray became a partial owner of the London *Daily News* and, upon his suggestion, Crawford was appointed in 1851 resident correspondent for the paper, in Paris. What Thackeray thought of his friend may best be learned from a letter which he wrote to Crawford, who had nursed him through a critical illness in 1849—one which wellnigh left the story of "Pendennis" forever unfinished. The letter was of the book in which Thackeray visualized Crawford

Rev. William Maine Fox

as George Warrington, the friend of Arthur Pendennis. In it he said:

> You will find much to remind you of the old talks in this book. There is something of you in Warrington, but he is not fit to hold a candle to you, for taking you all-round, you are the most genuine fellow that ever strayed from a better world into this. You don't smoke, and he is a confirmed smoker of tobacco. Bordeaux and Port were your favourites at "The Deanery" and "The Garrick" and Warrington is guzzling beer. But he has your honesty, and, like you, couldn't posture if he tried. You had a strong affinity for the Irish. May you some day find an Irish girl to lead you to matrimony. There's no such good wife as a daughter of Erin.

"The Deanery" and "The Garrick" were two well-known clubs of London. The Deanery was in Dean Street, Soho. Among the notables who had made it at least a temporary home were Goldsmith and De Quincey, and Hazlitt and George Morland, the talented but dissipated painter, for whom Crawford was named. It was rather a breeding house of journalists. Thackeray, George Augustus Sala, and Crawford all frequented it. The Garrick was, as it is to-day, a rendezvous for actors and press men.

The Irish wife whom Crawford was to find was Emily, the granddaughter of Amelia Fox Johnstone of Cleveland, Ohio, who was my mother's aunt. When a girl of seventeen, Emily went to Paris to study at the Sorbonne. While yet in her teens she sent some articles to the London *Morning Star*, which so pleased the editor that he appointed her Paris correspondent. Thus she and Crawford met, and in 1864 they were married. Thackeray was not privileged to attend the wedding. He died in 1863.

For twenty-two years, until the death of Crawford in 1885, the couple worked together in a literary partnership seldom likened. They were both journalists of the best type, having wide knowledge of affairs, keen sense of perspective, fine literary style, ceaseless industry, and a vivid appreciation of the responsibilities attaching to the office.

Richard Whiting, in his valuable contribution to the history of British journalism, "My Harvest," says of the twain:

Mrs. Crawford was as important, to put it mildly, as the man who had given her the name by which she was so widely known. She had extraordinary facility with the pen. The sex attributes of mind, as commonly generalized, seemed to have changed; hers was the will behind the instrument, the address, the energy to face the world. Under growing infirmities, his part declined to the practice of the domestic virtues. He was a dignified person who had been a good hand in his day, but that day was gone; and since he could no longer fill the part of the new man of the period, it was filled for him in their common interest by his partner, as the new woman. For the *Daily News* she wrote one kind of a political letter befitting the gravity of the subject, and for *Truth* quite another, a perfect storehouse of the anecdote of the day as it bore on the drama of public life. She knew all the leading men, especially on the Republican side; Gambetta was often to be met at her luncheon table.

With this she produced articles for the reviews, British and American, and I think had another correspondence for a New York paper. It was an all-devouring activity. Some of the work had the blemishes of haste, none of it was less than womanlike. There was a powerful mind behind it, too often doing less than justice to itself, but—one must live! A chance word of hers once put me on the track of an estimate of character in a common friend, at which I had been tinkering for years. She was handsome, but in a mannish way—a big, powerful head, lips apt for a smile or a resolve, a solid block of brow, with sparkling Irish eyes to light its recesses with promise of good fellowship and entertainment. As she advanced in age she looked like a marquise of the old school, with a mass of silvery white hair—warranted natural for the indispensable effect of the peruke.

In her husband's interest she fought the great De Blowitz in a struggle for the primacy of the press gallery at the Assembly. In their relations with the questor of that body the correspondents were represented by the suffrages of his colleagues. Blowitz sighed for the post, and began to make interest with the little constituency for the next sessional election. Crawford's prospects looked poor, but when the lady entered into the fray, they soon improved. She interviewed the authorities, she wrought by turn on the hopes and fears of the constituency, she stuck at nothing, and she won. The great one bated no jot of grandeur in defeat. When he saw how things were going, he took care to cast his vote on the winning side, with compliments addressed to the hearts of his supporters by inference at the expense of their heads.

The London *Daily News* was sold to a syndicate of which Henry Labouchere was a member. He was always a rover by nature. He went to Paris and fell in with the Crawfords. After the fall of the Emperor in 1870 the siege of Paris was on. The Crawfords went with their young children to Tours, where Gambetta, escaping from the metropolis by balloon, had established a branch of the Government of National Defence. "Labby" remained in Paris and wrote his memorable letters of a "Besieged Resident." A friendship between the correspondents sprang up, and when Labouchere founded *Truth* in 1877, Mrs. Crawford, in addition to her other work, wrote a weekly Paris letter which she continued throughout the rest of her life. Her husband died in 1885, and the post of Paris correspondent for the *Daily News* was given her without reduction of compensation. She, at my request, did occasional work for the Associated Press. Notably, in 1899, she contributed a most graphic series of pen pictures of the Dreyfus trial at Rennes.

Mrs. Crawford in her latter days took up her residence at Senlis, outside of Paris, and was there when the Germans invaded the place in 1914. She never survived the shock. She went to Bristol, England, to live with a son, and died in 1917.

Prof. Ormond Stone

My older and only brother, Prof. Ormond Stone, held the chair of higher mathematics at the University of Virginia, and was director of the Leander McCormick Astronomical Observatory at the same institution for eighteen years, and is now enjoying a well-earned retirement. My grand-nephew Alexander Stark, Junior, was the youngest major in our National Army, having won the position, and numerous decorations, because of great gallantry in the sanguinary struggle in the Argonne.

My Childhood Days

My father was a New Yorker by birth, but was taken to the West in his early boyhood. He met my mother when both were students at Knox College in Galesburg, Illinois. They were married in March, 1846.

I am grateful that my lines fell in pleasant places; that I was born on the boundless prairies of the West; that we were a people only reasonably good and in no sense transcendental; that our conscience was the homely Western conscience; that we did not measure a man's morals either by his manners or his money.

The Middle West, in the 'forties, and for years thereafter, was distinctly American, and I think more so than any other section of the country. The people were simple-minded, blunt, honest—none of them put on any "side." Many chewed tobacco and few men wore "evening clothes." Ladies of quality frequently smoked cob or clay pipes. Men frequently, as a substitute for a necktie, grew a full beard. One of this sort, whom I met in Paris many years ago, was an adept in profanity, and when I met him, he "blew off steam" in true Western fashion. I asked him his troubles. "This d—d country has no fine-cut chewing tobacco," he replied. It also touched him to the quick that when he crossed the Rhine and visited Frankfort not one of "the scurvy cabmen could speak English." It never occurred to him that the cabmen might have wondered that he did not speak German.

In many ways there was real advantage in the primitive life we led. We did more thinking on any given subject than is possible in these rushing, crowded days. We read less tittle-tattle in our newspapers. The mad passion for haste had not seized upon us. We enjoyed Dickens and Thackeray, or serious books on important subjects, instead of nibbling at a thousand trifling titbits respecting inconsequential affairs.

A buggy contented us instead of a law-breaking motor car.

If we desired to communicate with a friend a mile away, it served our purpose to write him a note, send it by messenger, and wait an hour for his reply, instead of fretting because there was a delay of a minute on a then non-existent telephone.

They were stage-coach days. The horse was an indispensable animal. He drew the carriage, the farm wagon, the plough, and the canal boat. I can remember vividly the days when the arrival or departure of the stage was an event in an Illinois town. It cost $10 and required ten days to send a letter from Missouri to California by the overland coach. Such advancement in human comfort as had been made on the seaboard was slow in reaching west of the Alleghany Mountains. Our food was simple and was provided by our own farm labour. Our clothes were, as a rule, homespun. The use of coal was not great. The home fires were made from wood.

Methodism seemed well fitted for the time. In some sense its activities doubtless furnished entertainment for the people. The sermons were largely argumentative. Methodist preachers advocated Free Will and Baptism by sprinkling and energetically denounced Predestination and Immersion. We had ordained ministers, local preachers, and class leaders. We had members on probation and those in full membership. In the absence of the cinema our diversions were the revival meetings in the winter and the camp meetings in the summer. Among our entertainers were a certain number of people who "went forward to the mourners' bench" and were converted every summer and winter and quite as consistently "backslid" every spring and fall.

But this was the Middle West, and the Middle West in the last half century dominated the country.

A pioneer Methodist minister in Illinois in the 'forties led a gypsy life. Under the rules of the denomination he could minister over one charge but two years and more often was limited to one year. The compensation was necessarily beggarly; it was missionary work. With little more than a horse and saddlebags containing a change of clothing, these evangelists rode from place to place, pleaded their cause in schoolhouses, or wherever possible; were housed by their adherents, and thus, obeying the divine call and injunction, they took no thought for the morrow. They uncomplainingly endured great hardships, and when they repeated the Lord's Prayer their petition for their daily bread was by no means a meaningless appeal. At best their hire was a pittance in money, sometimes supplemented by a "donation party," at which they received a curious collection of more or less useless trumpery. Now and then there was a parsonage to live in, but this was far from being assured. Their household belongings were scarcely worth moving from place to place. Frequently, if not indeed as a rule, the preacher was forced to add to his meagre income by something in the way of an avocation. None of these efforts was thought to be *infra dig*. The little earned by these outside occupations was all too small to be the subject of criticism. They were a noble band of God-fearing and God-serving men, who enjoyed the profound respect of everyone.

If any one would care to know what manner of man my father was, let me say, he was the gentlest, kindest I ever knew. There was ever the soft answer that would turn away wrath Yet he had conviction immovable. Patient to a degree, never stirred to anger, while stalwart in moral tone and unyielding in his endeavour. A fine Greek scholar, read in all the books of his profession, unswerving in his faith, believing absolutely in the plenary inspiration of the Scriptures, ardent in his defence of Arminianism, champion of the doctrine of Free Will, and uncompromising in his opposition to the dogma of Foreordination, very human and never at one with the Perfectionist class, liberal in his sympathies, so charitable that he would spend his last dollar in aid of the Bible or missionary cause, untouched through life by any breath of calumny.

The deprivations of the preachers' life were fully shared by their families. The hardships endured by my sainted mother in the period of my childhood are indelibly burned into my memory. With no help from any servant, she, like Martha, "was cumbered about much serving," yet found time to devote herself efficiently to the peculiarly burdensome duties incumbent upon a minister's wife. She made and mended the scanty wardrobe of her children, cooked their meals, scrubbed her floors, entertained visitors—of whom there were many—made pastoral calls when necessary, taught in Sunday School, and never missed a prayer- or a class-meeting. She was a generously good and not a meanly good Christian.

And we boys! The lot of a minister's son is not a happy one. With all of the cares imposed upon the parents, close attention to the children was scarcely possible. Yet there was always the benign Christian example in the home life which meant much. I never knew my father or mother to do an act which I could fairly criticize. In all respects and in every relation they led upright, godly lives. For this I must ever be sensible and sincerely grateful. Whatever have been or are my delinquencies, they cannot be charged to them. I know the age-old jibes concerning preachers' sons and deacons' daughters, but have no great concern respecting them. It is true that much, and far too much, is expected of the unfortunates. They are constantly in the eye of the members of the congregation, and little allowance is made for their shortcomings. Trivial offences are magnified, and they are rarely treated with real justice. Yet in a long life I have known many preachers' sons, and there have been very few "black sheep" among them. In nine cases out of ten they have proved to be high-minded, honourable, and respected citizens.

Moreover, I am convinced that the legacy of poverty left me was a priceless one. It is the rich man's son and not the poor man's who deserves pity. As Emerson so well said in his essay on Compensation:

Whilst he sits on the cushion of advantages, he goes to sleep. When a man is pushed, tormented, defeated, he has a chance to learn something; he has been put on his wits, on his manhood; he has gained facts; learns his ignorance; is cured of the insanity of conceit; has got moderation and real skill.

At Nauvoo

The first home I remember was at Nauvoo, a little city on the banks of the Mississippi River, made famous by the Mormons under the prophet Joe Smith. Smith had secured a city charter, which made him not merely mayor but autocrat of the whole neighbourhood. Even Mr. Lincoln and Judge Douglas found it politic to seek his political aid. At one time he announced himself as a candidate for the Presidency of the United States, but even this did not fully satisfy his ambition, and he prepared to found a monarchy of which he was to be king.

The Mormons led a stormy life and aroused such hostility on the part of their neighbours as to provoke a local war. Only five years before we moved there non-Mormons had murdered Joe Smith and his brother Hyrum, and had driven the whole outfit from the place. Then, but three years before my arrival, the wonderful temple which the Mormons had built was burned and nothing but the charred walls were left. On this ruin, as a child, I played. Though but five years old, there were incidents which have lived in my memory. I was taken to Carthage, the county capital, and shown the blood spot on the jail floor where Hyrum Smith was killed. Joe Smith's wife abandoned the church, and not long after married the captain of a Mississippi River steamboat, bought a Nauvoo hotel, and settled down to an orderly and comfortable existence. We made her acquaintance and found her a worthy woman. One of her sons, Joseph Smith, Junior, lived with her, and later became chief of a non-polygamous branch of the Mormon Church. I knew him for many years, and, while not accepting his faith in the tenets of his denomination, respected him greatly. He lived at Plano, Illinois, not far from Chicago, and published the *Saint's Herald*, the organ of his denomination. Later, he moved

Nauvoo Mormon Temple

to Missouri. I do not think he ever secured many followers.

The first half of the 19th Century was alive with both religious and socialistic developments. And Nauvoo was not exceptional. Besides the Mormon colony, there was an attempt by a Frenchman named Cabet to establish there a social organization of Icarians not unlike Robert Dale Owen's Harmony Enterprises in Indiana, the Oneida Community, and Brook Farm. It was famous for a while, but did not succeed. Its founder went to St. Louis for another trial, but soon dropped out of sight.

Carthage Jail

Under Brigham Young's leadership the Mormons in the year of my birth "trekked" away to Salt Lake City.

The Underground Railway

There was only the river between Nauvoo and the slave state of Missouri. My father's house and the houses of my maternal grandfather at Canton, and my uncle in Stark County, Illinois, were all stations on the Underground Railway, and the Negroes from Missouri and the other slave states were continually passed by night from one to the other and pushed along to Owen Lovejoy's house at Princeton—and thence to Chicago and to freedom in Canada. On one occasion a couple of Negroes arrived at our home in Nauvoo on their master's horses, which they had appropriated. These horses were put in our stable, and for safety the Negroes were buried under the hay in the loft. Some hours later, the masters came in search of their slaves. My mother was too honest to lie about it, and said that they might go out to the stable and see if they could pick out their animals. They were insulting and compelled her to get them their dinner. They went out to look for their horses, but were too drunk to identify them, and went away leaving the Negroes undiscovered. The next day my father put the poor creatures in a wagon, covered them with straw, and drove them to the next station on the Underground Railway.

Because of my mother's failing health, we moved to Chicago in 1854. My father, as other circuit-riding preachers, had been given a small commission on such subscriptions to the church periodicals as he could obtain and on the sale of Bibles and other religious books. With the little he had gained in this way it was possible to undertake the long and wearisome trip. The family was crowded on what was called a Democrat wagon and we set out. We stopped with the "brethren" of the denomination *en route*, and after several days on the road, reached our destination in the late summer of 1854. The experience of our family as conductors on the Underground Railway stood us in good stead as we sought houses of refuge.

We were welcomed on our arrival by two eminent Methodists, a distinguished doctor and a judge. The doctor, who for many years was accounted the leader in his profession in the West, speedily restored my mother's health, and the judge harboured us as visitors in his home. But it was no time for idleness, and soon, when my mother's health was sufficiently restored, my father was appointed as a "supply" at a small suburban town. To eke out a livelihood he manufactured and sold "Stone's Chinese Liniment, for man and beast." He also gave up his devotion to homœopathy and became an advocate of hydropathy. He practised on me, and I had frequent and exhausting "wet sheet packs" for ailments which, I am sure, were purely imaginary. Our intimate neighbour was a sister of the statesman, Anson Burlingame, and a cousin of the evangelist, D. L. Moody. The next year, 1856, Father was sent to the Libertyville circuit in an adjoining county. Here he added to his meagre income by setting up a daguerreotype and ambrotype

The Author at Eight Years
(From ambrotype taken by his father)

gallery. The first National Republican Presidential campaign was on and aroused great interest. It was a happy time, as always with an eight-year-old boy. There was no sense of responsibility, no fear for the future, perfect repose in the confidence that one's parents will provide, and no solicitude respecting their ability to do so.

Another year and another move. This time to DeKalb, in the western part of the state. Then it was more interesting. I was beginning to look upon a larger world. Then it was that my checkered career began. I was not yet striving to find what the French call their *métier*. But, during the summer school vacations, I went to work, alike because I could earn a little and because I became interested in things of practical value. In a limited way, and chiefly because it amused me, I learned to set type. My older brother was regularly employed at a wage, and I hung about the printing office, mastered the location of the various letters of the alphabet in the cases, and pushed the roller over the type on an old-fashioned handpress. For a half-dozen years thereafter I spent my summers first at one thing and then at another. It was a case of "everything by starts and nothing long." Yet it proved of value in the end. My health was never good. I was quite frail throughout my boyhood and early manhood. It was thought, when I was ten years old, that I was to be a victim of tuberculosis. Also I had little chance of an education. We moved from place to place and I was under instruction from so many teachers that I had no settled and continuous training. I was, however, an omniverous reader, and had great nervous energy and distinct power of concentration and persistency, which characteristics have followed me through life. As Byron once said of himself, "I often felt deficient in that which it was incumbent on any man to know." This, I am confident, is the feeling of every youngster as he seems to be passing from dependency to responsibility.

My father now engaged two bright young men as agents and sent them out to sell and put up lightning rods. Both of these young men were also teachers in the public school at which I was a pupil.

When nine years old I fell in love—with a young girl of eight. Her father, Joseph Glidden, was a farmer. To protect his lands he invented a barbed-wire fence, for timber was even then getting scarce and the fence rails were passing into disuse. He had no money to exploit it, but in the town was a retail grocery store, kept by the firm of Ellwood & DeLong, and Isaac Ellwood financed him. He subsequently became a multi-millionaire, as did Ellwood. In the same village was a member of my father's church named Jacob Haish, who ran a planing mill, and when he saw Glidden's success, started out to make a barbed wire of his own. There was a long contest against Haish's piracy, in which Haish was finally defeated.

I remember very well a church festival where for the first time oysters were served. They were of the old-fashioned canned variety which I do not think I have seen for half a century. One must acquire a taste for oysters, and in this instance, they were an unpleasant novelty. The affair gave rise to a new version of a church hymn. One stanza of the popular hymn ran thus:

>Far out upon the prairie,
>   How many children dwell;
>Who never see the Bible,
>   Or hear the Sabbath bell.

We parodied it, and sang with great gusto:

>Far out upon the prairie,
>   How many children dwell;
>Who never ate an oyster,
>   Nor even saw a shell.

There was a Sunday-School entertainment, at which a play called "The Treason of Benedict Arnold" was produced. I appeared as Major André. When I was efficiently hanged, there was loud applause.

I bought a rattan cane and came sailing jauntily into my father's house one day. Bishop Ames, an eminent Methodist divine, was calling. He turned to me and quietly asked in a serious tone: "My son, carrying a cane always argues weakness —either physical, or mental. In your case, which is it?" He cured me.

One Sunday, while we were living in DeKalb, I was in the pastor's pew, and my father was preaching. A curious old gentleman appeared and was seated by my side. A few moments after the opening of the service, and when the sermon was in progress, he dropped his head and apparently went sound asleep. I thought him most irreverent. When he went home with us for luncheon, I learned that he was Horace Greeley. He had heard every word of the sermon and earnestly discussed it with my father during the luncheon hour. The next night he lectured in the church. This lecture tour was one of the many occasions on which this strange, untrustworthy, and greatly overrated man was doing violence to the hopes of the sound-hearted people of the North. He was urging the election of Douglas, against Lincoln, for the United States Senate.

Norman B. Judd, chairman of the Illinois Republican Committee, wrote in a letter to Senator Lyman Trumbull:

> Horace Greeley has been here lecturing and doing what mischief he could. He took Tom Dyer [Democratic ex-Mayor of Chicago] into his confidence and told him all the party secrets that he knew, such as that we had been east and endeavoured to get money for the canvass and that we failed, etc.;—a beautiful chap he is to be entrusted with the interests of the party.

W. H. Herndon (Lincoln's law partner) wrote to Trumbull:

> There are some Republicans here—more than we had any idea of—who had been silently influenced by Greeley and who intended to go for Douglas, or not take sides against him.

Few of the famous journalists of my boyhood days were really ornaments of their vocation. They were largely responsible for the dislike, if not contempt, in which the editorial office was held. Turn back to their labours and examine their work. As I have said of Greeley, he was a shifty and wholly untrustworthy person, vituperative in the last degree, and a

My Father

My Mother

persistent office-beggar. Dana was a malignant who frequently misused his power. Thurlow Weed was primarily a political boss and was not in any sense a notable editor. The elder Bennett, while deserving of much commendation for his enterprise as a news gatherer, was little better than a blackguard in the conduct of his paper. George D. Prentice revelled in indecencies, as did Wilbur F. Storey, of the Chicago *Times*.

We moved from DeKalb to Kaneville for a year, and after that to Naperville. I was now in my eleventh year. I attended a German Sunday School and became grounded in the language. A famous divorce case was on trial. Isaac H. Burch, a wealthy citizen of Chicago, was the accuser of his wife, who was a niece of Erastus Corning, the famous politician of New York. The case had come to Naperville on a change of venue and Mrs. Burch and her small daughter Minnie were living with some neighbours of ours. Mr. Burch lost the case, but obviously the couple could never resume marital relations. The wife and her child went to France and lived in Paris. The little girl grew to womanhood and became the wife of M. Ribot, the famous French statesman.

Also there was a boy in the village who grew to fame. He became the agent for Haish, ur friend of DeKalb, having as his field the State of Texas, and finally became a well-known multi-millionaire. His name was John W. Gates. Also in the adjacent village of Warrenville, where my father preached, there was a family attached to whom as a nephew was a lad who subsequently became interested in the barbed-wire business, although a lawyer. It was Judge Elbert H. Gary, now chief of the United States Steel Corporation.

SECOND DECADE

The Year 1858

A NUMBER of notable things happened in 1858. Cyrus W. Field, in June of that year, successfully laid his first Atlantic cable. He had tried to lay one a year before, but it had broken in mid-ocean. This second cable was operated for four months, and 732 messages were transmitted through it. At the same time, William Thomson (later Lord Kelvin) invented his mirror galvanometer, by which he was able to locate the ends of a broken cable in the trackless waste of the sea, and to recover and splice the ends so as to make possible its use.

Still more important—it was in 1858 that the North and South really joined issue on the Slavery question. The hour which Judge Pope had prophesied, when the State of Illinois should bind the Union together, arrived. From the early days of the Republic a smouldering fire had burned on the altar of human justice. A few of the Fathers had felt keenly the barbarism of human bondage. Indeed, before the adoption of the National Constitution the Continental Congress of 1787 had voiced the conscience of the people of the colonies by for ever inhibiting the custom in the Northwest Territory. It was this act which made the Ohio River the dividing line between the free and the slave territories.

Yet compromise after compromise was resorted to in the vain hope that time would furnish a solution of the most difficult problem. The union of the states was of such overshadowing moment that anything and everything must yield to its maintenance. Two men of Illinois, Abraham Lincoln and Stephen A. Douglas, precipitated the crisis which put an end to the vexed question. Curiously enough, Douglas, Northern-born, a native of Vermont, espoused the cause of the slave-holding

South, while Lincoln, Southern-born, a child of Kentucky, spoke for freedom. The Missouri compromise, written by Jesse B. Thomas, United States Senator from Illinois, and agreed to in 1820, had fixed a line at latitude 36° 30′ north, as the divisional point between the contesting elements. In 1848, when California became our property by treaty with Mexico, it was admitted to the Union as a free state and there was temporary peace. Six years later, however, Douglas, another Illinois senator, introduced a bill for the admission of Kansas and Nebraska, leaving the question of slavery to the decision of the people resident in the territories named. This became a law and ended the famous Missouri Compromise.

Open warfare followed. The Republican party was organized, not in favour of the abolition of slavery, but as an effort to prevent its extension into the territories. It became a national organization, and in 1856 nominated John C. Fremont for the Presidency. Mr. Lincoln led the list of electors from Illinois. Fremont did not carry the state, but the Republicans elected their candidates for the state offices.

In 1858 the senatorial term of Judge Douglas was about to expire, and there was a campaign for the succession. Mr. Lincoln was named by the Republicans. He boldly declared the issue and challenged the slaveholders to a final contest. He said:

A house divided against itself cannot stand. I believe this government cannot endure permanently half slave and half free. I do not expect the Union to be dissolved. I do not expect the house to fall, but I do expect it will cease to be divided. It will become all one thing, or all the other; either the opponents of slavery will arrest the further spread of it, and place it where the public mind shall rest in the belief that it is in the course of ultimate extinction, or its advocates will push it forward till it shall become alike lawful in all the states, old as well as new, North as well as South.

Douglas was between two fires. The United States Supreme Court, in the famous Dred Scott Decision, had declared a Negro slave to be property which, like a horse, his owner could take into a territory. Douglas, in order to hold his Northern constituency together and secure a reëlection to the Senate, set up the claim that the people living in a territory could nullify this decision by hostile police regulations. This attitude did not, of course, please the Southern slaveholders. Lincoln was also between two fires. The Republicans of the Eastern states favoured the election of Douglas, thinking the measure he advocated the best obtainable.

A famous debate between Lincoln and Douglas followed. Douglas won reëlection as a senator, but Lincoln became a national figure. In February, 1860, he spoke at Cooper Institute in New York City. In manner he was not altogether "genteel"—but in matter he was a commanding influence. As the late Hamilton Mabie said of him:

> He had a style—a distinctive, individual, characteristic form of expression. In his own way he gained an insight into the structure of English and a freedom and skill in the selection and combination of words which not only made him the most convincing speaker of his time, but which have secured for his speeches a permanent place in literature.

This Cooper Institute address, which really made him President of the United States, was a remarkable incident in his life. The Republicans of New York invited him. But as they thought their Governor, Seward, the logical candidate for the high office of Chief Magistrate, they had little respect for their guest. He had been regarded as a "rough-and-tumble" sort of Westerner, and they assembled to hear an unpolished backwoodsman deliver himself. The hall was crowded, and William Cullen Bryant, the poet, presided. Mr. Lincoln's address proved a masterpiece.

Robert Lincoln, Mr. Lincoln's son, once told me a good story of the effect of the speech. He said:

> I was responsible for my father's nomination. I was at St. Paul's School at Concord, N. H., preparing for Harvard. I had failed in my exams. When my father came east to speak in New York, he arranged to go to Concord to talk to me, to tell me how he and my mother were denying themselves to give me an education, and how important it was that I should apply myself to my studies. The

people of the New England States learned of this, and after his Cooper Institute speech asked him to address meetings in several of their cities. Thus they came to know him and in the end to believe him a worthy candidate for the Presidency.

I remember one evening when, with my father, I went to hear a Republican speech by Owen Lovejoy. The evening was hot and the hall crowded. Chairman Judd presided. The speaker laid off his coat and removed his "stock" and collar. Handing them to the Chairman, he shouted in stentorian tones: "Here, Judd, hold my garments while I proceed to stone Stephen" [Douglas].

Mr. Lincoln's Election

And then Mr. Lincoln was elected. And how we Illinoisans followed him to Washington and his great office with all of our solicitude and our prayers. I doubt that there ever was another such occasion. He evoked our devotion. Before he left his home civil war was on; yet in him there was no hatred of Southerner nor of slaveholder. There was simply an obligation to duty—fealty to his oath of office. And from the hour of parting to accept the labours of the Chief Magistracy till the return, a corpse, slain by the assassin, there was in Illinois ever an affectionate devotion such, as I cannot help believing, has never followed any other public man in the country.

Many people have written of Mr. Lincoln. He has been painted in many colours. Yet, if the effort has been that of one not an Illinoisan, it has not been quite well done. None but one of his own state could ever fully understand him. His simplicity, his honesty, his straightforwardness, his clarity of vision—all these things we knew. We minded not his democracy of manner; his untidiness, sometimes, of dress; his *gaucherie*, if you please. Over it all was a great soul, filled with prophecy of the future—prophecy born of such a sense of justice as made prophecy easy and unerring. He was our idol.

And the part played by Judge Douglas when the Civil War came has never been fully appreciated. He had opposed Mr. Lincoln for the senatorship and the Presidency. But in the face of the threatened dissolution of the Union he stirred every loyal heart in the state by his gallant defence of the nation and his plea for the support of his long-time political antagonist. The speech he made before the State Legislature twelve days after the attack on Fort Sumter was of controlling influence in Illinois. It swung to the support of President Lincoln most of even the bitter partisans of Douglas's own party.

An illustration occurs to me. A crabbed old judge lived in a small city of northern Illinois, in the early days of the war. There was to be a Union meeting and the judge, a violent Douglas man, was asked to preside. He hesitated, but consented. The evening came, and the "Opera House," a hall over a grocery store, was crowded. As prearranged, a man rose and moved that "our distinguished citizen," the judge, be chosen as chairman. The motion was carried unanimously, with loud applause. Then a committee of three was named to conduct the chairman to the platform, and he began his speech with great dignity, thus:

Ladies and gentlemen; This is the happiest moment of my life. You have all known me as a true and tried Democrat, and therefore may be surprised at my contentment. But my reason is this: Life is a wheel of fortune, and when I have reached the point that I can officiate at a meeting of Black Republicans, I am sure that the wheel has touched the lowest level, and whichever way the darned thing turns, it must go up.

Douglas, by his speech before the Legislature, confirmed his title to the sobriquet of "the Little Giant." As Horace White said in his "Life of Lyman Trumbull":

He was the only man who could have saved southern Illinois from the danger of an internecine war. The Southern counties followed him as faithfully, and as unanimously as they had followed him in previous years, and sent their sons into the field to fight for the Union as numerously and as bravely as any other section of the state, or of the country.

In less than two months after his speech Douglas was dead, but he had done his work, and had done it so well that he had won a title to immortality.

Perhaps the most striking example of his influence was in the case of John A. Logan. Logan was a devoted adherent of "the Little Giant," and had been elected to Congress from the Ninth Illinois District by a vote of 20,000 against 5,000 for his opponent, yet he answered the call to arms from Lincoln, and became the great volunteer general of the war.

Boyhood in Chicago

It was during the campaign of 1860 that we moved back to Chicago, my father being appointed pastor of the Des Plaines Street Methodist Church. He served there for two years. We moved into the city from Naperville, a distance of thirty miles, by the usual lumber wagon, my mother and her children sitting high up on the furniture and my father walking a good share of the distance. He found a comfortable home, and we two sons resumed school life. I shall never forget a wise decision made by my father. Mother had traces of aristocracy still surviving, I suppose, as a heritage from her Irish "royal line." She thought her boys should attend a private school, or have a tutor. "No," said my father, "I have laboured for years under a distinct misfortune. Sunday after Sunday I have risen in the pulpit and preached a sermon, and there was no one to tell me that I did not know what I was talking about. It will be much better for our children to attend a public school, where they will be drilled in democratic notions, and where they will find independent companions to challenge their ideas." And so it was settled. I was sent to the Foster Grammar School.

It was necessary to help the family exchequer. I secured a position to carry the Chicago *Tribune* to its subscribers in a certain quarter of the city. This meant that I must be out of bed about four o'clock every morning, go to the newspaper office for my bundle of papers, and walk out to serve them. I reached home about eight o'clock, breakfasted, and was at school at nine. For a time I also had an afternoon task, the sweeping of the floor of the Board of Trade rooms, which were almost knee-deep with wheat and oats and corn after the day's session closed. I found time to attend on certain evenings a Palestine Class for the study of the geography of the Holy Land, and a lodge of Good Templars of which I became chief officer. And yet I was pursuing my studies so earnestly that for the year I ranked second in my class and was awarded the "Foster Medal."

I entered the Chicago High School, but after a year was forced to drop out for a twelve-month. I never finished the course. At the close of his two years' service, my father was sent to the church at Kankakee, and thither I followed him. I bought and sold old paper and rags for a time, and then secured a position in the leading dry-goods store of the place. Outside of the town there were two or three settlements of French Canadians. I soon picked up their *patois* and was able to serve them as a clerk in our store. One day there was a public examination for teachers' certificates, conducted under the auspices of the State Superintendent of Public Instruction. I attended, answered the questions, and was adjudged fit to teach. I was then fifteen years old. I was offered a school in a remote corner of the country, but on condition that I should "board around," that is, that I should live with one family or another a week at a time. On reflection I declined. Then I learned of a patent gong doorbell, for which there seemed to be a market. Doorbells were a novelty in Illinois in those days. I bought a stock of the bells and the necessary tools to affix them and set out. I peddled them from house to house with success for several months.

My father was next appointed to the church at Morris, Illinois. It was now the early spring of 1864. The Civil War was in full swing. I enlisted as a drummer and was anxious to "go to the front," but my father promptly cancelled the enlistment, as he had an undoubted right to do. His health was breaking and he retired from the ministry and engaged in the manufacture of saw-mill tools with his brother in Chicago. While in Morris there was a charming little girl who was running about the place, and who, in later years, became famous as Jessie Bartlett Davis, the opera singer.

Back in Chicago I began the study of law. I read Walker's

"Introduction to American Law," Blackstone, Greenleaf, Parsons, and other standard works, and was in a fair way to pass the bar. My mother dissuaded me. I then went into my father's factory and divided my time in aiding the bookkeeping and in learning the machinist trade. I qualified to run a lathe and planer and to do a certain amount of work with a file and a vise.

When I was in the Chicago High School, the war was on and there were recruiting, marching, and tearful good-byes everywhere. The city developed two of the best writers of war songs the world has ever known.

Dr. George F. Root of the music-publishing firm of Root & Cady wrote: "The Battle Cry of Freedom"; "Tramp, Tramp, Tramp, the Boys Are Marching"; and "Just Before the Battle, Mother."

Henry C. Work, a journeyman printer, wrote: "Kingdom Coming"; "Babylon Is Fallen"; and "Marching Through Georgia." He also wrote "My Grandfather's Clock." Later we organized brigades of various sorts—there was the Irish Brigade under General Mulligan, who fought in almost the first battle of the war, and there were the Germans, who went "to fight mit Sigel." Illinois contributed more than her share of men to the Union cause.

In the midsummer of 1864 Mr. Ballentine, commercial editor of the Chicago *Tribune* and father of a schoolmate of mine, asked me to help him in his work. This resulted in a short period of service as a reporter, although I was but sixteen years of age.

There were the makings of big men in Chicago at that time, but we did not know how big they were to become. For example, I used often to take our family washing to a neighbouring laundry. This establishment was maintained by one George M. Pullman who had just invented a sleeping car. He had set up a laundry to wash the bed linen of the cars, and took in consumers' work to help eke out expenses. He became one of the great millionaires of the nation.

I shall never forget a morning in April, 1865. We lived on West Madison Street in Chicago, and it was my habit to rise early and get the morning paper. I did so on this particular morning and came bounding through the house, announcing the assassination of Mr. Lincoln. I dressed at once and started for the *Tribune* office. When I reached there the street was crowded, and the windows were filled with bulletins announcing the death of Mr. Lincoln, Secretary Seward, General Grant, and Andrew Johnson. The wild burst of rage was beyond description. Unable to enter the Tribune Building because of the crowd, I made my way around the corner to the Matteson House, which was located on the corner of Dearborn and Randolph streets a block away. In it was an ancient lounging rotunda. It was packed. Very soon I heard the crack of a revolver, and a man fell in the centre of the room. His assailant stood perfectly composed with a smoking revolver in his hand, and justified his action by saying: "He said it served Lincoln right." There was no arrest. No one would have dared arrest the man. He walked out a hero. I never knew who he was.

THIRD DECADE

Election of General Grant

THE year 1868 was an exceedingly interesting one. It had much personal interest for me aside from the great public interest. As must be seen, I was hunting for a place in the world. For a month or two I was a reporter for the Chicago *Republican*. I attended the Republican National Convention, held at Crosby's Opera House in Chicago on May 20th. With great enthusiasm, General Grant was nominated for President and Schuyler Colfax for Vice-President. The rally song of the day was written by General Halpine (Miles O'Reilly), and ran thus:

> So, boys, a final bumper,
> While we all in chorus chant,
> For next President we nominate
> Our own Ulysses Grant.
>
> And if asked what state he hails from,
> This our sole reply shall be:
> "From near Appomattox Court House,
> And its famous apple tree."
>
> For 'twas there to our Ulysses
> That Lee gave up the fight,
> Now, boys, to Grant for President,
> And God defend the right.

Mr. Colfax was one of the many office-seeking journalists of the day. He had been the proprietor of the South Bend, Indiana, *Register*, and frequently visited Chicago. I knew him as he grew, step by step, to be member of Congress, Speaker of the House of Representatives, and in his later years, when he was on lecture tour, he and I corresponded freely.

Less than a week after the Convention President Johnson

was impeached before the Senate at Washington. I had seen him and heard him speak when he passed through Chicago "swinging around the circle" in denunciation of Congress. It was this tour and these speeches that aroused the hostility of Congress and precipitated the attempt to remove him from office. Years after I came to know him in Washington when he returned to the Capitol as United States Senator from Tennessee.

It was in the early summer of 1868 that I first travelled beyond the border of my native state. I went to New York City and assisted Franc B. Wilkie, a well-known Chicago journalist, in reporting the session of the National Democratic Convention, which nominated Seymour and Blair. There were some very interesting incidents connected with the work. Seymour did not want to be nominated, but Salmon P. Chase, of Ohio, did. He had been an ardent abolitionist and a member of Lincoln's Cabinet, and, strangely enough, appeared as a candidate for the nomination before a Democratic National Convention. His daughter, who afterward married a governor of Rhode Island and became the famous Kate Chase Sprague, conducted his headquarters in New York.

His case was not unlike that of a number of the leading Abolitionists. I have spoken of Greeley's attempt to defeat Lincoln and elect Douglas as senator in 1858. When the Civil War came on, very few of these Abolitionist leaders fought in the Union Army. They were for ever fussing and

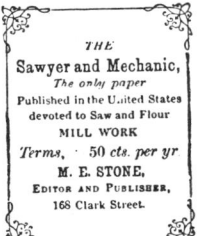  

Facsimile of letterhead, 1868

never fighting. Many of them had been advocates of secession, even before the Southern conspiracy developed. They held that any state had a right to leave the Union, and proposed that the New England States should set up an independent government. Wendell Phillips would not take an oath to support the Constitution of the United States. Greeley and Sumner both gave Presidents Lincoln and Grant infinite trouble. Greeley, as stage play, signed Jeff Davis's bail bond, and in 1872 he became the Democratic candidate for President.

In 1868 I began the publication of my first newspaper, the *Sawyer and Mechanic*. I issued it from the printing office of a friend. He was a kindly disposed gentleman who often employed reformed drunkards. One night a backslider was put abed in a room in a remote part of the building. He was suffering from delirium tremens, and I was asked to assist in keeping guard over him. About midnight I dropped off in a doze and my patient slipped from the room. In his condition he was quite irresponsible, and as, in his raving, he had tried to jump from the window and kill himself I was alarmed. I went off to hunt for him. There were no lights about the place and I was forced to feel my way. Suddenly I found myself passing my hand over what was obviously a nude corpse. I hastily lighted a match and discovered that I was in the

MELVILLE E. STONE,
MAKER AND FACTOR OF

| HARDWARE |

LAKE SHORE IRON WORKS,
371 TO 377 ILLINOIS STREET,
CHICAGO.

Author as an iron founder

dissecting room of a medical college. And there on his knees, sobbing and praying, was my charge, frightened stiff but perfectly sober. I led him to his own room and after explaining the situation, he passed into peaceful slumber and gave me no more trouble.

My paper did not last long. Then my father bought for me an interest in an iron foundry and machine shop. I was successful and soon after purchased the interests of my partners and became sole owner. On November 25, 1869, I was married. Shortly after, the folding iron theatre chair made its first appearance and took the place of the old-fashioned benches that had been in common use. I secured the right to use a patent and introduced a folding theatre chair of my own to Chicago. I furnished Wood's Museum with a thousand of these folding chairs in the spring of 1871, and in the later summer sold another thousand to Crosby's Opera House.

The Great Chicago Fire

On the evening of the 8th, of October, 1871, I had finished my contract in Crosby's Opera House, save some details that would occupy perhaps two hours. Mr. Crosby asked me to complete the work on the following morning, Sunday, because Thomas's Orchestra was to open the house on Monday night and would need the place for rehearsal on Monday forenoon. I objected and told him that I could easily finish the task on Monday morning in ample time for the rehearsal. It was then agreed that we should meet the succeeding evening and light the place for a sort of unofficial opening. As we stood upon the stage viewing the beautiful scene (Mr. Crosby had expended a vast sum of money in refurnishing the place) someone said that the stage carpenter had lost his all the night before in a fire in a remote section of the city. I casually remarked that it would be a horrible thing if the opera house should burn, to which Crosby replied, laughingly: "Oh, it will not. I have studied the statistics of theatre fires and they occur on an average of once in five years. We had a fire two years ago, so we are immune for three more."

Late that night I went home. I lived three miles away. I had scarcely gone to bed when there was a wild alarm and the great Chicago fire had begun. I dressed and started for my foundry. As I neared it, I found myself shut off by the flames and saw that it would be impossible for me to reach the place. Later it turned out that two of my iron moulders, in an effort to save the wooden patterns, had gone there and been burned to death. I wandered away aimlessly and finally sat down on the steps of the First National Bank Building on the corner of Washington and State streets. As indicative of the curious state of mind that one takes on in such disasters, I remember that a man sat at my side with a mass of sheets of postage stamps that he had evidently taken from some office to save. With scissors in hand he was calmly cutting them in shreds and throwing them into the street. It occasioned no surprise in my mind, but seemed to be a perfectly natural thing to do.

Pursued by the fire I wandered along the lake shore and reached a friend's house which obviously was soon to be destroyed. I set out to find something in the way of a cart to help him to remove his goods. I found a milk wagon and into that he and I very carefully put a sewing machine, and his wife and he and I marched for a mile to save this comparatively worthless thing. It was all that we tried to rescue.

I reached, by a roundabout road, my home about noon on Monday. On the way I met the chairman of the Board of Aldermen, and he and I talked over the situation and tried to think how to reorganize the city government. We finally engaged the First Congregational Church on Washington Street and prepared a notice that the City Council would meet there and signed the name of the mayor to the call. At home, I hitched up my horse and buggy and drove out on the North Side, whither the refugees had escaped, to tell them to come to the church, where food and clothing would be provided. I found the people in all stages of dress and undress. We gathered as many as we could, and the people living near the church who were not in the fire zone fed and clothed them as best they could.

A few weeks later, after the beneficence of the world was so remarkably disclosed, a vacant square was secured, and on it we built barracks in which several hundred destitute people were housed for the winter. In conjunction with General O. L. Mann, I was placed in charge of it, and devoted myself through the later fall of 1871 and early winter of 1872 to doling out coal, blankets, clothing, etc., to these poor people. With the lapse of fifty years people have forgotten to a great degree the extent of this calamity, which swept away nearly $200,000,000 worth of property, took 250 human lives, and left 100,000 people homeless and destitute. It was one of the great disasters of history, and the world as a whole came to the relief of the sufferers. But the factor at the terrible hour was the courage of the Chicagoans themselves. I do not believe that any community in the face of so great a calamity so quickly pulled itself together and embarked upon the task of rebuilding. Yet for years thereafter it was a ragged and unsightly town. Changes in the grades of streets were not promptly accepted by builders upon adjacent property, and even in the down-town districts pedestrians went up and down flights of steps in passing along the street where some new building blanked an old one. Frame shanties were side by side with brick- and limestone edifices, but everywhere was active business, everywhere men were making money fast.

In Daily Journalism

My foundry business did not revive, and after the winter given to executive work in connection with the relief of the destitute I was called upon to take charge of a newspaper, the *Republican*. Mr. J. Young Scammon, who had bought the paper, was president of the Chicago Astronomical Society, and my brother, Ormond, was an assistant teacher of astronomy in the Chicago University. Thus Scammon came to know of me. He asked me to take the editorship of the sheet; I was thoroughly incompetent for so responsible a position, and at my suggestion an adjustment was effected by which Colonel J. K. C. Forrest became editor-in-chief and I managing editor. I had some interesting as well as amusing experiences, of some of which I am not altogether proud.

Mr. Scammon located the office of his paper in a large brick stable, at the back of his palatial home, which was situated at the extreme southern limit of the burned district. Here, in what had been a wide hay loft, were all of the editorial and business departments, as well as the type-setting room. We made things lively.

A rich whiskey merchant, one Pat O'Neill, got into an altercation with one of his men and the man was killed. Whether or not it was a case of self-defence was never known. O'Neill was a very important citizen, and when I told the story in the columns of the paper, he took offence. He came up to our den to shoot me. One of our editors sat behind me. He took a revolver from the drawer of his desk and slipped it into my hand. I had the drop on O'Neill and ordered him downstairs. He went. But there might be a libel suit, and poor Colonel Forrest was greatly troubled. Scammon was absent from the city, he was a terrible autocrat, and what he might do on his return to town was appalling. So poor Forrest sat down and wrote an absurd editorial, apologetic to O'Neill, and saying he hoped Scammon would forgive us. The Chicago *Times* said there was but one possible excuse for the apology—beer. Forrest was heartbroken.

Colonel Forrest

Meeting with Ito

Across the street from our stable was the only surviving first-class hotel in the city. I took my luncheons there. One day a strange company of people arrived. They constituted the Japanese expedition to the United States under Iwakura. They were on their way to Washington and other capitals of the Western nations to secure release from the burdensome treaties which had been imposed upon their country at the time of the invasion of Commodore Perry. The secretary of the group was a young man named Ito. He told me the story of the opening of Japan, which was interesting. It was a southwest wind that did the business. The Japanese wanted to live the life of a hermit nation, or, as they expressed it, "like frogs in a well." It was the day of sailing vessels. The prevailing winds were from the southwest. So they thought that for their protection from the "foreign devils" it was only necessary to guard the southwest corner of their little empire, whence any sailing vessel must come. But there came into one of their ports a ship without any sails at all, with, instead, what seemed like a stove smoking lustily from the chimney. Of course, the watchman on the coast was useless and they must meet the new condition by finding out how this new kind of a boat was made to go. It was against the law of Japan for any one to leave the country without consent of the government, but two young patriots, Ito and Inouye, escaped, and with the aid of a shipping merchant at Shanghai, went to London. There they learned the secret of the steamship and came home to tell their countrymen how idle it was to attempt to keep the foreigner away any longer.

Ito in 1872.

I became acquainted with Ito and, although I never saw him again, we continued as friends through his long life. Also with the group was an eleven-year-old boy, the son of a great Japanese statesman, Okubo. His name was Makino, and I next met him as one of the Japanese Peace Commissioners in Paris in 1918.

My zeal ran away with my judgment, and on one or two occasions I stole important documents and printed them—documents that were ultimately intended for publication, but which I was not authorized to publish when I did. Among these was the first report of the chief of the Chicago Fire Department. I climbed over a partition in the City Hall under the eyes of the police to secure the report of the fire chief, and I lay back of an organ loft for half a day to get the report of a secret church trial.

These newspaper triumphs made me an important man for the moment with my fellow-newspapermen, but aroused a great deal of indignation on the part of the victims and also on the part of Mr. Scammon, who did not approve of that kind of journalism. The name of the paper was changed to the *Inter-Ocean*. I retired from the office of managing editor and E. W. Halford was called from Indianapolis to take the place, while I became city editor. One of my reporters was the young son of a Methodist preacher, who had learned a little of newspaper work at Erie, Pennsylvania. Later in life he worked for me for several years and grew to fame as a writing journalist. It was William Eleroy Curtis, whose letters and books upon his travels in foreign countries were notable. Mr. Halford was afterward private secretary to President Harrison, and now lives at Leonia, New Jersey.

Colonel E. W. Halford

The Case of Baron de Palm

I made the acquaintance of a remarkable character, one Baron de Palm. At first sight one would recognize him as a decayed voluptuary, of the sort that frequent the Continental watering places of Europe in the season. Habited faultlessly, with hair and beard carefully dressed, washed-out face and eyes, shaky on his legs, he had evidently, like Cousin John's profligate in Owen Meredith's "Lucille," never neglected an occasion to please himself. Such men were almost unknown at the time in bustling Chicago.

He told me his life's story. He was a Bavarian. He was Baron Johan Heinrich Ludwig de Palm; had descended from a line of German barons running back ten centuries. He was Grand Cross Commander of the Order of the Holy Sepulchre. His father was a prince of the Holy Roman Empire, and his mother a notable Countess of Thunefeldt. Born at Augsburg in 1809, he was educated for a diplomatic career, and served his king with distinction at almost every capital. Then he came to be chamberlain of Ludwig I, and here was experience. Ludwig was not the crazy Bavarian king, but in his veins ran the insane current which marked his family. Someone said of him that he was a "Lovelace with a touch of the Minnesinger about him—a mixture of Haroun-al-Raschid and Henry IV, the most meritorious and meretricious monarch of Europe." He built the Glyptothek, the Pinakothek, the Walhalla, and practically all of the show places of Munich. He came to the throne determined to give his people a liberal form of government, and for a time he honestly struggled to that end.

Withal he had pronounced weaknesses. It was De Palm's mission to minister to these.

One day an Irish girl arrived in Munich to fill an engagement as a Spanish dancer at the theatre. She was not a good *danseuse*, but was young and good-looking. De Palm made her acquaintance at once. He knew her as Lizzie Gilbert, then and ever after. Her stage name was Lola Montez, and under this pseudonym she earned world-wide fame. Her real name was probably Maria Dolores Eliza Rosanna Gilbert, although it was not quite certain. She was born at Limerick, Ireland, about 1818. Her father was a respectable country squire and her mother a Spanish chorus girl. The squire was sent to India for service and died there, leaving a young widow and her infant daughter.

Lola Montez

The daughter learned bad tricks from the Hindu servants, and it became necessary for her mother to take her back to England. Life in the homeland did not reform her, for when she was little more than fifteen she eloped with a certain Captain James of the British Army, and they were married. Again there was an assignment to service in India. Soon Eliza's conduct compelled her husband to divorce her.

She returned to Europe and went on the stage as a Spanish dancer. She made her début as "Lola Montez" at Her Majesty's Theatre, London, was hissed and dismissed at once.

Then she set out for the Continent, and appeared at one city after another, with varying success, but with ever-attendant scandalous incident, until, six years later, she arrived in Munich.

When De Palm saw her, he thought she might please his royal master. And he was not wrong. He introduced her to the King, and five days later the monarch called together his ministers and presented his "Lolita" to them as his "best friend." She was shrewd, and, indeed, intellectually brilliant. Very soon she had achieved complete mastery of the King. He created her Comtesse de Landsfeld, built her a villa, and gave her an ample income. She practically usurped the place of the Queen and also, and not unwisely, dictated the liberalizing policy of the Bavarian Government. Then came the wave of revolution which swept over Europe in 1848, and it burst upon Bavaria.

The court scandal was made the occasion for the revolt. The King was forced to decree that the Comtesse de Landsfeld had "ceased to possess the rights of naturalization in Bavaria," and to order her imprisonment as a disturber of the peace of the kingdom. She escaped, but secretly returned in boy's clothing and advised the King to abdicate, which he did. She floated around for a time, always getting into trouble. She married again and again, was charged with bigamy, escaped to Spain, and thence, in 1851, to New York.

With the downfall of the King, De Palm also left Munich, and for a time was with Lola Montez. Then they quarrelled and he went to one of his castles on Lake Constance. She came to America. She appeared a number of times on the Boston and New York stage. A clergyman wrote some lectures for her and she delivered them, with success, throughout the United States. She also published them in book form. Finally, when but forty-two years old, she broke down, came to New York, fell under influence of a worthy clergyman, did missionary work among the magdalens of the city for a few months, and then died in comparative poverty in Astoria, Long Island, and was buried in Greenwood Cemetery in Brooklyn.

Alone, on the ledge of a hill, surrounded by the imposing

tombs of the Van Rensselaers and the Barramores, and looking down on a quiet and restful lake separating it from the busy and rushing life of lower Brooklyn, lies a burial spot, on which is a marble slab, not quite upright, bearing the inscription:

Mrs.
Eliza Gilbert
Died
January 17, 1861
Age 42

And there any one may go to-day and see the last resting place of Lola Montez. It is on Lot 12,730 of Section 8 of the Greenwood Cemetery map; on Summit Avenue, at the end of Andrean path, not far from the Ninth Avenue gate.

When he heard that she was dead, De Palm sailed for this country. He went at once to Chicago and took out his first naturalization papers. As he later told me, he had had quite enough of the gay life, and, wishing to get close to Nature, he went to the Far West, and for some years lived with the Indian tribes, and greatly enjoyed it.

He returned to Chicago and lived there in comparative seclusion until 1878. Then he came to New York, joined the Theosophist Society, and on May 21st of that year died, a worn-out man, at the Roosevelt Hospital. There was a notable Theosophist furneral with orphic hymns and mystic liturgy in the Masonic Temple of New York City, and later a cremation in western Pennsylvania. It was the first cremation in the United States. He had always been a spendthrift and died penniless.

A Tour of the South

In the summer and fall of 1872 I did some editorial writing in the campaign for General Grant's second term, which we supported ardently. Then my health broke. The constant strain of working until the paper went to press in the early morning and then walking, as was necessary because of the absence of street railways at the time, through the burned district, for three or four miles, was too much for me. Mr. Scammon asked me to take a vacation and advised me that I should be free to write as much as I chose. I set out for an extended tour of the South, with the purpose of writing a series of articles for the *Inter-Ocean*, justifying Carpet-bag rule as the only sort of government possible during the period of reconstruction. I first, by way of diversion, visited and studied the battle-field of Shiloh. It was undeniably the scene of one of the decisive struggles of our Civil War. Although nearly eleven years had elapsed since the fateful days, abundant evidences of its sanguinary character survived. The wreckage of war was still distinctly visible. The visit was most instructive. I had read and reread the story of the battle, but as I walked over the field my concept of it changed, and I came to see that those two days of April, 1862, as much as any others during the whole war, bore testimony to the great tactical genius of Grant.

It was early in the period of the national strife. Even generals were limited in their knowledge of the art of war, and deficient in their sense of the first duty of a soldier—intelligent obedience. Grant's plan of battle was perfect. It has been said that he was surprised. And so he was. Halleck had ordered him to go to Pittsburg Landing and await General Buell's arrival. But Halleck had not ordered and could not order the Confederate general, Albert Johnson, to await Buell's arrival. And Johnson did not. He attacked the Grant forces a day too soon. But that obviously was not Grant's fault. It was Grant's duty to meet the situation. He did so in a manner which would have done credit to Bonaparte in his palmiest day. One man, a trusted subordinate general, failed him. It was Lew Wallace, afterward the author of "Ben Hur," who mistook a road and wandered away, as Grouchy did at Waterloo. Grant's troops were forced back to the river in some confusion, and it was again, as at Waterloo, "night or Buell." Fortunately night came; fortunately for the North the Confederate general, Johnson, was killed; and fortunately, finally, it was Grant, that cool, undaunted captain, who said in the moment of his apparent defeat: "I do not despair of defeating them yet." And the next day he did defeat them.

I went to New Orleans. I found the hotels crowded, and secured accommodations at Mrs. Edward's boarding house. It was the building occupied by General Butler as his headquarters when in command of the city. William Pitt Kellogg was governor, P. B. S. Pinchback, a Negro alleged lawyer, but really a race-track tout, was lieutenant-governor, and the Legislature was a compact Negro Carpet-bag outfit. Out of my contact with these people my view of the policy of reconstruction adopted by the North was completely changed.

I spent some time in Atlanta and made the acquaintance of Alexander H. Stephens and Ben Hill. Three young men, Henry Grady, St. Clair Abrams, and "Bob" Alston, were struggling with a daily paper, the *Herald*. They spent almost every evening with me talking over the profession of journalism. In these discussions we all learned much.

Henry W. Grady

At Richmond I met General John B. Gordon who acted as my guide for a very interesting visit to Libby Prison and the former residence of Jefferson Davis.

As a Washington Correspondent

In June I was back in Chicago, but it was obvious that I was not strong enough to take up again the strenuous life connected with a morning paper. Then I was invited to take the managing editorship of the Chicago *Mail*, a two-cent evening newspaper, and accepted. All the other papers in the city were five cents a copy. The Rev. Oliver A. Willard, a brother of Frances E. Willard, the famous temperance advocate, was the editor. In less than two months I effected a consolidation of the *Mail* and the Chicago *Evening Post*. The *Post* had an Associated Press service and the *Mail* had not. I then became the managing editor of the *Post and Mail*, but very soon went to the National Capitol as Washington correspondent. In making the arrangement I wanted to add one or two papers to my list, and I visited St. Louis to see Stilson Hutchins, the proprietor of the St. Louis *Dispatch*. As I entered the counting room of the *Dispatch* I found a curious creature sitting high up on the counter telling side-splitting stories to Hutchins and everybody about him. It was Eugene Field. Then and there began an acquaintance which lasted through his life. I went to Washington, and soon was added to the staff of the New York *Herald*, which was then operating under Howard Preston.

It was an interesting and exciting session of the Forty-third Congress. The service had a distinctly educational value. I widened my acquaintance with public men and public affairs. Out of my acquaintance with Alexander Stephens, who was once more in Congress, grew an affectionate intimacy, and I sometimes went to the National Hotel to play whist with him until very late hours.

That winter Andrew Johnson was elected to the Senate from Tennessee, and he came back to Washington. One Sunday morning I was assigned to interview him. It was the last interview that any newspaperman had with the ex-President. He stood in the parlour of his suite, with a number of flags of the country draped behind him as a background. He was dressed in the typical frock coat of the statesman, with a white tie. He had quarrelled with General Grant, who had become President, and there was great interest to learn his attitude. I shall never forget the manner in which he struck a pose in the traditional attitude of Henry Clay and said, with his deep, stentorian voice:

I come, sir, with the Constitution of my country in one hand and the olive branch of peace in the other, and if that damned liar in the White House plays decent, we will get on.

Nellie Grant was married to Algernon Sartoris by the Rev. O. H. Tiffany. I had their marriage certificate engrossed and presented it to them. I had frequent and very agreeable visits at the White House, and Fred Grant and I became lifelong friends.

On one occasion I interviewed General Sherman, and his declarations were distinctly sensational. He was bitterly opposed to releasing sons of important officials from their duties in the army to enable them to enjoy themselves in Washington, and among the number that he singled out for criticism was the President's own son.

I was a little timorous about publishing it, but General Sherman said it would not disturb his relations with President Grant, and afterward his point of view was confirmed in a talk I had with President Grant.

General Butler was the leader of the House and Samuel J. Randall leader of the Democratic side. As the Forty-third Congress was about to close I was with Randall when Butler came up, and Randall asked him to hold a Sunday session. Butler said no, he would not consent to it; he never would do any work on Sunday that was not necessary. Randall turned and chaffingly said: "Oh, that is your New England Puritanism, I suppose. That serves you to good purpose, and I expect to meet you some day, Butler, in another and better world."

Butler replied in a flash: "Oh, no, Sam: you will be there, as you are here, a member of the Lower House."

On another occasion an attack was made on Butler for his defence of the Jayne-Sanborn contracts. These contracts had been entered into by the Treasury Department and were contracts for the collection of delinquent internal revenue taxes and customs duties which had accumulated during the war. I think it was 50 per cent. of the collections that were to be given; I think the moiety was 50 per cent. The charge was—and it seemed to be well grounded—that these delinquent taxes could have been collected for the asking, as in the case of the Pennsylvania Railroad. A sub-committee of the Judiciary Committee, under the chairmanship of Charles Foster of Ohio, later Secretary of the Treasury, and known because of certain successful speculations as "Calico Charley," had investigated the cases and presented a report sharply criticizing Butler's action. Butler was instantly taken ill, and for three or four days it was announced that he was on the point of death. When the sympathy of the country had been duly roused it was announced that he would appear in the House of Representatives on a certain Friday evening to make the speech of his life in defence of his relation to the Jayne-Sanborn contracts. The house was crowded, floor and gallery. Butler rose and made his speech. He proceeded to denounce a leading firm of New York in unmeasured terms, and in the midst of it was interrupted by Foster.

Butler instantly clapped his hands, called a page, wrote something on a card, and sent the boy to his home on Capitol Hill—a big granite house still pointed out to tourists. The boy soon returned and handed General Butler a paper. The General was very near-sighted, and he handed this document to the clerk to be read and made a part of his speech. In loud tones the clerk proceeded to read "A letter to Mr. Tenny, District Attorney of Brooklyn," in which appeared a statement substantially as follows: "Have no fear for your friends Jayne and Sanborn. We are not going to hurt them. All we are trying to do is to get a rap at 'Old Cockeye.'"

This was signed "Charles Foster."

Then Butler proceeded with his peroration. Of course everyone recognized that he was "Old Cockeye." He asked what "Old Cockeye" had done to justify such an attack from a Republican committee. He told his audience how he, a Democrat, had voted for Jefferson Davis in the Charleston Convention in 1860, had bared his breast to the enemy's bullets and thereafter fought for his country, and he wound up with a most effective appeal. When he closed there was a hush over the hall.

Poor Foster was at a loss for something to say, and finally, as if he were at a Methodist prayer meeting, piped out: "Let us pray."

Butler had turned to take his seat, when he stopped and sang out in his peculiar whining voice: "*Yes, and spell it as you always do, with an 'e'.*"

Among the curious persons whom I knew very well was Colonel George Butler. He had led a checkered career, had been the husband of Rose Ettynge, the actress, at one time, and Consul General of the United States to Egypt at another, but had always so yielded to his love for alcohol that his life had been a failure. Nevertheless, as he was a nephew of General Benjamin F. Butler, he always maintained a certain standing. When I knew him in 1874-5 he was a pitiable object. He was personally untidy, usually the worse for drink, and spent his time sitting about as an idler in the public rooms of different hotels.

One day he visited the State Department in a state of intoxication. The State Department, as is well known, is the very embodiment of the dignity of our Government; and there was a gentleman of the old school connected with the service who still affected the blue cutaway coat with gilt buttons and buff waistcoat that came down from the former century. He was a veritable Colonel Newcome in politeness. Butler overheard him say he was about to visit New York and sidling up to him, said with a pleading voice: "So you are going to New York, Judge?"

"Yes, Colonel," replied the judge.

"Well," pleaded Butler, "will you do me a favour?"

"Certainly," replied the courteous judge, "if it is in my power."

Then Butler fumbled through his pockets and found a pawn ticket. Handing it to the judge, he urged: "When you reach New York will you go up to a pawn shop in Chatham Street and get my watch, pay the small charge on it, and bring it back?"

"Ah!" said the judge, "I never was in a pawn shop in my life, and I am afraid that I should find it difficult to do your errand. I want to accommodate you, but I think pawnbrokers are pretty bad people and they might easily trick me."

"Oh, no," persisted Butler, "they cannot do that; this watch is one that my uncle Ben gave me and I prize it very highly."

"But how should I know it?" asked the judge.

"Well," answered Butler, "I have had occasion to pawn it a good many times, and you will know it by the inscription that is under the back cover: '*I know that my Redeemer Liveth*'."

Mr. M—— was a congressman from southern Illinois. He delighted in a game of poker. Going home from an evening's sport with a couple of associates, he asked them to come in for a "nightcap." They thanked him, but were unwilling to disturb the family. "I'd have you understand," said he with a pompous air, "that I am Cæsar in my own house, and that I permit no interference with my wishes."

At that instant an upper window flew open, a woman in her sleeping apparel appeared, and in a gentle voice said: "It's all right, gentlemen, you can go on home and leave Cæsar to me. I will take care of him."

Stillson Hutchins, the well-known journalist, came to New York for a night at poker. The game broke up in the small hours with Hutchins a winner to the tune of some thousands of dollars. One of the players suggested the danger of walking the street with so much money on his person. "Yes, I know it," said Hutchins. "I'll accompany you," offered his friend. "*No,*" came the quick reply, "*you are the rascal I'm afraid of.*"

My service in Washington was an exceedingly pleasant period of my journalistic life. It seems to me that there was a richer and fuller intellectual interest in the Washington correspondence at that time than there is now. The correspondent had a wider editorial latitude than he has to-day, and the field for individual achievement in the collection of news was vastly greater. I must admit that the press associations now cover Washington news in such a way that there is little left to the initiative of the individual correspondent. Prominent statesmen or politicians who desire to put a matter of importance before the world send it direct to the Press Association themselves, knowing that it will go to all the principal papers in the country. There is less endeavour on the part of public men to keep in close touch with individual correspondents than there was thirty years ago, because the need of such intimacy is less.

More and more the special correspondent at Washington is limited to reporting or discussing matters of interest only in the limited field of his paper. The greater the field of his paper the more likely the matter is to be of national importance, and if of national interest it is covered in the manner mentioned above. Nobody is better aware of this fact than the present group of correspondents at Washington.

A few papers now maintain representatives who are given a semi-editorial authority and whose dispatches not merely transcribe the news but comment upon it. It is possible that this practice may grow, although the tendency of the American press to limit editorial comment rigidly to the editorial columns is rather against it. In the older countries of the world there is no precise parallel to the position of our correspondents at Washington, because elsewhere the political capital of the nation is at the same time the commercial capital and the great papers of the country are published there.

Our great papers are in New York, Chicago, Philadelphia, and San Francisco. It seems reasonable to believe that in time there will grow up in American journalism the practice of having the Washington correspondent in a certain sense an editorial writer, schooled in the policy of his paper, and authorized to express its views in his dispatches, enjoying as he does first-hand intimacy with the forces governing the country. I hesitate to offer predictions, but it seems to me that only by the development of this form of correspondent can the position of Washington correspondent again assume the importance that it had when such men as George Alfred Townsend, Henry Watterson, Murat Halstead, Whitelaw Reid, and others of their sort were prominent there.

Founding a Daily Paper

Early in the year 1874 my attention had been directed to the possibility of establishing a one-cent daily newspaper in Chicago. I studied the New York *Daily News* and the Philadelphia *Star*, both of which were successful. When the summer vacation of Congress came on I went home to Chicago and tried an experiment. Mr. William Dougherty, a well-known reporter, happened to be idle and I told him of my idea and said I would back him if he cared to start such a paper and see how it would be received by the public. He assented and, without any investment for a plant, issued for a couple of months, in an out-of-the-way location, the Chicago *Herald*. It could not be a permanent venture, as, indeed, it was not intended that it should be. It was what the French would call a *ballon d'essai*. Chicago was obviously the city of promise for my experiment. In forty years it had grown from a village to a metropolis with more than a million inhabitants. And, as in the Norse Saga the fabled Norns were weaving the fates of its people in their mystic looms, its possibilities were without limit. The hinterland was vast in proportion and rich in fruitage. So that, both as entrepot and depot, the city was certain to have a great future. I was convinced by this experience that there was a field and set out to prepare to occupy it.

I went back to Washington for the winter session of Congress of 1874–5. After the close of a special session of the Senate called for March, 1875, I returned to Chicago and to the managing editorship of the *Post and Mail*. But not for long. I was not pleased with the methods of the paper. It was in financial straits and the managers were anxious to force contributions for wealthy political aspirants. Also, I was obsessed with the desire to found my one-cent journal.

I had no money. For a short time, in conjunction with a fellow worker on the *Post and Mail*, I ran a correspondence bureau. George Lanigan, the then famous author of the "Ahkound of Swat," was a neighbour. He had been serving the New York *Herald* as its Chicago representative. He had received an offer to go to the Rochester *Post-Express*. Wherefore he surrendered his *Herald* work to me and departed. It was a windfall to me. A young Englishman, Percy Meggy, came along and I aroused his interest in my one-cent project. He had something like five thousand dollars in cash. He was ready to enlist in the undertaking. And so he, Dougherty, and I embarked on a very hazardous Odyssey. The winds seemed fair. Nevertheless, our craft required close attention if we were to make progress. On the 25th day of December we issued an experimental copy of the Chicago *Daily News*, with an announcement that on the first of the year, 1876, we should begin the publication regularly. This we did. There were four other evening newspapers in Chicago, all well established and supported by adequate capital.

Meggy was what the English call a "remittance man." That is, he depended on remittances of cash from his British home. Sometimes his remittances came as expected; sometimes they did not. This occasioned a certain degree of solicitude on the part of the partners and the employees. Not so, however, with Meggy. He never had any solicitude about anything. He was the capitalist of the institution, and stoutly maintained all of the prerogatives of your ideal capitalist. His rôle was that of the idle rich. So far as labour went he was on a perpetual strike. His mind was on his brierwood pipe and the matinée tickets. Although ostensibly an editor, he wrote nothing, read no copy, and as to any other kind of work, did as little.

Dougherty was the fighting journalist, and as the paper was avowedly aggressive, and deservedly so in a city where corruption was running riot, he had an abundant opportunity for the exercise of his talents. He filled his office with distinct credit.

If we were to succeed and create a permanent institution, we must take an original line, appeal to and win public approval, and, above all, be patient. We were not building for a day but for all time. Therefore we had certain definite and quite novel rules. Unlike our competitors, we must with single-mindedness accept as our only masters, our readers. We should aim at a reputation for veracity and fair dealing in all our relations with the public. Our quest was for public respect and permanency. To create a newspaper which should endure must be our sole aim; that is, the newspaper must be the end of our ambition, and in no sense the means to some other end. It followed that the paper should be independent of any political party. I had had experience in service upon a party organ, the *Inter-Ocean*, and had seen what such service meant. Assured of the paper's support, the party managers and heelers never visited the office except to give orders. They put their feet on our tables, smoked our cigars, now and then invited one of the "boys" to a luncheon, but went to the opposition papers to consult about their policy or the fitness of their prospective candidates.

Likewise, the paper must be independent of any other selfish interest. As a precautionary measure, its proprietors should not be permitted at any time to hold stock in any public-utility corporation. The paper must have no axes to grind, no friends to reward, no enemies to punish. In its every phase as a news-purveying organ, or as a director of public opinion, it must be wholly divorced from any private or unworthy purpose. It must have only two sources of revenue—from the sale of papers and the sale of advertising. Its hallmark must be dignity and decency.

The first intent of the publication was the collection and presentation of the world's news. It was recognized that in its editorial department there were three offices to perform: First, to print news; second, to endeavour to guide public opinion aright; and, third, to furnish entertainment. I used this order because I believed it to be the correct one. I believed it to be even a business mistake to invert this order and to make the entertainment of the reader of first importance. I think the business of guiding public opinion, while obviously involving large responsibility, is, after all, secondary. Following this order, the proper presentation of the news was the first thing of consequence. The news was put upon the first page of the journal, the most conspicuous place, and an effort made to present a true perspective of the world's real developing history. I had a view that the relation of a newspaper to a community was not very different from that of an individual. And so, in our dispensing the news, we were not unlike the witness in court, bound to "tell the truth, the whole truth, and nothing but the truth." This, subject to the limitations that the news was of a character proper to publish. The paper, while independent in all things, must be neutral to none.

I suppose there are no two journalists in the world who would agree precisely as to the relative value of the various news articles before them. I sought, however, to establish certain approximate standards, which seemed to me wise, to determine alike what should and what should not be presented. In a certain sense the counting room must have no influence in the matter, and yet in a larger sense it must have everything to do with it. There must be no pandering to the vitiated taste of the unthinking. There must be no publishing of so-called sensational and exaggerated or scandalous material for the purpose of making sales. The paper must be cheap only as to its price. There must always be a sense of responsibility. We were engaged in something else than a mere business enterprise in which we should seek to provide anything and everything that the public might crave.

Therefore, a rule provided that in his relation to the public every man's activities were a proper subject for attention, while in his domestic relations he was entitled to privacy which no newspaper was privileged to invade. Also a rule that nothing should be printed which a worthy young gentlewoman could not read aloud in the presence of a mixed company. Still another rule, that every effort should be made for accuracy and impartiality, and that if we were ever led, through error, into a mis-statement, there should be a fair, frank, and open acknowledgment and apology. I discarded utterly the common effort to assume the editor's infallibility, believing it was much easier and infinitely more important to gain a reputation for integrity.

With these principles which were obviously wise, yet practically revolutionary, as newspapers were then conducted, we began business. As workshop, we secured accommodations in the building occupied by a daily Norwegian paper, the *Skandinaven*. The composing room was on the fourth floor, and one corner was partitioned off roughly to serve as an editorial department. The writing was done on inverted packing cases. As a number of other papers were published in the building, we were able to rent press facilities. Our business office was a space about ten feet square ruled off in a corner of the counting room of the *Skandinaven*. Scarcely had the paper begun its career, however, before serious problems were presented. First, initial issues were larger than expected. The first day we sold about 9,000 copies. At once additional printing-press facilities were demanded. In time we bought an old-fashioned four-cylinder Hoe rotary press capable of turning out ten thousand copies an hour. Second, the capital in sight was limited, and naturally there was very limited credit. Third, there were a number of important news developments, which, being adequately reported, stimulated the circulation in such a measure as to threaten, with the limited press facilities and the limited capital, a collapse.

The employees of the paper were a fine lot of men. They enlisted as soldiers, ready and anxious to share in the trials, the disappointments, all of the vicissitudes of the enterprise. It was never a case of "master and man," but a family. John J. Flinn was chief editorial assistant and was very efficient. In later years he became leading editorial writer on the *Christian Science Monitor*. Andrew B. Adair was the foreman of the composing room on the first day of issue, and has held the place with greatly widening responsibility through a half century to the present day. Cornelius McAuliffe was a journeyman typesetter at the same eventful beginning, had ambition to become an editor, and so developed that he later, and for a considerable period until his death, directed the news columns of the Chicago *Record-Herald*. Kirk La Shelle in the early days of the paper was also a typesetter. He became interested in the drama, showed capacity, was made critic, and grew famous as a theatrical manager. And Elwyn Barron was a reporter. He developed into a well-known dramatic author, collaborating with Wilson Barrett on several pieces and being the sole author of others, all of them successful.

Frequently, in those strenuous days, pay hour came and "the ghost" did not walk, for there was no money in the shop. But there was no complaint. There was ever sympathy and confidence for the struggling proprietor. My gratitude and affection for my fellow workers of that period have ever been measureless.

In less than a week from the first issue we were refusing advertisements, because we could not permit them to encroach on the space reserved for news. The very novelty of such a daily newspaper, so conducted, proved a sensation. The largest department store in the city thought to see what the bantling was like and sent us a column advertisement. Back it went with a polite note that if reduced to a half column and held over for two days, we would find room for it. Then they returned it with a three-line editorial item calling attention to it. It was the custom of the Chicago papers to insert such items. Of course we refused, as we did their demand for a given location. At first we were told that all this was a "bluff," later that it was arbitrary, and we were notified that they would never patronize the paper if these "reasonable" requests were not met. When they saw that we were in earnest they not only backed down, but confessed their approval of our policy.

An adverse criticism upon a play appeared, and the proprietor of the theatre summarily withdrew his advertisement; but when he found that it made no difference whatever with the treatment of his playhouse, that good plays were commended and bad ones condemned, he thought better of his action and resumed his advertising.

Undeniably, so far as I was concerned, there were enthusiasm and energy about the business, but there was also no small measure of good fortune. First, a fine collection of enemies developed. The Chicago *Tribune*, which was conducted upon the theory that it was justified in publishing whatever it believed the public would enjoy reading, attacked the enterprise even before the first copy of the *Daily News* was issued, despite the fact that the projected newspaper was to be in no sense a competitor, the *Tribune* being a morning paper and the *Daily News* an evening paper. This assault was so ungenerous that it aroused for us the sympathy of very many people.

One evening, shortly after the *Daily News* was founded, I was invited, with the editor of another paper, a veteran in the business, to address the Commercial Club of Chicago on journalism. My associate speaker had been censured rather severely for the publication of scandalous matter and was on his mettle. He was to make answer to a company of merchants, men of distinctly commercial type, and here was his opportunity. In a defiant tone he told them that the journalist, like themselves, was in business to make money, and was perfectly justified in giving the public anything it might want. If the newspapers were low in tone, it was because the readers craved sensation. If his hearers did not like his paper, they had better start one of the kind they liked and see how it would succeed.

Then it was my turn. I flatly challenged the view of my confrère. I agreed that every merchant had certain responsibilities in the conduct of his business, but held that the limitations upon the journalist were infinitely greater; that in the conduct of so important an educational force as the daily newspaper, the editor was chargeable with a very high duty in respect of the decencies of his publication—a duty which he could not escape.

A very eminent citizen closed the discussion by calmly saying that the "give the public what it wants" doctrine was that on which keepers of dissolute houses justified their vocation, and that, if a journalist were willing shamelessly to take his place with such people, he must be privileged to do so.

No line of paid reading matter was admitted to the news columns. Everything in the way of advertising was printed as advertising so that the reader could easily distinguish it.

And as to the business department; it was recognized that advertising was legitimate. But our theory was that everyone was free to advertise or not, precisely as he was free to buy groceries at a grocery, or dry goods at a dry goods store. And no one lost standing with the paper if he neglected to use its advertising columns. Indeed, it was not unusual to advise people who brought advertisements to the office that they would get better results by taking their notices elsewhere. For instance, if a man wished to sell an engine, he would be thanked for coming to us, but told that it would be wiser for him to put his advertisement in some journal making a specialty of mechanics. And with the earliest issue the actual paid circulation, day by day, was printed at the head of the editorial column and sworn to. Our belief was that the advertiser should be perfectly free to advertise, or not to advertise, and that if he did want to advertise he had the same right to know the extent and the character of the circulation of the paper that you would have if you entered a dry goods store to buy prints and demanded to know whether they were fast colours, and a yard wide, or not. We had no right to expect him to buy a pig in a bag. Our aim was, therefore, to give the fullest possible information and to invite the advertiser to verify our statements by any method that might suggest itself.

There was no boasting of circulation, no bragging of the increase in sales. We were content to permit the sworn statements to speak for themselves. Now and then when, because of a violent storm—not an infrequent occurrence in Chicago—or on the opening of the school term in the autumn, the newsboys were less active than usual, an editorial mention of the decline in the issue was inserted. As a result, the faith of the people in our sworn declaration grew until it was not uncommon for men to make bets as to the circulation of the paper for an ensuing month.

Having no liking for the quite common theory that a newspaper was somehow entitled to a man's advertising, and in case of his failure to "come across" resentment was justifiable (a sort of genteel blackmail), we had no employees to go begging as mendicants for patronage. We engaged a young man who had never been connected with a newspaper, and his sole mission was to go to the merchants, tell them that he was not soliciting from them, but if they thought of advertising in the paper, it was his duty to tell them all about it and to put them in the way of verifying his assertions.

If our sworn statement was questioned, my answer was that at least twenty employees of the paper knew the facts, and we were not such fools as to put ourselves at their mercy by issuing a falsehood. This, of course, was conclusive.

After we began publication, I found that, through inadvertence, we were accepting and publishing so-called "Personal" advertisements, which in reality were of an immoral character. A letter came to the office asking for the insertion of a "Wanted" for two girls for an establishment at South Bend, Ind. It opened my eyes as to the "Personals." I published a notice that they would be refused, and thereafter every advertisement was accepted subject to editorial censorship, to the end that no improper notices should be admitted.

A disreputable quack doctor engaged a lawyer to begin an

action to compel us to print his announcement. He failed, but, in the attempt, disclosed our policy, much to our benefit.

Inasmuch as we regarded the reader of more value than the advertiser, and inasmuch as our first duty, as we conceived it, was to the reader, while aiming to deal fairly with the advertiser at all times, we insisted that he should take second place. We therefore made it an inflexible rule that all locations of advertising must be at publisher's option, and we made no contracts whatever for "top of column next to reading matter." In the make-up of the paper the news was considered paramount and the advertising relegated to a less important place.

The rule was also absolute that there should be no cutting of rates under any circumstances. One day the junior partner of a leading dry goods firm called. With no small degree of pomposity he said he would talk of advertising; that he never dealt with underlings and therefore had called to see the proprietor of the institution. He was good enough to say that he might be induced to make a contract, but he wanted me to bear in mind that ours was a poor, struggling journal, while his house was a very important one, and that if he patronized us it would result in others doing likewise, so that any business between us was likely to be of as great benefit to the paper as to his firm. Of course this meant that he wanted a special rate. I asked him if it was not so, and he readily assented.

"What concession would you think fair?" I suggested.

He thought 10 per cent. would do.

"You mean from our lowest price?" I rejoined.

"Certainly," he replied.

Then I told him that we had established a rule that we would never cut our rates; that we had in no case violated the rule, and that we had regarded it as inflexible. "But," I added, "I recognize the force of what you say, and in order to secure your patronage I will break the rule on one condition."

"What is that?" he asked eagerly.

"That you will permit my family to buy such goods as they may choose at your store 10 per cent. cheaper than any one else and give me a writing to that effect which I may publish."

"Good heavens!" he shouted, "we run a one-price store, and such an announcement would ruin us!"

He went away in high dudgeon, but a week later made a contract upon our terms.

It was the period when the telephone was introduced. The telephones were first installed in the drug stores. We seized the opportunity to make contracts with a considerable number of the drug stores to act as advertising agents. We allowed a small commission, and the advertisements were phoned in. Their appearance in the paper was prompt, and our patrons were saved the delay and expense of making a journey to the office. The *Daily News* was a pioneer in this method of locating branch agencies.

Creating 99-Cent Stores

One of the difficulties encountered was to induce people to use the one-cent coin. The smallest denomination current in the city was the five-cent piece. The smaller coin was practically unknown. I imported from the Philadelphia Mint some barrels of pennies and persuaded certain merchants to mark their goods at 59, or 69, or 99 cents. Thus began in Chicago what were known as "99-cent stores." The customer (frequently to his disgust) would be returned a penny in change, and the only use he could make of it was to buy a copy of the *Daily News*. The pennies which the newsboys paid into the office for the purchase of papers were put up in packages of 25 or 50 and each morning distributed to the stores selling 99-cent goods. It was a slow process, but in time resulted in a general circulation of the coins.

As I have said, the founding of such a paper required patience. And neither of my partners had the necessary power of endurance. They were in no mood for a prolonged struggle. They wanted to quit. Meggy wanted to go home to England and Dougherty to find a new position. And so we took the money from the till and gave it to them, and I was left alone in my glory.

Meggy spent a short time in England and then, charged

with his experience of perpetual strife in the *Daily News* office, went out to Australia and became, as a high priest of idleness, a leader in the political labour movement which eventually secured control of the Government. Later, Dougherty died. His daughter married Stuart Robson, the actor, and is still a worthy member of the theatrical profession.

I struggled on. The paper was successful; indeed, far too successful. The demand was so great that it was clearly impossible to provide the necessary facilities for its production on the slender pocketbook at my command. I must find a moneyed partner. Henry Demarest Lloyd was in sight. He was a brilliant young journalist, employed on the Chicago *Tribune*. More important, he had a rich father-in-law, Governor William Bross, and might get the desired funds from him. He joined me, without definite commitment, for a month or two, and then we tearfully parted. The father-in-law would neither put up nor come down, and again I was alone.

When my partners withdrew I assembled three or four bright assistants. It was a day when every competent journalist was expected to be a drunkard, and my staff lived up to such requirements. Chicago had a notable reformatory for "habituals" called the Washingtonian Home, and it was a poor week for the institution when I did not have one or more of my staff imprisoned there. When they were "sobered up" they proved quite efficient.

One evening I was forced to dismiss one of our derelicts who had exhausted my patience by his too-frequent lapses. He was the brilliant son of a former governor of Missouri. Somewhat after midnight I was aroused from my bed at my home several miles distant from the office. The man whom I had discharged appeared with a carriage and told me that the boiler upon which we depended for steam to run our press had exploded. He had been carousing in a neighbouring saloon at the time and had hastened to notify me. I dressed hurriedly and went with him. After surveying the scene of destruction I drove to the house of a man who dealt in machinery, and before daybreak had a portable engine installed and was able to print an extra edition giving the first news of the accident. This was a hard blow, but gave us a reputation for enterprise, which made the paper the talk of the town.

With the disappearance of Lloyd as a possible associate, it became evident that I had neither the physical nor financial strength to carry on the work alone.

Enter Victor F. Lawson

Then I turned to Victor F. Lawson. He and I had been fellow students at the Chicago High School, and his father being a partner in the firm publishing the *Skandinaven*, I was

Victor F. Lawson in 1876

Melville E. Stone in 1876

A Life Partnership Begun

brought into daily contact with him. He had a desk in the office of his father's paper and was developing a business career. He was a witness of my effort, my code of newspaper ethics, and the measurable success that I was achieving. After consideration he took over the interests of Meggy and Dougherty, and there began a partnership which lasted twelve years and proved to be the happiest period of my life. He sympathized fully in my views of newspaper responsibility and approved of all the rules I had adopted for the governance of the enterprise. He became business manager, and I was free to devote my whole attention to the editorial department.

There never was the slightest trace of friction in our most intimate relation. Out of it all grew a close friendship, which has continued to the present hour.

The Chicago *Post and Mail,* owned by the McMullen brothers, enjoyed the Associated Press privilege. Nevertheless, the *Post and Mail* was daily pirating our news. No sooner would a dispatch appear in our early edition than it would be seized upon by that paper. Mr. Flinn, who, as I have said, was chief editorial assistant, set a trap. The morning paper of that day announced great distress in Servia. We framed a dispatch, and published it in our noon edition on Saturday, December 2, as follows:

John J. Flinn

SAD STORY OF DISTRESS IN SERVIA

London, Dec. 2.—A correspondent of the *Times* writing from Servia, where he has spent many weeks, says that the country presents a gloomy picture to the traveller. The land is devastated and the people are starving.

Everywhere he found men and women crying for food. He could see in any large village hundreds of young women in a state of seminudity. It has been a hard matter for the priests to keep the populace under their control. Children are starving by thousands throughout the country.

The men, young and old, go through the streets shouting for bread, cursing the rich for not coming to their aid. A few days ago the mayor of the provincial town of Sovik issued a proclamation ending with the ominous words: *"Er us siht la Etsll iws nel lum cmeht"* (the municipality cannot aid).

Upon reading this, the people, led by the women of the town, organized a riot, in the course of which a dozen houses were pillaged and over twenty persons were brutally murdered.

The three-o'clock edition of the *Post and Mail* for the same day contained the dispatch word for word, the only change being made in the caption, which appeared in the *Post and Mail* as "Horrid Starvation in Servia."

The dispatch was dropped from the three-o'clock edition of the *News* and it did not appear in the five-o'clock edition of the *Post and Mail*, as some friend of the McMullens, who owned that paper, called their attention to the fact that reading the supposed foreign words backward, they became: "The Mc-Mullens will steal this sure." It was too late, however, for they had been decoyed by the item and the harm was done.

As the *News* did not issue a Sunday paper and as we wished the widest publicity given to the hoax, we asked the *Times* and the *Tribune* to reprint it with explanations on Sunday. They did so, and the *Post and Mail* was literally laughed to death. In less than two years we bought all that was left of it, including its franchise in the Associated Press and its material, for $15,000.

It was a great news year. Primarily the Hayes-Tilden Presidential contest engrossed public interest. When the Republican National Convention assembled at Cincinnati we were able to touch high-water mark in enterprise by issuing an extra announcing the nomination of Hayes before it was declared in the Convention Hall. The process was very simple, but then very new. As the balloting progressed we were keeping tally, and when a sufficient number of votes to insure Hayes's victory was reached the forms were sent to press, and in a moment the papers were selling on the street. In that day the performance was accounted something wonderful.

Then came the campaign, the indecisive election, and the succeeding electoral commission. All this furnished exceptional opportunity for an enterprising newspaper. We admittedly took the lead in journalistic activities and maintained it.

One of our competitors was the Chicago *Evening Telegram*, owned by Wilbur F. Storey of the Chicago *Times*. Storey spent money without stint and enjoyed great fame as a news gatherer. But he found that we set a pace too swift for him, and he abandoned the enterprise.

We were a happy lot. We had no "office politics." There

were no jealousies, no attempts to secure advancement by undermining an associate. Each man sought to aid his fellow, and all to make the paper decent, truthful, entertaining, and a force for the right. I have great pride in the fact that all the men who worked with me have throughout my later days been abiding friends. We all struggled earnestly and never counted the hours.

Story of "Ross Raymond"

In 1876 an attractive young fellow called on me and asked for work as a reporter. He said his name was Ross Raymond, and told me of his belief in his capacity and of the work he had done. I employed him. He proved an energetic and altogether competent employee. As time went on he grew in favour and was advanced. I sent him to the State capitol to report the Illinois Legislature. Suddenly he asked to return to Chicago, and, without apparent reason, tendered his resignation. He had overdrawn his account a trifle, but that was of small consequence. His resignation was accepted, and he took his leave.

"Ross Raymond"

Some months later he turned up in Baltimore; wrote a play in which I was made the hero. It had a short run, and thereafter I heard no more of him for a long time. Then one day he appeared. He had been working, meanwhile, for the Philadelphia *Times* and the New York *Herald*. He had served the *Herald* at Elberon, N. J., while President Garfield lay there dying. He had been married, but had deserted his wife. He told me that the managing editor of the *Herald* had treated him badly, had promised to pay him space rates but had repudiated the agreement and had forced him to take a weekly wage which was much less than he was fairly entitled to. He wanted nothing, only called to pay his respects, and went his way.

Next I heard that he had been arrested in New Orleans for passing a draft upon the *Herald*, acceptance of which had been refused in New York.

There was another long period of silence. How he escaped punishment in New Orleans I do not know. Then, one day in September, 1882, I received a cable message from Cairo, Egypt, advising me that a battle had been fought against the forces of Arabi at Tel-el-Kebir; a victory won; and that the sender of the message, who had been present, would like to wire me an account. It was signed by Ross Raymond. I replied at once, asking him to send the story. So it happened that the Chicago *Daily News*, even before the London papers, printed a graphic story of Wolseley's decisive battle. And again I heard no more.

Months later Raymond appeared in Chicago. He said he had left us in debt to the office and would accept no payment for his valuable message from Egypt. Again he disappeared.

Two years later he wrote me from Allahabad, India, where he was editing the *Pioneer*, the paper on which Rudyard Kipling had made a reputation. And again there was silence for months.

Then I learned the reason for his sudden and mysterious resignation while serving as my legislative correspondent at the Illinois capital. He had met William J. Calhoun (then an Illinois lawyer of note and later American Ambassador to China), and had been recognized by him as an old-time fellow pupil at a little school at Poland, Ohio, where William McKinley also received his preparatory instruction. Calhoun knew Raymond's history and Raymond feared he might betray it. His real name was Frank H. Powers, not Ross Raymond. He was born at Beaver, a few miles east of Poland, in Pennsylvania. From there he enlisted in the Navy and later passed the required examination and was admitted to the Naval Academy at Annapolis. He failed to pass his first semi-annual examination and was dropped from the rolls. He then, a "bilged middy," began a criminal career.

"Powers, after leaving the Academy," writes Mr. James A. Campbell, who knew him in the navy, "had no home and he wandered about the country. He called on wealthy fathers of his former classmates in the Academy and told them some cock-and-bull story of having obtained leave to settle his mother's affairs and running short of funds, and as he was able to talk glibly about the Academy and the middies, he succeeded in making a number of touches. His exploits were made public after the victimized fathers had communicated with their sons in the Academy, and by the boys were informed that they had been swindled by the "bilged middy." Captain Charles King, the well-known author of army novels and short stories of fiction, based one of his stories on the exploits of the "bilged middy.'

"In the early part of 1871 the writer, still a naval apprentice, was a member of the crew of the U. S. S. *Richmond*, flagship of the Mediterranean squadron of the American fleet in Europe, Commodore J. R. Madison Mullaney commanding. One day when on shore leave at Naples, Italy, I visited the Royal Museum and in the department devoted to relics of Pompeii and Herculaneum, I met Powers. He wore the uniform of a seaman of the British Navy. Her Britannic Majesty's ship *Monarch* was in port and Powers was one of her crew, serving under the name of Frank Palmer. We talked over old times and parted, not to meet again until we encountered each other in Philadephia some years later, when I learned that he came to this country on the *Monarch,* when that vessel brought home from Europe the body of George Peabody, the eminent philanthropist, who had died abroad. I gathered the impression that Powers deserted the *Monarch* after her arrival in this country, and then blossomed out as Ross Raymond and became a newspaperman."

He had been singularly successful in leading a dual life. On one hand, under one alias, he was a brilliant journalist commanding a high salary and always in demand. Under another name he was an accomplished rascal, engaged in swindling, blackmailing, forgery, and like offences. His mysterious disappearances were due to the fact that he was frequently taken into custody and sent to prison.

 On one occasion he appeared under one of his many assumed names at the Hotel Bristol, on the Place Vendôme, in Paris. It was the hotel at which the royalties visiting the French capital were accustomed to stop. Raymond announced himself as the avant-courier of the Khedive of Egypt, who, he said, would arrive late that evening, accompanied by a large suite of attachés. And, as it was the Khedive's birthday, His Highness would desire to give a befitting dinner to his staff. Raymond engaged, with scrupulous care, rooms for his party, and selected a menu of rare delicacies. Then, with perfect nonchalance, he told the hotel manager that he must select a suitable souvenir for each of the guests, and he asked that a quantity of jewellery be sent for from which he might make choice. The unsuspecting boniface hastened to comply. Raymond indolently picked out thirty or forty pieces which he wished put in the hotel safe to await the evening dinner, and asked that the rest of the collection of valuables be returned to the jeweller. Then he called a carriage and drove for an hour in the Bois de Boulogne. Returning to the hotel, he had the jewels he had chosen sent to his room that he might wrap them and affix the name of the recipient to each. And now he quietly slipped out of the place with his plunder and escaped to England. He had no relation to the Khedive, it was not the Khedive's birthday, and His Highness was not en route to Paris. It was all a cunning and successful scheme of robbery. It was not until years after that his identity was discovered. And then he was in prison. He was never punished for the crime.

Adopting once more his *nom de plume* of Ross Raymond, he settled down quietly in London and found no difficulty in gaining a handsome income by writing for American newspapers. He made the acquaintance of Henry Irving and a number of other notables, who years afterward assured me of his attractive qualities and who had no suspicion of his real character.

In 1889 I spent a week-end in Manchester, England. Late Saturday afternoon I read in an evening paper the story of the arrest and arraignment of an American, under an obviously assumed name, for swindling. He had called on Joseph Chamberlain, introducing himself as a New Jersey gentleman farmer who made a specialty of orchids. As orchids were Chamberlain's weakness, he was, of course, interested, and gave his visitor a hearty welcome. "He told me more about the cultivation of my favourite flower than I had ever had the time to learn," said the Birmingham statesman in forced admiration.

After having established suitable confidence Raymond suggested that he had a bank check for one hundred pounds sent him by the famous English journalist, George Augustus Sala, and as he was a stranger, and for the moment a little short of funds, he wondered if Mr. Chamberlain could arrange to have the check cashed. Nothing could give Mr. Chamberlain greater pleasure. So Raymond pocketed the amount and said "Good day!"

He called upon Pain, the fireworks man, in another guise, and sold him another Sala check for a like amount. Both checks were forgeries, cleverly executed. The police found little difficulty in tracing the culprit, and when I was in Manchester it was he who was in jail in that city.

Although Raymond's name did not appear in the newspaper story, I was convinced from the nature of the offence that it was he. And if so, I determined to call on him and see whether I could properly aid him. Sunday morning I saw the high sheriff and told him of my belief that the man was a former employee of mine, in jail under a fresh alias. He courteously offered to go to the jail, see the prisoner, and, if my suspicion was well founded, arrange for me to visit him. He saw Raymond, who frankly admitted his identity, but said that while he was grateful for my interest, he shrank from the ordeal of a meeting. He said he was guilty and purposed pleading so in court. He thought it better that he be sent to prison, because, if by any chance he was permitted to go free, he knew he would get into trouble again very soon. The next day he was sentenced to ten years at hard labour in Dartmoor Prison.

He took his punishment with singular stoicism. He picked oakum uncomplainingly, and signified no wish for a release. His faithful wife was living with relatives in the State of Nevada. She believed, and I have no doubt rightfully, that her husband was a victim of a peculiar form of insanity. So long as he avoided alcoholic stimulants he led a perfectly orderly and honourable life. But given one glass of intoxicant, he would instantly set about swindling someone. His devices were most ingenious and rarely failed. With the proceeds he would order expensive suits of clothing, take a costly suite of rooms at a leading hotel, order a supply of champagne of some priceless vintage, and, all alone, indulge in an orgy. When his spree was over he would return to his newspaper work and slave without relaxation.

Later, as I was about to visit England, Mrs. Raymond and a number of newspaper friends urged me to make an effort for a ticket of leave. I presented the facts to the then Home Secretary, Mr. Asquith, who said a release could probably be arranged if I would take the prisoner to America and give an assurance that he would never again set foot on British soil. This, of course, was not possible. And, therefore, the term of imprisonment was served. Raymond returned to the United States, and for some time led an orderly life. He was appointed city editor of the Philadelphia *Times*, and proved highly efficient. Just as we hoped his reform was lasting, however, he appeared in Milwaukee, posing as a colonel of distinction in the British Army. He was accepted as a welcome guest of the Wisconsin Club, and entertained the members with recollections of his services for his "Queen and country."

Then he perpetrated one of his swindles, was arrested, and sent to the workhouse. There was another period of sobriety and hard work. And then another disaster. He went to New Haven and called on President Hadley of Yale, representing himself as an Oxford professor temporarily visiting this country. He was short of funds and was accommodated. He paid a like visit to Mr. Seth Low, then president of Columbia University, and finally to General Thomas L. James, president of the Lincoln National Bank of New York. Once more he was arrested. His wife asked me to visit him in the Tombs, and I did so. His lawyer was with me. I said that I thought he might be given a light sentence if insanity should be pleaded. He turned on me in anger and said: "No, sir! Never will I leave my wife as a legacy the memory of a crazy husband." He was imprisoned at Sing Sing for about two years. While there he edited the *Star of Hope*, the prison newspaper, with great brilliancy.

On his release he and his wife took a little apartment in an inexpensive quarter of New York City, and he and she worked together, upon a very small income, but for the first time in years were really happy. He had no more escapades, but a year or two later died.

He was a handsome, impressive person always. His ability to pass for a clergyman, a college professor, a distinguished soldier, or a scientist of fame was amazing. His stock of information on almost every conceivable subject was sufficient to deceive any one.

Dick Lane, My Burglar Friend

After years of maladministration there was a reform government in the city of Chicago. Not a Puritan government, but an honest one. For a long time there had been whispers that the police force was corrupt. And there was much reason for believing that the suspicion was well founded. The plan of operation was very ingenious. There was a conspicuous keeper of a gambling house. He was also the chief Democratic "boss." He had as a partner a lawyer who was noted as a "jury fixer." Such a combination was almost unbreakable. It owned the police, the prosecuting officers, and even certain of the judges. The situation was such that even a bank robber or a house burglar was safe.

Dick Lane

He made his compact with the "boss." He agreed to commit no depredations within the limits of the city. It was arranged that he was free to operate in any outlying town. And then he was to run into Chicago, share his plunder with the "boss," and if arrested was to be defended by the lawyer partner. With the aid of the jury commissioner it was always easy to secure one "safe" man among the twelve in the box, and a failure to convict was certain.

In such circumstances the honest but stupid citizens were easily cozened. They looked with pride upon their municipality. There were no burglaries, no bank robberies in the city. Indeed, there was little evidence of crime anywhere about them. Therefore, the government of the place was admirable! But Chicago was an asylum for all sorts of criminals. This was a condition to be changed.

I learned that over in Michigan State Prison there was a famous bank robber who felt that he had been unjustly convicted. He had been guilty of all kinds of crimes short of murder, but not of the particular one for which he was incarcerated. He was said to be very sore against the Chicago police. His name was Dick Lane. I went to the prison at Jackson, Mich., and saw him. He "opened up" freely and frankly. He told me, in detail, of the "criminal insurance" plan of the Democratic boss and his lawyer partner. He told me how bank robbers and house burglars were protected by the Chicago police. He told me where I might find his burglar's tools—one set under a haystack, fifty miles west of Chicago, in DeKalb County, another in the hayloft of a Chicago detective's barn, and a third in a window box of his "girl's" place on South State Street.

I returned to Chicago and reported the result of my journey to the chief of police, a gentleman of unquestioned integrity. It was Mr. Elmer Washburne, who later was chief of the United States Secret Service at Washington. He and I set out to confirm Dick Lane's statements. We found the burglar's tools in all the places he had indicated. Then, of course, there were retirements from the police force. They were retirements in disgrace. It could not be shown that there were criminal offences by the city detectives, but there was a wholesome measure of moral sanitation. After a while Lane was released from prison. And one afternoon, as I was leaving my office, I met him in the street in the custody of a policeman. He appealed for help. In his long and efficient career as a veggman (bank-safe man) he had had many exciting and dangerous experiences. He had served more than half his life in jails of one sort or another. In one affair he had lost an eye.

"Mr. Stone, I am in trouble," he quite unnecessarily explained. "It was like this: Yesterday I broke my glass eye, and, needing another, last night I opened the store of Doctor Walker, the oculist, over there on Clark Street. In the dark I couldn't pick out one of the right colour to match my real eye, and so I had to take a trayful. I hadn't more than stepped into the street when they pinched me. I told the cop that you were my friend, and he came round here with me."

Experience with his natural enemies, the police, had taught him that political influence was too often more valuable for the accused criminal than any perfect legal defence. With him also friendship was a cardinal virtue. He had proved his friendship for me by squealing on the police when I asked him to. Now, why should I not protect him when he was in trouble? It did not occur to him that any moral element in the business deserved consideration. And he regarded my suggestion that, as he was admittedly guilty of theft, he should be punished, as an inconceivable attitude for a real friend to take.

There was another phase of the case, however. He was afraid that, having caught him, they might "railroad" him to prison for a long term on a trumped-up charge in retaliation for the disclosures he had made concerning the corruption of the Chicago police force. They talked about his complicity in a certain robbery. And of that he assured me he was wholly innocent. I promised him that I would do what I could to prevent any unjust punishment of him. The penalty for robbing the oculist was light. I lost sight of him for a number of years.

Then one day he appeared at my office for a private interview. He told me that he was tired of criminal life and wanted to "go square." I laughed and frankly said I had no faith that he could reform. "You do not want to pay the price necessary to real reformation, Dick," said I. "It means hard work at small pay, and I do not believe you have the strength of character to persist in the effort."

"Will you try me?" he pleaded. "I have thought it all over, and I want to quit this life that I am leading. There isn't anything in it. I do a 'job,' get a little money, hurry to town, square myself with the 'boss' and his lawyer, give a bunch of money to a worthless woman who pretends she cares for me, but who does not, and then I gamble away the rest. In a few days I must go out and do another 'job' or starve. Then I'm nabbed and sent up for a year or two. When I get out of the penitentiary the thing is simply repeated. And I tell you I am tired of it. I will go straight if I can have a chance."

I telephoned my friend, Mr. H. H. Kohlsaat, editor and publisher of the Chicago *Record Herald*, and asked him to step over to my office. He came, and I introduced my burglar friend. I told him that Lane wanted to reform, and Kohlsaat agreed to employ him as an assistant janitor at $5 a week.

Dick was delighted. He went to work. He proved faithful and was promoted. He was converted in a mission Sunday School and became active in religious effort.

More than twenty years passed, and Dick Lane lived in Chicago until his death an orderly Christian life.

The Case of Judge Blodgett

In the publication of the *Daily News*, at a very early stage, we took up the investigation of public wrongs. Perhaps the first notable instance was the Blodgett case.

Henry W. Blodgett was the judge of the United States District Court in Chicago. He had been a politician of many years' standing, and his reputation was not altogether savoury. A close scrutiny of his administration of the office led me to believe him an unjust judge. There were three young lawyers in Chicago of very high character who shared my views. They were John S. Cooper, John J. Knickerbocker, and Henry I. Sheldon. After no little hesitation, in view of the responsibility assumed, in 1877, we framed a petition to Congress, asking an investigation with a view to Judge Blodgett's impeachment. This was sent to Mr. Carter H. Harrison, a member of Congress from Chicago, and he presented it. A sub-committee of the Judiciary Committee of the House of Representatives, under the chairmanship of J. Proctor Knott of Kentucky, was appointed to conduct the inquiry.

Blodgett had for some years been a railroad attorney and a lobbyist on behalf of the railroads, and since Chicago was the most conspicuous railroad centre in the United States, the atmosphere of the place was murky with railroad influence. The moment the attempt to impeach Blodgett was disclosed, a large coterie of the leading lawyers of Chicago, who had enjoyed railroad practice, as well as the newspapers competing with the *Daily News*, took up the cudgels, denounced the three young men roundly and set out to defend the accused. It thus happened that when Proctor Knott's committee arrived, even before it began work, there was a round of wining and dining for the members, and the whole accusation was stigmatized as an outrage.

As the hearing went on, however, it was evident that it was serious. It was clearly shown that there was a backstair influence which was wholly improper and which undeniably affected Blodgett's judicial actions. It was shown also that he had borrowed money from bankruptcy funds in the registry of his court with which to speculate in Wall Street.

In the end Proctor Knott's committee found that the investigation was quite justified, but impotently reported to Congress that it was so late in the session that no impeachment proceedings were possible, and thus Blodgett escaped.

Several years elapsed and then the judge faced his deserts.

Judge Drummond, the United States Circuit Judge for the Circuit, was in his declining years and about to retire. This came to my knowledge privately in the spring of 1884. I went to Washington at once and called upon General Arthur, then President of the United States. I asked him to read the record in the case as presented by Proctor Knott's committee. He did so, and when I suggested that Blodgett would be a candidate to succeed Judge Drummond, he very promptly assured me that such an appointment would not be made.

But then there was a complication. General Walter Q. Gresham, who had previously served with distinction as a Federal judge, but had retired from the judicial office to enter politics, was postmaster general under President Arthur. The President knew that Gresham had tired of politics and would like to return to the bench. But his name had been suggested as a candidate for the Presidency against Arthur, and any appointment of him as Judge Drummond's successor before the meeting of the Nominating Convention might be construed as a ruse to prevent his running as a candidate. President Arthur asked me to see him, find out how he felt, and if he still desired a judicial office, to offer him Drummond's place, the appointment to be made months later.

I called on General Gresham and we went for a long ride. I told him frankly of the situation. He promptly and vigorously denounced any effort on the part of his friends to make him a Presidential nominee. "It would be disgraceful," said he, "for any member of General Arthur's cabinet to try to run against him for the Republican nomination after the splendid administration he has given the country." I then told him that I was commissioned to offer him the Circuit Court Judgeship to be made vacant by Judge Drummond; but it must be understood that the arrangement was to be held as confidential until after the National Convention, to the end that it must not be regarded as a political arrangement. This was assented to; I reported the situation to the President, and went back to Chicago.

I told Judge Drummond the whole story and he withheld his retirement for some months and until the proper moment for Gresham's appointment. Then, as I had anticipated, a petition for the appointment of Judge Blodgett for the post was prepared and signed very generally by the railroad lawyers of Chicago and backed by the corrupt forces. It was presented to President Arthur, but was ineffective. General Gresham was appointed.

In April, 1877, the Mayor appointed me as a member of the Board of Education, a position in which I served three years and then declined a reappointment because of my other duties. There was no compensation attached to the office and I accepted only as a public duty. I started a campaign against the teaching of German or any other language than English in the primary grades. I was not successful at the time, but later the seed sown came to fruition. I also urged the appointment of well-trained teachers for the primary grades. It had been the policy to hold purely scholastic examinations and to make appointments upon the results thus disclosed. This meant that the youngest children were given over to inexperienced teachers with small pay but much knowledge of the higher branches, while the later grades were taught by splendid elderly women, many enjoying the experience of motherhood, but rusty in erudition. I was able to effect a change in this business.

In the summer the great railroad strike and riot wave reached Chicago. There were several days of bloody battle between the officers of the law and an insensate mob. The event was reported by the *Daily News* in a fashion that had no precedent in the history of western journalism. A corps of reporters, mounted on horseback, went through the riotous districts and telegraphed or telephoned the situation hour by hour, almost minute by minute. Some of them were even disguised as rioters; and one at least fell into the hands of the police because he was in the front ranks of the mob. Extra editions of the paper were issued hour by hour and the circulation ran up to over 70,000 copies a day.

Detective Journalism—The Spencer Case

All our fine theories would be of little avail unless we could compel attention of the public. The admonition to Sempronius did not in the least deter us. We set out to command success as well as to deserve it. We made the paper sensational. Not, as I have said, in the ordinarily accepted signification of that much-abused word. Not by parading the noisome details of commonplace crime, nor the silly so-called "human-interest stories" of cats born with two heads, or like babble having no real value and only presented for the purpose of pandering to the prurient taste of groundlings. But in a larger and better sense. It is easy to edit a newspaper if one does no thinking, has no initiative capacity. He then labels all murders and suicides and hangings and prize fights and chicken fights as news, and his task is a simple one. These are the editors who, like the three Japanese monkeys, never see, hear, or tell us anything. But the field of human activity is quite large enough for better work—work which will give an individual character to a paper, wake an echo, and conduce to betterment of the readers.

After this fashion the *Daily News* was sensational and intensely personal. How we pursued public plunderers and uncovered their misdeeds, and sent them to prison, constitutes a chapter in the history of Chicago of which no one connected with the paper has reason to be ashamed.

In 1877 there was no provision in the State of Illinois for legal inspection or control of savings institutions. As editor of the *Daily News* I began urging such legislation. That there was need for such supervision was evident from the fact that the three or four leading savings banks of Chicago were publicly offering suspiciously high rates of interest for deposits. But, preventive of any action, was a conspiracy of the officers and directors of the involved concerns, including a considerable number of the important people of the city. What with influence and money, they were able to stifle any move at the State capital. The clamour of the *Daily News* was denounced as improper and even disgraceful.

So it happened that public sentiment was with the culpable bankers, and when the suspension of one bank after another was announced there was amazement and almost a panic. This was true on the 29th of August of that year, when the State Savings Bank of Chicago, the largest institution of the kind west of New York, suddenly closed its doors upon over twenty-five thousand depositors, and with liabilities of many millions of dollars. Of assets of value there were practically none in sight. And the president of the bank, Mr. D. D. Spencer, had decamped.

Then some leading citizens stepped into the breach, effected an assignment to a co-conspirator, and named a protective committee—designed to be protective, not of the depositors, but of the absent president and of his equally guilty directors.

More than two weeks elapsed, and, although the city was in a state of wild commotion, there was no move for the apprehension of Spencer. Then, it being obvious that the authorities would do nothing, I took the matter in hand. The pursuit of the fugitive bank president and his final location in Europe is the story I have to tell.

Spencer left Chicago on Sunday afternoon, August 26th, on a Michigan Central Railway train, accompanied by his wife and adopted daughter. They left the car at some point in Canada. Such was the information furnished by a Mr. Washburne of Chicago, who was a fellow passenger of his. With this clue I determined to find the fugitive and, if possible, to bring him to justice.

The first step in the plan of pursuit was to learn definitely Spencer's movements from the moment he left until he alighted in Canada. It was known that the family took berths in a sleeping car.

The books of the company were searched by the Chicago agent, who learned that on the train in question there were three sleepers, but one alone took through passengers. The car was in charge of Conductor Humphreys, who remembered the party. He helped them to alight at Hamilton; they took a train for Toronto. The train had started, and he called to the conductor to hold it, which was done, and he helped the people aboard. In the hurry of this departure Spencer said he had to leave his baggage, and he asked the local baggageman to forward it to Toronto, giving him his checks.

This much was learned in Chicago. The rest was clear. Go to Canada and follow the baggage from Hamilton and Toronto. With a photograph of Spencer and a facsimile of his signature, I set out. I went to Hamilton and was soon in conversation with a bright young fellow who ran the baggage room at that station. I showed him Spencer's picture and asked if the original had passed that way recently.

"Do you remember," I asked, "a man who arrived here at eleven-forty-five on the afternoon of August 27th, just as the Toronto train was leaving, and who gave you his checks and asked you to forward his baggage to Toronto?"

"Oh, yes, that's him; I remember it all now. He said they were small pieces, and I have occasion to recollect it. He lied. They were very heavy. Let me see. There were two canvas covers and a Saratoga. Yes, I sent them to Toronto at three that afternoon, double-checked to the Union Station. That's where he wanted them sent.

"Come here a bit," he continued after a pause, and, entering his office, he opened his register and began searching the dates. "There," he said when he reached the page on which the work on the 27th of August was recorded, "these are the numbers of the checks on those trunks—442, 7,752, and 10,484. Now, you go up to Toronto, stop at the Union Station, and ask Jimmie Foster, the baggage-man there, what became of that stuff. He can tell you whether the trunks were sent to a hotel or whether they went off on the Grand Trunk."

I took the next train for Toronto and called on Jimmie Foster. He remembered the incident well. The party arrived there on the one-fifteen train, intending to take the Montreal boat at once, and was very much put out that the luggage did not arrive until after the boat had gone. "They came from Chicago, didn't they?" said he. "Chicago was stencilled on the trunks, anyway. Let's go and see Duffy; he'll remember them, I know."

Duffy was the baggage-man for the Grand Trunk Company at the Union Station, Toronto.

When shown the photograph he thought he recognized that face, but was not certain. Foster described the baggage, and then it all flashed over him.

"Oh, yes," he said, "that party came in early in the afternoon and stayed about the depot here until evening. He had a tall, slim girl with him around the platform, and I think his lady waited inside in the waiting room. He was going east. I remember him for a foolish little eccentricity of his. I came out here on the platform and found him picking the labels off of his baggage. They were all covered with marks of the hotel and railway and express companies into whose hands they had fallen, and that seemed to annoy him. I saw him working away at it and took pity on him, and went and got a sponge and spent a good half hour with him, sponging the marks off of his trunks. He was greatly pleased to see how well they looked when they were cleaned.

"There," continued Duffy after a glance at his books, "that's the party—three pieces of baggage on the afternoon of August 27th, checked by myself through to 'Sixty-five over.'

'Sixty-five over' means across the ferry at Quebec. This party was going to take an Allan Line steamship."

A clerk in the office of the Allan Steamship Agency, in Toronto, remembered a visit from Spencer and his daughter on the afternoon in question. Spencer there obtained a plan of the *Circassian*, which was to sail on the following Saturday, and promised to call again.

Having thus established his course beyond question, I set out for Montreal. There I found they had spent the day and taken a night train for Quebec. At daybreak on Wednesday, August 29th, they landed at the depot at Point Levi. The ferryboat was on hand, and they immediately passed to Quebec, on the other side of the river.

While here, stopping at the St. Louis Hotel, Spencer, *alias* Williams, read the announcement of his crime in the Quebec *Chronicle* and afterward in the NewYork *Herald*, copies of which he bought at a news stand in St. Louis Street. The party went aboard ship on Saturday morning, and the boat steamed out promptly at ten. There was no one present to see them off or bid them God-speed.

Having thus made certain of their departure for Liverpool, I set about overhauling them on their arrival. I immediately telegraphed the information I had received to the superintendent of police at Chicago, and he in turn sent the following cablegram:

Supt. Williamson, Scotland Yard,
    England.
  Arrest D. D. Spencer, absconding bank president from here; charge, forgery and embezzlement, $1,000,000. Supposed to have gone from Quebec, September first, on steamship *Circassian*, with young wife and child, under assumed name. Full description by mail will reach you Wednesday.

M. C. HICKEY
Chief of Police, Chicago.

Then there was a period of waiting—and disappointment, for Spencer and his family had quietly left the boat at Moville, on the north coast of Ireland, had slipped from the clutches of

Scotland Yard, and had gone away, unchallenged, to, in present-day phrase, "somewhere in the world."

It took time to renew the hunt. Then I set out again. I went to Europe. I bore letters to the English, French, and German police authorities. Nothing was to be learned in London. In Paris, with the aid of the Secret Service, the city was searched from end to end without result. Berlin was, as ever, better organized. The *Fremden* list disclosed that a person who was unmistakably Spencer had been there, had witnessed the army manœuvres, and had left.

When the search seemed hopeless I received a cable from Chicago that Abner Taylor, the assignee of Spencer's bank, and always suspected of aiding the runaway, had sailed on a certain ship for England. I trailed Taylor, finally faced him, and told him that he would be shadowed until his meeting with Spencer. He promised to notify me when he found Spencer, which he did. As a result a *Daily News* man walked in on Spencer unexpectedly at Cannstadt, Germany, and obtained a full confession. Later there was an adjustment of the crime in Chicago and a dismissal of the indictment.

As a result of this exposure there was the passage by the State Legislature of an act providing for the rigorous inspection of savings banks, and Spencer and his coterie never figured in the banking business again.

Such was our activity. As Dean Swift would have said, we lived all the days of our life. This case was among the earliest in which we resorted to detective journalism in the public behalf. For years thereafter the detective methods of the *Daily News* were notable and of great value to the community.

FOURTH DECADE

A Tour in Europe

IN AUGUST, 1878, as I began the fourth decade of my life, the average daily issue of our paper reached about fifty thousand copies, and we bought the *Post and Mail*, thus securing a very good perfecting press, as well as the service of the Associated Press. With this acquisition and the eclipse of Storey's *Evening Telegram*, we felt that our permanency was practically assured. Things were going so well in our business and so ill in my own condition that a vacation in Europe was planned for me. I had broken down from overwork, and developed nervous prostration, with accompanying melancholia. Utterly unfit for such a journey, I sailed from New York City in the spring of 1879. I found myself without an acquaintance on the boat, and before we were a day out I was quite ready to jump overboard and end my wretched, desolate exsitence. As I was walking the deck, medi-

William H. Crane

tating on the thing, a kindly woman, who divined my agony, boldly introduced herself. I have no thought of hinting that there was anything unwomanly in her manner. Quite the contrary. As an angel of mercy might have done it, in the gentlest fashion possible, she asked a question, told me who she was, and suggested that we walk the deck. Then she introduced her husband. I have no doubt she saved my life.

She "mothered" me until, in London—a World's Congress of Physicians being in session—she handed me over to a company of Chicago doctors, who took me in hand, trailed me over the Continent with them, and enlisted my interest in the things about me. Out of it all Will Crane, the actor, and his wife were numbered among my most valued friends.

I not only continued my search for Spencer, the absconding banker, as I have already said, but was able to engage in other work which proved of value in my after life.

I went to Ireland. I bore letters of introduction from Colonel Forrest to a number of conspicuous persons. One of these, addressed to the Lord Mayor of Dublin, Sir John Barrington, resulted in a dinner in my honour at the Mansion House in the Irish capital. One of the guests was old Doctor Shaw, the famous professor of Greek at Trinity College, a school from which years before an uncle of mine was a graduate. The doctor also held the chair of editor of Saunders's *News Letter*, an important daily of Dublin. I attended by invitation a number of his lectures and wandered with him about the city and learned much of the Home-Rule question then to the fore in the "distressful country."

· I went down to County Wicklow for a lawn party at a gentleman's demesne. I was presented to a young woman named Lady Mary. What her real name was, or who she was, I have never known. It was quite enough to be presented to Lady Mary. We fell to talking. "You are from She-*kay*-go?" she asked in a truly English drawl. "Yes," I replied. And then one may imagine my consternation when she continued with: "And is that anywhere near where the dear young prince was killed?" meaning South Africa, where the Prince Imperial of France had lost his life a month earlier.

A few weeks later, while coaching from Cork to the Lakes of Killarney, we halted at a wayside shrine between Mallow and Glengariff. The usual group of barefooted beggars attacked us. "Where are ye from?" asked a ragged old woman. "From Chicago," I answered. "And how's it gettin' along since yer fire?" she returned. It was not that she knew her geography so well, but, in common with so many other Irish peasants, she had relatives in our city from whom she had heard and in whom she was interested.

At Cavan, my mother's birthplace, I met Captain Boycott, the agent of Lord Erne. His brutal evictions won for him unenviable notoriety, and (because of the ostracism meted out to him by the peasantry) fixed the word "boycott" in the language.

I met Charles Stewart Parnell and told him of the Lady Mary episode. I shall never forget the quizzical, cynical look he gave me, nor how he fell to talking of conditions in Ireland. There was nothing of the emotional Irishman about him. Rather he was the cool, practical, analytical American type. "I am not surprised," said he. "I have no doubt the young woman could have told you with whom the Queen drove out yesterday afternoon. These people live in the atmosphere of the British Court. They know nothing else."

He impressed me as a self-contained, almost taciturn, person. The Home-Rule movement was well under way, but he was not at one with its leader, Doctor Butt. He had great respect for him, but did not believe his methods could ever achieve success.

Charles Stewart Parnell

I next met him in New York Harbour. He had come over on the steamer *Scythia* with John Dillon to plead his cause before the people of the United States. I, in turn, had been chosen as chairman of a committee to welcome the gentlemen to the American shore. So it happened that I travelled to New York, went down the Bay, and, on January 2, 1880, made a speech of greeting to Parnell and Dillon. And so also it happened that I came to be rather close to them and to those associated with them thereafter.

I shall never forget the appeal they made. In simple phrase, and without any attempt at eloquence, but much as Louis Kossuth had told the story of Hungary's wrongs years before, they pleaded the cause of their downtrodden people.

The task was not easy. Irishmen in America were by no means at one in respect to the steps that should be taken in opposition to government by Britain. Over here was a large band of radicals grouped as the Clan-na-Gael, the Irish Revolutionary Brotherhood, or Fenians, and Parnell was to them a Conservative. They wanted physical warfare; he believed in political methods. His visit had a twofold purpose, namely, the collection of funds to feed the famished people of Ireland, and the unifying, if possible, of the discordant American elements, to the end that he and his associates might be able to rely on a solid and compact backing from American sympathizers in the Irish cause. He faced two hostile classes, the friends of England, who would have none of Home Rule, and the hare-brained Irish, who had no faith in constitutional methods, but wanted to use guns and powder and ball. How he won was full of dramatic interest. There was an element of tremendous surprise. And I think upon this fact his success was largely dependent. Here was a Protestant Irish landlord pleading with quiet dignity but great earnestness the wrongs of the emotional tenantry against the crushing iniquity of landlordism. As he spoke "those who came to scoff remained to pray." A leading anti-Home Rule journal of New York suddenly found itself forced to open a subscription in aid of the starving people of Erin. And within a week the fighting men, those who had talked in loudest terms against Parnellism, began to bend the knee.

Some of us took active measures to forward the public enthusiasm. The tour was an extraordinary success. Money was contributed in surprising measure. Parnell and Dillon were the idols of the hour. More than that, their cause became the popular cause.

Yet their visit was not a long one. Indeed, they had scarcely begun their work before they were called back to Britain by an announcement of the dissolution of Parliament and a consequent impending general election.

Parnell found himself confronted in Ireland by three hostile classes: the Catholic bishops, who distrusted him as a Protestant; the Orangemen and pro-British, who did not want Home Rule; and the uncompromising radicals, who wanted to try by force to create a wholly independent nation. All of the antagonists whom he had met in America were present at home, but in larger measure.

Parnell went into the campaign undaunted. He was warned of trouble when he landed at Queenstown, and he was mobbed when he undertook to speak at Enniscorthy. Yet he stood as a candidate for Parliament before three constituencies: Meath, Mayo, and Cork City, and was returned by each. Then he was formally chosen leader of his party, and his marvellous career was fairly begun.

I had occasional letters from him, as well as a number of cable messages, for publication in the Chicago *Daily News*.

While in the United States he had met a young woman whom he had engaged to marry. At her instance the affair was broken off. Very soon after his return to Europe he met Mrs. O'Shea and fell desperately in love with her. Politically, he was carrying on a terrific contest against the Clan-na-Gael both in Ireland and in America; against the British and their allies in Ulster, and against the followers of Isaac Butt, who advocated an innocuous form of Home Rule agitation, and all the while he was living over a social volcano ready to burst into an overwhelming flood of scandal at any moment. It was not surprising, therefore, that he should write me apologizing for not writing as frequently as he could have wished.

That he should make any headway, much less win, in such an obstacle race gives proof of his marvellous capacity. Only those who knew how he was surrounded by adverse, sinister, and malicious opponents, ready to arrange pitfalls for him on every side, can appreciate his fortitude as well as his cunning. On one occasion a Chicago woman, the wife of a leader of the American Clan-na-Gael, having knowledge of Parnell's liaison, went to Paris, employed a courtesan of surpassing beauty, took her to London, introduced her to the House of Commons and to the "Uncrowned King" of Ireland, but without success. Her object was blackmail.

Parnell was a hard master of his party. He brooked no opposition in his own camp, and he treated every Briton with undisguised contempt. Even Dillon and Davitt broke with him for a while after the Kilmainham imprisonment and the

Phoenix Park murders. Dillon, who had memories of 1848, and his father's revolutionary campaign with John Mitchell and Smith O'Brien, became restive under Parnell's cold-blooded leadership, pleaded ill health, and came to this country to visit his brother William in Colorado. On his way he stopped over in Chicago and gave me the pleasure of a visit. He was a bookworm. I took him to the greatest bookstore in the world, then, as now, located in that city, and there he and I spent some happy hours and days poring over the works of

". . . the dead but sceptered sovereigns who still rule our spirits from their urns."

Davitt, too, came to the United States. He, like Dillon, could not approve of Parnell's moderate methods. They had suffered too much. Yet Davitt, while carried away for the moment by Henry George's propaganda, and burning with a desire for urgent and drastic action, resented in terms which no one might misunderstand any suggestion of disloyalty to his chief.

John Dillon

All the while Parnell was plodding on. He calmly refused to make answer to "Buckshot Forster's" attempt to implicate him in the assassinations of Burke and Cavendish, saying that he declined to appear as a defendant in any matter at the bar of an English tribunal. Taunting and contemptuous ever of the Briton, he enforced from the controlling government respect and even deference. Always this man, by sheer force of character, and alone, was making progress toward a recognition of the justice of the cause of Ireland. He was the very embodiment of courage.

Once only I saw him timorous. The celebrated Parnell Commission was in session, investigating the accusations of the London *Times*. He was impaled as an accessory in the Phoenix Park murders, and the Piggot letters, incriminating him in no uncertain fashion, had been offered in evidence. It was in the summer of 1888. I was in London. Parnell and I had a meeting. He was conscious of his innocence, he knew the Piggot letters were forgeries, but, also, he knew the temperament of England at the moment, and the consequent personal danger to himself. A common friend, John Finerty, back in Chicago, was publishing a paper, railing at the investigation and practically defending the assassination as an act of justice. "Does this man know that he is putting a noose about my neck?" asked Parnell in distress. And then he urged me to cable Finerty to stop. Which I did.

Piggot was exposed, ran away to Spain, and committed suicide. Parnell was exonerated. There was a fine reaction in British sentiment. Gladstone and the whole Liberal party made obeisance to Parnell, and Home Rule seemed assured. I returned to America, and the following year a delegation of Irish National leaders came over to plead their cause and to collect funds for a final campaign. They reached Chicago in the autumn and we were together night and day during their visit to the city. In the delegation were T. P. O'Connor, John Dillon, William O'Brien, T. D. Sullivan, and T. Harrington.

Suddenly, as out of a clear sky, burst the storm. Captain O'Shea had sued for a divorce, naming Parnell as co-respondent. There was no defence; the divorce was granted. I shall never forget the emotions aroused. On the one hand there was a recognition of the measureless need of Ireland for relief and the priceless value of Parnell's services for the cause; there was gratitude for him and confidence in his matchless leadership. On the other hand was the doubt that in the face of the O'Shea disclosures there was further hope for usefulness from him. Then came Gladstone's letter to Morley, dissociating himself from Parnell, and all the great dream of so many years that British misrule in Ireland—so graphically portrayed by Froude, and so confessed by every English statesman—was about to end, suffered a piteous awakening.

Parnell made a brief final struggle, met disaster, and died. And Irish Home Rule still is not yet.

Meeting Gambetta and Clemenceau

I went to Paris. I met Gambetta and Clemenceau. Both were intimate friends of my cousins, the Crawfords. Gambetta was the godfather of Mrs. Crawford's only daughter, Leona Crawford, a beautiful girl, who was accidentally drowned in a Swiss lake while yet in her teens.

The dramatic story of Gambetta's tempestuous life had rarely been equalled. The son of a small grocer of Cahors, in the south of France, he was apprenticed by his father to a watchmaker. Hating the occupation, and ambitious to become a lawyer, it was said that he tore out an eye and unfitted himself for the business to which he had been assigned. A maiden aunt helped him to take a course at the Sorbonne, in Paris, and achieve his goal. As in the cases of Byron and the younger Dumas, he awoke one morning to find himself famous. It was in the days of the Second Empire, two years before the Battle of Sedan and the downfall of Louis Napoleon. Gambetta was thirty years old. He had been known for a number of years as a hare-brained radical, who mounted chairs in the cheaper cafés and harangued the crowds in denunciation of the Imperial Government. He was a briefless lawyer. He was not punished for his treasonable indiscretions, because he was thought by the authorities to be unworthy of notice. Finally, however, his hour came. He was called to defend one of several journalists who started a subscription for a monument to Baudin, a deputy who was shot on the barricades of Paris at the time of the coup d'état of 1851. His speech was a masterpiece of invective. In terms of measureless audacity he arraigned the culprits who had destroyed the Republic of 1848 and erected an autocracy upon the ruin. Thereafter he was a leading figure among the Republicans of France.

When I met him he was at the zenith of his power. But a few months before he had turned General MacMahon out of the presidency and installed Jules Grévy. His challenge to MacMahon and his consequent victory at the general election established the Republic. Notwithstanding the suspicions and misgivings born of his earlier radicalism, he proved a great constructive force, and when, two years after our meeting, he was killed, he left to his people a priceless legacy of orderly self-government. When he was charged with responsibility he made heroic answer to the accusation that he was a Communard; he showed himself a genuine Republican. He had a great admiration for the American form of government, and, had he lived, would certainly have striven to model the French system much more closely upon our own.

Clemenceau and Gambetta worked to the same end, yet not in the same groups. Clemenceau was a far greater radical, and in the end the two were not at one as to either their aims or methods. The "Tiger" was viciously uncompromising in his urgency for an untainted democracy. He regarded the Republic as an experiment, well enough in its way, nevertheless an experiment. He sturdily battled against colonial expansion, because he felt that France needed all her strength to complete the task of reconstruction—moral and economic—after the débâcle of 1870. A brilliant journalist and a master of parliamentary tactics, he unseated one government after another for years. And he did great things for his country. He, more than any one else, made possible the impossible. He so stabilized the democratic spirit of France as to keep the Republic in existence and in growing efficiency for now half a century.

Emily Crawford also made me acquainted with Labouchere and Horace Voules, his manager on *Truth*. So it happened that the Associated Press was able to report the coronation of King Edward in 1902 in a fashion theretofore unknown in England. Our correspondents occupied a pew in the south transept of Westminster Abbey, not far from a door. Sheet by sheet their copy was smuggled out by a messenger, who took it to Voules's house in a near-by street. There it was telephoned to our main office and put upon the cable. Wherefore the American papers had a much quicker service than the journals of London.

Still another valued friend whose acquaintance I made through the intermediation of my cousin was Percy Bunting, for many years editor of the *Contemporary Review*, the great Liberal periodical. He was the grandson of the Rev. Jabez

Bunting, a famous Wesleyan Methodist preacher. I found Percy Bunting of great assistance in determining my view of British politics.

The European journey restored my health. On my return to Chicago in the early fall of 1879 I resumed activity in the *Daily News* office. It was again a case of "full steam ahead."

More Detective Journalism

One day the city was startled by the announcement that Mr. Moore, a trusted citizen, had decamped, leaving a shortage of several thousand dollars in his accounts as supervisor of the West Town of Chicago. While he was in the full enjoyment of a reputation which any one might envy, he was arrested at his own house on a charge of embezzlement. The following day the public was advised in one breath of the defalcation, the arrest, and the sudden and mysterious flight of the prisoner while under guard of a police officer. From that time, for nearly a year, his whereabouts remained a profound secret. Finding once more that the Police Department was doing nothing, the *Daily News* again set on foot an inquiry. By a very simple decoy it was learned that the man must be in Canada. The investigation was pursued a little further, and he was located in the oil-producing districts about Sarnia. I went to Detroit, up the St. Clair River, and into Canada to hunt until the man was found.

I left the boat at Sarnia and climbed up the bluff to the hotel, a large, two-story frame structure with a wide-spreading veranda, overlooking the St. Clair River and the little city of Port Huron on the opposite bank. I found landlord, clerk, porter, and, indeed, every available employee busy in the bar-room serving liquor in a wholesale fashion, for a civic holiday excursion from London, Ont., had thrown two dozen carfuls of merry-makers into the town. While they were thus engaged I ran back over the hotel register to see what Chicago people had been there of late. When I reached the page devoted to the arrivals of August 3d I was struck with a specimen of chirography which seemed very familiar. In plain characters, just as I had seen it hundreds of times in Chicago, was: "*A. Moore, Petrolia, Ont.*"

I again turned the leaves of the book and found a similar inscription on July 18th. I examined both signatures very closely, and very soon was convinced that "A. Moore of Petrolia" was none other than Mr. Moore, late alderman, school inspector, and town supervisor of Chicago.

After journeying through a wild barren country I finally reached Petrolia. I entered one of the two hotels which flanked the railway station and laid down my valise. I then took a turn about town, and at an apothecary's asked the clerk if he knew Mr. Moore.

"A large man with gray beard who came over from the States a few months ago?'" he returned.

"That's the man," said I.

"He's boarding at the Corry House. You will find him there. Just ask for Mr. Moore."

I did so.

"He's up in his room," said the landlord. "Will you go up?"

I thanked him, but would prefer meeting Mr. Moore downstairs, if he would be kind enough to call him.

Pretty soon, as I stood in the dimly lighted hall at the foot of the stairway, I saw him descending, not the man who had left Chicago so abruptly a year before, but wan and broken, his well-worn clothes hanging close about his shrunken form, his beard thin, and his whole appearance betraying all too plainly the struggle he had undergone.

"Mr. Moore, I believe," I said, audibly, as he reached the lower step, and looked inquiringly at me.

Then I was assigned a room, and, after some preliminary, Mr. Moore came in and sat upon the bed, and told me the full story of his misadventures.

"It was on the evening of Wednesday, the 6th of June, a year ago," he began, "that my affairs in Chicago culminated. I had then lived long in that city and had held several honourable offices, such as alderman, school inspector, etc., and I can say truthfully, and my record will prove it, that I was always opposed to corruption, always voted against steals, always conducted myself, both as a citizen and as a public officer, in an honest and upright way.

"Along in the early spring I was taken sick. I don't know what my disease was, but it was some trouble with my heart. It so affected my head that at times I really had no command of myself. Everything I had touched from the time of the panic had gone against me; I had a family to provide for; one of my daughters was, and is, an invalid—these things worried me more than I can tell you. Things seemed to be going from bad to worse. I have no doubt that my financial troubles preyed upon my mind. I struggled along day after day and got no better. I don't want to plead the baby act, and I suppose a good many people wouldn't believe the facts; but I tell you there were a good many days, along about that time, when I know I was not morally accountable for all my acts.

"A good many times I went downtown and went through the form of a day's work when I was physically unfit. But I had to keep my head above water. Finally, I found my town accounts $300 short, and I really had nothing with which to make it good. I was in such a state of distress that I couldn't sleep nights, nor keep a clear head during the day. I didn't drink. I never drank. My habits were all good and I was economical. But my health was such that I couldn't do anything, and the accumulating misfortunes and prospects of misfortune unmanned me.

"I went on 'Change' when I should have been at home in bed. I did unaccountable things—things that I would never have thought of doing when in my right mind and health. Whereas before I had always bought and sold with extreme caution and in small lots, I now launched out as if I had been a millionaire. The tide turned against me, as of course it would, for I had bought and sold without the exercise of any sort of judgment—bought and sold like an insane man.

"It is of no use to talk about it now, of course, but you can see that if I had intended to play the villain, I should have taken a very different course. Only a few months before—

about the first of the year—I could have pocketed $33,000 and come away to Canada and had enough to insure me a good living the rest of my days. Instead of that I came away without anything.

"When my situation burst upon me in its full force, broken in health and short in my town accounts, I became despondent. My doctor told me to quit business and rest. I could undoubtedly have adjusted my affairs, but my mental and physical condition was such that I didn't accomplish anything. About that time I can only recollect that I, for the first time in my life, seriously contemplated self-destruction.

"I went to bed more insane than sane. They came for me at night when I was not looking for them. If it had been in the daytime I should have gone right along and faced the issue in court. But the thing burst upon me in such a way that I couldn't endure it. The officer came in, and after we had talked over matters a while, he left me in my bed and took a seat in the parlour, and went sound asleep. I lay there turning the situation over in my mind, and finally, when I couldn't stand it any longer, I told my wife that I was going to get out of there. She begged me not to. But I drew on my trousers and slippers, and went out into the kitchen and got a hat, and walked out of the back door.

"I went to the house of a friend, woke him up and got a bed. When morning came, I sought the advice of a lawyer. My friends thought I had better wait a while and see what turned up.

"That night, or the next, a carriage called for me and I was driven to the house of another friend, where I stayed fourteen days. During that time I saw the papers every day, and was very much interested in the efforts which the police were making for my apprehension. All the time I was in the hands of my lawyer. I thought some arrangment of my affairs would be reached. Finally, I was advised to go to Canada, where I could recuperate my health and await an adjustment in personal security.

"Acting upon that advice, nearly three weeks after my arrest, I one day took a carriage, drove to a suburb, and took a train for Canada. I went first to Toronto and then to Sarnia, where I met my present associate in business. He had a good deal of experience in the oil fields. After investigation I became convinced that, with the means I could control, the chances for me were good, if not better than in any other business I could enter."

The next morning we strolled out over the oil fields of Petrolia, and I took advantage of the opportunity to inspect his wells.

"You are doing finely," said I, at length.

"I run the engine," said the ex-alderman, "and since I have been here I think I have made $800 to $1,000 over investment and expense. At the same expense of running, had I the money, our capacity would easily be doubled. It costs $450 to sink a well, and the cost of pumping additional holes, now that we have the engine in, would be next to nothing."

"What is your notion as to your future?" I asked.

"Well, I don't know," he replied, slowly. "I am very anxious to settle up my affairs in Chicago, and to that end would be only too glad to bend all my energies for years to come. But it is a very difficult case to adjust. The amount involved is not so large, but I am tied up here and am practically powerless. Now I have a little piece of property in Chicago. If the town board would take that at its value and give me time to work out the rest, I want to do so. With what my brothers have put in here for my benefit, I think I could earn the balance in a comparatively short time. But I can't tell, you know, whether the town authorities could or would make an arrangement by which I could get time to fix the thing up. If they don't, of course, much as I would dislike to do it—self-preservation is the first law of nature, my duty to my family is imperative—I shall be forced to give up Chicago and live and die here. Now, mark you, that is not my wish. If they will give me half a chance, I will earn and pay back every dollar I owe, with interest, if it takes me ten years to do it in. All I ask is the chance."

"What kind of a chance do you want?"

"I would like to have the town officers take my Chicago

property at a valuation, and then permit me to give my notes for the balance, payable at such time as I can meet them. By so doing, they stand some chance of getting their money. By continuing the present policy, they are only postponing the day of payment and they put me in such a position that I can never make the restitution which I honestly desire to make."

"Have you made such a proposition to the town board?"

"No; I tried to have it done. But my affairs have not been managed as I wished."

"And now," said he, as he finished his story, and we were about to part, "I may be all wrong, but it seems to me that I am offering all the reparation for my offence that can be reasonably expected of me. I have told you, and the books in Chicago will prove my assertion, that if I had been disposed to be a rogue my shortage would not have been $7,000, but over $33,000. Put my offence in the very worst light: I took $7,000, and am forced to live in Canada; the city treasurer of Chicago took $500,000 and walks your streets unmolested. It may not be delicate for me to say so, but I confess I don't see the justice in such a course. I want to live and die in Chicago; I am an American, and want to remain such; I want to pay, dollar for dollar, every debt I owe; I will do these things if they let me."

I was on the train; it started, and the man went back to his prison in the oil fields.

Convinced that, while overtaken in a fault, he was nevertheless inherently honest, I took up the matter and had it adjusted. His shortage was repaid with interest and the indictment against him dismissed. He returned to Chicago and lived there for some years as an honoured citizen, and then went to a distant city, where he held an important post for more than forty years. After the event narrated his life was an unblemished one.

It was worth as much to save Moore as to outlaw Spencer.

The Campaign of 1880

As we neared the Presidential campaign of 1880 it was obvious that Blaine, whose candidacy of four years before had gone down in shame at Cincinnati, was to try his luck once more and that his opponents were to present General Grant for a third term. The General was back from his triumphal tour of the world. He was to come to Chicago. I conceived the idea of bidding him welcome in a souvenir issue of the *Daily News*. I telegraphed to a great company of the leading men of the nation, South as well as North, asking them to wire me for publication some word of greeting. I received a large number of responses, and printed them on the morning of Grant's arrival in our city. One only of the replies was ungracious. This came from "Bob" Toombs of Georgia, who had a large share in projecting the Civil War upon the country and who was until his death a wholly unrepentant rebel. He wired as follows:

ATLANTA, GA., Nov. 12, 1879.
M. E. STONE, Editor, *Daily News*, Chicago.

Your telegram received. I decline to answer, except to say, present my personal congratulations to General Grant on his safe arrival to his country. He fought for his country honorably and won. I fought for mine and lost. I am ready to try it over again. Death to the Union.

R. TOOMBS.

Then there was a reunion of the Army of the Tennessee in honour of the returning chieftain. There was a memorable banquet with six hundred covers and fifteen speakers. The flow of eloquence surpassed anything theretofore known in Chicago. Mark Twain contributed a side-splitting speech on "Babies." Stephen A. Hurlburt, Colonel Ingersoll, and others were all at their best. But the effort of the evening was that of my cousin, William F. Vilas of Wisconsin. I sat at his side at the speakers' table, and I shall never forget the thrill that ran through the company as he, who was then comparatively unknown, rose and, in well-modulated yet quite modest tones, told the story of the first great tocsin call to victory, Grant's "No terms but unconditional surrender," at Fort Donelson.

As the preconvention campaign progressed, a surprising situation developed. A number of Illinois and Wisconsin districts elected delegates favouring Elihu B. Washburne as a candidate for the Presidential nomination. As Washburne had been the avowed friend of Grant, this circumstance was inexplicable and caused more or less alarm to the Grant following.

Some weeks before the convention assembled, and preparatory to the event, Roscoe Conkling, J. Don Cameron, and John A. Logan gathered in Chicago to further the Grant interests. They sent for me, called attention to the Washburne move, and asked me to learn whether it was a friendly or an antagonistic effort. So I called upon Washburne one evening at his residence, on North La Salle Street, in Chicago. I suggested that a campaign was on for his nomination as the Republican candidate for the Presidency. I asked if he was to be an opponent of General Grant. We met in the parlour of his home. He rose in stately fashion and replied:

"Mr. Stone; everyone knows that I am a friend of the great commander. It was I who in 1861 recommended him to Governor Yates for his first army command. No one can doubt my position."

"But," I answered, "the enemies of Grant are pushing you as a candidate against him. Will you authorize me to say for you that they are doing so without your consent or approval?"

"Ah," said he, "that I cannot do. You may say that I am not seeking the place. But the office of President is one neither to be sought nor declined."

And so I left him, and the delegates elected in his name voted against Grant, an eventuality for which we were prepared.

While the convention was impending, there was a celebration at Springfield on May 5th. In the parade which preceded the ceremony Governor Collum rode with General Grant. And he told the General of my interview with Washburne, and expressed solicitude as to the attitude of Grant's former friend. Grant listened attentively and then said: "Well, Governor, during the war I sometimes had interesting experiences. Perhaps it was during the progress of a battle. Off on the horizon I saw a body of troops marching, not in any direction contemplated by me in my plan of action. They were too far away to permit me to identify the character of uniform they wore.

The thing puzzled me. Even with a glass I could not make them out. I could not tell whether they were our troops or the enemy's. But before the battle was over I found out."

This was the answer.

That day Washburne was also at Springfield. But about noon, and before Grant made his speech, he quietly slipped away, took a train, and left for the State of Maine. He pleaded as an excuse that he was needed to look after the fences on some property he owned in the distant state. The phrase "looking after one's fences" thus took origin.

There were many things about the Presidential contest of the year that were disturbing to any one born and bred a Republican in the Illinois political school. Our State had given to the war, for the maintenance of the Federal Union: Lincoln, the immortal president; Grant, the unconquerable general; Yates, the beloved war governor; Logan, the great volunteer captain, and Oglesby, Palmer, McDowell, Baker, Elmer Ellsworth, the brothers Wilson, James and Bluford, and a long line of other heroes.

Lincoln and Grant had been nominated for the chief magistracy in Chicago, and there, too, had been held the Copperhead Convention of 1864, which in the midst of the contest declared the war a failure.

But the Republican Party of 1880 was no longer that of former days. It had drifted away from its moorings.

We had noted, to be sure, the tatterdemalion crew that met in Cincinnati in 1872, called themselves Liberal Republicans, and played a farce comedy ending in the nomination, defeat, and tragic death of Greeley. But this only strengthened our admiration for the "old commander." We appraised his service in the White House as a worthy and altogether befitting sequel to his service in the tented field. We minded how he had, as president, taken hold of a chaotic South, and in his quiet but effective way had reëstablished all the functions of government. We knew how during his administration scandals had developed, and how some of them involved his friends, but we felt that his loyalty to his friends was a fine quality, and we did not forget that in the midst of his perplexities he had coupled with his famous aphorism of his letter of acceptance of the Presidential nomination of 1868, "Let us have peace," another equally sterling: "Let no guilty man escape." No one ever dared to hint that his escutcheon was tarnished. And so, in 1880, Illinois was for Grant. There was no alarm over the clamour about the danger of a third term or the "man on horseback." We knew that Grant was a private citizen, had been out of office for four years, and had no political machine. He was, to us, the last man in the world to seek a crown or become an autocrat. So we did not share in any measure Jefferson's fear of the danger of more than one term for our chief magistrate.

What I Knew About Grant

My knowledge of Grant began before the Civil War. In the fall of 1860 my father attended the annual session of the Rock River Methodist Conference, then held at Galena, and he was billeted on Orville Grant. There he met the members of the family, and on his return he told us of the high esteem in which they held their brother, Captain Ulysses, who had just come up from St. Louis to find employment in his father's leather shop. Later Orville Grant came to live in Chicago, and he and his sister, Mrs. Cramer, were frequent visitors at the home of our neighbour, the Rev. Mr. Boring, the Methodist presiding elder. So we followed the fortunes of the developing soldier with unusual interest.

I was in the Crosby Opera House in Chicago in 1868 when Grant and Colfax were nominated, and I was captain of the "Grant Guards," a company of "Tanners," which led the torchlight processions in the campaign of that year.

I was also present at the first great reunion of the Army of the Tennessee, held in the same auditorium in December, 1868, when Sherman, Sheridan, Thomas, Logan, Custer, and practically every surviving Union general, came to do honour to their chief. It was then that Belknap delivered the stirring address which made him Secretary of War.

In 1874 and 1875, when Grant was serving his second term

as President, and I was a newspaper correspondent in Washington, I was a frequent caller at the White House.

Throughout his entire career he seemed to give no evidence at any time of personal ambition. At least there was never any self-seeking. Even as to the contest of 1880 it could hardly be said that he was a candidate. He said in response to an early appeal to him to disclose his attitude: "I will neither accept nor decline an imaginary thing. I shall not gratify my enemies by declining what has not been offered me. I am not a candidate for anything, and if the Chicago Convention nominates a candidate who can be elected I shall be glad. All my life I have made my decision when the time for the decision arrived. I shall not depart from my usual course of action."

And later, yet also before the convention assembled, when Washburne was seeking to induce him to issue a declination of the honour, he wrote in reply:

There are many persons I should prefer to have the office than myself. I owe so much to the Union men of the country that if they think my chances are better for election than for other probable candidates in case I should decline, I cannot decline if the nomination is tendered without seeking on my part.

Such was his course of conduct in every emergency presented. On one occasion we were talking quietly of physical courage in battle. He said:

You newspapermen have given me credit for one thing for which I am undeserving. You have spoken of my going off and smoking a cigar during an engagement as if it was evidence of great bravery. It was not so. I had brought all the intelligence of which I was capable to bear on the situation, and, as I could think of nothing that had escaped, I felt powerless to do more and could only leave the outcome to fate.

Of the unsolicited honours conferred upon me in my long life I am most deeply sensible of two. Many years ago, when I was still a young man, the Lincoln Memorial Association was founded in Illinois, and I was amazed and gratified to find myself selected as one of something like a dozen men as incorporators. And after my removal to New York I was again surprised by my selection as one of the trustees of the Grant Monument. I think I am the only person thus placed. The purpose of these two organizations was the same—the guardianship of the ashes of Illinois' illustrious dead and the annual remembrance of their birthdays.

The National Republican Convention assembled on May 20, 1880. The great hall was crowded to suffocation. The Committee of Arrangements put me in charge of providing seats for the members of the press. It was no easy task. Somewhat over one thousand places were allotted. But, by reason of an accident, the tickets were not delivered to me until the morning on which the body convened. As a consequence, as frantic a company of journalists as one could imagine hunted me out for the necessary means of admission to the hall. The thing was likely to resolve itself into a riot when what seemed to me to be a direct interposition of Divine Providence saved me. As I was hunting for a place at which I could distribute the tickets in an orderly and expeditious fashion, I met Mr. George Starr, the one-time well-known publicity agent for Barnum. The circus was in Chicago and exhibiting in a substantial building adjoining the Convention Hall. And there was an ideal ticket office therein, behind solid stone walls. Thither Starr led me with my precious cargo of cardboards, secured a detail of husky policemen, formed my frenzied newspaper friends in line, and in ample time everyone was provided for and happy.

The Grant and Blaine forces were very equally balanced. Three days were spent in "jockeying for place," and then the naming of candidates for the Presidential nomination began. James F. Joy of Michigan led off with a speech, which was a model of stupidity, naming Blaine. With Ingersoll's perfervid presentation of the "plumed knight" at Cincinnati in 1876 in mind, it seemed inexcusably dull. And he closed with a grandiloquent flourish: "And now bearing the mandate of the Commonwealth of Michigan, I offer as our candidate one whose name is a household word throughout the world, the Hon.

James H. Blaine." Of course there was a great guffaw at this blunder respecting Blaine's name. I don't think Joy saw it.

Then Conkling arose and electrified the great audience by quoting from General Halpine's verse, in his opening for Grant:

> When asked what State he hails from,
> Our sole reply shall be,
> He comes from Appomattox
> And its famous apple tree.

His speech was full of fire and very effective. But it was Garfield, who, in naming John Sherman (who never had a ghost of a show), carried away the oratorical honours. At the mention of either Blaine's or Grant's name the assembled multitude had gone off into paroxysms of applause, lasting in each case nearly half an hour. Garfield took the platform and began his address quietly and in rather an appealing fashion. His audience was tired from shouting and ready for repose. Garfield touched a sensitive chord when he said:

As I sat in my seat and witnessed this demonstration it seemed to me a human ocean in tempest. I have seen the sea lashed into fury and tossed into spray, and its grandeur moves the soul of the dullest man; but I remember that it is not the billows, but the calm level of the sea from which all heights and depths are measured. . . . Not here in this brilliant circle is the destiny of the Republic to be decreed for the next four years. . . . But by 4,000,000 of Republican firesides, where the thoughtful voters, with wives and children about them . . . there God prepares the verdict.

It was an oratorical triumph. Garfield captured the convention and was himself nominated for the Presidency. Chester A. Arthur (Conkling's chief lieutenant) was named as the candidate for vice-president in an effort to placate the Grant element.

There was measureless treachery throughout the whole business. To begin with the composition of the convention: there were the usual collection of unjustifiable contests for delegate seats. In making up the roll call for the body these contests were ruthlessly decided against the Grant faction. The merits of the cases did not count. Then, in New York and Illinois and other states, there were a considerable number of delegates who had accepted their places under pledge to vote for Grant, but who had been "reached" and shamelessly violated their instructions. And, to meet the case, the unit rule, which had governed such conventions theretofore, was abolished so that those betraying their trust might cast their votes and have them counted. Finally, it was clear before the convention met that the chances were against Blaine, and he and Garfield entered into a secret agreement by which the Blaine vote should be turned over to Garfield and assure him the nomination. This, although Garfield appeared in the convention as the leader of the Ohio delegation pledged to the support of Senator John Sherman. And Sherman never forgave the betrayal. While as a good sportsman he supported the nominee, there ever rankled in his bosom a conviction that he had been betrayed. As he put it in his autobiography:

When I proposed to him [Garfield] to be a delegate at large to the Chicago Convention, he no doubt meant in good faith to support my nomination. When his own nomination seemed probable, he acquiesced in and perhaps contributed to it.

Following the nominations there was no assurance that the ticket would be elected. The Democrats named General Hancock as their candidate for the Presidency. He cut a sorry figure. He was a fine soldier, but not all a politician. The Sherman adherents were lukewarm and the Grant forces recalcitrant. And Garfield's personality was not all that could be desired. Definite accusations of misconduct were numerous. One of these was known as the De Golyer Paving Affair, with which I was familiar: Under the administration of Governor Shepherd there was a physical reconstruction of the national capital. Among the things to be done was the paving of the streets. A Chicago paving firm of my acquaintance, De Golyer & Co., put in a bid and were anxious to secure the contract. In that emergency they engaged Garfield as their attorney to plead their cause before the government of the District of Columbia. But Garfield at the moment was chairman of the Committee on Appropriations of the House of Representatives and had practically a determining voice in the appropriation by Congress of all the funds for all of the work. Of course his appeal for the De Golyers was equivalent to a command. His participation in the business for an attorney's fee was inexcusable.

The exposure of this and other delinquencies was damaging. To offset it a huge fund was provided and expended where, to use the phrase of the day, it would do the most good. The campaign was notoriously corrupt.

There was good fortune in the character of the opponents. Near the day of election a letter purporting to have been written by Garfield to one H. L. Morey of Lynn, Mass., and defending the right of "individuals and corporations to buy labour where they can get it cheapest" was published in facsimile form in the New York *Truth*, a not altogether reputable daily paper issued by a fine company of reckless journalists.

The letter, which was obviously a plea for the importation of Chinese cheap labour, created a sensation. It was immediately denounced as a forgery.

There was a judicial inquiry and two or three indictments. One of the most active members of the staff of the *Truth* newspaper was Louis F. Post, who in the Wilson Administration came into prominence again as the Assistant Secretary of Labour, and came into conflict with the Attorney General concerning the release of persons arrested as dangerous aliens. The *Truth* confessed the forgery and claimed to have been imposed upon. The indictments were dismissed. The thing proved a boomerang of distinct benefit to Garfield.

Garfield was elected. On the popular vote he exceeded the return for Hancock by less than 9,000 ballots.

Promptly on his accession to office he appointed Blaine Secretary of State and proceeded to reward the delegates who had betrayed their trust and violated their instructions in the Chicago nominating convention.

Garfield's cruel assassination a few months later evoked universal condemnation, and closed every critical mouth for the time being.

And now things were going so famously with us that Lawson and I could not let well enough alone. We had established the leading afternoon paper in Chicago. But this was not enough.

Founding the Morning News

So, on March 20, 1881, we issued the first number of the Chicago *Morning News*, price two cents per copy. Again, as six years before, we faced important competition, and again it was imperative that, if we were to succeed, we must present a new type of journalism. There were four existent and well-to-do morning papers. We set out for a departure from their methods of operation.

All of the rules which had proved so valuable for the six years during which the *Evening News* had grown to success were, of course, still observed. There was the same divorcement of the editorial and business departments, the frankness with respect to advertising, the publication daily of the exact paid circulation of the paper, as indeed it has been to the present day.

In the editorial department, I still held to the view that there were three functions: news gathering, editorial, and entertainment. Or, if you choose: information, interpretation, and amusement. The principal thing was the chronicling of events. As I have said, in the *Evening News*, by the purchase of the *Post and Mail* we acquired the evening dispatches of the Associated Press. It was not so with the *Morning News*. And not only were these dispatches indispensable, but to conduct our morning paper without them involved serious complications. By a rule then in force we were forbidden to patronize a news-gathering concern in competition with the major organization. The sword of Damocles hung over our heads. At a meeting of the Associated Press, which I attended in virtue of the rights of the *Evening News*, I was called to account because the *Morning News* was doing business with a rival, the United Press. My answer was that it was none of their business—that I should continue to buy news wherever I could and wherever I chose. But there was another rule forbidding us to patronize any telegraph company other than the Western

Union. I answered that I would bring my news by an ox team if it suited me. There was no further attempt to enforce these clearly illegal restrictions. Yet the receipt of the Associated Press dispatches for our morning paper was desirable, and I set out to get them.

They could only be had by consent of our Chicago competitors. Such consent in like circumstances had never been secured by any one. And I was assured that my quest was hopeless. Nevertheless, it was well enough to try. And so I did. For the first time in the history of the Associated Press I succeeded. In less than a year after the *Morning News* was founded we were able to publish the desired dispatches, and, on October 17, 1883, I was elected a director of the "A. P." We were now on even footing, so far as news facilities were concerned, with any of our competitors.

John Ballantyne

This, however, was not enough. I called to service a remarkable corps of special correspondents. The Irish situation was still the exigent matter. Parnell wrote me that he was so occupied that, much as he regretted it, he could not continue his telegrams. Then I employed William Dillon, brother of Parnell's associate, and T. P. Gill. They were prominent in the Irish National Party and sent me a series of most illuminating messages. Grace Greenwood served us with specials from Paris, while Joseph Hatton, in that day a famous journalist, was our London correspondent, William Eleroy Curtis, our representative at Washington, and Dr. Albert Shaw, now of the *Review of Reviews*, was the North-

Joseph Hatton

William E. Curtis

western correspondent, located at Minneapolis. My former schoolmate, John Ballantyne, was the efficient managing editor. Out of it all I am sure that our news columns surpassed in interest those of any of our rivals. But even chronicling events was not all. We were living in a wonderful age. There had never before been such progress in discovery and invention. To make note of this and to inform our readers of the developments in science was plainly important. There was no attempt to usurp the functions of the technical or the trade papers but we sought to present in popular form so much of the dramatic march of the world in material advancement as would be interesting and profitable to every reader. This field included the amazing changes in electricity, mechanics, surgery, medicine, sanitation, etc.

How to Edit News

We made no boast that we had all the news, as did many of our contemporaries of that day. It was our business to have it all, else there was no excuse for our existence. Having the news and publishing it did not, after all, determine the character of the paper. It was too much like judging a man from the fact that he was properly dressed. There must be something more to give individuality and standing to the journal. We had another obligation. This was to edit the news so as to give each item its relative importance and to save the time of the reader. One day I was talking with a young man employed on the Chicago *Times.* "What do you do?" I asked.

"Edit the telegraph," he replied.

"And how?" I returned.

"By inserting the words which the correspondent eliminates to save telegraph charges," he explained.

"Then," said I, "you do not edit at all. Your correspondents do the editing."

Therefore our "desk men," who really edited, were quite important. We made it a rule that the paper should never exceed eight pages in size, and that only such matter should be inserted as we believed would be of interest to a majority of the readers. This very brevity turned out to be popular.

For the editorial page I adopted certain methods which were old in England but altogether new in the United States. The usual custom with us was to employ three or four "leader writers," who were expected to write intelligently upon any subject assigned to them. Such editorial writers must know everything about everything to be of real value to a paper, for the daily newspaper should be prepared to discuss editorially all of a myriad topics, any of which might at any hour call for attention. But there were no such wonderful writers existent. Wherefore the usual course was for the poor wretch who must make his contribution, willy-nilly, to have recourse to an encyclopedia, hastily cram on a subject and then, in his article, do the best he could to disguise his ignorance. Having often done this myself, I knew how weak was, as a rule, the editorial page of an American daily. It was this very weakness that made notable the vigorous, yet far from scholarly, diatribes of our early-day journalists.

It was the second John Walter of the London *Times* who followed the obviously correct course of conduct, and thereby made his paper the great "Thunderer" of Europe. He went out into the various fields of human interest and activity and secured specialists in each line, and either employed them steadily or kept them on call and paid them liberally for each article. Delane, his great executive editor, himself an Oxonian, was able to bring to the service of the paper the best among the scholars of England.

F. W. Reilly

Here was an example which impressed me. I engaged specialist editors to write upon many topics. I employed Dr. Frank W. Reilly, executive head of the Illinois Board of Health, to cover sanitary, medical, and surgical topics. He was a brilliant writer and a delightful personality. He surrendered his governmental office and devoted his entire time to us. He was not only the recognized authority on sanitation; he was a student in many other departments of science, and an exceptionally well-read man in classical English literature. He set the whole office going over Chaucer, Spenser, Addison, and all the mid-Victorian authors. He, through his articles in the paper, began a campaign for a canal to connect the Chicago and Illinois rivers. The sewage of the city of Chicago ran into the little river that flowed through the city, and thence was deposited in Lake Michigan. From this lake we drew our drinking water. The plan for a canal involved changing the current of the Chicago River so that, instead of flowing into Lake Michigan, it should flow south into the Illinois River and thence to the Mississippi.

Professor W. S. B. Matthews, admittedly the most competent man in the West for such service, wrote upon musical topics; Walter Cranston Larned, author of several well-known books on European architecture and painting, was art editor; and Colonel Gilbert A. Pierce, who later was the distinguished governor and United States Senator from North Dakota, made a specialty of national politics; Mrs. Helen Ekin Starrett, who wrote with a masculine pen, dealt brilliantly with almost every conceivable topic; for pure literature we had William Morton Payne, later the well-known editor of the *Dial* and having national fame as a critic. Payne was the author of a notable hoax which created a great sensation in the world of journalism.

One day a charming young woman showed me some verses written by a young Chicagoan. They disclosed such genuine merit that I sent for the young man and took him into the service of the paper. He was a very efficient dramatic critic for a while. It was Harry B. Smith, the famous librettist of comic opera.

Prof. James Laurence Laughlin of the Chicago University wrote upon finance, and Prof. Richard T. Ely of the Wisconsin University on sociology. Among the other graduates of the *Daily News* office were Col. George Harvey, now the American Ambassador to Great Britain. He came to us when he was nineteen years old,

W. S. B. Matthews

and displayed such capacity that he was later taken to the New York *World* and finally became its managing editor. George Ade, the well-known playwright and author of "Fables in Slang," joined the *Daily News* staff very soon after his graduation from Purdue University in Indiana, and he and John T. McCutcheon, the caricaturist, another graduate of the same school, won fame by their work on the paper. Slason Thompson, author of the Life of Eugene Field and of the plays "M'liss" and "Sharps and Flats," and compiler of "The Humbler Poets," served with great efficiency and distinction as an editorial writer upon general topics. Finley Peter Dunne (Mister Dooley) served a term as reporter on the paper. And there was Henry Guy Carleton, poet, dramatist, and former officer in the United States Army. He, among other things, contributed editorials upon military topics. He was a very brilliant fellow and subsequently became managing editor of *Life*. Morgan Bates and his talented wife, Clara Doty Bates, and Mr. and Mrs. Alexander Sullivan were members of the staff.

Colonel Harvey

Slason Thompson

"Bill" Nye

George Ade

And for pure entertainment we had Eugene Field and Bill Nye, as well as Thomas E. Powers, the caricaturist. James Whitcomb Riley, Kate Field, and other equally well-known authors furnished contributions. Altogether, it was a great newspaper staff. Indeed, I think it was the greatest in point of ability ever assembled in this country.

As in the case of the *Evening News*, it was our plan that the paper should be cheap in nothing but its price. It was the farthest removed from "yellow journalism," alike in matter, policy, and typography. It favoured ardently civil-service reform, and I was elected president of the Chicago branch of the league. While not advocating prohibition, it was outspoken in its opposition to the saloon and the malign influence of the pothouse in politics and social order. It was independent of party control, but supported vigorously the candidates who seemed most deserving. Regardless of the fact that its constituency was naturally—because of its price—very largely composed of the working classes, it strenuously insisted that trades unions must stand by their contracts as honestly as must employers.

John T. McCutcheon

In the phrase of the London bobbies, the rule of the office was to "keep on movin'." We were never idle. We were always doing something. If it was not the publication of the sensational news of the day, it was a thrilling detective story provided by our own activity and clearly of value to good government, or some interesting disclosure in the field of science, or some side-splitting presentation in the field of entertainment.

The routine of the day was about like this: We, the chiefs of the editorial departments, reached the office about half-past ten in the morning. After a short delay, for the purpose of caring for our morning mail, we assembled for a conference about eleven. Eugene Field called it the "Senibodi." Everyone came surcharged with suggestions. We had no "office politics." Everyone was ready to help his fellow. No one was striving to supplant his fellow. Everyone was proud of his connection with the paper. No one felt that he was liable to be asked to write something which he did not believe to be true. As I have said, we were yokefellows, and it was never a case of master and man. One day Slason Thompson said he was entitled to an increase in salary.

"And why?" I asked.

"Because," he replied, "I am the man in the editorial conference who is always ready to say that you do not know what you are talking about." His salary was promptly increased. And, as I look back through the years, I think Thompson's judgment was quite often better than mine. Anyhow, I am

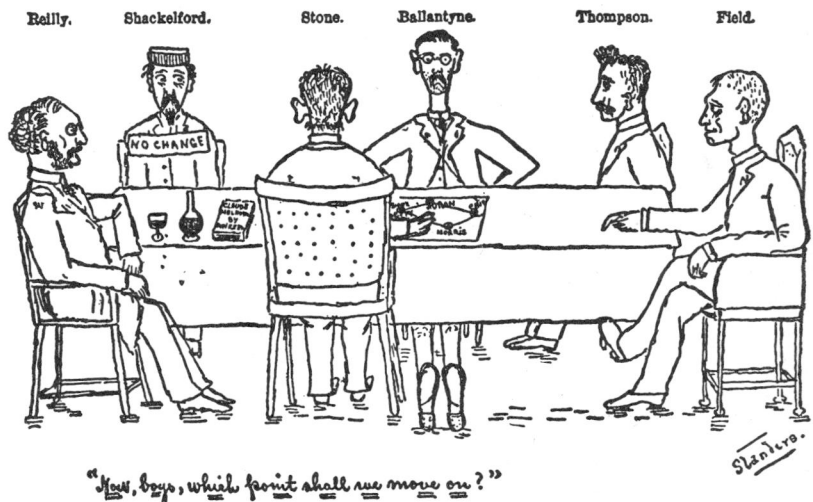

The Senibodi in the *Daily News* Office
(Drawing by Eugene Field)

convinced that it is not the man who always acquiesces in your opinion who is most helpful.

Our first effort at these morning meetings was to try for a proper perspective of the newspaper interest of the day. We had a theory that the mind of the reader centred primarily on some one thing. It might be an event in Chicago, or it might be an event in Senegambia. And the second day's story of the event usually meant more to the reader than the first day's. We set out to gratify his curiosity, to answer any question about the event that he was likely to ask.

When we had traversed the news field, and determined how we should deal with it, we turned to our preachments. This meant the editorial guidance of our constituency, so far as we felt qualified to undertake it. And I am bound to say that we were not at all modest as to our offerings. We had views, and we did not attempt to disguise them. Our very frankness, as a rule, was gratifying to our readers, for I believe that, whether they agreed or disagreed with our opinions, they believed us to be honest and also recognized that we were considerate of the people whose minds were not at one with ours.

We devoted ourselves to entertainment and earnestly sought for something worth while. If it was to be fun, it must be real fun and not stupid buffoonery to make the unskilful laugh and the judicious grieve. There was no department of humour in the paper, no compulsory comic page. There was no crying aloud: "This is funny," any more than was there any shouting as to the growth of circulation or vaunting of the number of advertisements in a given six months. The reader was quite likely to find a gem worthy of Douglas Jerrold or Voltaire buried in an out-of-the-way corner, anywhere on the sheet. It paid him well for buying the paper, and the next day he bought it again. And he continued to buy it.

We were always doing novel things. For instance, on the occasion of Henry Irving's arrival on his first American tour, I engaged four of the leading clergymen of Chicago to write signed criticisms of his opening performance.

After the editorial conference we went over to a Viennese pie shop, Henrici's, and bought luncheon and dyspepsia. I am not sure that Henrici's pies did not in the end kill poor Field. And we bowled at Tom Foley's. Back to the office and our work. Home to dinner. To a theatre in the evening and thereafter back to the office for our proofs. We cut them ruthlessly, so that out of the matter we gleaned the best.

We established the "Saints and Sinners Corner." It was in an unpartitioned department of McClurg's bookstore; reserved for the sale of rare books. Here there gathered a notable company of bibliomaniacs. Among those who frequented the place were: Eugene Field, Slason Thompson, Doctor Reilly, Frank Larned, and others of our own staff, as well as the Rev. Dr.

Frank W. Gunsaulus, Bishop Frank M. Bristol, the Rev. Melancthan Woolsey Stryker, dear old Dr. Robert Collier and the Rev. Father Hogan. Also a number of non-residents resorted to the "Corner." There was Paul du Chaillu, Dr. W. F. Poole, the famous librarian, Henry Ward Beecher, Charles Dudley Warner, Francis Wilson, the comedian, John H. Finley, the famous educator, Joe Jefferson and Sol Smith Russell.

The meetings in the "Corner" of a late afternoon continued for a number of years and enduring friendships were established. Now and then we had a formal evening, at which it was my duty to preside. For one such occasion Eugene Field wrote his well known poem of "Dibden's Ghost," which he recited in low voice and in a dim religious light.

My forte was "sleuthing." My exploits in detective journalism created a great sensation in the West and prompted me to further attempts. And, Heaven knows, there was field enough. If editors could only see that they are the eyes of the citizenry, as well as the mentors, the gossips, and the grinders of moving-picture cameras, they would do more good, achieve greater fame, and make more profit. In a popular government it is all-important that someone shall play sentinel, watch the sleeping tents where lie the well-meaning but inactive sovereigns, and prevent the invasion of corruptionists and revolutionists. Eternal vigilance must not be expected from the man who is busy with selling his needles and pins. And if we are to maintain our liberty someone must be on guard, not to chatter about duty in editorials, but to go out, discover offences against the law, and bring the offenders to justice. Detective work always requires a painstaking examination of all the known facts and, from these, careful, intelligent deductions. A puzzling case is as fascinating as a chess problem. You have only to follow the footsteps of Sherlock Holmes to be led to an agreement with my view.

Origin of a Famous Phrase

In 1882 Clarence Dresser was a free-lance reporter in the city. He was one of the offensively aggressive type—one of those wrens who make prey where eagles dare not tread. Always importunate and usually impudent. Such reporters are not the best. And Dresser had, because of his tireless audacity, proved a failure as a news gatherer and been employed and speedily dismissed by all the papers. Then he became a "free lance."

He prowled among the railroads, gathered what he could, betrayed confidences generously, and sold his output at something an article. His situation was precarious, but railroad officials were afraid of him and they fed him liberally with annual- and trip-passes, and one way or another he made a living.

One evening Mr. William H. Vanderbilt arrived with some friends. He was on his private car which was side-tracked in an out-of-the-way corner of the Michigan Central yards. Dresser learned of his whereabouts and posted off for an interview. Vanderbilt was at dinner. But it was useless. Dresser forced his way in and cheerily accosted the magnate. Intrusion of this sort was not uncommon with him. He was nothing abashed when Vanderbilt said sharply: "Don't you see, sir, that I am engaged?"

"I want an interview," replied Dresser.

"Well, sit down at the other end of the car until I have finished dinner, and I will talk with you," pleaded the victim.

"But it is late and I will not reach the office in time. The public——"

This was too much for the infuriated Vanderbilt, who interrupted his tormentor with the ejaculation: "The public be d——d; you get out of here!"

Dresser scurried off to the *Daily News* office, told in great glee the story as I have recalled it, and wanted to sell an article based on Vanderbilt's phrase which he had extorted: "The public be d——d." But our night editor would have nothing to do with it. Instead, he roundly denounced Dresser for the whole business.

Then Dresser went off to the Chicago *Tribune* and, cautioned by his experience at the *Daily News* office, avoided any suggestion that he had aroused Vanderbilt's anger, and made a sale.

The result was a publication which did the whole railroad business incalculable damage and, as much as anything, led to the war on transportation companies which followed.

About this time my attention was engaged by another railroad man, one Charles T. Yerkes. I was in Philadelphia for a few days. I left the city for Chicago on an evening train. "Bill" Singerly, owner of the *Record* and a friend of mine, found me in a Pullman car. "You can't stay here," he said. "There is a crowd of good fellows, some of them friends of yours, in a private car ahead. We have a vacant drawing room and you must occupy it." I accepted his invitation. I found myself in the company of a band of as jolly a lot of "highbinders" as one might care to see. Among them was "Charley" Yerkes. They were going to Chicago to make a raid on our traction lines. There was no secret about their purpose. How they expected to do up the guileless Chicagoans was made plain. There was much drinking, much Bacchanalian singing, some dancing, and little or no sleep throughout the night.

And so they came to the city of Chicago. Everything was ripe for their plucking. The street-car systems were primitive in their methods, the public officials were incorrigibly corrupt and zealously corruptible, and the citizens were asleep. Very soon the accomplished craftsmen from Philadelphia were in full swing in our burg.

I was watching the onslaught with interest. When the bribery of officials became an open and unblushing business, I opened fire. I published Yerkes's record, including his term in prison. He threatened to kill me, but I went on. And finally life in Chicago became unbearable for him and he moved to New York. It must in fairness be said that, with all his misconduct, he really did a great service in improving the transit facilities of the city.

Acquaintance with Diaz

My acquaintance with General Diaz of Mexico began in the spring of 1883, when he came to Chicago. I happened to be on the citizen's committee of entertainment and was thrown into relation with him. He was accompanied by his wife and his father-in-law, Señor Romero Rubio.

The General was then in the full vigour of life, a perfect type of stalwart manhood, firmly knit, swarthy of complexion, hardened by service in the tented field, but betraying singular intellectual strength withal. Señora Diaz presented a sharp contrast to her masterful husband. He, from top to toe, was an Indian. She was a Spaniard, who might have passed for a Castilian. There was no Mexican strain visible in her. Perhaps Andalusian, but surely and undeniably Spanish. Adorned with a mantilla, and wearing a crucifix she was obviously a Catholic. He a Mason; she a faithful daughter of the Church.

President Diaz

But, after all, the father-in-law, Romero Rubio, was in some respects the most interesting of the party. He was a member of the Cabinet of President Diaz—Minister of Gubernacio. His ethical standards were not those of his distinguished chief, who, whatever errors may be attributed to him, will for ever live as an example of unimpeachable probity. Romeo Rubio was not above making the most of his official position. A good story is told of him. At a time when from purely patriotic motives General Diaz was striving to enlist capital from the United States for the development of Mexico, and was granting concessions for railroad building, gold- and copper-mining, and like enterprises with a free hand, certain Americans called upon Romero and being advised of his thrifty character offered him fifty thousand dollars for some sort of a license to do something, I have forgotten what. They assured the Minister he could accept the bribe without danger of exposure. "You say you will give me $50,000 and will tell no one," he replied. "Make it $100,000 and tell everybody."

His career was a brief one. Diaz got rid of him.

Early in 1896 I went to Mexico and called upon the Chief

Executive at his palace. We talked at length and with intimacy of the outlook for Mexico and of his purposes in respect of his country. His frankness was delightful, his perceptions remarkable, and his sterling integrity beyond question. He was a great patriot and a great statesman. "I wish my country to profit by its proximity to yours," he said. "We have many things to contend with. Our peons are a good people, well meaning but densely ignorant, and our *intelligensia* are for the most part of the easy-going Spanish type. We can gain much from an infusion of the intelligence and the energy of the United States." To him this did not mean the slightest personal advantage, but solely a contribution to the welfare of the Mexican people.

I ventured to speak of what seemed to me the two crying needs of his country: first, such a division of the great *haciendas* as would give homes to the peasantry; and second, education for the common people. "Yes," he replied, "and if I live to do it, I intend to see the land divided and compulsory education enforced." But, even then, he was an old man and not equal to the task he had set for himself. He was an Indian with all the forceful characteristics of his race; he was wholly unselfish, he was highly resolved to leave a monument of acknowledged well-doing; yet it was not to be. His life had been one of never-ceasing battle, he had drawn upon his strength in a measure of which he little dreamed, and in the end was surrounded by associates having little sympathy with his purposes and little capacity to aid him in the undertaking.

As evidence of his simple-mindedness, on one occasion a thirty-third degree Mason from New York City arrived. To Diaz free masonry meant much. It represented the element which in a Latin country contested the political field with the Roman Catholic Church. And Diaz was a Mason. As he jocularly told me, "My wife is a good Catholic and goes to Church and to the Sunday bull-fights, while I am a Mason and stay at home on Sunday." When the distinguished Mason from New York arrived, Diaz gave him a state dinner at Chapultepec. Later, he was much chagrined to learn that his guest was a New York hack driver.

For the succeeding years Diaz and I corresponded frequently. Then came the revolution and his departure for Europe. And comparative poverty for him, with the deluge for his country. There were vicious rumours that he had made a fortune and had gone to Paris to live in luxury. This was a wicked falsehood. He died in Paris, July 15, 1915.

On February 27, 1919, with M. De la Bara, one-time President of Mexico, I called upon Señora Diaz, the widow of the great President. I found her living in quiet seclusion at 16 Rue Leonardo da Vinci and in moderate, not to say humble, circumstances in a third-story apartment in a remote corner of Paris. She had selected the location because a few steps away, in the Church of Saint-Honoré d'Eylau, rested the remains of her beloved husband. She had grown older than when I had last seen her. But she had all of the grace, all the charm, all of the intellectual brilliancy of her earlier day. With tears and love for Mexico, and love and tears for her dead hero, she awaits with dignity and patience the hour when she may be freed from her grief.

An Invitation from New York

I received the following letter from the General Manager of The Associated Press:

The New York Associated Press, No. 195 Broadway, New York,
March 12, 1883.

Dear Mr. Stone:—

Do you and Lawson want to undertake a newspaper enterprise in New York?

If so, you can make an arrangement with Cyrus W. Field for the *Mail and Express*, not requiring payment of money except as you make it out of the concern.

Yours truly,
William Henry Smith.

Some time after I was in New York and called on Mr. Field. He offered to sell us a half interest in his paper at a satisfactory price and to permit us to pay him out of the profits that we should make from our interest. He did not even ask us to give up the conduct of the Chicago *Daily News*. It was an attractive and quite flattering tender. But, I asked him, who was to own the other half of the property? When he said he was to be our partner, I said I must decline his proposition—that his ownership in and control of the elevated railway system of New York made it impossible. He could hardly understand my attitude and was plainly grieved. Later he sold the paper to Colonel Elliott F. Shepard.

On the day of my refusal of Mr. Field's proposal, and immediately after I had left his office, I ran into Joseph Pulitzer on Broadway. He asked me to go with him to the Astor House. We sat down in a corner and he told me that he had that morning bought the New York *World* from Jay Gould. He invited me to share in the purchase, taking either the editorial or the business department. It would involve so much that I felt again forced to decline with thanks.

Both Field and Gould had learned the lesson that the ownership of a newspaper cannot successfully serve to aid in the management of a public utility.

It became evident that the Chicago *Tribune* was gaining

The William H. Smith Letter

much fame from its foreign service, a good share of which was pirated from the *Daily News*. A trap was set. Matthew Arnold had just made a tour of the United States, had lectured in Chicago, and had returned to England. As everyone knew, he was an acrid critic. Perhaps the reader remembers the story of Robert Louis Stevenson, if it has ever been told in print. I am not sure.

Stevenson lay out in Apia, in the Samoan Islands, nearing his end with tuberculosis. The death of Matthew Arnold was announced.

"Ah," said Stevenson, faintly, between paroxysms of coughing, "that is too bad. He won't like God!"

With Arnold's temperament in mind, we saw an opportunity to deal with the *Tribune*. After talking the matter over, I shut William Morton Payne up in a room and he prepared what purported to be a cable message from London, quoting an article, on his visit to Chicago, contributed by Matthew Arnold to the *Pall Mall Journal*. It was admirably done.

Whitelaw Reid joined me in the scheme. I sent him Payne's "dispatch." He caused it to be printed in one copy of the New York *Tribune*, which found its way into the hands of the New York correspondent of the Chicago *Tribune*. The correspondent, acting under instructions, telegraphed the whole thing to his Chicago paper, and the next day it was printed and created a sensation in our city.

We of the *Daily News* assumed that it was genuine and interviewed those whom Arnold was credited with having roundly scored for bad manners and undeniable ignorance in the *Pall Mall Journal*. The men whose names were mentioned in Arnold's alleged article spoke back bitterly. The *Tribune* on its editorial page chimed in with the denunciators of the caustic British critic. The thing went on for two or three days, and, after everyone had had his say, I cabled Arnold a full personal explanatory message, and of course received from him a reply to the effect that he had made no such communication to the press. This I published, adding that there was no such paper as the *Pall Mall Journal*, and indeed exposing the whole business.

The Chicago *Tribune* was not merely convicted of having

Matthew Arnold's Cable

stolen the "dispatch," which was not worth stealing, but of adding humbug and deluding the readers.

Founding the Fast Mail Train

Our morning paper had been going about a year when we struck a snag. The Chicago *Herald*, which had been founded as a Republican Party organ at two cents a copy, within a week of the date when our own sheet began issue suddenly became involved in a serious libel suit and was forced to change ownership. Mr. John R. Walsh became the chief factor in the new proprietorship. At the same time he was at the head of the Western News Company, which for years had controlled the distribution of all of the Chicago dailies in the out-of-town districts. It was the practice of the news company to collect in the early morning from each paper as many copies of the sheet as they had orders for, to assemble these in packages, and send them by express to the country dealers. It had been cleverly arranged that the express companies should refuse to carry a package for less than ten cents. This resulted in giving the news company a monopoly, and as Mr. Walsh, our immediate competitor, was president of the news company, discrimination against us was easy, and the situation became intolerable.

At the time General Arthur was President of the United States, Judge Timothy O. Howe of Kenosha, Wis., was Postmaster General, and Frank Hatton of Burlington, Iowa, First Assistant Postmaster General. They were all friends of mine, and Judge Howe and Frank Hatton, being from cities adjacent to Chicago, were easily made acquainted with my predicament. After deliberation with them, we devised a plan to circumvent the manifestly unfair methods of Walsh. The mails for China, Japan, and other Oriental countries passed through Chicago. At that point they were divided among the various transcontinental railroads. Tom Potter, general manager of the Chicago, Burlington & Quincy Railroad, was called into consultation and agreed that, if given enough of this mail for the Orient to compensate him, he would run a fast train to leave Chicago about three o'clock in the morning and reach Omaha at two o'clock in the afternoon. This was the first fast mail train in the United States. There was no increase of expense to the Government, but, as these trains became general, they greatly expedited the delivery, not only of newspapers, but of all first-class mail. It was a notable reform. The morning papers of Chicago, which theretofore had left the city by express at eight in the forenoon, now reached their subscribers in middle Iowa, 300 miles distant, about that hour. We were freed from Mr. Walsh's control, our distribution costs markedly reduced, and not long after the Chicago *Herald*, unable to profit by such unfair methods, was offered for sale.

Days with Eugene Field

They were rollicking, happy days—those that I spent with Eugene Field. As I have said, I met him first in October, 1873. Not long after, he and his brother Roswell went to the St. Louis *Journal* and I frequently called upon them. Gene, for everyone so called him, had hardly begun to betray his extraordinary genius. His environment was not such as to awaken him. He plodded, writing well but not brilliantly. Then, dissatisfied, he went to Kansas City and St. Joseph, Mo. At "St. Joe," the home of his wife, he felt more at ease. There he wrote "Little Boy Blue," that tender, heart-racking verse which has brought comforting tears to the eyes of so many thousands of bereaved mothers. There, too, finding as his editor-in-chief Major Bittinger, a brave old fire-eater, he began the pranks which ever after delighted his soul.

There, too, I fear, he for a brief period indulged in the flowing bowl, and earned a reputation which altogether quite unjustly followed him through his after life. They tell a story of him that he owed an account at a saloon. He always owed an account. On this occasion the debit was written on a slate and hung upon the wall. One evening he entered the place. The proprietor felt that whatever the indebtedness, Gene's delightful society had furnished ample compensation, and forthwith wiped off the score and with some degree of pride announced to his debtor that the bill was settled.

"Indeed," said Field, nothing abashed, "I believe that it is the rule here when a man pays his shot, you treat the house; is it not so?"

"Yes," reluctantly and dubiously replied the saloon keeper.

"Then," said Field, "everybody will step up to the bar and have a drink on the house."

In each place he became famous. What Gene had done, what he was doing, and above all what he would do next— these were the topics that absorbed all interest. He was doing something, and that something was always original. He might write a story or a poem; his composition might be exquisite in diction, classical in construction, or it might be clothed in what the French happily call the argot of the street, or in the rich dialect of the western plains. In any case, it was faultless of its kind. Or he might tell a story, or recite, or play a practical joke, or, indeed, preach a sermon. His versatility was beyond comparison. His life was a veritable kaleidoscope, and each new picture was startling and full of interest. All the while he was a hard, conscientious student. His power of absorption was marvellous. If he had not been a writer, he could easily have become an actor or a painter. He was for ever drawing pen-and-ink sketches of himself and others.

His school days were few; some months at Williams, a year at Knox College at Galesburg, Ill., and a short course at Columbia, Mo.—graduating nowhere and hardly a creditable pupil anywhere. Yet I dare say he entered upon his life work with a better mental equipment than 90 per cent. of varsity men. He read everything and remembered everything he read. In Denver he wrote the "Tribune Primer." It was not a great thing and did not compare with his later work. But it attracted widespread attention and served notice that a new humorist was born to the world, one ranking above Artemus Ward, Josh Billings, Nasby, and Bill Nye, and worthy a place beside Dean Swift or Charles Lamb. It revealed a quality of mind theretofore unknown on this continent and gave promise of the greatest possibilities. It was not mere horseplay. It was not a mere jester who had come among us with cap and bells and humped back and motley—it was something better and worthier.

Eugene Field by Himself

Early in 1883 William Eleroy Curtis, the well-known newspaper correspondent, and I took our wives for an outing in the West, having as our destination a visit to the wonderful Zuni Indians in Arizona. On the way we stopped over at Denver, and one evening went to Taber's Opera House to hear Emma Abbott. I went out for a stroll between the acts. When I returned who should be sitting in the back row but my old-time friend Eugene Field.

He had tired of "St. Joe" and had gone over to Kansas City and back to St. Louis and had finally taken leave of the effete Middle East and landed in Denver. He joined O. H. Rothaker and F. J. V. Skiff, two of the most brilliant editors of their day, in the conduct of the Denver *Tribune*. Here Field made his paper and himself famous by the publication of certain beautiful verses, and by certain characteristic practical jokes which set everyone aroar. He wrote his charming poem, "The Wanderer"—the moan of a sea shell far from its home on a Colorado mountain top—and issued it as from the pen of Helena Modjeska, the actress. He went out to Ouray, made the acquaintance and the undying friendship of Daniel Day, editor of the *Solid Muldoon*, a fine type of the editorial cowboy, and penned at Gold Hill, under the shadow of the peaks of the Rocky range, in a primitive frontier tavern, "Casey's Table d'Hôte." Then back in Denver, when Oscar Wilde was announced for a lecture, he dressed his associate Rothaker in velveteen jacket and knickerbockers and decorated him with a huge chrysanthemum, drove through the Denver streets and received the plaudits of the citizens, who thought him the host of the veritable Irish poet. Here, too, he sent for Bill Nye, then editing the Laramie (Wyo.) *Boomerang*, and gave him a dinner which has not been forgotten to this day. And he tilted his lance at "Brick" Pomeroy, who at the moment was a Denver editor.

When I met him the *Tribune* was about ready to quit. To this end he had contributed his full share. The field was too small and the times were too strenuous for him. I asked him to come to Chicago and take a place on the *Daily News*. We left the theatre, walked the streets for an hour, and his engagement was settled. That is, if upon reflection he should conclude that he would like to join me. There was no contract. Neither of us wanted one. The only indenture was the amusing letter which follows:

DENVER, April 26, 1883.

DEAR MR. STONE—

Had I supposed you were going to be in Denver a day longer I should have tried to have another talk with you and I believe we could have settled the question of my coming to Chicago. I repeat that I was much pleased by the way you talked relative to my casting my lot with the *News*, and I want to assure you once more that when I go to you it will be with the intention of staying. As I intimated to you while you were here, I cannot leave the *Tribune* people in the lurch. I have a contract with them till August 2, and, while I could get out of that contract, I would prefer abiding strictly by it. Would it suit you as well, providing we agree as to other details, that I delay my coming to you till September 1? I will contract with you for two or three years, to do the work you specify, for $50 per week the first year, $50.50 per week the second year. If you choose to contract for three years, I shall want $55 the third year. The reason I tack on the 50 cents for the second year is to gratify a desire I have to be able to say I am earning a little more money each year. This is a notion I have happily been able to gratify ever since I began reporting at $10 a week.

Will you people allow me $100 for the expense of breaking up housekeeping here and removing to Chicago? I am a deucedly poor man or I would not suggest the thing. An attempt at honesty in the profession has kept me gloriously hard up, with a constantly increasing family. However, as you are not running a charity enterprise, I beg you will not consider this last suggestion if it seems an improper one. I trust to hear from you at your earliest convenience.

Yours very truly,
Eugene Field.

To Melville E. Stone, Esq.

The very engagement was characteristic. He wanted to join me, he was tired of Denver and distrustful of the limitations upon him there. But if he was to make a change he must be assured that it was for his permanent good. He was a newspaperman, not from choice, but because in that field he could earn his daily bread. Behind all, he was conscious of great capabilities. Not vain, nor by any means self-sufficient, but certain that by study and endeavour he could take high rank in the literary world and win a place of lasting distinction.

Then he came to Chicago and an intimacy of twelve years, duration began. There was no stipulation as to the precise sort of work he was to do, but we were both anxious that he should have the largest opportunity. After talking it over, we agreed that he should have a column of his own. He wished it so that he might stand or fall by the excellence of his work. Salary was less an object than opportunity. And so it happened that the "Sharps and Flats" column of the Chicago

Morning News was established, and Field wrote practically every line that appeared in that column from its beginning until his death. The title was borrowed from the name of a play—"Sharps and Flats"—written by Slason Thompson of the Chicago *News* staff and played with notable success by Robson and Crane. Field was given the utmost liberty of action. To fill his own column meant that he should write something like two thousand words a day. But this he could easily do. He was the most prolific writer I have ever known. How day after day and year after year this column laughed and wept, how it sparkled and crackled with jollity, how it swept the tenderest chords of the human soul, needs no word of explanation.

No sooner had Field arrived in Chicago than he began his pranks. He came in the early fall. A month later we reached Thanksgiving Day. It was our custom to give each married employee of the paper a turkey on that occasion. But not for Field. He would have none of it. A day or two before the holiday I received a formal letter, written in his inimitable script suggesting that if it was all the same to me he would prefer a suit of clothes, as he had no particular use for a turkey. The state prison was forty miles away and the warden was a personal friend. From him I obtained a suit of "stripes" that would fit my petitioner, and when Thanksgiving Day arrived, the "suit of clothes" was presented in a package which when opened surprised and delighted him beyond measure. He was tall, slender, smooth-shaven, almost bald, the little hair he had being cut very short.

The home of the *Daily News* was a primitive place. As the paper grew, we rented adjoining buildings and connected them by doors cut through the walls. I converted the top floor of one of these structures into editorial offices. It was really a loft. There were three small offices in front and rear where the light could be secured and between was a long hall practically vacant. To heat the place—there was no steam—there was an ·old-fashioned "cannon stove."

Now and then a country editor would call and I would assign a reporter to show him over the establishment. In his wander-

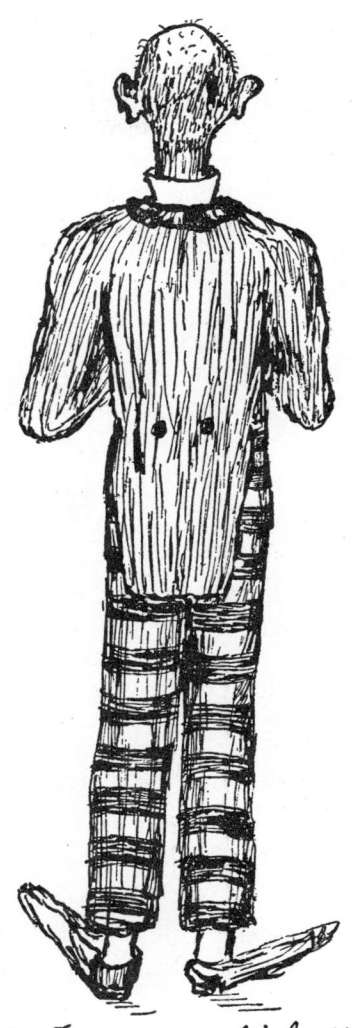

Mr. Field reading his beautiful poems at the Press Banquet.
(Drawn by Himself)

ings he would reach this loft. While the conducting reporter dilated upon the wonders of a metropolitan newspaper, the door of one of the petty dens would open and a tall, gaunt creature, almost bald, and smooth-shaven, in prison stripes and an old pair of carpet slippers, would step out, seize a poker and proceed to shake down the ashes in the stove. This done, he would set about sweeping the floor and raising a cloud of dust that would choke a behemoth. The visiting editor, gasping, would ask what this meant. With well-simulated embarrassment, the reporter would reply that he was afraid to explain. This was the skeleton in our closet. It was the one thing about the place that all the employees disapproved of but did not dare to discuss. In strictest confidence, however, he would tell. The editor of the paper was a friend of the warden of the penitentiary, and took advantage of that fact. "The man before you," he would say, "is a life convict. He is a trusty. To save expense, Mr. Stone has induced the warden, Major McClaughry, to let him have this poor wretch to serve as janitor for the *Daily News* office. It is all wrong, but, you can well understand, we cannot afford to open our mouths about it." The editor would join with the sympathetic reporter in denouncing the outrage, while Field, the wretched convict, was chuckling over the prank. In one case, a week later, down in Central Illinois, a weekly paper appeared with an editorial pouring out its vials of wrath upon McClaughry and myself for this shameless performance.

Correcting Some False Ideas

Not only did Field write every line that appeared in the "Sharps and Flats" column, but practically everything that he wrote after 1883 appeared at one time or another in that column. His books, which have had such general circulation, and have given the public as much of pleasure and of exquisite pain, are simply selections from his work for the Chicago *Daily News*.

In the opening lines of his admirable little book, "The Eugene Field I Knew," Francis Wilson says: "There were many

A Dedication from Eugene Field

President Arthur

Eugene Fields. Like the Apostle, he was all things to all men and much to many." I think I may add in justice that very many people do not know, nor ever have known, what the real Eugene Field was and that to this too widespread misconception of his character Field himself was unconsciously, yet very largely, responsible. In a certain sense he was his own worst enemy. He so enjoyed a good story that he quite frequently invented one—not to give offence to others—at his own expense.

He never took any pains to deny a story concerning himself, although the story may have done him a rude injustice, provided only that the story was a good one and had a point. I know that people imagine from stories they have heard that he was a high liver, if not, indeed, addicted to stimulants. As a matter of fact, he was a man of most simple and exemplary habits, and during my entire and very intimate acquaintance with him, was, in fact, although not by profession, a teetotaler, nor did he smoke. I have never seen him drink so much as a glass of claret.

It is also true that a great many stories of an unpublishable character have been given currency by crediting them to Eugene Field. All of this, as I have said, did him great injustice, and those who knew him best naturally resent it.

The Puritan Strain

It is true, nevertheless, that he was a many-sided character. *Au fond*, he had a profound religious, even spiritual, nature. The Puritan strain of his ancestry frequently cropped out in his daily life. He had a secret fondness for Cotton Mather and Jonathan Edwards and all the other sturdy captains of the Church Militant. Yet over all there spread the warm, mellow rays of a human sympathy which prompted some of the

Eugene Field at Work

sweetest and most pathetic verse of our language. He sounded all the depths of tender emotion and voiced the agonized cry of bereaved motherhood and sisterhood and childhood with the tone and timbre and *tempo* of a master. What grief-stricken maternal heart is there that has not wept itself to consolation with reading "Little Boy Blue"? What sobbing bosom has not found comfort and relief in "The Singing in God's Acre"? What unruffled hero "grunting and sweating under a weary life," has not felt his burden lifted on reading "Father's Way"? Would one stand in that field where both eyes weep, the one for joy, the other for grief, then let him read "Casey's Table d'Hôte" or "Two Opinions." Or would one laugh and laugh alone, then let him read "Café Molineaux," or "Mynheer of Kalverstraat." Either for tragedy, comedy, history, or pastoral, as old Polonius said, his muse was attuned.

Practical Jokes

Is it the man behind the pen that one would know? Well, those who knew him best quite often felt that they did not know him at all. He was genial, fraternal, affectionate; yet as much as any one I ever knew, he was a victim to the isolation of greatness; he impressed us that he was in the world but not of it. He sometimes seemed to have been dropped out of another and a former generation. He had nothing whatever in common with the hustling workaday life of the great city in which he spent his latter days. The mighty forces making for material progress meant nothing to him; he lived and moved in another world. Books were his companions, and day by day he worked with the old masters and the old minstrels and heeded not the things about him. It may surprise those who have heard so much about his quips and pranks to be told that he took life very seriously. He worked very rapidly, yet with scrupulous care. Often a manuscript would lie for months in his drawer awaiting a final revision which should render it acceptable to his keenly critical eye. The mechanism of his verse was ever perfect. He was a close student of words and knew their value to a nicety. His success was not achieved without constant and earnest toil. From this labour his active mind found relief in the humorous pranks which endeared him to his friends and which have, in a measure, given the public a false idea of him. He was tireless in his efforts at a practical joke.

A room adjacent to Field's was occupied by the society editor. She was a modest little person, the very pink of propriety. Her duty required her to attend an evening party, return to the

> To Melville E. Stone, Esqr.,
>
> Once my employer,
>
> Always my friend
>
> and invariably my creditor,
>
> I present this book with much love.
>
> Eugene Field.

Inscription in a Book by Eugene Field

office about midnight, write her "copy," hand it to the city editor, and go home. With his impish instinct, Field waited one night until she had gone and then, with a bit of chalk, he traced a man's footprints from the street up three flights of stairs to her room and all the way down again. And the next morning I received a formal note of complaint from him charging that Miss —— was receiving callers in her office at an unseemly hour; that she was not a discreet person, and as damning evidence he asked me to make note of the footprints on the stairs.

There was a public celebration. I do not remember the reason for it. But while the procession was marching by, with beating drums and waving banners, my office door opened and there entered Eugene Field and his three children "Trotty," "Pinney," and "Daisy." The youngsters were in rags, patches on their garments and their toes bursting from old borrowed shoes. "I must have an increase in salary," said our joker as he pointed at the example of abject poverty he had carefully prepared.

We went to the theatre. They were playing "The Mikado," with Roland Reed as Koko. We sat well down in front. Sud-

Field Bursts into Song

denly while Reed was singing one of his best lines Field, who was an actor of great ability, screwed his face into unspeakable shape and poor Reed was forced to stop and begin all over again. Often if there was a child in the seat back of him, Field would turn and make a face which would set the infant bawling. The mother, having no idea of the cause, would search in vain for an offending pin, while Field's sides were shaking with delight. Yet again, he and I were seated near the stage, and "East Lynne" or some equally tear-forcing play was being produced. At the moment of high tension, when there was profound silence throughout the house there burst out a loud "Ha! ha! ha!" and then Field turned to a quiet old gentleman seated by his side and silently denounced him with a look of amazement and condemnation. The audience took it up and all recognized the poor old fellow as the culprit. He blushed and, when the curtain fell, quietly took his hat and slipped out, and did not return. Field, who was almost a ventriloquist, was the real offender.

One day he gave a very elaborate luncheon in honour of Dr. Edward Everett Hale. Among the guests were F. Hopkinson Smith and Thomas Nelson Page. The menu was most carefully prepared. The list of toothsome viands presented for his friends was as follows:

Blue Points on the Shell.

Consommé Royal.   *Sauterne Château Yquem,*
                      Bottled at the Château.

Terrapin à la Maryland.
Canvasback Duck.
(Hominy Balls).

Old Madeira, rich and rare.

Camembert and Roquefort.

Champagne, Perrier Jouet et Cie.

Coffee.   Cigars.

Suitable glasses for each wine were provided, and under instructions the waiters, with bottles clothed in napkins, poured out, with great dignity, cold water for each as a beverage. And the actual food was corned-beef hash, pork and beans, soda biscuits, and apple pie.

At another time my wife and I were entertaining Madame Modjeska at a formal dinner. Paul du Chaillu, Edward S. Willard, the English actor, and Major Moses P. Handy were there. And, of course, Field. It was a cold winter night. As a delicacy hot-house strawberries were served. Field promptly refused them on the ground that they would spoil his taste for prunes.

I had a place in the country to which he was always welcome,

How Mr. Stone Rewarded a Faithful Vassal.

Quoth generous, genial Mr. Stone —
As once he brooded all alone —
    "It doth amaze me highly
To climb up here and see no sign
Of Thompson or of Ballantyne
    Of Hawkins or of Reily!
These persons are employed to write
Their lucubrations, fair and bright,
    Upon my paper's pages;
But, by my soul! I ween they shirk
For wine and actresses the work
    For which they draw their wages.
"Ay, all are false — save one alone!"
Fiercely continued Mr. Stone —
    "And he alone is dutiful!
At all times sober and on deck,
Calmly he issues from this wreck
    And whoops his work up beautiful.
And seeing him in yonder room
Mocking the incandescent gloom,
    I venerate my joker;
And lo! how eagerly he chews
His humble plug — would he refuse
    A mild Havana smoker?"

#

Nov. 26, 1885

A Field Appreciation

invited or uninvited. He would throw himself on my bed and write by the hour. Also, if he was short of anything, he did not hesitate about helping himself from my wardrobe. One day he called on me in the city, carrying a bundle under his arm. This he deposited with:

"There is something my wife told me to bring you. I don't quite know what it is. I believe there's a shirt, and I know there's a pair of socks of yours, that have spoiled our wash for three weeks."

Casey's of Table d'Hôte Fame

Then he turned and walked out.

In the spring of 1895 he went to California for a vacation. His health was not good. He tired of the continuous chatter about the "glorious climate." A cousin lived at Alameda. Eugene went to visit him. One morning, at breakfast, his cousin being absent, he began thus to his cousin's wife:

"I had a horrid dream last night. Yet now that I think of it, it was not so bad. I dreamed your husband was dead. And he approached the

Field Invites Himself to My Country Home

pearly gate. St. Peter was on guard. Edwin [that was the cousin's name] tried to enter, but Peter stopped him to find if his name was in the book. 'Who are you?' asked Peter. 'Mr. Field,' replied Edwin. 'Ah,' said Peter promptly, 'Mr. Eugene Field, walk right in. You are welcome.' 'No,' replied Edwin, 'not Eugene Field, but Edwin.' 'Then,' said Peter, 'I must examine my book.' He did so and Edwin's name was not there. So Edwin was told to go below. At the gate of the infernal regions was another guardian with cloven hoof and forked tail. And he, too, had a book. Edwin attempted to enter, but was not enrolled and was again turned away. I heard him cry in anguish: 'Great heavens, must I go back and live in the glorious climate of California?'"

Appeal for a Small Loan
(Drawing by Field)

Eugene Field died in his sleep, November 4, 1895, aged forty-five years.

When all too young, and much before his time, he died, there passed from us one who, though he had done much, and not a little that will endure, was surely at the threshold of a very great career.

Emory Storrs and His Tailor

One day, in 1883, it was announced that Baron Coleridge, grand-nephew of the poet, and Lord Chief Justice of England, who was visiting the United States, would come to Chicago. He was engaged in what the Thomas Cook people would call a personally conducted tour, and Col. Elliot Shepard, Vanderbilt's son-in-law, was his courier. Then there were great doings to arrange a befitting reception and a high-class banquet for his lordship. The Chicago Bar Association took the matter in hand, but, wishing to make it really a memorable occasion, they widened the scope of their undertaking and invited certain citizens to participate. So it happened that I was asked to serve on the "Committee on Speakers" for the feast, and actually became chairman.

Lord Coleridge

For years Emory Storrs had been the prize orator for such occasions. He was a brilliant lawyer. I think he had a better concept of the fundamentals of jurisprudence than any member of his profession whom I have ever known. But in his personal character, he was, to say the least, peculiar. He was not a teetotaler. His standards, in respect of conventional morals, were angular. In his commercial relations he was a Dick Swiveller. At the moment he was my attorney in one or two rather important cases. Despite this fact, I was unwilling, because of his well-known delinquencies, that he should represent the Bar of Chicago and make the speech of the evening. And I frankly said so. My committee agreed with me. We selected Melville W. Fuller, who later was Chief Justice of the United

States Supreme Court. He acquitted himself with credit, as one might have expected.

A day or two after our committee meeting and our decision, Storrs called upon me. He knew what had happened. He knew that he was not to be the spokesman at the great feast and he knew that I was responsible for the fact.

Nothing abashed, however, he presented himself. "I have a favour to ask," he began. "The public dinner to Coleridge is to occur on Wednesday evening. You have chosen Fuller to speak for the Chicago Bar. I do not complain. Your selection is all right and quite fitting. Now I have arranged to give a dinner on my own account to his lordship on Thursday night at the Leland Hotel. I am here to ask you to be one of my guests. You must not refuse. You and I are long-time friends, and I insist upon your acceptance."

I demurred, but after some pleading on Storrs's part, yielded.

The public dinner went off with appropriate éclat. There was a very large and representative attendance, the cuisine and wines were good, and the speeches all that could be desired. Storrs was conspicuously absent. As his *coup* had been pretty well noised about, we all looked forward with interest to the succeeding evening. We knew that he would strive to outdo in the matter of decorations, cuisine, and general appointments.

Late in the afternoon I went home to dress. I had hardly entered my house when there was a call upon the telephone. It was from my office. My astonishment at what followed may be easily imagined. I was advised that a certain tailor, named Walsh, to whom Storrs was indebted, had gone into court, sued out an attachment, and a sheriff's officer was on his way to the Leland Hotel to levy on the forthcoming feast.

It was a pretty kettle of fish. Without delay I telephoned to the hotel and asked for Storrs. He promptly responded. I told him what had happened and said that, if he wished, I would go down and sign his bond and release the attachment. He laughed and said he would be grateful if I would come at once and attend to the matter.

I hurried down, but on my arrival found that Samuel Allerton, a wealthy pork packer, had dropped in by accident, given bail, and relieved our host from his dilemma.

No one could have been in a happier mood or better form than was Storrs that evening. There were about fifty guests, including many of the most distinguished citizens of Illinois. I do not think any one at the table, except Storrs, Allerton, and myself, knew of the attachment episode. Storrs's speeches were brilliant, and everything went off with such spirit that I doubt if Lord Coleridge enjoyed a more notable entertainment during his American visit.

After the company had assembled and participated in an informal reception, and about as we were to pass to the dining hall, Storrs took my arm and whispered in my ear: "There was only one thing that annoyed me about that Walsh matter this afternoon, and that was the sacrilege of that d——d sheriff's officer, *that he should think of laying his unholy hands on the Lord's Supper!*"

The Campaign of 1884

The campaign of 1884 was what Sir Edward Creasy might have called one of the decisive political contests of our Republic. It was momentous because a dominant party, voicing the sentiment of the victorious North, was beaten finally by a party burdened by a former advocacy of human slavery, by an attempt to destroy the union of states, and by a more recent history of twenty years in which it had been stupidly opportunist, passing from one futile campaign of negation to another. The campaign was notable because a long-time leader in the field of American politics, brilliant, forceful, and supported by a vast company of personal devotees, was defeated by a man new to public office, with no reputation as a speaker or writer, modest, even taciturn, and scarcely known beyond the limits of the state in which he lived. It was decisive, because the general sentiment of the electorate was distinctly changed, and the spiritual being of the nation took on a new birth.

Mr. Lincoln's great task in the four years of storm and stress was really to conquer the whole North and to free the whole

South. And he had not finished the work when he died. Therefore it happened that after Lee's surrender we forced the rule of carpet-bagger and contraband upon the subjugated South. We trusted no rebel. With the best of intentions, and for reasons which at the time seemed obvious and compelling, the right of suffrage was given to the former slaves. Many of our leaders were camp followers who either had fought badly or had not fought at all in the Civil War, but who were now widely clamorous for revenge.

The real soldiers, footsore and weary, went quietly from the battle-field to their homes, and left the conduct of affairs to those who from their shouting one might suppose had done all the fighting. As someone has said, our national affairs went off into a witches' dance. Scandal followed scandal in quick succession, such as the Jayne-Sanborn contracts, the Black Friday episode, the Whisky-Ring exposure, the Belknap-Post-Tradership transactions, the Spencer-Arms jobbery, the Crédit-Mobilier rascality, the De Golyer Paving Affair, and the Star-Route robberies. And in the South the rapacity of the Northern mercenaries allied with the ignorance and incapacity of the Negro vote, sustained by the Federal arms, begot a condition altogether insupportable. Matters were not helped by the struggles of the Southern people for relief. The Ku-Klux manifestations and similar acts of reprisal were worse than vain. They merely stimulated the North to renewed measures of repression, which produced a solid South. Following the theory of Alexander Hamilton, who once declared to John Adams that he believed the safety of the Republic depended upon corruption, high protective tariffs were imposed, with an unwritten but no less distinct understanding that in return for these special privileges those benefited by them should contribute liberally to the Republican Party purse. The Presidential campaign of 1880 had been notoriously corrupt. The phrase "Blocks of Five," referring to the purchase of voters in Indiana in that year, has passed into the literature of American politics.

So it happened that, as the campaign of 1884 was approached, the question uppermost in the minds of the electorate was political purity. Not that this question of corrupt politics was entirely new. As early as 1866 James G. Blaine and Roscoe Conkling, both members of Congress, engaged in a bitter debate bearing on a public expenditure. As the years went on, the line of cleavage between the two widened, and there grew up within the Republican Party two factions, with these men as leaders. The Blaine partisans never doubted his integrity, while the Conkling followers never believed in Blaine's honesty. A number of official acts, which his best friends characterized as "indelicate," stamped Mr. Blaine as a man with whom Conkling was unwilling to affiliate. His marvellous personality and undeniable magnetism, however, carried Blaine through contest after contest, and the loyalty of his followers remained unshaken. At Cincinnati, in 1876, Colonel Ingersoll drew his portrait as that of a "plumed knight walking down the halls of Congress and throwing his shining lance full and fair against the brazen foreheads of the defamers of his country and the maligners of his honour."

But the Conkling followers would have none of Blaine, and Colonel Ingersoll, after Conkling's death on April 8, 1888, eulogized him before the New York Legislature. In that memorial address he said, with sinister design, as he once confessed to me:

Roscoe Conkling was an absolutely honest man. He was the ideal representative, faithful and incorruptible. . . . He made no bargains. He neither bought nor sold. . . . He neither sold nor mortgaged himself. He was in Congress during the years of vast expenditure, of war and waste—when the credit of the nation was loaned to individuals—when the amendment of a statute, the change of a single word, meant millions, and when empires were given to corporations. . . . He had the taste of a prince and the fortune of a peasant, and yet he never swerved. No corporation was great enough or rich enough to purchase him. His vote could not be bought for all the sun sees, or the close earth wombs, or the profound seas hide. His hand was never touched by any bribe, and on his soul there never was a sordid stain. Poverty was his priceless crown.

Yet, with the distinct merit of probity, Conkling had weaknesses which chilled the ardour of many and put serious limits upon his strength as a leader. He delighted in stinging sarcasm, and frequently used it in inexcusable fashion. He was arrogant and pompous to a degree that was ludicrous.

In the campaigns of 1876 and 1880 Blaine, as an aspirant for the Presidency, was subjected to merciless attack. The nomination of Garfield, a Blaine partisan, in 1880, was offset, as a compromise, by the selection of General Chester A. Arthur for vice-president. But Garfield's administration had not fairly begun when he was assassinated, and Arthur became the chief executive. It was inevitable that he should be regarded with no small degree of suspicion by those who know little of his real character. The descendant of a long line of rugged Scotch-Irish ancestors, the son of a Vermont Baptist minister, from boyhood he had been an ardent Abolitionist. After the war broke out, he gave up a fairly lucrative law practice to become quartermaster general of New York State, and in less than four months, by his admirable management, he clothed, uniformed, and equipped, supplied with camp and garrison equipage, and transported to the seat of war, sixty-eight regiments of troops. In 1871 he was appointed collector of the port of New York by President Grant, and held the office for over six years. An effort was made to remove him by the Hayes administration. The accusation was that both he and Alonzo B. Cornell, the naval officer, had been too active in politics and that their offices had been used for partisan purposes. The Secretary of the Treasury pleaded with Arthur to resign, accompanying the request with an offer of an important foreign diplomatic mission. General Arthur not only refused to resign, but presented indisputable evidence that during the six years he had managed the office the yearly percentage of removals from all causes had been only $2\frac{3}{4}$ per cent. against an annual average of 28 per cent. under his three immediate predecessors. He also showed that in making promotions, the uniform practice had been to advance from the lower to the higher grades, and that the expense of collecting the revenues had been greatly reduced. Nevertheless, Hayes nominated a successor, whom the Senate refused to confirm. After a two-years' struggle both Arthur and Cornell were displaced, but at the succeeding state election Cornell was elected governor of New York by a substantial majority, and Arthur became the leading candidate for United States Senator, an aspiration checked by his nomination for the vice-presidency.

Putting aside all factional spirit, Arthur ceased to be a partisan, and moved carefully forward in an effort to carry out faithfully Garfield's announced policies. The Pendleton Civil Service Reform Bill was passed, and the first national commission, composed of men of the highest character, was appointed; oppressive internal taxes were abolished; and there was a first, though not altogether satisfactory, scientific revision of the tariff by a special commission; the fast-mail service was established; domestic letter postage was reduced from three to two cents; the national indebtedness was reduced by $500,000,000; wooden warships were discarded, and a new navy of steel vessels begun. The annual River and Harbour Bill, which for years had been the object of widespread and justifiable criticism, was vetoed, and in its stead a proper method for the protection of the Mississippi River levees was urged.

In the late summer of 1883, after nearly two years in the White House, President Arthur visited Chicago, and on that occasion I asked some two hundred of the leading men of the country to give expression to their judgment respecting his administration, the same to be published by me in the *Daily News*. In responses from clergymen, college presidents, literary men, and politicians, from those who had opposed his nomination, from Democrats who had opposed his election, there came a virtually unanimous declaration of approval and confidence. About the only qualifying word came from Mark Twain, who replied:

MELVILLE E. STONE, Editor *Daily News*,
Chicago, Ill.

I am but one in the 55,000,000; still, in the opinion of this one-fifty-five-millionth of the country's population, it would be hard indeed to better President Arthur's administration. But don't decide till you hear from the rest.
MARK TWAIN.

Hang the Telegraph—it would be a year getting there—I send by mail.

In his demeanour as well as in his official acts Arthur was an ideal chief executive. I had personal knowledge of the poignancy of his grief at Garfield's assassination, and of his patient suffering under the malignant accusation that he was indifferent. No man could have had a keener sense of the dignity or responsibilities of the Presidential office. He was at all times kindly, even a model of urbanity, but he never ceased for a moment to betray a punctilious regard for the proprieties of his position. It was once reported that in an after-dinner speech, where jocularity was pardonable, he had discussed campaign contributions freely; spoken rather approvingly of the corrupt use of such funds, because, after all, it was only "fighting the devil with fire"; and that, as he stood washing his hands in invisible water, he had said that "while there was life there was soap." He assured me that the whole story was a reporter's invention, which offended him very greatly. Though he had shared in the rough-and-tumble of practical politics, he was unwilling to suffer any loss of dignity or to yield in any measure his devotion to the highest ideals.

Toward the end of Arthur's term the Republican conventions of state after state adopted flattering resolutions, calling for his reëlection. So when the Republican National Convention met in Chicago on June 3, 1884, the candidates were Arthur and Blaine.

Ten years before I had been a correspondent at Washington, when, in the Forty-third Congress, Blaine was speaker, and like virtually all of the men who represented newspapers at the national capitol at that time, I distrusted him, and if for no other special reason, I favoured Arthur.

General Arthur's interests were put in direct charge of half a dozen men, several of whom were not delegates. Among these were George H. Sharpe and Elihu Root of New York, Omar D. Conger of Michigan, Frank Hatton of Iowa, and Benjamin F. Butterworth of Ohio. On the opening day the situation was uncertain. A substantial majority of the delegates were opposed to Blaine's nomination, but were so divided in their preferences that he was undeniably the favourite. The first skirmish was over the temporary chairman. Of this Senator

President McKinley

Mr. Kaneko

George F. Hoar in his autobiography [Vol. ii, p. 61] says, speaking of John R. Lynch of Mississippi:

I was the means of procuring for him a national distinction which very much gratified the men of his colour throughout the country. The supporters of Mr. Blaine in the national convention of 1883 had a candidate of their own for temporary presiding officer. I think it was Mr. Clayton of Arkansas. It was desired to get a Southern man for that purpose. The opponents of Mr. Blaine also desired to have a candidate of their own from the South. The coloured men were generally Blaine men. I advised them to nominate Lynch, urging that it would be impossible for the Southern coloured people, whatever their preference might be as to a candidate for the presidency, to vote against one of their own colour. Lynch was nominated by Henry Cabot Lodge, afterward my colleague in the Senate, and seconded by Theodore Roosevelt and by George William Curtis.

It would be difficult to frame a paragraph more inaccurate. The truth is that Senator Hoar had nothing whatever to do with the selection of Mr. Lynch. During the convention, I took a room at the Grand Pacific Hotel in the city. Next to it, and communicating, was a room occupied by James D. Warren of Buffalo, N. Y., an active friend of General Arthur.

A day or two before the convention assembled the National Republican Committee met and agreed upon the nomination of General Powell Clayton of Arkansas as temporary chairman. I had had some experience with Clayton, and felt it was important that he should be beaten. As far back as July 30, 1883, he had written me a letter in which he said:

Mr. Arthur's accession to the presidential office was under circumstances of the most difficult and trying nature. Many people, anticipating failure, stood ready to proclaim their criticisms. If any official of his has afforded them that opportunity, I am not aware of it. Should the same wisdom, care, and fidelity mark his course to the end, I think history will place his administration among the very best the Republic has been blessed with.

"*Not for Forty Nominations!*"

Some months later, and within a few days of the national convention, I was at the White House. In the course of conversation with the President, he told me he was puzzled at the attitude of the Arkansas delegation. It had been elected as an Arthur delegation, and he had had a letter of personal assurance from General Clayton. Nothwithstanding this, however, the New York *Tribune*, the leading Blaine organ of the country, persisted in crediting the fourteen delegates from Arkansas to Blaine. General Arthur handed me a letter he had received from Clayton, and asked me to see him on my arrival in Chicago which I did. Clayton told me that, while he was personally devoted to President Arthur, he was embarrassed by the attitude of his colleagues. He said there was a widespread feeling that the southwestern territory should be recognized in some important way, and that the members of the Arkansas delegation, with certain men from Texas and adjacent states, eighteen in number altogether, had concluded to vote for Arthur if he was willing to promise, if elected to appoint Clayton as postmaster general. I replied that I had no authority to encourage such a hope, but would submit the matter to General Arthur himself.

Leaving Clayton, I went at once to the Palmer House and sent a cipher message covering the case to Fred Phillips, Arthur's private secretary. Scarcely a moment elapsed when an answer came back in plain English: "Not for forty nominations."

The next day I informed General Clayton that the proposed arrangement could not be carried out, and thenceforward he and his delegates were open and avowed Blaine men.

When General Clayton was proposed for temporary chairman, General Arthur's friends, knowing the facts as I have recited them, were naturally exceedingly anxious to accomplish his defeat. On the night of June 2nd, Mr. Warren and I were sitting in our rooms discussing the matter. I think Mr. H. G. Burleigh, an Arthur delegate from Whitehall, N. Y., was present and took part. Very likely General Sharpe was also there. My recollection is very clear that I suggested that there was one way to meet the issue, and that was by the nomination of a coloured man. I did not believe that the convention would dare to defeat such a candidate. The plan was agreed to.

The first name offered was that of Blanche K. Bruce, who had been a member of the United States Senate, and seemed to us the logical person. We found he was living in a remote part of the city, and hurried a messenger with a carriage to him. He arrived at our rooms about three or four o'clock in the morning. As the convention was to meet the next day, there was no time to lose. We presented the matter to Bruce with all the earnestness we could command, but were unable to induce him to enter the contest. After he left, some one suggested Lynch's name. It was nearly dawn when he arrived. He was an original Arthur man, and it therefore took little entreaty to enlist him in the enterprise.

I do not know who communicated the matter to Mr. Lodge and his associates, but the following afternoon, when the convention was called to order, Mr. Lynch's name was presented as a candidate against General Clayton, who was proposed by the national committee, and on the call of the roll, Lynch secured a majority of forty votes.

As I have said, the situation in respect of a nominee for the presidency was uncertain. The two leading candidates were Arthur and Blaine, but the balance of power was held by a contingent of reformers, real or pretended. In a number of cases, as in that of General Clayton, personal reasons unquestionably played a controlling part. The Massachusetts delegation was under the leadership of Senator Hoar. He had quarrelled with President Arthur over the appointment of Worthington as collector of the port of Boston, and as he said frankly in his autobiography, his opposition to Worthington grew out of the fact that the latter had supported Ben Butler in Massachusetts, and Butler in turn had woefully defeated Hoar's brother when the latter ran as a bolting Republican candidate for Congress in 1876. "But for the indignation caused by this appointment," wrote the Senator, "I think the delegation from Massachusetts would have supported Mr. Arthur for reëlection. There would have been no movement for Mr. Edmunds, and but for that movement, Mr. Arthur would have received the Republican nomination." One of the New York delegates at large, who was open in the denunciation of Blaine, yet helped to make his nomination certain by supsporting Edmunds against Arthur, also had his personal reasons. This was Theodore Roosevelt. It was his father who, in 1879, had been nominated as Arthur's successor for collector of the port of New York, and refused confirmation by the Senate.

Out of it all, Blaine was nominated for the Presidency with General John A. Logan as running mate. A platform was framed with great care to meet the peculiar situation. Naturally Blaine's friends made an earnest effort to put the tariff to the fore as an issue. They had no stomach for a revival of the charges of corruption that had been freely discussed for the eight preceding years.

But a storm of protest broke throughout the nation. I do not think any newspaper correspondent who served in Washington while Blaine was Speaker ever thought of voting for him. I met one of them, General Henry V. Boynton, the dean of the corps, in Chicago after the convention, and asked him what he proposed to do. He was a Republican, and for years had been a leading political writer for his paper, the Cincinnati *Gazette*.

"I do not know," he replied; "I am a poor man, and dependent upon my work for a livelihood. One thing I know I shall not do; I shall never write a line in advocacy of Mr. Blaine. That probably means that I must resign my position and look for something else to do." He did tender his resignation, but was given a vacation for the campaign.

A great number of conspicuous Republicans declared they would not vote for the nominee. Among them were such men as Henry Ward Beecher, George William Curtis, Thomas Wentworth Higginson, Carl Schurz, Wayne MacVeagh, Moorfield Storey, Sherman Hoar, and the Rev. James Freeman Clarke. These recalcitrants formed what was known as the "Mugwump" contingent. I was among the earliest of the number in the West. The name had been applied in derision by the New York *Sun*. In 1877 it had originally been used to stigmatize General Logan by Isaac Bromley, an amusing editorial writer on the New York *Tribune*. When the epithet was revived, in 1884, General Horace Porter, on being asked what it meant, replied that a Mugwump was "a person educated beyond his intellect." When the Chicago *Daily News* was asked the same question, I replied that a Mugwump was "a Republican with a conscience."

The Republicans having made their nominations, all eyes turned to see what the Democrats would do. At that time I happened to visit New York, and one day called on Mr. Conkling, who was out of politics and practising law. The interview was an amusing one. Although we were alone, he struck his familiar senatorial attitude, and proceeded to deliver himself of an oration. He had parted company with Arthur almost immediately after the latter's accession to the Presidency because his former lieutenant would no longer do his bidding. He therefore felt little regret at Arthur's failure to secure the nomination. But his hatred of Blaine survived, and was his absorbing interest. He closed his grandiloquent and distinctly didactic effort by turning to me and saying: "Well, there will be a funeral, and you and I will at least have the consolation that neither of us will ride in a front carriage."

The National Democratic Convention assembled at Chicago a month later, and of the presidential possibilities Grover Cleveland was the most conspicuous. In some respects he bore a resemblance to General Arthur. As I have said, Arthur was the son of a Baptist minister. Cleveland's father was a Presbyterian minister. Both were born in rural parsonages. To both was left the priceless legacy with which the American minister of the gospel is usually able to endow his offspring: a sound moral training, a limited education, and no wordly estate. Each was a lawyer of no mean ability, but of distinctly local fame. Each had the taste of an amateur for politics, which he indulged freely, but without reaching the height of a recognized boss. The integrity of neither had ever been questioned.

On the other hand, no two men ever differed in greater measure than Blaine and Cleveland. Beginning his political career early in life, Blaine had been a conspicuous figure through a long term of years, and from his youth he had always been in trouble, but he'd "turn a corner jinkin', an' cheat auld Nickieben."

Cleveland, on the other hand, was a village Hampden. In his earlier years his progress was slow, and gave no promise of a notable future. After his admission to the bar he served for a short time as assistant district attorney of Buffalo. Some years later he left the practice of his profession to become sheriff of his county. He had been defeated once for the office of district attorney. This made up the measure of his public service until 1881, when he was suddenly nominated for mayor of Buffalo. Unlike Blaine, his motto had ever been that of the Prince of Wales: "*Ich dien.*"

Two rather interesting coincidences marked the careers of the two men. In their young manhood both had served in the same year as teachers in institutions for the blind—Cleveland in New York City, and Blaine in Philadelphia. Both of them, also, had been drafted into the army during the rebellion, and both had paid for substitutes. Cleveland's substitute did his duty, and Cleveland's two brothers enlisted and served with distinction, while Blaine's substitute deserted at the first opportunity.

The nomination for mayor of Buffalo came to Cleveland altogether unsolicited; but with his sense of duty he had no alternative. His speech of acceptance was the only personal appeal made by him during the campaign. In that, however, he used a phrase which later passed into an apothegm, and became inseparably connected with his whole public career. He said: "We consider that public officials are the trustees of the people." He was elected mayor by a fair majority, and began service on January 1, 1882, without any formal inaugural ceremony. He promptly struck out for an administration in which the sentiment that "a public office is a public trust" became the watchword. He vetoed one corrupt ordinance after another, and within six months was "recognized as one of the strong, virile figures, both of his city and of his state."

Then there was an election for governor of the State of New York, and a number of the party managers turned their eyes toward him. The leader of these was Daniel Manning of Albany. It was wholly characteristic of Mr. Cleveland that by no hint or sign did he attempt to better his own fortunes. The Democratic State Convention met at Syracuse on September 22, 1882. Mr. Manning asked Cleveland to go to Syracuse to meet the delegates, to whom he was personally almost entirely unknown. Cleveland reluctantly accepted the invitation and then for the first time he was introduced to Mr. Manning and the others who were championing his cause. He was nominated, and two weeks later, in his letter of acceptance, made a strong plea for economy, efficiency, and integrity in the public service. During the campaign he wrote no other public letter and made no speeches. He was elected by the unparalleled majority of 192,000. He went quietly to Albany the day before his inauguration, and assumed office without ceremony on January 1, 1883.

Grover Cleveland

The national convention of his party the following year found him at once the idol of those who believed in honest government, and a bitter object of hatred to the machine politicians. The delegation from his own state was uninstructed, and its attitude for some time was in grave doubt. Tammany Hall was solidly against him, and such men as John Kelly, Bourke Cockran, and Thomas F. Grady openly asserted that he could not carry New York, and without it he could not be elected. Then sturdy General Bragg of Wisconsin took the floor and made a short speech which electrified the Convention. His phrase, "We love him most for the enemies he has made," became the shibboleth of his followers and made his nomination certain.

During the canvass, there was a striking difference in the attitude of Blaine and Cleveland. Blaine, true to his instincts, kept himself constantly in the public eye. Cleveland wrote his letter of acceptance and made two speeches. Soon all attempts to discuss public questions such as the tariff, civil-service reform, etc., were abandoned, and the contest resolved itself into a round of crimination and recrimination. It was the most intensely personal campaign we have ever had.

All the charges against Blaine's misuse of his official relations for personal profit, which had been effectively used in 1876 and 1880, were reënforced by fresh disclosures, and proved most damaging. Joseph Keppler, the cartoonist, pictured him week after week, as the "tattooed man," a characterization that in the end became as famous as Thomas Nast's cartoons of Tweed. The New York *Independent, Harper's Weekly*, and other leading journals, which had always been sturdy supporters of the Republican Party, revolted.

A number of important newspapers, including the New York *Tribune*, Chicago *Tribune*, and Cincinnati *Commercial*, which in 1876 had led in the campaign against him, suddenly changed front, and because they disclosed no reason for the change, did neither Blaine nor themselves any good.

The election was close, and for days after the polls closed the result was in doubt. On the final count, it was admitted that Cleveland had carried New York, the pivotal state, by a narrow plurality, and was therefore elected. A number of reasons were assigned. It was said that Blaine was defeated because of an indiscreet remark by the Rev. Dr. Burchard, who in an address to Blaine a few days before the close of the contest had said the constituent elements of the Democratic Party were: "Rum, Romanism, and Rebellion." It was said that extensive frauds in Queens County had deprived Blaine of enough votes to change the result. It was said that heavy rains in Jefferson and St. Lawrence counties, Republican strongholds, had made it impossible for the farmers to get to the polls, and therefore Cleveland had won his victory. On the other hand, a large number of New York City Democrats bolted their party and voted for Blaine. All of these things doubtless contributed, but the vital fact remained that, whether justly or unjustly, Blaine was the recognized candidate of and apologist for corruption, and that from his defeat there followed a change in the moral tone of the nation which was of great moment, and made for better government. That this did not persist, and that it did not lead on immediately to perfection, is true.

Nevertheless, there can be no such triumph without some lasting influence. So it was in this case.

The Famous Mackin Case

In 1884 the "Mackin Case" was of moment in Chicago and, indeed, throughout the nation. Upon its issue depended important things. When the presidential contest was over an interesting situation arose in Illinois. The election took place on the 4th of November. For two weeks the result, both in state and nation, was in doubt. There were 204 members of the Illinois Legislature on joint ballot. And that legislature was to elect a United States Senator. And one vote would determine whether the senator would be a Democrat or a Republican. Also, the United States Senate was so evenly balanced between the two leading parties that a single new Democratic member would tie the body politically. In these circumstances, to the amazement of everyone, it was announced that the Democrats had carried, for the office of state senator, a district which was notoriously Republican and which, indeed, for every other office than state senator, was admittedly and overwhelmingly Republican. For State Senator Rudolph Brand, a well-known and reputable brewer was apparently chosen over Henry W. Leman an equally well-known and reputable lawyer. And Leman had apparently run 200 votes behind every associate upon his ticket, while Brand had seemed to run an equally astonishing number of ballots ahead of his fellow candidates. Here was a how-de-do.

Joseph C. Mackin

Immediately there was a charge of fraud. It was before the Australian ballot had come into use. The party tickets, which in presidential elections contained the names of a large number of nominees, were printed from peculiar type and were held in the greatest secrecy until the morning of the balloting, to prevent counterfeiting. After the polls closed they were strung upon thread, and, with the tally sheets, were sealed and deposited in the custody of the county clerk to await the inspection and decision of a canvassing board.

When, under the law, they were opened by the returning board it was evident that the Second Election Precinct of the Eighteenth Ward of Chicago presented matter for consideration. It was here that Brand had seemingly run away ahead to everyone and Leman had, with like unaccountable reason, run behind. And yet everything was technically proper in the returns. The tickets, as strung upon the thread, appeared perfect in form, and the tally sheet corresponded with the count of the tickets and seemed undeniably correct.

In an effort to prove rascality, the Republican managers secured affidavits from many more of their partisans than were credited with votes for Leman, that they had voted for him. But to this the Democrats laughingly made answer that these people had not closely scanned their ballots on Election Day and, therefore, had unwittingly voted for Brand.

Several weeks went by and I paid no heed to this clamour, because I thought it the usual cry of a defeated and disappointed company of partisans. Then, on Thanksgiving Day, sitting alone in my office, it occurred to me that, in the light of the fact that my newspaper had supported Cleveland, I was rather bound in honour to make an investigation. I called a reporter and asked him to get a specimen of the genuine Republican ticket as it had been voted at the polls. Very soon, from the *Evening Journal* office, in which the printing had been done, he brought me an original of the desired ballot. I scanned it closely and found several styles of type that were clearly uncommon. Then, looking over the list of type founders and type-founders' agencies in Chicago, I sent the reporter out to them to learn who, if any, of the printers in the city, had recently, or since the election, ordered the rare kinds of type in question. He returned after a couple of hours and reported that the job-printing firm of P. L. Hanscom & Co. had made such purchases. I next, by a liberal wage offer, took into my employment a lad who served as "devil" in the Hanscom shop. He disclosed the fact that a Mr. Wright, a junior partner in the concern, had kept the boy up throughout a night ten days after the election to assist in the printing of certain tickets. And then the youngster brought me the "tympan sheet" used in the work. Every printer knows what the "tympan sheet" is, but others may not. In "making ready" for the use of such a press as was utilized on this occasion, the type is fastened in a frame, technically called a chase, on one jaw of the machine, and on the other jaw is fixed a pad of paper, the "tympan," against which the type presses. The top sheet of this pad was the "tympan sheet," and it bore a facsimile of the ticket which Wright had produced.

Meanwhile, excitement was running high, and a grand-jury inquiry had been instituted in the Federal Court in Chicago. This forced the county clerk to present the tickets and tally sheet in his custody awaiting inspection by the Canvassing Board. I took advantage of this to have these documents photographed. It was fortunate that I did so, because after their examination by the grand jury the Judge ordered them sealed up again and forbade any one to see them in advance of the official count.

Now my course of action was clear. I promptly swore out a warrant for the arrest of the printer, Wright. One Wednesday evening I took "Long" Jones, who in that day was the famous United States marshal for the Northern District of Illinois, for a ride. We drove to Wright's house, and I asked for him. His wife said her husband was a Methodist and had gone to prayer meeting. Jones and I said we would sit in the parlour and await his return. Finally he came, and the following conversation ensued. Disclosing my name and vocation, I said:

"Mr. Wright, a crime has been committed, and I have reason to suppose that you have been an innocent participant in the business. I have evidence that since the recent election you printed certain tickets which were imitations of the Republican ballots voted in the Second Precinct of the Eighteenth Ward, but upon which the name of Rudolph Brand was placed instead of that of Henry W. Leman. These tickets so printed by you have been substituted for the real ones voted and are now held as the genuine ones by the county clerk. I am here to ask you for whom you did this work."

"I do not recognize your authority to ask me any question respecting my business," said Mr. Wright.

"Quite true," I replied. "I assumed that you were a good citizen and that you would be glad to aid me in uncovering the fraud that has been attempted. As a precaution, however, I have sworn out a warrant for your arrest, and the gentleman here with me is the United States marshal. He will now take you in custody."

Mr. Wright was staggered, but there was no escape for him, and Jones and I bundled him into our carriage and took him to jail and saw him safely locked in a cell. The next morning he changed his mind. He sent for me and told me that he had printed the tickets upon the order of one Joseph Mackin, a well-known Democratic saloon keeper and ward heeler of the city. I had Wright taken before the grand jury, and he testified that he had delivered his fraudulent ballots to Mackin. I then swore out a warrant for Mackin and caused his arrest.

The forged tally sheet now demanded attention. I had, as I have said, a photograph of it. I set about an effort to find the man who had produced it. I secured specimens of the chirography of every well-known Democratic politician. The letter *G* upon the forged tally sheet proved important. Wherever it appeared it was written thus: G. For instance, the word Chicago was like this: ChicaGo. Here was a clue. One William J. Gallagher was a Democratic city employee, and in executing a receipt for his weekly salary wrote *G* in the singular fashion spoken of. I followed up the matter and found a saloon loafer who had seen Gallagher at work upon a tally sheet several days after the election. I then swore out a warrant for Gallagher and had him locked up.

By this time public attention was thoroughly aroused. A meeting of the leading citizens was held and funds were subscribed for the employment of competent counsel to aid the Federal district attorney. Chief of these was General I. N. Stiles, who for many years was known in Chicago as "the People's Lawyer." The Democratic bosses were also at work.

They furnished bail for Mackin and Gallagher and employed eminent lawyers to defend them. Of these United States Senator Turpie of Indiana was leader. We were now in for a fight.

When the trial came on I produced my evidence, which seemed unanswerable. I offered two outstanding facts, which seemed conclusive. First, as a practical printer, I directed attention to the palpable difference between the genuine and the fraudulent tickets. The type was, to the casual observer, the same, as was the paper. But a careful measurement of the size of the two ballots necessarily betrayed the crime. As printers would understand, the paper in each case was dampened. So it happened that the genuine ticket shrunk, and when it was used by Wright he measured this dry and shrunken ticket, set his type to provide for shrinkage of the damp paper he must use, but did not calculate well, and his product was therefore longer than the original.

Again, in the list of presidential electors upon the ticket was the name of Judge Humphrey, who was later the presiding Federal judge of the Southern District of Illinois. His name was originally Otis Humphrey, but for reasons of his own, early in life, he adopted the letter "J" as an additional and first prenomen. In the genuine ticket his name was printed properly, J Otis Humphrey, there being no period after the J. But Wright naturally supposed this to be an error and affixed a period.

Other differences noticeable only to the eye of the trained printer betrayed the inexactness of the counterfeit ballot. The engraved caption, placed under a microscope, was clearly printed from a "reproduced cut," and the titles, "For Lieutenant Governor," "For Secretary of State," etc., on close inspection presented unlike appearances. Wright had been unable to duplicate the type used in printing the genuine ticket, and had obtained the closest imitation he could find.

All seemed to be going well with the trial until the State rested its case and the defense began. Then some startling things happened. A self-confessed "tramp" printer named Sullivan took the witness stand and swore that just before the election he had secured a copy of the Republican ticket from a fellow "jour" who, working with the company having the official contract for the printing, had stolen a specimen ballot and, attaching it to a brick, had thrown it to Sullivan from a window into an alley. Then, said Sullivan, he had rented an unheard-of little printing shop from one Titman and there had produced the facsimiles. Titman appeared and swore that he had rented his place to Sullivan, and a political "handy man" testified that he had received the tickets from Sullivan on the morning of the election and had peddled them all the day at the polls. When Sullivan had finished his direct evidence, at my suggestion, General Stiles asked leave to defer cross-examination. I had gone out and obtained a warrant for the arrest of the witness for perjury. So, when he left the court room, he ran into the arms of a deputy marshal, who took him to jail. The "gang" did not dare to bail him out, and at daybreak, after spending fourteen of fifteen hours behind the bars, he sent for me and "squealed." He had been coached by Mackin and his lawyers. I am not sure that Senator Turpie had guilty knowledge of the business, but he never escaped suspicion. When court opened, General Stiles called Sullivan for cross-examination.

"Sullivan," said Stiles, "you testified that you received a copy of the genuine Republican ticket before the election. What did you do with it?"

"I didn't do nuthin' with it," replied the tramp, sheepishly.

"Didn't do nothing with it?" queried the lawyer. "But you swore that you did. Was that a lie?"

"Yes," said Sullivan.

"And was all of your story about printing facsimile tickets in Titman's place a lie?"

"It was."

And thus the carefully prepared defence of perjury was exploded. Senator Turpie at once pledged his honour that he had no part in the affair, but he narrowly escaped an attempt at disbarment.

Mackin and Gallagher were promptly found guilty. The verdict was set aside on a technicality, but ultimately both were sent to the penitentiary and served adequate terms. Mr. Leman's title to his seat in the State Senate was established, and as a result a Republican, General John A. Logan, was elected to the United States Senate.

The Case of McGarigle

After the inauguration of President Cleveland in 1885 I called on him at the White House, and we briefly considered his policy. I told him of a rule of self-conduct which I had early established in my newspaper career and which I had never broken; namely, that I should seek no favours at the hands of a public officer. Nor should I sign any petition or write any letters seeking an appointment from a public officer. I told him that I should be glad to be of any service to his Administration, and that at any time he desired to know anything respecting the fitness of any applicant in Illinois and chose to make any inquiry of me, I should endeavour to aid him by telling him the truth.

It happened, therefore, that one day long after, when I was with him at the White House, he told me there was a vacancy in the office of the United States marshal for the Northern District of Illinois and that he thought of appointing a certain William J. McGarigle to the place.

McGarigle was an active Democrat and had been an acceptable chief of police of Chicago, but with a change of the local administration had become warden of the County Hospital. It was within my knowledge that as warden he had become corrupt. A new hospital had been built and required furnishings and McGarigle and one or more of his intimates had been paid commissions upon these. An unsuccessful bidder had "squealed" to me. I told the President that I regarded the applicant as wholly unfit. He challenged my judgment and said that McGarigle was a fine-looking fellow, that he had come recommended by practically every banker, railroad president, politician, and clergyman in Chicago. I certainly must be prejudiced. I replied that if he would take the contract to appoint McGarigle as marshal, I would undertake to move his marshal's office to Canada within six months. I had been busy with other investigations, but should take up McGarigle's case very promptly. Mr. Cleveland was altogether unhappy at this declaration, but the next day he sent for Senator Logan, an ultra-Republican, asked him respecting the character of another applicant for the marshalship, a former Union soldier named Marsh, and upon being assured that Colonel Marsh was an honest man, promptly sent his name to the Senate.

Then I took up the McGarigle case. With the aid of the always efficient prosecuting attorney, Mr. Julius Grinnell, the evidence was secured. A prominent firm of merchants, who had sold curtains and bedding for the hospital and paid McGarigle a commission, called on me at the *Daily News* office and protested strongly against being forced to go before the grand jury and confess their misconduct. They even threatened to withdraw their advertising from the *Daily News* if I should push the matter. This, of course, was amusing but not effective. An indictment was promptly found and McGarigle was arrested.

The sheriff, one Canute Matson, who was not over bright, served the warrant; but upon McGarigle's plea that he would like to go to his home and tell his wife of the happening, the sheriff entered McGarigle's home and was seated in the parlour while the culprit went upstairs to break the news. After sitting there some time Matson found that the bird had flown.

There was a great sensation in Chicago and, of course, severe condemnation of Matson. I took up the investigation and found that on the evening of the arrest McGarigle had been spirited away by some of his friends to a boat lying in the harbour and controlled by a Doctor St. John. On this boat he had set out for Canada. I immediately took train for the Straits of Mackinac and chartered a small boat to intercept the fugitive. My movements were betrayed by a rival newspaper, and McGarigle escaped. The story of this betrayal is told, in his interesting autobiography recently issued, by the offending reporter, Charley Chapin, who is serving out his sentence in Sing Sing prison for wife murder. If I could have caught him at the time, I should have been tempted to kill him, and might myself be the "lifer" to-day. Not long after, however, I located McGarigle in Canada safe from extradition, and supported by a Chicago merchant named Lehmann. The disclosure of his whereabouts and exposure of Lehmann's connection produced a situation which was intolerable for them. Later McGarigle felt forced to come back to Chicago and face the music. The power of their political friends and the merchant's co-partners was sufficient to influence one of the judges to arrange for a secret return and hearing, a plea of guilty and a fine of the ridiculous sum of a thousand dollars.

As I have said, Mr. Cleveland was nettled at my prompt assertion concerning McGarigle. But his annoyance soon wore off and when, in 1887, he was passing through Chicago, en route to Milwaukee, he asked me to join him on his private car. There was a vacancy in the office of Chief Justice of the United States, owing to the death of Mr. Waite, and Mr. Melville W. Fuller of Chicago had been recommended for the position. He asked my opinion of Mr. Fuller, and laughingly suggested that he hoped I had no such prejudice as I had in McGarigle's case. I commended Mr. Fuller highly and he was appointed.

Organizing the Linotype Company

Early in 1885 Mr. William D. Eaton, a well-known Chicago journalist, called my attention to a new device for mechanical type-setting. Otmar Mergenthaler, a young German inventor in Baltimore, was at work on it. Eaton suggested that I look into the matter. On my way to Washington I stopped at Baltimore, and in a little upper room found the machine and the inventor. The invention impressed me very greatly.

I had spent more or less time and study upon the subject and had investigated the machine in which Mark Twain was interested and in which he lost so much of his fortune. Here was something new and something which obviously would do the work.

Mergenthaler had been financed by certain residents of Washington, but they had reached the limit of their ability and more money was needed. I invited a number of friends to meet me in Baltimore for a further examination of the machine.

Among the number were Whitelaw Reid of the New York *Tribune*, William H. Rand of the firm of Rand, McNally & Company, and William Henry Smith, general manager of the then existing Associated Press. They were impressed, as I was.

On March 14, 1885, an agreement was entered into on behalf of the parties in interest, Mr. Stilson Hutchins, then proprietor of the Washington *Post* representing Mergenthaler and the Washington group of earlier financiers, and I representing the group of associates whom I had enlisted in the matter.

The original syndicate was somewhat modified, Messrs. Richard Smith, Haldeman, and New dropping out and being replaced by others. The patents were examined and certain defects discovered. I found that what has been known as the "justifying" apparatus had been in use before and was covered by a patent to a Mr. Shuckers, who had been experimenting with a device not altogether unlike Mergenthaler's. Shuckers had been the private secretary of Salmon P. Chase, the illustrious Chief Justice of the United States. He was living in Atlantic City for the time being, and thither I went and negotiated with him for the purchase of his patent.

That done, on behalf of the syndicate which I had organized I paid Mergenthaler something more than $300,000 for the control of the company. As Mergenthaler said in his autobiography, it was doubtless the largest payment ever made in this country for an incomplete invention.

I became the first chairman of the Board of Directors, and the first twelve machines when completed were placed, at my suggestion, in the office of the New York *Tribune*, and the second twelve in the office of the Chicago *Daily News*.

It was Mr. William H. Rand who gave the machine the name of "line-o-type," which was abbreviated into "linotype."

Before the organization began to make any profit, I sold my entire interest to my partner, Mr. Lawson, at precisely what it had cost me. To-day the device is in universal use.

Convicting the Chicago Anarchists

At the same time I was active in the famous anarchist case. With the amazing development of the Middle West the drift

of immigration to Chicago was inevitable. The great fire of
1871 increased the tide. In the rebuilding of the city un-
numbered thousands of labourers and adventurers were attracted to the city from Europe. And it was observed that
they did not come from northern Europe in the same proportion
as formerly. The Germans and the Scandinavians, who had
in the earlier days constituted the bulk of the immigrants and
had enriched the population of Chicago by their industry, integrity, and general good citizenship, were now replaced by a
less acceptable class from more southerly latitudes. Germany
was beginning her period of unexampled prosperity following the
war of 1870–71 and the unification of the Teutonic states, and
there was a noticeable tendency on the part of her people, for
the time being, to withstand the temptation of foreign adventure.

As a result of this change in the population of Chicago there
grew up great colonies of uneducated newcomers. They had
little of the underlying spirit of American institutions. They
brought with them and preserved their hatred for all forms
of governmental restraint. They were peculiarly fitted to yield
to the influence of the demagogue. After the extraordinary
period of activity occasioned by the rebuilding of the burned
city there was left a considerable body of discontented working-
men ripe for trouble. The railway strike of 1877 betrayed the
condition; there were several days of bloody struggle with
the angry mob, few of whom had any real or direct interest in
any of the points at issue, and the police.

It was natural under such circumstances that every possible
panacea should have been offered, and for three or four years
the city was filled with advocates of social and political reform.
George Jacob Holyoake, the famous English agitator, appeared
upon the scene and a futile attempt was made to establish such
a system of coöperation as had proved so successful in the Midland counties of England.

As early as March, 1876, a small group of people had attempted to establish a social democratic party and later had
named one Albert R. Parsons for alderman in one of the wards.
But his defeat was overwhelming and the plan attracted little

attention. Following the railway strike, however, the Socialist Party nominated a candidate for mayor, a Doctor Schmidt, who polled 12,000 votes, and from that time on the movement was one to be reckoned with. Doctor Aveling and his wife, who was a daughter of Karl Marx, the great German state socialist, came over from England, advocated anarchy, and precipitated a division in the ranks of the Chicago socialists. There was thereafter marked activity among those who advocated revolutionary socialism as opposed to political socialism, and who became open and avowed anarchists.

Two daily papers were established as organs of the militant faction, the *Arbeiter Zeitung*, in German, edited by August Spies, and the *Alarm*, in English, edited by Albert Parsons. The advocates of state socialism weakly attempted to maintain themselves, but finally dwindled into insignificance, while the revolutionary anarchists grew more aggressive with each succeeding month. The bitterness between the two factions became very great. Finally, in October, 1884, the National Federation of Labour Unions met in Chicago and decided upon May 1, 1886, as the day upon which an eight-hour system should be introduced throughout the country. At first the anarchists displayed little interest in the movement, but as the agitation progressed they seized upon it as a means for furthering their propaganda.

At this time, while editing the *Daily News*, I was deeply interested in what was transpiring. Mr. Carter H. Harrison was mayor of the city. While an avowed Democrat, he was essentially a politician whose chief motive and largest capacity lay in the direction of gathering votes. In some respects he was an amusing character. It was his habit to attend the gatherings of each of the foreign elements and plead for popularity by claiming himself as their particular and only friend and spokesman. A dangerous situation arose. Mayor Harrison made no effort to check the anarchists in their excited and revolutionary movement. His attention was frequently called to it and to the possible result, but he ignored every warning. Finally in March, 1886, the leaders of the anarchist movement grew so bold as to solicit from me the publication of an interview, and I sent a reporter to see August Spies and George Schilling. They gave him a long statement in which they announced that they intended to join in the demands of the trades-unions on the first of May for an eight-hour law and that if strikes resulted and the police interfered they proposed to give battle.

The statement went on to say that the anarchists had fully arranged their plans. They were to place dynamite bombs in the manholes of the sewers and explode them. As a tangible evidence of their purpose they sent me by the reporter one of the bombs which happily had not been charged with explosives. I subsequently presented this to the Chicago Historical Society, but for some time it remained upon my desk, although nothing was necessary to remind me of the danger of the situation.

Upon the receipt of the statement I was greatly perplexed as to what course I should pursue. On the one hand, I knew that Spies, Parsons, and the rest were anxious for the advertising which a publication of the interview would give them and their cause. They fattened on notoriety, and every boastful statement of theirs when made public tended to attract to them the unthinking labour element. On the other hand, it was most important that I should do everything in my power to arouse the law-and-order element, and particularly those charged with the administration of the city government, to the menacing condition of affairs. The mayor of the city must be made to act if it were a possible thing.

It was my belief that at no time was there danger of any general social upheaval in the city; it was a developing community with unlimited material possibilities. While there had been a temporary check in certain undertakings, such as the erection of buildings, the population of the back country was growing apace and this meant consequently increasing wealth for the metropolis. On the other hand, the unbridled clamour of a band of anarchists, though small in numbers, was very likely to lead to mischief.

I spent some hours upon the interview and finally printed about one half of it. It served to awaken the public mind to the danger, but Mayor Harrison made no sign. As the weeks went on incendiary meetings continued to be held by the leaders of the anarchists with inflammatory speeches.

Warfare in Earnest

The first day of May finally arrived, and with it the strikes. These occurred wherever the eight-hour day had not been accepted, and included most of the larger industries of the city. A repetition of the Paris Communal riots was freely predicted, and there were many small battles between the strikers and those employed to fill their places. At one time a wild rumour spread over the city that the butchers of the stockyards were marching on the city in a body.

One of the most important strikes occurred at the McCormick Harvesting Machinery Works, and a battle took place between the police, who stood guard over the "scabs," and the strikers. A few shots were fired and some of the strikers injured, though probably no one was killed. In the rioting in the stockyards district the members of the mob pillaged every drug store and drank everything that looked at all like liquor. As a result there was much suffering and perhaps some fatalities.

During all this time the anarchists were goading the strikers on to desperation. They espoused the cause of labour merely to secure the support of the workmen and used them and their troubles for their own ends. Forty thousand men were on strike in Chicago alone at this time, and many of these, aroused to a frenzy by the anarchists' leaders, were armed and prepared to make resistance. The anarchists announced that six of the strikers had been killed by the police in the riot at the McCormick works, and sought by this announcement to arouse the strikers to further violence. It was to protest against the killing of these men and to take measures for avenging their deaths that the anarchists called a meeting for the night of May 4th at Haymarket Square.

I was living in West Adams Street at this time, and on the night of May 4th was at home with my family when, a little after eight o'clock, we were startled by the noise of an explosion which did not appear to be very far away. And this was shortly followed by the noise of heavy wagons hurrying west on Adams Street. These were police patrol wagons filled with wounded policemen. I at once called my office by telephone and learned of what had happened. A dynamite bomb had been hurled into the midst of the police at the Haymarket Square meeting, and many had been wounded.

Words Can Kill

The meeting had been held on Desplaines Street near the old Haymarket, and within one hundred yards of a police station, where the anarchists knew a large force was waiting to interfere if any provocation should arise. A wagon was improvised as a speakers' stand, and from it August Spies was the first to address the meeting. During the course of his remarks he shouted that it was the duty of the strikers to hang McCormick and all other employers, and some one in the crowd had cried: "Let's hang them now."

Parsons, who spoke next, asked the strikers in the names of their wives and children to arm themselves and stand firmly against the law.

The end of Samuel Fielden's speech, which followed Parsons's, was reported in shorthand as follows:

You have nothing more to do with the law than to lay hands upon it and throttle it until it makes its last kick. It turns your brothers out on the wayside, and has degraded them until they have lost the last vestige of humanity, and they are mere things and animals. Keep your eye upon it. Throttle it. Kill it. Stab it. Do everything you can to wound it, to impede its progress. Remember, before trusting them to do anything for you, prepare to do it yourself. Don't turn over your business to any one else. No man deserves anything unless he is man enough to make an effort to lift himself from oppression. Is it not a fact that we have no choice as to our existence, for we can't dictate what our labour is worth? He that has to obey the will of any one is a slave. Can we do anything except by the strong arm of resistance? Socialists are not going to declare war; but I tell you war has been declared on us, and I ask you to get hold of anything that will help to resist the onslaught of the enemy and the usurper. The skirmish lines have met. People have been shot. Men, women, and children have not been spared by the capitalists and minions of private capital. They had no mercy, so ought you? You are called upon to defend yourselves, your lives, your future. What matters it whether you kill yourselves with work to get a little relief or die on the battlefield resisting the enemy? What is the difference? Any animal, however loathsome, will resist when stepped upon. Are men less than snails and worms? I have some resistance in me; I know that you have too. You have been robbed and you will be starved into a worse condition.

As Fielden uttered these last sentences the mob showed signs of becoming unmanageable; they had gradually been worked up to a high pitch of excitement and the police were summoned. One hundred and eighty men, under Inspector Bonfield, appeared upon the scene, and as they halted before the wagon on which the speakers had stood, Police Captain Ward raised his hand and shouted in a loud voice: "I command you, in the name of the people of Illinois, to immediately and peaceably disperse." Fielden had barely shouted back a reply: "We are peaceable," when there was a flash, followed by a terrific explosion. Someone from the sidewalk had hurled a bomb into the midst of the platoon of policemen. One was killed and sixty-six injured, seven of whom subsequently died.

The wagons which passed our house were taking the wounded to the Cook County Hospital in West Harrison Street. The facts which I could get from my office were for the moment very fragmentary, but they were sufficient to convince me that it was a time for immediate action. What we had feared for so long had at last come to pass.

Hunting Down the Guilty

I called up Mr. William Pinkerton, of the great detective agency, at his house, and asked him if he had a number of reliable operatives on call, and when he assured me that he had, I instructed him to put shadows over August Spies, Albert Parsons, Samuel J. Fielden, and such other of the anarchist leaders as could be reached, at the earliest possible moment.

Their names were well known to us, for the same little coterie had been preaching anarchy for months.

Early the next morning I hurried to my office, and shortly afterward a messenger came with an urgent request that I go at once to the court house to confer with the prosecuting attorney, the city attorney, and the coroner. A very few minutes later I joined them in the basement of the court house, where the coroner was anxious to discuss the form of verdict to be rendered over the body of Police Officer Mathias J. Degan, who had died the night before. Julius S. Grinnell, the prosecuting attorney, and Fred S. Winston, the city attorney, had been discussing with Mr. Herz, the coroner, various questions of law concerning the case when I joined them. They were in trouble. No one knew who had actually thrown the bomb, and they both felt that this was important in the conduct of the case. I at once took the ground that the identity of the bomb thrower was of no consequence, and that, inasmuch as Spies and Parsons and Fielden had advocated over and over again the use of violence against the police and had urged the manufacture and throwing of bombs, their culpability was clear. It seemed to me that there was a well-settled principle of law which governed the case and I cited certain decisions which seemed to me to have a bearing.

Julius S. Grinnell

I finally went to a standing desk in the room and wrote out what I considered to be a proper verdict for the coroner's jury to render. In terms it was something like this: that Mathias Degan had come to his death from a bomb thrown by a person or persons unknown, but acting in conspiracy with August Spies, Albert Parsons, Samuel J. Fielden, and others unknown.

After some more discussion my draft was accepted by Messrs. Grinnel and Winston, and Coroner Herz hurried away to hold his inquest. Parenthetically, it may be said that such verdicts are usually dictated to juries. It was really a question of giving them the law on a case and not dictating as to their opinions.

There now remained nothing but to cause the arrest of the

guilty. Mr. Pinkerton notified us that Spies, Fielden, and some others were under shadow, and soon warrants were issued and they were lodged in jail charged with murder in the first degree. Parsons had disappeared. Scores of suspects were arrested and released for want of evidence, but the following ringleaders of the movement were held: August Spies, Michael Schwab, Samuel Fielden, Adolph Fischer, George Engel, Louis Lingg, and Oscar Neebe. It was understood that one Schnaubelt had actually thrown the bomb, but he could be found nowhere. Years after he was located in Germany and confessed his guilt.

The trial began on the 14th of July and lasted until the 20th of August. Joseph E. Gary presided, and Julius S. Grinnell and William P. Back were, respectively, the representatives of the State and the defence.

Throughout the various campaigns which we carried on against grafters, ballot-box stuffers, and anarchists, I was able to maintain a singularly personal relation with the men I was seeking to punish. In Mackin's case, after he had served something like two years in the State prison, I signed and circulated a petition for his pardon, which the governor of the State granted. I felt that the punishment imposed was adequate. And when I caused the arrest for corruption of the brother of the Democratic boss of the city, and while I was striving to see that he should be given a term in the penitentiary, both brothers said they really liked the *Daily News* because it always fought "face front."

While the anarchists were plotting I had in my employ certain of their number who wrote nightly reports, addressed them to me confidentially, and mailed them in out-of-the-way parts of the city. Not only that, but Joe Greenhut, a German socialist reporter, and George A. Schilling, who wrote the lives of the conspirators, frequently called at my office and told me of the progress of "the impending revolution."

As I have said, Parsons made his escape on the night of the Haymarket meeting. He went to Wisconsin, where he was in hiding for some time. Finally, as the trial began, he came back to Chicago and, with his wife, appeared at my office to ask me to surrender him to the court. It happened that I was not in my room at the moment, and they went to Captain Black, the leading counsel for the defence, and he performed the office.

The trial was a memorable one, and while it lasted the most intense excitement prevailed in Chicago; some further demonstrations by the anarchists were to be expected. They had threatened to blow up the court-house and to kill everyone who was influential in the prosecution. Menacing letters written in red ink, symbolic of blood, were sent to my wife, and the wives of Judge Grinnell and Judge Gary were warned that their children would be kidnapped and their homes destroyed by dynamite.

Finally the case closed with a verdict of guilty. There was an appeal, but in the end Judge Gary's view of the law was sustained, and the verdict was confirmed. The sentence to hang applied to seven men. Lingg secured a dynamite cartridge and, inserting it between his teeth, exploded it and committed suicide.

Tense Days

As the day for the execution drew near the situation in Chicago became very tense: there was a marked evidence of fear that something desperate was about to occur, this something to be by way of revenge by the advocates of anarchy. The atmosphere seemed surcharged with trepidation. The 11th of November, 1887, a year and a half after the explosion of the bomb at the Haymarket, was the day fixed for the hanging. On the preceding Sunday I received a message from Parsons asking me to visit him in the jail. Accompanying the request was a note written in pencil, as follows:

M. E. Stone. Please bring along a Box of good Havana's, medium. P—

I made haste to comply with the request. On my arrival I was admitted to Mr. Parsons's cell and took a seat at his side upon the prison cot. He at once began an appeal. He urged me to intercede with the governor for a commutation of his sentence. We talked for two or three hours. I had no doubt then, as I had had no doubt from the beginning, of his honesty of purpose.

As we sat talking in his cell I told him of my belief that the only safety of society lay in the maintenance of law and that I could not arrange a commutation or a pardon unless he was ready to admit his error. It was a very trying situation. I longed for some chance to help him, and it was heartbreaking that our minds could not meet. It was inevitable that my respect for him was greatly increased by his steady refusal to yield in the slightest degree. But my sense of duty was equally compelling. Finally a fit of desperation seized him. He cried out that he could never leave his children a legacy of dishonour; that at least he was not a coward, and that I was responsible for his fate, and that all that was necessary to save him was that I should make an effort. When I replied that greatly as I grieved over it, I must follow the path which seemed to me to be right, he suddenly became violent and made an attack upon me. At that instant the door of his cell opened and a bailiff entered and seized him while I withdrew. His paroxysm of rage lasted but an instant. The bailiff followed me into the corridor and locked the cell door.

Albert R. Parsons

The next day a Mr. John Worthy called upon me. He was the owner of extensive stone quarries and was a well-known citizen of Chicago. Samuel Fielden had been a teamster in his service. He told me that Fielden had been a local Methodist preacher in England, that he loved to make a speech, that he became intoxicated with his own verbosity, that he was not a man of evil intent, but one, to use Mr. Worthy's phrase, who set his mouth to going and then went off and forgot it. He was anxious to save Fielden's life, and he wanted me to intercede for him with the governor of Illinois. I said precisely the things that I had told Parsons, that penitence must precede pardon, and that unless Fielden was ready to admit his error I could not lift a finger in his behalf. He asked me to have a talk with Fielden, and I said that I was quite ready to do so if Fielden desired it. I saw Fielden and he wrote a letter of abject recantation. Schwab heard of it, asked an interview, and wrote a similar letter. Spies solicited an interview, was told of Fielden's and Schwab's action, but like Parsons, stood his ground.

I took Fielden's and Schwab's letters to Springfield and presented them to the governor. He made haste to commute the sentences of Fielden and Schwab to life imprisonment, but declined to interfere in any of the other cases.

Over a quarter of a century has passed, and I am unable to see how I could have taken any other course. I had no reason to believe that in the circumstances I could have saved the lives of either Spies or Parsons. Nor can I see that it would have been right for me to attempt to do so unless they were ready to recant. They were engaged in an effort to destroy all law, and under our form of government, which I then believed and still believe a necessary and proper institution among men, they were not justified in asking the governor, a law officer, to exercise the power which he derived from the law to save them.

The fateful Friday having arrived, threats of assassination were by no means infrequent. There was a widespread expection that the jail would be destroyed by dynamite. A cloud of apprehension lowered over the city. There was a hush, and men spoke in whispers. Everyone awaited the hour for the execution of the dread mandate of the law with solicitude, indeed with fear. I have never experienced quite the like condition. Then, at the appointed hour, four men were hanged. The announcement went out, and as by the wind of the morning, the cloud lifted and the business of the great city moved on in its wonted way. The tragedy was over. And it was a tragedy.

Punishing Corrupt Public Officials

At this time it was evident that corruption was running riot in the affairs of Cook County, in which Chicago is located. My attention was directed to the Board of County Commissioners, and it was evident that there should be a house-cleaning. Julius Grinnell, the prosecuting officer, and I were working together. One F. W. Bipper, a butcher who supplied meats under contract to the various charitable institutions, had grown rich in an amazingly short time. His shop had taken on palatial proportions. We also found that the county was paying for more meat for the charitable institutions than it was possible for the inmates and employees to consume.

One evening Grinnell and I wandered into Mr. Bipper's place and in true Russian fashion demanded that he give us his books of account. He did not dare to refuse. We found that we had become possessed of a gold mine.

Then Bipper offered to turn State's evidence. He said that he had been paying each of the county commissioners, as well as the supervising attendants of the county institutions, several thousand dollars a year. He furnished us the evidence to confirm his confession. I took him, a willing prisoner, put him in charge of Harry Wilkinson, one of my reporters, and sent him off into a neighbouring state—this to prevent the "boodlers" from either bribing or assassinating him.

Our disclosures created great excitement, and my personal safety was threatened. One of the commissioners named Wasserman kept a saloon which was the place of resort for the accused. One evening he came to my office to kill me. He found me alone, but was so drunk that he was easily disarmed and sent about his business. One or two of the other commissioners, notably "Buck" McCarthy, who was the political boss of the stockyards, brought libel suits against the *Daily News*. McCarthy, who was a giant in stature, also encountered a *Daily News* reporter, Paul Hull, and beat him so badly that he was sent to a hospital, and his life was in danger for some time.

I was surprised one day to receive a call from this ruffian. I did not dare to refuse him admission to my office. My surprise was increased when he said he wanted to "get rid of that damned libel suit." He was very mild and wholly tractable.

"Well, McCarthy," said I, "you have charged me with being a libeller. Are you willing to acquit me of that offence? If you will write a letter, which I will prepare, saying that the *Daily News* has not libelled you in any way, I will consent to a dismissal of the case."

He said he would, the letter was written and published, and the case summarily dismissed. His lawyer, the notorious Alfred S. Trude, met me the evening after the publication and was very angry because I had, as he expressed it, made a "monkey" of his client. "The poor fool didn't know that he could dismiss his libel suit without your consent," said Trude.

The case of the corrupt public officials came to trial, the evidence was ample, and on August 5, 1887, eleven county commissioners and one warden of the insane asylum, were found guilty. Eight of the culprits were sent to the penitentiary for two years, and four were fined a thousand dollars each.

Retiring from Journalism

I trust that the patient reader has not reached the conclusion that my activities as the editor of a daily newspaper were wholly confined to thief catching. It is undeniable that such a view would be measurably natural. The *Daily News*, however, was not simply a detective agency. The exposure of crime and the punishment of criminals were of great value to the community and gratifying to the business office of the paper, because they created sensations, made us notable, enlarged our circulation, and filled our coffers. If commercial success was all there was to journalism, our progress left nothing to be desired. We had grown from nothing to fame and fortune and there was great promise for the future. As I have said, I had a staff of unequalled capacity. But—and there was the rub—I alone was unequipped. Our very success was embarrassing. I was prematurely prominent. I had reached a dizzy and dangerous height. In the phrase of an anonymous writer, I found it impossible to impersonate my reputation.

One day a Vermont school of which I had never heard, the Middlebury College, to my utter amazement, made me an LL.D., *in absentia*. I felt as might one who had stolen the sacred relics from the altar of a Roman Catholic church. I had no education justifying such distinction. Day by day there was borne in upon my consciousness the conviction that an editor of an American newspaper should, in the old Latin phrase, be fitted to treat *de omni re scibili et quibusdam aliis*—that is, of everything that was knowable and of certain other matters. The fact that I had both initiative and industry was not enough. And so, when in May, 1888, my partner, Lawson, to whose personality I was devoted, and for whom I had the largest respect, was ready to buy my interest, I jumped at the chance. I felt like a prisoner to whom freedom was suddenly possible.

The "better half" of our household had some misgiving about my retirement from an enterprise so promising, but she was of New England origin and had the Yankee sense of thrift, while the Irish blood which controlled my veins was naturally financially profligate.

There was no trafficking as to price. We agreed without difficulty. Lawson gave me an extra $100,000 for a stipulation that I would keep out of newspaper work in Chicago for the ensuing ten years. And one memorable evening I invited my staff to a dinner and broke the news. I was out. And in the *Daily News*, the following morning, appeared my valedictory and Lawson's salutatory:

Upon the issuance of this number of the *Daily News*, I retire from its editorship and from all participation in its management. I have sold my entire stock interest to my long-time friend and business associate, Mr. Victor F. Lawson, and he now becomes sole proprietor, editor, and publisher.

As it may gratify some measure of curiosity to learn the reason for this step, the following facts are made public:

From the day on which I founded the *Daily News*, in December, 1875, until recently, I have been engaged almost without remission in the work incident to the editorial service. How arduous such labour is only those who have struggled to found a metropolitan daily newspaper can ever know. Taking the years together, it has impaired my health. A few weeks ago I offered to sell my shares in the paper to Mr. Lawson, and, after reflection, he reluctantly accepted my terms, and the transfer has been effected. I leave the paper in the hands of a gentleman concerning whose good character there can be no question—whose purposes are the very best, whose judgment and ability I esteem most highly. The public may rest assured that under Mr. Lawson's editorial control the earnest endeavour of the *Daily News* will be in the future, as in the past, to make for those things which are true and honest and just and pure. The editorial staff, admittedly without rival in the West for brilliancy or efficiency, will continue unchanged.

And so, not without a goodly share of regret because circumstances thus force me to abandon the one ambition of my life and to sunder a thousand ties which seem well-nigh unbreakable, but with a clear sense of duty to my family and myself, with a sincere acknowledgment of the great debt of gratitude which I owe the people of Chicago and the Northwest for a more than generous support, I bid the readers of the *Daily News* a final farewell.

Chicago, May 16, 1888. MELVILLE E. STONE.

Life is measured not so much by years as by achievement. To have exercised the responsibilities of the editorial conduct of the *Daily News* from its first issue to the present time and to have seen that responsibility steadily widen in its application until it touches a daily constituency the largest, with a possible single exception, in America, may well fill the measure of one man's ambition, and as well discharge one life's duty. In his withdrawal, therefore, from the exacting cares of journalism Mr. Stone only claims his well-earned right to much-needed rest and recovery of health. And yet Mr. Melville E. Stone is too young a man to long face a purposeless future, and that new interests will in proper time engage his efficient abilities may not be doubted; but it may well be doubted whether any most successful future accomplishment on his part can add, except by way of a consistent endorsement, to the reputation of the founder of the *Daily News*.

The confidence which Mr. Stone so generously expresses touching the management which now continues its responsibility, in undivided measure, for the conduct of the *Daily News*, shall be at least so far assured as sincerity of purpose and faithfulness in endeavour may contribute. The *Daily News* will continue to be an impartial, independent, American newspaper, whose highest ambition shall be to give its million-a-week constituency all the news, and to tell the truth about it.

Chicago, May, 16, 1888. VICTOR F. LAWSON.

My bonds were broken. And I had left the paper in the hands of one who shared in the largest measure all of my views as to an editor's responsibility, whose integrity was beyond question, and whose fidelity to the public weal was assured. I was too proud to confess, either at home or to the public, the real reason for this sudden and surprising abdication. I had been forced to become something of a *poseur*, and hadn't the courage to admit my lack of learning. And so I pleaded ill health.

I found this quatrain, in Eugene Field's inimitable penmanship, in my mail the next day:

> I am a light of other days,
> A quenched and scattered fire,
> Or, to adopt a finer phrase,
> An old and broken lyre.

FIFTH DECADE

A Sentimental Journey

AFTER selling my interest in the *Daily News*, I made haste to set out upon my "sentimental journey." In a little more than a month I was on the ocean, chanting the old Gascoigne roundelay:

> *Viva la joia!*
> *Fidon la tristessa!*

Did any one ever know a happier hour? Such a fortune as fully satisfied all of one's dreams of avarice, care free, and in the family treasure chest three beautiful and brilliant children. And so we sallied forth.

On the British steamer they celebrated the Fourth of July. Judge Daly of New York presided, and the Reverend Doctor McArthur, famous pastor of Calvary Baptist Church of New York, and I delivered the usual chauvinist speeches. Our English fellow passengers were most considerate, so that we got off with our lives.

On March 9th of this year, the old Kaiser died, and on June 15th, while we were about to sail, his son, "Unser Fritz" passed away and William II became German Emperor.

Some weeks of sightseeing for the children in London and then off for the Continent. We made our way by easy stages to Geneva, Switzerland, and found an anchorage at the Château Bellerive, some five miles out of John Calvin's city. We made no mistake in choosing this as an abiding place. Built away back in the early days of the fourteenth century by the Duke of Savoy, it was ancient enough to interest any one of the newest of new America. It was on the shore of the wonderful Lake Geneva, in full view of Mont Blanc on one side and the Jura Mountains on the other. A fraction of an old moat guarded one angle and a row of protecting poplars another. It had come down from its lordly creator with few changes, and relics of Bourbon days and Napoleonic days and all the days that followed were at your hand in every quarter. The Byron cottage, where George Gordon and Shelley spent some happy, if not altogether reputable months, was at our door. So, also, was the home of Dreyfus, the wronged. Here was obviously the place of our quest, and here we made our foreign home for over two years. Not that we spent much time there; it was a haven of rest, but one from which to roam.

This is not to be a detailed story of our journeyings in Europe. What with the inexpensive personally conducted tours, "travelogs," and moving pictures, interest in a traveller's printed descriptions of foreign scenery and customs has ceased. So it follows that a reader would not, or at least should not, waste his all-too-limited time on any travel recollections which I could recount. Save a few things perhaps.

Our peregrinations reached from the Cataracts of the Nile to the North Cape, and east as far as Nizhni Novgorod in Russia. It was over two years of vagabond life. We visited every country in Europe except Spain and Portugal, which we saved for a future journey.

In Goethe's phrase, we made all of our journeys "without haste and without rest." Mr. John J. Knickerbocker of Chicago, an eminent lawyer, came over to travel with us. He didn't stay long. On his return to Chicago, being interviewed by a newspaper and asked why he had gone abroad, he replied, "For a rest."

"You travelled with Mr. Stone, did you not? Why did you come home?"

"Again for a rest," said he.

J. J. Knickerbocker

We were not at all like the American girl who was asked how long she, her father, and her mother, had spent in Florence. "One day," said she. "My father saw the shops and restaurants; my mother the churches, and I the galleries." We aimed to do more than the ordinary tourists did.

I had been interested, from my boyhood, in the activities of Bonaparte, and, as we wandered, seized the opportunity to visit and study almost every one of his battlefields from Italy to Egypt and Germany and Russia, winding up at Waterloo.

We set out early in the winter of 1888-89 for the Levant. It was perhaps as instructive a portion of the earth as we could have turned to. And it was, I doubt not, a most edifying hour for our visit. The world was preparing, all unconsciously, yet with certainty, for the contest of the ages. The struggle between the missionary spirit and the mercenary aim of mankind was on. As we viewed the scene, the admonition of Paul to Timothy, that "the love of money is the root of all evil," had a new meaning. Before I reached Europe, William II had ascended the German throne and begun his disastrous career.

We went to Egypt. The year 1888 touched high-water mark in the appropriation of African territory by the Christian nations of western Europe. There had been protests against these invasions, but they had been ineffectual. In 1882 Arabi Pasha, foreseeing the predatory attitude of the so-called civilized powers, had opened a campaign for "Egypt for the Egyptians." In his suppression Britain took the lead. Lord Charles Beresford bombarded the rebels at Alexandria, and Sir Garnet Wolseley with his guns and his disciplined troops, won the battle of Tel-el-Kebir. Arabi's forces were massacred and he was sent in exile to Ceylon.

Britain thus added Egypt to her African conquests. Then the other European states set out for their share of the plunder. They worked so assiduously that five years later Bishop Arnett, of the African M. E. Church, said at the great Parliament of Religions in Chicago:

> Every foot of land and every foot of water in Africa have been appropriated by the governments of Europe. If it please God, He may raise up, not a Washington, not another Toussaint l'Ouverture, but one who, with his sword will, at the head of his people, lead them to freedom and equality. He will form a republican government whose cornerstone will be religion, morality, education, and temperance,

acknowledging the fatherhood of God and the brotherhood of man; while the Ten Commandments and the Golden Rule shall be the rule of life and conduct in the great republic of redeemed Africa.

Up in the north, in Turkey, another sort of missionary spirit was forcefully at work trying to impose the Moslem faith upon the Christians of Asia Minor by fire and sword. Between these extremes lay Bethlehem, Gethsemane, and Calvary, with all the memories of two thousand years, enjoining the gentle doctrine of the Golden Rule, the promises of the Beatitudes, the new commandment, and "On earth peace, good will toward men."

The cupidity of the European nations impressed me as quite as malign as the ferocity of the Mohammedans. And so it has seemed to me through all the years that have succeeded. We Christians who have been ruthlessly encroaching upon the rights of our weaker fellows, by the partition of Africa, of Asia, and of South America, cannot hold ourselves blameless. War after war has resulted, and the end is not yet. It will not do to say that our merciless creation of an overlordship over a powerless people is always justified by the spread of our civilization. The "white man's burden" is far too often the burden of a wholly unjust course of conduct which is certain to cause a violent yet quite proper reaction. The Boer War and the Boxer rising were perfectly equitable appeals to the *Lex Talionis*. Even the great World War, which has just closed, was born of the feeling on the part of the Germans that they had not been given their share of the world's loot. So far as it is possible to see, we are to go on sowing dragons' teeth.

Enterprising men go to China or Mexico, or where you will, and secure a concession. At first they find no difficulty. But the instant they, by modern methods, reap a large reward, the native population feel that a birthright has been sold for a mess of pottage, and trouble ensues.

And our missionaries, who deserve all honour for their self-denying labours, are, after all, engaged in a service which does not go hand in hand with these mercenary efforts. Komura a Harvard graduate, who became a leading statesman of Japan, once said, when he and I were talking of the unhappy differences thus caused and of the possibilities in store:

I do not think your missionaries have made many converts among our people. Yet they have done us great good. They have brought with them doctors and nurses and hospitals, and taught us how to heal the sick and to prolong life.

Wherefore, in the recent past, while we have been engaged in predatory incursions upon the Asiatics and the Africans, we have at the same time been building them up physically and fitting them to give us battle. Meanwhile, we have just sent to their death something like ten millions of the very flower of western civilization. And the birth rate of Europe and America is notoriously declining.

But this is wandering afield.

When we reached Egypt, Britain, as I have said, was in control, and Sir Evelyn Baring, later Lord Cromer, was on the throne, although the Khedive was the titular sovereign. Cromer was a great constructive statesman, but at the moment of our visit had not really begun his beneficent work. Later in his life I came to know him and to esteem him very highly.

In the winter of 1888–9 the marauding spirit of Drake and Clive and Warren Hastings had not become altogether extinct when dealing with "the white man's burden." We saw poor blind Egyptians cut across the face with a *kurbash* by arrogant British officers. The *corvée* (enforced unpaid labour on the government work) was still exacted. Torture to compel confession of crime was still resorted to, and the purchase of girls as slaves was not uncommon, although clandestine. I do not mean that any of these practices were approved by the British authorities. They were not. On the contrary, for some years there had been an effort at reform. But the chief business of Sir Evelyn Baring was to look after the payment of the Egyptian debt, and it was not until some years later that he was able to reform, not only the methods of the native government, but the conduct of some of his own countrymen.

A party of thirteen was arranged, and we set out for a camping tour through Palestine. No railroads had yet been constructed in the Holy Land, and, therefore, we travelled by carriage or on horseback. Our stay in Jerusalem was the more gratifying because we encountered a number of friends from Chicago. Among these was the Methodist Bishop, Charles H. Fowler. He was not alone one of America's most eloquent pulpit orators; he was as well a travelling companion of most agreeable character. He knew his Palestine as well as Bædeker, and was far more at home in its historical interest. In common with all visitors to the hills of Judea, we were woefully disillusioned. To find the Holy Sepulchre and the scene of the Crucifixion under a single roof was enough to tax our credulity to the utmost. But everywhere the rule of an American shop applied: "If you do not see what you want, ask for it." And to ask meant to receive.

We went down to Hebron to see the Cave of Machpelah, where Abraham and Jacob were buried. On the way we were pelted with stones by hostile Moslems, and on our arrival were permitted to see no more than the walls inclosing the alleged tombs. The way to the Jordan was infested with brigands, but we greased the palm of an Arab sheik and got through safely to Jericho and the Dead Sea.

After visiting the massive ruins of Baalbek and going again, like St. Paul, to Damascus, we wandered away to Smyrna, and the Temple of Diana. We met King Milan of Servia, who shared our visit with us.

We turned to Greece, and at Athens were entertained by Mr. Schliemann, the famous archæologist. He greeted us with singular cordiality, chiefly because of his pride in the fact that he was an American citizen, having been naturalized long before in California. His father-in-law asked me innocently enough if I knew anything about the Pennsylvania Railroad in my country. When I said I did, he wanted to know if I thought it well managed, because, he said, he was the largest individual stockholder in the corporation. And he had never been in the United States. On my return to America I found his statement fully confirmed.

Mr. Oscar Straus was the American Minister at Constantinople. He gave us a most cordial welcome. My friend, "Sunset" Cox, had preceded him as our envoy. When I knew Mr. Cox in Washington, some years before, he had been a persistent critic of the American diplomatic officers because of their alleged extravagance. It was somewhat amusing to find that Mr. Straus had at his disposal a legacy from Mr. Cox's incumbency in the shape of a fine fast-going yacht. On it we had a delightful journey up the Bosphorus to the Black Sea.

At Constantinople we also encountered Dr. Andrew D. White of Cornell University, and established a friendship that lasted as long as he lived.

Thence we journeyed on to Budapest and Vienna, halting leisurely for some days at each city.

Days with Andrew D. White

One morning, as we were breakfasting at our hotel in Vienna, Doctor White's card was presented. On it was written: "I am here and lonely; let's get together." And so we had another visit with this most attractive gentleman. His brain was a perfect storehouse of valuable information. And we enjoyed many things in common. I had long been interested in the story of the French Revolution and the career of Bonaparte. I had visited and studied a great number of the Corsican's battlefields. Doctor White had a like penchant.

Years after, when he was for the second term our ambassador to Germany, I was in Paris. I received a telegram from him asking when I expected to be in Berlin. I answered it, and a few days later arrived to find that he had cancelled an engagement to go for an outing with Mrs. White on the island of Rügen, and had taken a suite for me next to his own at the Hotel Kaiserhof. We had a great week together. We went down to Wittenberg and lived with the memories of Martin Luther. I believe it was largely at my suggestion that Doctor White wrote his exceedingly interesting "Recollections." He had passed his seventieth year and had grown quite deaf. And Roosevelt had hinted to me that he wanted the Berlin Embassy for another friend. I told the doctor of the situation. He resigned and went to the Italian Riviera and completed his life story.

The Diedrichs Affair.

While I was in Berlin at a later date, Baron Richtofen, the German Minister of Foreign Affairs, gave me an interesting account of the famous Diedrichs episode at Manila. This was his version: After Dewey's victory there was a period of a year and a half in which the American people were in doubt as to what should be done with the Philippine Islands. The United States was not a colonizing nation and not a few American citizens felt that we had a white elephant on our hands. Doctor White, then American Ambassador to Germany, shared this view. One day he called at the Foreign Office and asked Richtofen why Germany would not take the Islands and relieve America of her burden. The German Minister was surprised at the suggestion but said that he would confer with the Kaiser and let the ambassador know the result. After some delay Doctor White was notified that Germany would accept his suggestion as a solution of the problem. Thereupon the ambassador cabled to the State Department at Washington a recommendaton in accordance with his plan. He received a summary reply rejecting the whole proposition. Meanwhile, however, Admiral Diedrichs had been ordered to the Philippines.

Baron Richtofen

I breakfasted with Prince Henry of Prussia, and while he confirmed Baron Richtofen's story, he said he thought he had some responsibility in the matter. He was at Hong Kong when Diedrichs sailed and he approved the expedition, not alone because it was supposed to be in accordance with the American desire, but also because there were a number of German merchants in Manila who desired protection at the hands of their government.

Richtofen's account was fully confirmed by at least two former attachés of the American Embassy. Then one day when talking with the Kaiser he asked me to make no use of the explanation given by Richtofen as coming from Germany because, as he said, it would be arousing the unpleasant incident afresh, and if the explanation was credited to them, would be regarded as an attempt to excuse an impropriety. "You can doubtless get the facts from Washington on your return to America," he said.

I came to America and saw Judge Day, who had been Secretary of State under President McKinley. He remembered the incident and the cable message from Doctor White, but thought it was in the nature of a personal message which had never been placed in the files of the State Department and that therefore it was impossible to be secured textually. In his autobiography Admiral Dewey treated the subject, but his explanation was wholly at variance with the accounts published at the time in the newspapers. He said the differences with Diedrichs grew out of a misunderstanding upon Diedrichs's part as to his rights, that Diedrichs said: "I am here by order of the Kaiser"; that later when the subject was fully discussed Vice Admiral von Diedrichs was able to understand Dewey's position and that a difference of opinion about international law had been adjusted amicably. When Dewey returned to Washington and at a dinner at the White House on October 3, 1899, President McKinley mentioned the newspaper statements respecting the friction. McKinley said: "There is no record of it in all the files." Thus confirming fully Mr. Justice Day's statement to me. Later, Doctor White, in talking with me, vigorously denied any statement that he had offered the Philippines to Germany. He said that his conversation with Richtofen was a purely personal and not in any sense an official communication. It seems probable, however, that Diedrichs was sent to the Philippines with the understanding that the American Government would be glad to give Germany possession of the Islands.

I remember that about this time while riding on a train with Senator John C. Spooner, he said that he proposed to introduce a bill in the Senate to give the Philippine Islands to the three nations which had shown a capacity for colonizing—England, Germany, and France—and thus settle the problem. This he never did.

The whole question of the final disposition of the Philippines hung in suspense until the evening of October 9, 1899. Chicago was celebrating the anniversary of the great fire of 1871. There was a banquet at the Auditorium with something like one thousand participants. I presided, and among the speakers were President McKinley, Premier Laurier of Canada, and Vice President Marescal of Mexico. It was at this dinner that the President announced our purpose to hold the Islands for an indefinite period. He had come fresh from the conference of a week earlier, with Admiral Dewey.*

We set out for the North Cape by way of Hamburg and Christiania. When near the Lofoton Islands, we encountered the German Kaiser, we on a Norwegian boat, he on his imperial yacht, the *Hohenzollern*. It was early evening. To do him honour, we dipped the Stars and Stripes and fired a shot. In white sailor's costume, he mounted the bridge of his vessel and sailed all about us, firing as he went, I should say, fifty guns at least. He was not to be outdone in politeness. We saw the midnight sun five nights in succession and were exhausted for lack of sleep. He was less than forty miles away, but, clouds intervening, never saw the midnight sun at all. This was my first sight of a man whom later I came to know with some degree of intimacy.

One journey to the North Cape, if the midnight sun is visible, will suffice any one. It is a very trying expedition. Bishop Charles H. Fowler and his wife were on our boat. He was asked to preach one Sunday to the passengers, and suggested that I give him a topic. "Why," I replied, "do you not take as your text the 25th verse of the 21st Chapter of Revelations, which declares, descriptive of heaven, that 'there shall be no night there'?" "They would throw me off the boat," he answered.

---
*Olcott's Life of McKinley. Vol. II, p. 96.

He always had an uncontrollable sense of humour. One day he was presiding at the Methodist General Conference. The Reverend Doctor Buckley of New York, who also loved a *bon mot*, sought the floor for a couple of hours, but was denied recognition. Finally, when he got the floor, he opened with great solemnity: "Beware of the snare of the Fowler!" and the Bishop instantly finished the quotation from the 91st Psalm: "and the noisome pestilence!"

We toured the land of the Vikings in carioles and then went by way of Stockholm and Helsingfors to St. Petersburg. The American chargé d'affaires at the moment was John Martin Crawford of Cincinnati, the brilliant translator of the Finnish Saga, "Kalevala," from which Longfellow derived "Hiawatha." We were made guests of Czar Alexander III at a review of 60,000 household troops at Tsarskoe Selo. It was an amazing sight. The Czar improvised a staff for the occasion, inviting Nicholas, the hereditary Prince of Montenegro, the American general, Daniel Butterfield, and the Crown Prince, later Nicholas II, to accompany him. We also witnessed a review of the Russian monitors off Kronstadt. These were a reproduction in modified form of Ericsson's famous boat. It was curious to note how they moved along. They were from time to time lowered until their decks were awash, a process which ultimately led to the submarine.

We visited the famous fair at Nizhni Novgorod, whither the people of Turkestan, Siberia, and almost every Asiatic country, came in droves to sell their wares. On the Volga River we saw a Mississippi River steamboat, which had been moved from St. Louis to do duty in central Russia.

I took the treatment at Carlsbad, where in my daily walks I was associated with Mr. William M. Evarts and Senator William E. Chandler of New Hampshire. Mr. Evarts was practically blind and Senator Chandler and I took turns in guiding his footsteps and enjoying his brilliant observations. We rose each morning at six o'clock, paid our visits to the particular springs to which we were directed by our doctors, and then went off for a five-mile walk before breakfast. It did not worry me. I had learned how to walk before breakfast in the days when I was a carrier for the Chicago *Tribune*. This was long ago, yet to-day, whenever the weather permits, I take my morning walk. The lure of the fields at daybreak is one which, to those who have been caught by it, will endure. It is a most stimulating practice, both from a mental and a physical point of view.

There was a visit to the Paris International Exposition, at once amusing and edifying.

Then it was necessary to come to America on a business journey. I left my family in Geneva. On my arrival in New York I found the papers filled with alarming accounts of the prevalence in Geneva of a new disease, "La Grippe." There were something like 20,000 cases. As a result my family hastened away, first to Munich and then to Dresden.

In Chicago on January 11, 1890, I was honoured with a public dinner arranged by a committee of well-known citizens.

I set out for a return to Europe, taking with me my father and my mother. We met the family at Dresden and spent some months in the cities of Germany.

Then off to the British Isles and particularly to Ireland. We went to my mother's birthplace, Rice Hill, adjoining Cavan. It pleased her greatly to see the spot where she had spent her early girlhood. The old barn where John Wesley had preached was still standing. Down at Clara in King's County was the ruin of the old castle which had been for centuries the seat of the Fox family of Kilcoursey, from which my mother's maternal line had descended, while at Galtrim House, very near the Hill of Tara, we visited "The Fox," the living chief of the ancient sept. We went down through Wicklow, stopping at Bray for an hour with Michael Davit and calling at Avondale, the home of Parnell.

Banking and Other Activities

We sailed for home from Queenstown in the early summer of 1890. My holiday must end. It was requisite that my children be educated in the United States. Herbert, our older son, began "tutoring" and entered Harvard College that fall;

Melville Edwin, the younger son, entered Phillips at Andover, and later went to Harvard.

I bought some thirty-five acres at Glencoe, twenty miles north of Chicago, and built a country home. The land was on the shore of Lake Michigan, eighty feet above the water level, beautifully wooded, and through it ran the famous boulevard, the Sheridan Drive. We lived here in the summer, and at the Virginia Hotel, in Chicago, in the winter.

Back in Chicago, with nothing to do, I proposed a "lazy men's club," and suggested that I would be a candidate for its presidency, but this was not to be. After a few months without my initiative two or three gentlemen set out to organize a new national bank. They invited me to take some stock. Then, much to my surprise, I was asked to become president. I declined on the ground that I had no experience to justify such an undertaking, but said I would accept the vice presidency if a suitable chief officer could be secured, with the understanding that if all should go well within a year and then I should feel justified and the directors should concur, I might become president. With this understanding, Mr. O. D. Wetherell, a wealthy lumberman and former city treasurer of Chicago, was made president and I took second place. Thus the Globe National Bank began its activities. In a year Mr. Wetherell and I changed places.

Very soon after the trustees of the famous Drainage Canal unanimously elected me as their treasurer. I accepted on condition that no compensation be attached to the service. I marketed many millions of dollars of their bonds and thus financed the business, purely as a public service. It was in the construction of this canal that the contractors learned the way to dig the Panama Canal a quarter of a century later.

Fresh opportunities and responsibilities crowded upon me in quick succession. I found myself busier than I had ever been before. I had not been a banker for a year when I was elected president of the Bankers' Club of the city.

The presidency of the Citizens' Association, an organization looking to the guardianship of the civic weal, and of the Civil Service Reform League, and the vice-presidency of the Union

League Club, followed. Also membership in the Commercial Club, a select body of fifty of the leading citizens of Chicago. And a member of the board of governors of the Chicago Club.

I received the following letter:

Mayor's Office, Chicago, March 30, 1892.

Hon. M. E. Stone, City.

Dear Sir:

The law requires that in the month of July next the mayor must appoint seven members upon the School Board, to fill vacancies occurring at that time.

It will afford me great pleasure if you will permit me to send your name to the Council as one of the seven members whom I must appoint in July next. Your long, active, and unselfish efforts in behalf of public morality and good government render you especially qualified for this position, and I should esteem myself fortunate if you will accept this nomination, inasmuch as it is my desire to place upon this board only men whose positions in this community are such as to become a guarantee that its affairs will be ably, honestly, and impartially administered.

Trusting I may receive a favourable reply, I remain, with great respect,

Your obedient servant,
Hemp Washburn, Mayor.

I was forced to refuse the offer.

I was more than "mentioned" for mayor of Chicago, and if I had not declined the nomination I might have been elected.

More important, Judge Gresham, who had retired from the bench in 1893, when he was appointed Secretary of State in President Cleveland's second term, died in 1895, and then a ridiculous effort was made in Chicago, entirely without my knowledge or approval, to induce President Cleveland to appoint me as his successor. There was a two- or three-day stir about the matter, and then it died out as it should have done, and Richard Olney, of Boston, was appointed. While the tempest was brewing in the teapot in Chicago, however, there was room for an amusing incident. Although I had been a Mugwump in the campaign of 1884, and although Mugwumps were anathema in the Union League Club of Chicago, they had done me the honour of electing me vice-president. One morning as I entered the club a somewhat distinguished judge, who was a close personal friend, but always a rabid Republican, accosted me with, "I see, Mr. Stone, they have presented you as a candidate to succeed Judge Gresham as Secretary of State." I laughed in a stupid apologetic fashion as I replied that I hoped the President had sense enough to appreciate that no such appointment should be made, that I was not an aspirant for the place, and added that I had great confidence in Mr. Cleveland's wisdom. I am certain the Judge had no idea of the malapropos nature of his reply when, with all seriousness he said, "Well, I don't know, Mr. Stone, Cleveland has done a lot of d——d strange things."

At the unveiling of a statue to Franklin in Lincoln Park, the orator, Henry Estabrook, said:

He [Franklin] was elected alderman, assemblyman, postmaster, and the president of more things of a public and quasi-public character than Melville E. Stone ever thought of.[1]

This was a time in which, however, I was occupied with serious matters; as John Morley said, "like many another man of grave [or dull] temperament, I sought snatches of relief from boredom by clapping on a fool's cap at odd moments."

Before my return from Europe, Congress had passed an act providing for a world's fair to commemorate the 400th anniversary of the discovery of America, and had chosen Chicago as the city in which the fair should be located. A number of organizations were set up for the entertainment of our guests. A large houseboat was moored within a breakwater off the lake shore and fitted up as a club to be resorted to on hot summer nights. There was a quaint "hole in the wall" in a back alley, a veritable chamber of horrors, bedecked with coffins, human skulls, a bit of rope on which a culprit had been hanged, and a hundred other mementoes of crime. It was the "Whitechapel Club" where a band of jolly Bohemians made merry with the truly conventional Uitlander.

---
[1]Estabrook's Speeches, p. 85.

There was the famous Fellowship Club which for some years gave a series of winter-season dinners of a most elaborate sort. Badinage and repartee ran riot. · There were only fifty members, but these were carefully chosen.

The first great dinner was on the evening of October 20, 1892, following the dedication of the Fair. Some six hundred guests were present. There were: the Vice-President of the United States, many members of the Cabinet, the Chief Justice and most of the associate justices of the Supreme Court, Cardinal Gibbons, several Episcopalian and Methodist bishops, twenty-nine governors of states, and other notables too numerous to mention. Mr. James W. Scott presided and there were several toast-masters. It was my duty to introduce a man who later became president of the nation, William McKinley, Jr., Governor of Ohio.

Eugene Field and I wrote topical songs to popular airs for these dinners. When the president, James Scott, died in 1895, I was chosen as his successor. And when I left Chicago, the club ceased to exist. I was sovereign at a Twelfth Night frolic where the literati of our really cultivated city assembled.

A number of eminent artists came to arrange the decoration of the buildings for the Great Fair. Among them were Frank Millet, Hopkinson Smith, Elihu Vedder, and Walter Crane, with all of whom we soon became friends. Conan Doyle was with us for a short time. He had been writing the Sherlock Holmes adventures and we had frequent interesting talks on detective methods. George W. Cable, Charles Dudley Warner, Edmund Clarence Stedman, Edward Everett Hale, Mr. Howells, and Mark Twain were also of our visitors. There was Paul du Chaillu, the famous African traveller—Friend Paul. He was always full of good cheer, entertaining us with his wonderful tales of Ethiopia and the Land of the Vikings and Russia. And Paul Blouet, "Max O'Rell." He was a fellow of infinite jest. I found him one day at the Union League Club. He was tearing mad. "What troubles you?" I asked.

"That scoundrel, Mark Twain," he snapped out. "He is at least no gentleman. I wrote a serious paper on the United States, giving my impressions of this great country, as many other foreign literary men have done. I noted certain aristocratic tendencies, and remarked upon the large number of persons studying their geneological tables to learn whether they were qualified for membership in such societies as the Sons of the American Revolution or the Colonial Dames. They all seemed to be trying to find out who their grandfathers were and what they had done, I said. Now, how do you think Sam Clemens commented on this perfectly proper observation. He said I was quite right in all I said, and that the only difference between France and America was that every Frenchman seemed to be trying to find out who his father was."

My most intimate friend was George Royal Peck, who had come from Kansas to Chicago to become general counsel of the St. Paul Railway. I think of all the men I have ever known, he knew more about more things. His fund of information upon literary topics was marvellous. I think he was the one man who had ever declined a gubernatorial appointment to the United States Senate. I had met him back in 1884 when as a delegate to the National Republican Convention, he had ardently favoured the nomination of Arthur, while his co-delegates were for Blaine. He was a brilliant orator.

One day Senator Thurston of Nebraska, and Henry Watterson were sitting as Tam and the Souter were wont to do.

"Oratory is a thing of the past," quoth "Marse" Henry. "The days of Webster and Clay and Calhoun are gone for ever. There are only three great orators, you and I and George Peck, to-day."

"Why lug in Peck, he isn't here?" retorted Thurston.

While living at Topeka, Peck and his friend Rossington, another eminent lawyer, went to Europe. It was their first ocean voyage.

They were stout, hearty fellows, full of fun, and their journey in Europe was a veritable lark. They paid tips with lavish hands, and did all of the regulation things that "first-timers" are wont to do when visiting Europe. They returned, and one evening in a Topeka club, were relating their wonderful experiences. "But," said Peck, "we Americans are fools to buy our clothes of English tailors simply to save a little money.

They never give a good fit." He wore at the moment a London-made suit.

"What is the trouble with the garments you have on?" asked some one.

"They are too small. Can't you see," replied Peck.

"Well," came the quiet retort, "you should bear in mind, Mr. Peck, that you were not nearly so big a man in England as you are in Kansas."

And there were almost daily luncheons and dinners in honour of the distinguished visitors to the World's Fair. This "keen encounter of our wits" was enjoyable but exacting.

Visit of W. T. Stead

In the fall of 1893 William T. Stead came to Chicago, and I enjoyed an interesting, and in some respects, amusing intimacy with him. He was an amazing zealot in respect of any mission to which he felt that duty called him. One night as we "philosophized" before a blazing hearth he broke out with this exclamation "Stone, there is this difference between us: you are a journalist first and reformer thereafter, while I am a reformer first and a journalist thereafter."

W. T. Stead

However candid was his personal thrust, there can be no doubt of the accuracy of his self-estimate. He was a great journalist, but before that he was even more than a reformer. He was an evangelist.

In his work, all his life, he had a profound contempt for anything like conservatism. He was nothing if not militant. When he enlisted in a cause he stopped at nothing to gain his end. The suspicion sometimes raised by the very sensational character of his exposures, that he was a reformer for notoriety and profit, was wholly unjust. He was undeniably sincere. He would cheerfully sacrifice everything for a conviction.

So it was when he made his attack in the columns of the *Pall Mall Gazette* on London as "The Modern Babylon." One may in fairness doubt the wisdom of certain things he did, but no one should doubt either his honesty or his courage.

After his retirement from the editorship of the *Pall Mall Gazette*, and his release from a three-month term of imprisonment, early in 1886, he floated about, doing desultory writing, and then founded, first, the English *Review of Reviews*, and soon thereafter, in partnership with Dr. Albert Shaw, who had worked for me on the Chicago *Daily News*, the American review bearing the same name. Both enterprises were successful, but they by no means filled the time of the energetic Stead.

He had been told, as had many others, that of all places on earth, Chicago was undeniably the wickedest, and therefore it was obviously the fittest spot for an evangelist's missionary effort.

He had not been in the city a week before I received a note from him, reading as follows:

Chicago, December 8, 1893.

M. E. STONE, Esq.,
DEAR SIR:
Mr. McClaughry, late chief of police in Chicago, told me that there was no one who had more information about Chicago as it is, and better judgment as to what ought to be done there, than yourself. What he said naturally made me anxious of having an opportunity of meeting you, if only for half an hour. I shall be glad to wait upon you at any hour that may suit your convenience.
W. T. STEAD.

I may say in passing that Mr. McClaughry was a Christian gentleman who enjoyed the esteem of every good citizen, and whose service as chief of police had contributed in large measure to make Chicago a well-governed city.

I invited Stead to dine with me, and he came. I tried to tell him frankly the story of the place, which in some aspects had no counterpart anywhere on earth; how in a man's lifetime it had grown from a petty Indian trading post into a great metropolis with a million of inhabitants; how men well under middle age had accumulated great fortunes, not by speculation, but in legitimate commerce; and how all this had made for an inordinate devotion to dollars; and yet how there was a countervailing public spirit and civic pride which a few months before had found expression in the great Columbian Exposition, which for artistic beauty and real dignity had never been equalled, and it was difficult to see how it ever could be surpassed. And, as for the morals of the place, it was rather better than worse than other like cities of the world. Its faults were many, but its virtues plenty.

This was unconvincing to a man who had come four thousand miles to see the modern counterpart of the "cities of the plain." So thanking, but all the time doubting me, he went his way. He went to find the seamy side of things, and, of course, he found what he was looking for. Because it was there, as it always is in any large agglomeration of human beings.

He took up his residence in a little room over a disreputable saloon and consorted wholly with the lost souls of the underworld. All this, be assured, for a high and holy purpose. He was in the mire, but not of it. He wallowed for a month. Then he came out and wrote his sensational book: "If Christ Came to Chicago." It was an honest effort, but its author had seen but one side, and it was therefore grotesquely unfair.

Quite satisfied with his work, Stead came again to see me. He bore a letter from his partner, Doctor Shaw. It seemed that he had written Shaw, telling him the work was done and asking advice as to his future movements. And the reply puzzled him. He came to me as a common friend, to solve the riddle.

Doctor Shaw, who greatly respected Stead, but had little sympathy with his bizarre methods of reform, wrote something like this:

You say you have finished your work in Chicago, and you ask what I think you should do now. My reply is that you should fix a very early date for your sailing to England, and should bend all your energies to that end.

Poor, sincere Stead did not at all see the fun of Shaw's reply, and when I burst into laughter, he was offended.

And yet he had a sense of humour. When Albert Edward of England went down to visit the Wilsons at Tranby Croft and have a game of baccarat, and Lady Brooke told of Sir William Gordon-Cumming and the charge of cheating at cards, and there was a national scandal, Stead quietly said of it:

Let us study the power of prayer. Edward was born in November, 1841; even before his birth there were prayers that the heir to the throne would prove a worthy Christian sovereign. And there were so many hundreds of thousands of churches in the world offering this prayer. They have offered it morning, noon, and night through all the years. Compute it and you will find that untold millions of such prayers have gone to heaven. The "baccarat scandal" is the net result.

It was more impressive than Tyndall's famous prayer gauge. Yet Stead was not sacrilegious. On the contrary, he was a devout Christian, as he understood Christianity.

After he had written his book about Chicago, after he felt the power of sin in that pioneer western city, he wondered if it was not his duty to spend his life there in a work of reformation. And he came again to me to consult about the matter. We spent an evening together. I frankly told him of a burning hope that I might again edit a paper in the place and do something of value in the city in which I had lived from childhood. But I also spoke of a call to print a paper in Boston. The next day he wrote me the following letter:

January 8, 1894.

My dear Mr. Stone:

I left your hotel last night with a sense of relief—of having come out into the light. I do not think you will start that paper in Boston. I think you will start it here in Chicago, and I am right glad. Glad for public reasons, because you are the only man to do it. My suggested weekly would be a miserable *pis aller* compared to your daily, and glad for selfish, personal reasons of my own, because with one so immeasurably more competent than myself in the field, there will be no longer any imperative demand for the sacrifice of my home life and English work, which, but for your stepping into the breach, I was beginning to fear would be exacted from me.

In the English-speaking world there are only two centers—London and Chicago. If the immense possibilities of leadership in Chicago seemed to summon me from London, they will not let you dream of Boston. If I can help you in any way—not that I think you are in the least likely to need any help—you can rely upon my loyal and enthusiastic support, either here or in London, where perhaps in the future I may be able to serve you in some way or other at present not clearly revealed to me.

I am extremely glad to have had that talk last night.

I am,
Yours very sincerely,
WILLIAM T. STEAD.

And so we parted.

I told him in our conference of a new type of newspaper of which I had dreamed, to be in tabloid form, with small pages and many of them. He went back to London, tried it, but without success.

After that we frequently wrote each other. But I never saw him again. He intended to give me the pleasure of a visit, when he went down on the ill-fated *Titanic*, bound for New York.

Evolution of News Gathering

Less than a year after I became a bank president I was called to the Associated Press. A crisis had developed in the affairs of the organization.

*The business of news gathering and news publishing, as we know it, is wholly an American idea, having taken its rise in this country in the early years of the last century. There were coffee houses in London and New York, where the men had been accustomed to gather to exchange the current gossip, and letters on important topics had occasionally been published; but before this time no systematic effort had been made to keep pace with the world's happenings. Then came the newspaper, supplanting the chap book, the almanac, and the political pamphlet.

In the new development half a dozen men were notable. Samuel Topliff and Harry Blake were the first news-mongers.

---

*From articles on ".The Associated Press," *Century Magazine*, 1906.

Topliff established a "news-room" in Boston, where he sold market reports and shipping intelligence; and Blake was a journalistic Gaffer Hexam, who prowled about Boston Harbour in his rowboat, intercepting incoming European packets, and peddling out as best he could any news that he secured. Both became famous in their day.

Later, in 1827, Mr. Arthur Tappan, the merchant, philanthropist, and reformer, founded the *Journal of Commerce* in New York to combat the growing influence of the theatre, which he regarded as pernicious. But the playhouses proved too strong for him, and within a year he sold the paper to David Hale and Gerard Hallock, two young Boston journalists. They were familiar with the work of Topliff and Blake, and promptly transplanted their methods to New York. They discarded the rowboat, and built a handsome seagoing yacht, which they named the *Journal of Commerce*, and ran twenty or thirty miles beyond Sandy Hook to meet incoming vessels. There had previously been a small combination of New York papers to gather ship news; but the building of the *Journal of Commerce* incensed the other members, and they promptly expelled Hale and Hallock, who replied in a card, which was printed in their newspaper on October 9, 1828, as follows:

Yesterday our new boat, the *Journal of Commerce*, went below for the first time, fully manned and equipped for service. We understand that her rival, the *Thomas H. Smith*, is also in readiness for similar duty. An opportunity is now afforded for an honorable competition. The public will be benefited by such extra exertions to procure marine news, and we trust the only contention between the two boat establishments will be, which can outdo the other in vigilance, perseverance, and success. In one respect, and in one only, we expect to be outdone; and that is, in collecting news on the Sabbath. This we shall not do, and if our Monday papers are, as we trust they will not often be, deficient in giving the latest marine intelligence, we must appeal to the candour and moral principle of our subscribers for a justification.

Hale and Hallock also erected upon the Highlands, near Sandy Hook, a semaphore telegraph, to which their schooner signalled the news, and which in turn transmitted it to Staten Island. Thence the news was carried to the publication office in New York City. In this way they were able to outdistance all competitors. They also introduced to American journalism the "extra edition." The scenes about the office of the *Journal of Commerce* in those days aroused great public interest, and before long the proprietors enjoyed a national reputation.

Not content with outdistancing their rivals in European news, they also established a pony express from Philadelphia, with eight relays of horses. By this means they were frequently able to publish Southern news twenty-four hours in advance of their competitors. This system worked so successfully that the Federal Government took it over; but Hale and Hallock extended their express to Washington, and thus maintained their supremacy. They frequently published official news from the capital before it had been received by the Government officers in New York. In one instance a Norfolk paper, published two hundred and thirty miles south of Washington, copied the Washington news from the New York *Journal of Commerce*, which it received by sea before it had any direct advices. In time this enthusiasm waned, but with the advent of James Gordon Bennett and the New York *Herald* it revived, and the zeal then displayed has never been surpassed.

The battle royal which was carried on between General James Watson Webb of the New York *Courier and Enquirer* on the one hand and Bennett of the *Herald* and Hale and Hallock of the *Journal of Commerce* on the other, is historic.

When the war with Mexico broke out, Mr. Bennett was able, through his system of pony expresses, to publish accounts of battles even before the Government despatches were received. He also had a carrier-pigeon service between New York and Albany for the annual messages of the Governor, which he printed ahead of everyone. The Cunard liners ran between Liverpool and Boston, and Bennett, with characteristic energy, instituted a scheme for hurrying the news by pony express from Boston to New York.

Topliff and Blake had been succeeded by D. H. Craig, who established himself as an independent news collector and vender at Boston, and displayed extraordinary alertness. As the Cunard boats approached the harbour, Craig met them and received on his schooner a budget of news from the incoming vessel. Then by carrier-pigeons he communicated a synopsis of the news to his Boston office, frequently releasing the birds forty or fifty miles from port.

Meanwhile, Professor Morse was struggling with his invention of the magnetic telegraph. In 1838 he completed his machinery and took it to Washington on the invitation of President Van Buren; but it was not until 1843 that Congress appropriated $30,000 to build an experimental line. It took a year to construct this between Washington and Baltimore, and it was not until the latter part of 1844 that it proved of any service for the transmission of news.

D. H. Craig

The First Associated Press

With the advent of the telegraph Craig determined to make use of this novel agency in his business, but encountered the hostility of those having a monopoly of Morse's patents, who desired to control the news business themselves. There was a sharp contest. The New York papers joined forces with the telegraph people, and in 1848 organized the Associated Press, with Mr. Hallock as president and Dr. Alexander Jones as manager.

Gerard Hallock

Alexander Jones

Its membership was limited to the proprietors of the six or seven New York dailies, and its purpose was to gather news for them only. Later, other newspapers in the interior arranged for exchanging news with it, and thus the enterprise developed into one of great importance.

A hundred interesting stories are told of the experiences of Manager Jones. Because of the excessive cost of transmitting messages by the imperfect telegraph lines of that day, he devised a cipher, one word representing a sentence. Thus the word "dead" meant, in the Congressional reports, "After some days' absence from indisposition, reappeared in his seat." When they desired to convey this information respecting Senator Davis of Massachustts, they wired, "John Davis dead." But the word "dead" was not recognized as a cipher by the receiving operator, and all the papers of New York and Boston proceeded to print post-mortem eulogies, much to Davis's amusement.

When the Whig convention of 1848 assembled at Philadelphia, Jones planned to score a great "beat." The wires did not cross the river at Jersey City, and therefore he arranged for a flag signal across the Hudson River. If General Taylor should prove to be successful, a white flag was to be waved. Unfortunately, another company was also signalling by white flags on another subject, and so Jones was misled into announcing Taylor's nomination before it happened.

Jones was a better general manager than prophet. In the light of to-day, the following declaration, which he published in 1852, is interesting:

All idea of connecting Europe with America, by lines extending directly across the Atlantic, is utterly impracticable and absurd. It is found on land, when sending messages over a circuit of only four or five hundred miles, necessary to have relays of batteries and magnets to keep up or to renew the current and its action. How is this to be done in the ocean, for a distance of three thousand miles? But by the way of Behring's Strait the whole thing is practicable, and its ultimate accomplishment is only a question of time.

Craig, against whom the efforts of the association were directed, did not, however, surrender. As the Liverpool boats touched at Halifax en route to Boston, to this point he turned his attention. He had a synopsis of European happenings carefully prepared in Liverpool and placed in the purser's hands; and, on the arrival of the vessel at Halifax, the purser sealed this budget in a tin can, which was thrown overboard and picked up by Craig's representative, who hurried it on to Boston and New York by pony express, completely outstripping all rivals. The New York and Boston newspapers then chartered a steamer to express news from Halifax to Boston, with the idea of telegraphing it from Boston to New York. But Craig was equal to the emergency. Putting a pair of his best carrier-pigeons in a basket, he travelled by the land route to Halifax in season to take passage on the press express boat for Boston; and when the steamer approached the shores of Massachusetts his pigeons, heavily freighted with the European news, were sent off from a window in his state-room. This was so adroitly done that, long before the express boat landed, Craig's pigeons had reached the city and the news they brought had been published. His opponents then gave up the fight, and elected Craig their general manager.

For the ensuing forty years they had no rival worthy of note. Hallock retired in 1861 and Craig in 1866. David M. Stone succeeded as president and James W. Simonton as general manager. In 1882 there came a change.

J. W. Simonton

The Associated Press had grown to be all-powerful in its field, and an offensive and defensive alliance had been formed with the great Reuter News Agency, which had meanwhile grown up in Europe; but the Association was owned by seven New York papers, which gathered such news as they desired and sold it to the newspapers of the inland cities. Important subsidiary associations, such as the New England Associated Press and the Western Associated Press, had been organized. They bought the news of the New York association and made payment in money, as well as a contribution of the news of their own localities; but they had no voice in the management. The Western Association finally revolted. There was a short-lived contest that ended in a compromise. The West was admitted to a partnership in the direction of the business. Two Western men, Richard Smith of Cincinnati and W. N. Haldeman of Louisville, joined Whitelaw Reid and James Gordon Bennett in an executive committee; Charles A. Dana was added as a fifth member and chairman; and William Henry Smith, who had served the Western association as manager, was appointed general manager. The compact ran for a term of ten years.

William Henry Smith

All this while the Association had confined its energies to the gathering and distribution of what is known among newspapermen as "routine news"—shipping, markets, sporting, Congressional reports, and the "bare bones" of a day's happenings. The owners of the great metropolitan dailies who controlled it preferred to hold the management in leash so that they might display enterprise with their special reports of the really interesting events. The smaller papers, which were wholly dependent upon the Association for general news, could not afford extensive special telegrams, and therefore desired the organization to make comprehensive reports of everything.

In the earlier days telegraphic facilities were so limited and the cost of messages was so great that it was necessary to report everything in the briefest form. It was enough that the facts were disclosed, and little heed was paid to the manner of presentation. Moreover, a great majority of those writing the despatches were telegraph operators destitute of literary training.

The advantages of an Associated Press newspaper were very great. It was scarcely possible for a competitor to make headway against the obstacles which he was compelled to face. Not only was the burden of expense enormous, but the telegraph company which was in close alliance with the Association frequently delayed his service, or refused to transmit it at any price. It followed that the quantity of news which an editor was able to furnish his readers became the measure of his enterprise and ability. It was his proudest boast that his paper printed "all the news." James Gordon Bennett, Sr., of the New York *Herald*, and Wilbur F. Storey of the Chicago *Times*, set the pace, and won much fame by lavish expenditures for telegrams, which were often badly written.

During Mr. Smith's administration substantial improvements were effected. Arrangements were made with the telegraph companies for leased wires, which were operated by the Association itself. There was also not a little display of real enterprise.

The Western papers which had been admitted to a share in the management demanded more enterprise and a report of more varied character. The policy of limiting the field to "routine news" was abandoned, and the institution began to show evidence of real journalistic life and ability. It startled the newspaper world by occasionally offering exclusive and well-written items of general interest. When Mr. Blaine was closing what promised to be a successful political campaign in 1884, it was an Associated Press man who shattered all precedents, as well as the candidate's hopes, by reporting Doctor Burchard's disastrous "Rum, Romanism, and Rebellion" speech. This was then an unheard-of display of enterprise.

Two years later the same reporter scored again. He had been sent to Mount McGregor with many others to report General Grant's last illness. He was shrewd enough to arrange in advance with the doctor for prompt information of the final event. A system of signals had been agreed upon and when, one day, the doctor sauntered out upon the veranda of the Drexel cottage and drew a handkerchief from his pocket and wiped his hands, the reporter knew that the General was dead and telegraphed the fact throughout the world. For months afterward it was spoken of with wonder as the Associated Press "scoop."

A Masterpiece of Reporting

Then came the Samoan disaster, in 1885, and with it a disclosure that an Associated Press man might not only be capable of securing exclusive news, but might also be able to write it in a creditable way. Mr. John P. Dunning of the San Francisco bureau happened to be in Apia when the great storm broke over the islands. In the roadstead were anchored three American war vessels, the *Trenton*, *Nipsic*, and *Vandalia;* three German warships, the *Adler*, *Olga* and *Ever;* and the British cruiser *Calliope*. All of the American and German ships were driven upon the coral reefs and destroyed, involving the loss of one hundred and fifty lives. The *Calliope*, a more modern vessel with superior engines, was able to escape. As she pushed her way into the heavy sea, in the teeth of the hurricane, the jackies of the *Trenton* "dressed ship," while her hand played the British national anthem. It was a profoundly tragic salutation from those about to die.

Mr. Dunning's graphic story, which will long be accepted as a masterpiece of descriptive literature, was mailed to San Francisco, and a month later was published by the newspapers of the Associated Press. It was a revelation to those who had long believed the organization incapable of producing anything more exciting than a market quotation. It was also an inspiration to those who were to succeed Mr. Smith in the administration of the burden. It revealed the possibilities in store for the Association.

Unfortunately, however, too many of the employees were chosen because of their familiarity with the technical side of the telegraph business, and were incapable of writing the news in interesting fashion. In addition, the organization was loosely planned, or perhaps it would be more accurate to say was not planned at all. It had grown up through constant compromises by more or less conflicting interests, and the special concessions which were constantly being made led to a very considerable degree of friction. Many of the papers in the association enjoyed an exclusive right to the service, and it was almost a cardinal principle that no new paper could be admitted to its privileges without the consent of all Associated Press papers in the city of publication. As the country grew, such a plan made a rival organization inevitable. There was a close alliance, offensive and defensive, between the Associated

Press and the Western Union Telegraph Company, by the terms of which the Association was given special advantages, and it in turn refused to patronize any rival telegraph company.

From time to time enterprising men founded new papers which, under the rules, could not gain admission to the Associated Press. Rival telegraph companies also appeared in the field and established rival news services. Owing to the great strength of the Associated Press, these rival concerns struggled against heavy odds, but constantly grew in importance, until finally there were enough papers which had been unable to secure admittance to the Association and enough telegraph companies contesting the field with the Western Union Company to organize a formidable competitor—the United Press. Behind it the two most important papers were the Boston *Daily Globe* and the Chicago *Daily Herald*, both of which were enterprising and financially strong. In London also there was established a rival to Reuter, called the Central News Agency, not very formidable, to be sure, yet sufficiently enterprising to furnish a fair summary of the world's news. It had a distinct advantage in the fact that the five hours' difference in time between London and New York enabled it to glean from the London morning papers the most important happenings in time to transmit them to America for publication in contemporaneous issues.

It was one of the rules of the Associated Press—both of the parent organization and of all the tributary associations—that a member should not traffic with any rival association; but the rules were so loosely drawn and so ineffectively enforced that the United Press was able to sell its report to a large number of papers. In many cases members of the Associated Press bought the United Press report, paying a considerable weekly sum for it, simply in order to prevent its use by a rival newspaper. All of this gave the United Press a considerable revenue and an important standing. Finally, it menaced the supremacy of the older organization.

Then an unfortunate compromise was effected. Those in the management of the Associated Press privately purchased a controlling interest in the stock of the United Press, and made a secret agreement that the two associations should work in harmony. The existence of this private arrangement was disclosed in 1892, as the ten-year alliance between the New York Associated Press and the Western Associated Press was about to terminate. It created great commotion. The Western Associated Press refused to go on under such an agreement. Finally, the New York Associated Press was absorbed by the United Press, and the Western Associated Press set out to operate independently. There was a period of attempted compromise, and, all such efforts having failed, my friends incorporated on December 13, 1892, as "The Associated Press" of Illinois. Then I was invited to become general manager. I had been a member of the Board of Directors and of the Executive Committee of their former organization during the years that I had edited the Chicago *Daily News*, and I was reasonably familiar with the business.

One evening, having attended a theatre, I returned to the Virginia Hotel, where I was living for the winter, and found two gentlemen awaiting me. They—Colonel Frederick Driscoll of the St. Paul *Pioneer Press* and Mr. Charles W. Knapp of the St. Louis *Republic*—represented the Executive Committee of the Associated Press. They told me that at a meeting of their organization a resolution had been unanimously adopted asking me to accept the office of general manager, and they had called to secure my acceptance. All I could say was, in the phrase of the young lady, that their proposal was "rather sudden." There were things to think of.

Their outlook was certainly not inviting. Against them was arrayed the wealth of the entire Eastern journalistic field and they had apparently been cut off from all relation with the foreign news agencies. There were but sixty-three members. None was very rich and several were not even well-to-do. And three or four were under well-grounded suspicion of disloyalty. Then, also, there was my responsibility to the bank of which I was president.

On the other hand, the business of banking had never greatly appealed to me, although I had been undeniably successful in the enterprise. I had a secret longing to return to the

printers' craft. And much more controlling than any personal interest was the question of public duty. My friends of the press and I talked it over. And this is the way we reasoned:
The United Press was controlled by three men, only one of whom was a journalist. These men were William M. Laffan, of the New York *Sun*; John R. Walsh, president of the Chicago National Bank and the Western News Company; and Walter P. Phillips, general manager of the United Press. My friends felt it unsafe to leave so important a business under a privately owned, money-making control. We took it for granted that the need of an intelligent, well-informed electorate in a self-governing people must be admitted. Through all the days from Gutenberg and his invention of printing there had never been an hour when the first aid to autocracy had not been the placing of the press in leash. And it was equally true that there had never been an effort to break the bonds of tyranny that had not turned at the outset to a struggle for untrammelled printing. For ages freedom of opinion had been forbidden and the army of martyrs who had gone to the stake was large. Freedom of communication of opinion by printing was even more often anathema. Hand in hand, free government and a free press had come to us through the centuries.

It was quite true that control of the press was wrested from governments at the beginning of our Republic. The first amendment to our Federal Constitution did this. It forbade any attempt in the United States to stop free speech or a free press. But, unhappily, this was not sufficient. Government might not enchain the press, but private monopoly might. The people, for their information—indeed, for the information upon which they based the very conduct of their daily activities— were dependent upon the news of the world as furnished by the newspapers. And this business of news gathering and purveying had fallen into private and mercenary hands. Its control by three men was quite as menacing as that of the governmental autocrats of the ages agone. There could be no really free press in these circumstances. A press to be free must be one which should gather the news for itself.

A national coöperative news-gathering organization, owned

by the newspapers and by them alone, selling no news, making no profits, paying no dividends, simply the agent and servant of the newspapers, was the thing. Those participating should be journalists of every conceivable partisan, religious, economic, and social affiliation, but all equally zealous that in the business of news gathering for their supply there should be strict accuracy, impartiality, and integrity. This was the dream we dreamed.

The directors of the bank were impressed, and they said: "Go ahead." So, for something like five years, I held both offices.

I assumed the duties of general manager of the Associated Press in March, 1893. Twenty-four hours later I was on my way to England to see what could be done in the foreign field. I spent one week in London, made a contract with the great group of foreign agencies, and was back in Chicago in less than a month.

We were ready for a fight. It seemed a very unequal one, a sort of David-and-Goliath affair. Our little band seemed no match for the terrible "army with banners" arrayed against us. Yet we were not in the least downhearted. We had right and justice on our side, and with this consciousness we had faith in our ultimate success.

Suddenly, in the first week of May, the National Cordage Company failed, and a financial panic resulted. Walsh had no stomach for a Press Association war at that moment. He began to bluff.

"You and I must attend to our banks," said he to me one day.

"Not at all," I replied. "I have no concern about the panic."

"But," he added, "what will you do if they start a run on you?"

Then I laughed at him. And I explained: "As treasurer of the Drainage Canal Board, I have several millions on deposit in yours and the other banks of the city. I will withdraw this, deposit it in my own bank, and pay on demand."

"Oh," he said in alarm, "we can't stand that."

Then we arranged a truce and devoted ourselves to the financial situation. The World's Fair was with us, bringing an enormous volume of cash to the city, and we weathered the storm with ease.

It did not surprise us that in a few months the United Press violated the truce. Such a course was to be expected. In August we concluded to "have no more nonsense" about the business, and on September 7th the war was on. The contest lasted for four years, and was waged with great bitterness. Mr. Victor F. Lawson, my former partner in the ownership of the Chicago *Daily News*, was elected president and devoted himself with great persistency and disinterestedness to the upbuilding of the organization. He and I set out for New York, where we began a prolonged missionary effort. It happened that Mr. Horace White of the New York *Evening Post*, Mr. Joseph Pulitzer of the New York *World*, and Mr. John Cockerill of the New York *Commercial Advertiser*, were all Western men who had been long-time friends of mine, and it was not difficult to convince them of the wisdom of our plan of organization.

When I called upon Mr. White I found him busily writing an editorial. Scarcely pausing in his work he said: "I am with you. I do not believe in an association which is controlled by three or four men. The *Evening Post* will join your company. But I am under pledge to make no move in the matter without consulting my friends of the New York *Staats-Zeitung* and the Brooklyn *Eagle*." Very soon the *Evening Post*, the *Staats-Zeitung*, the *World*, the *Morning Advertiser*, and the *Commercial Advertiser* of New York, as well as the Brooklyn *Eagle*, abandoned the United Press and joined us. The fact that we retained the name—"The Associated Press"—which for over forty years had been a household word in the United States, was of great value, editors, as a rule, recognizing the desirability of advertising (as they had done for many years) their connection with the Associated Press rather than their alliance with the United Press. The title "The Associated Press" was a most valuable trade-mark.

In time the Philadelphia papers, certain New England papers, and a number of journals in central New York also abandoned the United Press and joined the Associated Press. The contest resulted in placing a heavy burden of expense upon both organizations. The normal revenues of neither were sufficient to maintain its service at the standard of excellence required by the competition. The members of the Associated Press promptly assembled and subscribed to a large guaranty fund to provide for the deficits, while the four or five New York papers behind the United Press were compelled to contribute in like manner in order to hold their clients to any degree of allegiance. Month by month and year by year the converts to the Associated Press grew in number and the burden of expense upon the New York papers became heavier.

All through the days when I was sharing in the Press Association contest I was equally busy with other things. I not only piloted my bank through the panic of 1893, I was a member of the Clearing House Committee, and we were forced to look after a number of "lame-duck" banks which required our financial aid to save them from failure.

The Campaign of 1896

The Presidential campaign of 1896 was fought over measures rather than men. As I have said, the issue, bimetallism, was not a new one. In 1526, more than three centuries before, Nicolas Copernicus had offered a plan to reform the currency of the Russian provinces of Poland, and in it had declared against the possibility of maintaining a double standard of money. A few years later Sir Thomas Gresham of England had repeated the axiom, which thereafter was known as the incontrovertible "Gresham Law" of finance. When Alexander Hamilton, in 1795, opened a mint for the United States, he fixed a standard of $15\frac{1}{2}$ to 1 between silver and gold, and thought it would work. But in 1834 gold had disappeared from circulation because, in confirmation of the Gresham Law, the ratio of $15\frac{1}{2}$ ounces of silver to 1 ounce of gold made silver the cheaper and more popular metal. Then a new effort to adjust the matter resulted in fixing the ratio at 16 to 1. But in 1848 gold was discovered in California, and three years later in Australia, and again, as always, a statutory enactment proved futile as against the immutable economic law of supply and demand.

It was only necessary to read Benton's "Thirty Years' View," which was easily accessible, to convince one that bimetallism was a dream that could never be realized. In these circumstances it seems incredible that the issue should again come to the fore. But it did.

In February, 1896, I was on my way, with my wife and daughter, to Mexico. We were halted five hours at El Paso, until the connecting train on the Mexican Central Road was made up. My daughter was urgent to cross the border to the foreign land, and, of course, had her way. So we set out for Juarez to while away the time. We climbed into a little street car, drawn by a donkey, and trundled along over the bridge which crossed the Rio Grande. My family very soberly seated themselves within the car, while I lighted a cigar and stood on the rear platform. In a few moments a man came from the interior of the car and, calling me by name, introduced himself.

"I am Mr. William Jennings Bryan," said he. "I was a congressman from Nebraska, and I met you in your office when you were editor of the Chicago *Daily News*."

Then I remembered him, and we fell into a conversation. He joined us for our visit to Juarez. This was my first conscious acquaintance with Mr. Bryan. I say "conscious acquaintance" because, in fact, I had met and known him years before when he was a law student in Chicago in the office of Lyman Trumbull, and later when he was a congressman from Nebraska and made a remarkably able speech for tariff reform, with which I fully sympathized; but all this I had forgotten.

However, this meeting on the quaint little car en route to Juarez was agreeable, and the visit of that day a pleasant one. We went to the Mexican cathedral, or maybe it was only a church, and after that to see Fitzsimmons, the prize fighter, who had rented a small shop on the main street and was in training for a forthcoming contest with Maher. He gave a private exhibition of boxing for us, and I remember that Mr.

Bryan was greatly interested in "speckle-faced Bob's" cub lion, and held him in his arms as I did in mine.

Well, we had our visit, and I went my way to Mexico City. Mr. Bryan had gone to the Mexican Republic to study the silver question, and I believe had completed the inquiry in the five hours we spent together.

Time crawled on, and I next met him in Chicago. The St. Louis Convention had been held and McKinley had been nominated as the Republican candidate for the Presidency. There were some interesting things concerning this. The "Major," as we called McKinley in those days, was a friend. Four or five days before the St. Louis Convention he had asked me to come to his home at Canton, and I went there. We sat for a long afternoon on the porch of his cottage. He had received at the hands of Mr. Robert W. Patterson, managing editor of the Chicago *Tribune*, a proposed plank for the platform to be adopted at the St. Louis Convention. It referred to the monetary question and declared in a modified way for bimetallism. I was president of the Globe National Bank of Chicago at the time, and he did me the honour to ask my view of Patterson's proposal. I promptly told him that there was no such thing as bimetallism possible. I used the well-known illustration of the yardstick, and assured him that two yardsticks of different length could not be. In truth, Major McKinley had no settled opinion in respect of the matter, and he said he was convinced that the financial question would, after all, not be the issue of the coming campaign. I challenged this view, and, having in mind some things that had happened, said that neither he nor the National Convention could determine the issue, and that the people would in the end do this. Finally, he told me that Charles Emory Smith was drafting the platform, and he asked me to see him in St. Louis and try to settle the matter.

The thing that had happened, and which forced me to believe that the silver question and not the tariff was to be the issue, was the action of the Peoria Convention of the Democratic Party in Illinois, which had already been held. The controlling force in that convention was a very astute politician,

Governor John P. Altgeld of Chicago. He had thrust the issue of bimetallism into the Peoria Convention and secured the passage of a resolution declaring for a 16-to-1 standard. But for the fact that he was born in Germany, and therefore ineligible to the office of President of the United States, it is not unlikely that he would have been the national Democratic candidate that year.

The story of the adoption of the gold-standard plank at the Republican National Convention has frequently been told, yet not always accurately. When I arrived in St. Louis I found a good deal of confusion. I was called into a conference of Major McKinley's friends. Those present were H. H. Kohlsaat, editor of the Chicago *Record-Herald*, ex-Governor W. R. Merriam of Minnesota; the Hon. Myron T. Herrick of Ohio; Senator Redfield Proctor of Vermont; the Hon. Henry C. Payne of Milwaukee, and Mark Hanna. As manager for the McKinley forces, Mr. Hanna found himself in a difficult position. Several Western states were earnestly for free-silver coinage. Mr. Hanna, therefore, while personally a gold-standard man, was unwilling to take the responsibility of actively participating in the fight against a declaration for bimetallism. After repeated conferences a resolution committing the Republican Party to the gold standard was agreed to. The most urgent and uncompromising advocate of a gold plank was Mr. Kohlsaat. My only part in the framing of the plank was to write in the word "inviolable" in the pledge to "maintain [inviolable] the obligations of the United States at the existing standard."

After the wording of the resolution had been finally agreed upon it was necessary to submit it to Major McKinley. A long-distance telephone line between the Southern Hotel in St. Louis and the McKinley cottage in Canton had been established, and Mr. Hanna and I went to the St. Louis end of the wire in the basement of the hotel to read the plank to the waiting candidate at Canton. It was a new experience for Mr. Hanna, and he could not make himself heard. I therefore read the resolution. Major McKinley asked if that had been fully agreed upon by his friends, to which I replied that it had. Reluctantly he acquiesced in it, but asked if it was not possible to introduce a modifying phrase pledging the Republican Party to promote an international agreement for the free coinage of silver. In obedience to this suggestion such a phrase was introduced, and the plank was later adopted by the Convention.

Mr. McKinley's campaign, carried on from his cottage at Canton, was a remarkable one. Although he had never given the financial question very serious consideration, and certainly had no adequate conception of the business when nominated, he delivered speech after speech of such cogency as to command the attention and admiration of every student of finance.

Then the Democratic National Convention assembled in Chicago. Here also there was great confusion respecting the financial question. The New York and Massachusetts delegates were pronouncedly for a gold standard, but a number of the Western states were again advocates of bimetallism. One morning as I was going to the Convention Hall, which was located at some distance from the centre of the city and reached by the Illinois Central Railway line, I encountered Mr. Bryan. We rode together to the Convention. Naturally we discussed the probabilities. He said that he did not know what the Convention would do, but logically he should be the nominee. I sat within a few feet of him while he delivered his famous "Cross of Gold" speech. It was, of course, a remarkable forensic effort. Then the balloting for a nominee began, and we witnessed a sight the like of which I think had never developed in a national party convention before. The Ohio delegation was pledged to John R. McLain, and McLain himself was chairman of the delegation. On each roll call he rose and announced the vote of Ohio as solidly for John R. McLain. On the final ballot he personally withdrew his name.

He retired to a room under the platform which had been set apart for newspaper work and sent a request for me to come to him. Bryan had been nominated for the Presidency, but the Convention was to adjourn for the night before nominating a vice-president. McLain asked me if I would see Bryan during the evening and ask him if it would be agreeable for McLain to be nominated as vice-president. "Bryan is poor," said Mc-

Lain, "and I can finance his campaign." That night I called upon Mr. Bryan, who was lodged at a small hotel called the Clifton House. I bore McLain's message to him and asked him how he felt about it, making no recommendation or suggestion. He at once and with no little vehemence said that he would not run on a ticket with McLain at all. The next morning I carried Bryan's answer to McLain and he disappeared from the contest, while Mr. Sewall of Maine was nominated.

During the campaign party feeling ran so high that I was charged by both of the campaign managers with bias. Each was convinced that I was using the Associated Press to further the interest of the opposing party. At the close, however, McKinley and Bryan voluntarily sent me the following letters:

Canton, Ohio, Nov. 5, 1896.

MY DEAR SIR:—It gives me pleasure to acknowledge (and I sincerely thank you for) the enterprise displayed by your great association in reporting and transmitting so fully the news from Canton during the campaign just closed. I desire to thank you especially for the faithful and efficient services of Mr. George B. Frease, whom you detailed to take charge of this arduous and exacting work.

Very truly yours,
W. McKINLEY.

Mr. Melville E. STONE,
General manager, the Associated Press,
New York.

MR. MELVILLE E. STONE, General Manager, Associated Press,
Chicago, Ill.

MY DEAR SIR:—Now that the campaign is over, I desire to thank you for the fairness and thoroughness with which you have reported my speeches and also to express my appreciation of the correspondents whom you have detailed to travel with our party.

Yours truly,
W. J. BRYAN.

Collapse of the United Press

The final *coup de grâce* to the United Press was given by a fellow "Mugwump" of the campaign of 1884—Mr. Haskell of

WILLIAM MCKINLEY
CANTON, OHIO, Nov. 5th, 1896.

My Dear Sir: — It gives me pleasure to acknowledge (and I sincerely thank you for) the enterprise displayed by your great Association in reporting and transmitting so fully the news from Canton during the campaign just closed. I desire to thank you especially for the faithful and efficient services of Mr. George B. Frease, whom you detailed to take charge of this arduous and exacting work.

Yours very truly,

W. McKinley

Mr. Melville E. Stone,
General Manager The Associated Press,
New York.

Letter from William McKinley

the Boston *Herald*. This was particularly gratifying, because my experience in the long contest seemed to disillusion me

William J. Bryan.

Lincoln, Neb. Nov 6 — 1896

Mr Melville E. Stone Gen Manager Ass't Press
Chicago, Ill.

My Dear Sir —
Now that the campaign is over I desire to thank you for the fairness and thoroughness with which you have reported my speeches and also to express my appreciation of the correspondents whom you have detailed to travel with our party.
Yours truly
W J Bryan

Letter from William Jennings Bryan

"sairly" respecting New England. Through my youthful days I had conceived a passionate love for the Yankees. Faneuil Hall was to me the cradle of liberty. I thought we should have no difficulty in inducing the New England editors to shake off the chains that bound them to our mercenary enemy. Instead, I found them more interested in their shekels than in their shackles. Daniel Webster had said that Massachusetts needed no encomium. She got none from me.

On April 8, 1897, Mr. Charles A. Dana of the New York *Sun*, as president of the United Press, applied to the courts of New York City for a receiver and the service of his organization was abandoned. A large number of United Press newspapers applied for admission to the Associated Press. The sharp competition between the two rival associations had resulted in heavy losses on both sides. Each of the parties to the contest was carrying a substantial indebtedness. We had been frequently notified by the managers of the United Press that if they should finally triumph, the members of the Associated Press would be taxed to pay all these liabilities, and the conditions of adjustment would be far from agreeable to the unfortunate papers which should continue faithful to our associates up to the time of the final triumph. None of these threats, however, seemed to justify any departure from our purpose to take into membership the United Press papers free from any attempt at reprisal or punishment.

A small number of papers still found it impossible to join, and formed another association, which grew into "The Publishers' Press" organization, serving many papers, chiefly afternoon issues, with a creditable report.

At the annual banquet of the Associated Press in Chicago, on May 19, 1897, a silver set was presented to Mr. Lawson and a loving cup to me. Mr. St. Clair McKelway, on behalf of the members of the organization, made the presentation. He said:

Mr. Stone has only friends around this board or in journalism outside it. He has confirmed the regard of those who know him, and he has conquered the regard of those who misunderstood him. He found a world of interest in the war of news. He has made it a concert of powers on behalf of general intelligence and the just diffusion thereof. He has conquered peace with honour, and when we ask him for his enemies he does not have to reply, as did the boastful road-agent in California, who told the shriving priest that he had no enemies, because he had killed them all.

A Princely Offer

No sooner was the contest with the United Press ended than Joseph Pulitzer came at me with a proposition that I take the editorial management of the New York *World*. He was urgent. He sent old Mr. Merrill of his staff to Chicago to try to persuade me. I said the offer was most flattering but I feared the work would be more strenuous than I cared to engage in. Merrill returned to New York, reported to his chief, and then I received the following telegram:

Washington D. C., May 2, 1897.
MELVILLE STONE,
   Chicago, Ill.
   Extremely desirable and important because I am perfectly sure you overestimate difficulties and time required. Please telegraph exactly what day you will be in New York. Will go over.

                      J. P., Calumet Place, Washington.

Joseph Pulitzer

I saw him at Washington and at Bar Harbour. As an inducement, the compensation he named was princely, and, to ensure my absolute control of the property, he said he would enter into a hard-and-fast contract for five years, go away on his yacht to the China Sea, and leave me undisturbed. Still I hesitated. In the fall I received the letter which follows:

                              Bar Harbor: 2 September, '97.
MY DEAR MR. MELVILLE STONE,
   With September I am beginning to make plans for the fall and winter. I wonder whether you can let me know exactly when you will be back here. I need not say that I am looking forward to see you with pleasure.

I wish you would make it before the middle of September, because we are apt to have a rainy spell at that time and I do not want your stay to be more tiresome than is absolutely necessary. Rain here means a great deal of confinement.

Very faithfully yours,
JOSEPH PULITZER.

In the end, as it seemed to me that the work I was engaged in was a public trust which I should not desert, I definitely declined Mr. Pulitzer's proposition.

I do not think Joseph Pulitzer ever quite forgave me. At least we were never again quite as good friends. I was not a little surprised, after his death, to find that he had named me in his will as a member of the advisory board for the conduct of the School of Journalism which he had provided for at Columbia University.

Reporting the Spanish War

It was in the war of 1898 that the Associated Press of which I was general manager achieved its first notable success. Although by the terms of the existing compact the field of operations, both in the Caribbean Sea and in the Philippines, was territory which the French agency had engaged to cover, early preparations were made for an American service. In the Cuban insurrection special correspondents were stationed at various points of interest and did creditable work. Neither of the contestants desired publicity, and following midnight marches and early morning raids, and transmitting news to New York by surreptitious means, were efforts which taxed the courage and ingenuity of the best-trained men. When General Weyler was in command at Havana he forbade all newspaper work. Nevertheless, thrilling accounts of the horrors attendant upon his *reconcentrado* system were smuggled out by Associated Press men at imminent risk of being shot for their pains. It was an Associated Press story of the destruction of the United States battleship *Maine* in Havana harbour that was published exclusively throughout the world the morning after that unhappy event.

But the work of these correspondents ended when the United States and Spain joined issue. A new plan of campaign was then organized. The situation presented serious problems. Land battles had been reported many times. But this must be a naval contest, and prompt newspaper reports of battles upon the high seas were unheard of. It must be remembered that wireless telegraphy had not been developed. The outlook was made more unpromising when all the ocean cables touching Cuba were cut. But the Federal Government was reasonable, and lent its aid. A capable reporter was installed upon the flagship of each of the squadrons, and both Sampson and Schley gave them every facility to enable them to do their work. A number of fast sea-going despatch-boats were chartered and sent to the Cuban coast. The whole service was placed in charge of my assistant, Colonel Diehl, who managed it wisely and succeeded in making a new record in the business of war reporting. A splendid staff of correspondents was landed at Santiago with General Shafter's army, and their copy, as well as that of the men at the flagships, was carried by the despatch-boats to the cable stations on the Jamaican or Haitian coast.

When Hobson sank the *Merrimac* at the mouth of Santiago harbour, four men wrote a composite story which was so skilfully interwoven that the reader thought it all the work of a single pen. In the actions before Santiago the Associated Press men showed great courage and transmitted reports which, for descriptive power, accuracy, and comprehensiveness, have never been surpassed. The story of the fateful encounter with Cervera's fleet cost, for cable tolls alone, more than $8,000, and the total expenditures for reporting the war exceeded $300,000.

It was dangerous work. Menaced by innumerable forms of tropical disease, exposed to death on the firing-lines as often as any trooper, braving the horrors of a Caribbean hurricane in a wretched little vessel, or taking the chance of being sunk at any moment by either friend or foe, our men performed gallant service; and happily, all came out alive. It was a cruel fate that compelled them to write anonymously, while much less capable men were written into temporary notoriety by the newspapers which employed them as "specials." The public never heard of these Associated Press men, but in newspaper offices and in army and navy circles they have always been recognized as the real historians of the war. Poor Lyman, one of the most conscientious of them, contracted a disease from which he afterward died. "Ned" Johnstone and "Nat" Wright became newspaper managers. Collins is the London manager for the Associated Press. Roberts is chief of the Paris office. Goode, who served on Sampson's flagship, is now Sir William Goode of England. It was Thompson who wrote the story of the dramatic surrender of Cuba from the position of a prize of war of the United States, to self-government, and by a unanimous and voluntary act of Congress his account was made a part of the Congressional Record.

Leonard Wood's Protégé

At the close of the Spanish War of 1898 one Major Bellairs, who seemed to bear adequate testimonials, was appointed by a subordinate of mine as Associated Press correspondent at Santiago, Cuba. At the moment General Leonard Wood was the commander at that post and was actively engaged in cleaning up the city. Bellairs's work seemed excellent for a time, but soon it was observed that there was a departure from the imperative rule of impartiality in his despatches. He had evidently become a protagonist of the commanding officer. This defect was believed to be chargeable to his lack of experience in the Associated Press organization. His telegrams were edited so as to remove any partisan colour, and he was cautioned respecting his obvious favouritism. Not that there was the slightest antagonism in our organization to the efficient officer referred to, but there was an earnest purpose to keep the service free from bias.

Later the General was transferred to Havana to succeed General John Brooke, and Bellairs was assigned to accompany

"Major Bellairs"

him. Once more there seemed to be insidious references in his service which caused remark. Then I received a letter from Florida suggesting vaguely that I look into Bellairs's record. I set out to do so, when the general appeared on the scene and vouched for the man's character in unmistakable terms. He assured us that Bellairs was the victim of malice and was wholly trustworthy.

Finally, there was a transference of both men to the Philippines, and again apparent fulsome praise of his friend on the part of the correspondent was noted. Then the charge against Bellairs was renewed in more definite shape, and I renewed my investigation. To my amazement I found he was a notorious criminal. His real name was Charles Ballentine, but he had used many aliases in his checkered career. Perhaps the best known were Ernest Allaine Cheiriton, E. Elaine, and E. A. Cameron. He was of British birth, his father being a clergyman of Norfolk, England. He entered Cheltenham College, England, in 1876, when but fifteen years of age. He began at once a career of swindling, which he followed for years. While at school he made a book on the principal English races as shrewdly and as profitably as the most expert gambler. His schoolfellows paid dearly for his acquaintance.

On leaving college he set out to live on his wits. He visited almost every country on the globe, and his victims were innumerable. He proved a successful society confidence man. His first professional operation was at Dieppe, the famous French watering place, where he appeared as an English swell, spent a month in riotous living, and left a large number of victims. In 1886 he ran a notable course in swindling in Australia. He was arrested in New York in 1891 on a charge of forgery in Florida; was extradited on a requisition of Governor Fleming of Florida; tried, convicted, and sentenced to seven years' imprisonment in the State prison at Chattahoochee.

On learning of his true character he was promptly dismissed. It is fair to say that his case was a unique one in our service, and for his employment or retention I do not think any one blamable. He was so clever that one might easily have been deceived. Later, in 1910, I saw him in Tokio, where he was in the employ of the London *Times*.

A Rascal Named Smith

Based upon the good name of the Associated Press and the silly vanity of some of the multi-millionaires of the country, a number of shrewd swindlers have been able to gather in considerable sums of money. One day, after I had entered the Associated Press service, Marshall Field, the well-known merchant, called me to account in the Chicago Club for what he was pleased to say was a very unworthy course of conduct on my part. Then he told me how he had been victimized. A fine-looking young fellow had called upon him as from our organization and told him that we were engaged in a very proper work which he thought would interest Mr. Field. The fine young fellow's explanation of the "very proper work" ran about as follows: "Mr. Field, my name is Smith. I have been commissioned by the Associated Press to call on you. You know how anxious our people are that every statement of ours shall be accurate. To that end we want to write an appreciation of the work of every really great American citizen, a copy of which is to be placed on file in the office of each of our leading papers for use in an emergency, as for instance, if the subject of the sketch should be honoured in any way, or if unhappily he should die. We have in mind to issue copies of these appreciations to one hundred of our most important papers, the idea being that the smaller papers will reprint them when they appear. For this service the Associated Press has fixed the nominal price of $10 a paper, or $1,000 for the one hundred."

The Rascal Smith

Of course it was a clear case of swindle. And I reminded Mr. Field that before paying his money, or criticizing me, perhaps it would have been wiser to telephone our Chicago office to ask if Mr. Smith's statements were true. In that case he would have learned that we were engaged in no such scheme of petty blackmail; he would have saved his money, and he might have put us in the way of catching and punishing the rascal. But this had not occurred to him.

Thus put upon notice, I awaited further news of Smith's activities. I did not wait long. He turned up in Detroit and called on General Alger, former Secretary of War. The General manifested interest, but was slow in making up his mind and asked the fellow to call again the next day, fixing an hour. Then our Detroit office was asked about the business. There was an exposure, and when Smith called the next day he was arrested. I hastened to Detroit and seized his trunk at a hotel. In it I found a most interesting mass of paraphernalia. He had taken great pains to prepare for his enterprise. He was operating both in the name of the Associated Press and that of our rival, the United Press. He had laboriously gathered facsimiles of the signatures of forty or fifty well-known men, and had them reproduced and printed upon a form of address commending his undertaking "to whom it might concern." One of these approved the "proposed action" of the Associated Press; the other the "proposed action" of the United Press. He also had secured the visiting cards of a number of notables and had numerous packages of lithographed reproductions of them. He had also learned where the notables kept their individual bank accounts; had obtained blank checks of these banks, and had filled in each with an order to pay a thousand dollars to himself, and affixed a forged facsimile signature of a notable. When he approached General Alger he sent in what seemed to be a genuine visiting card of Chauncey M. Depew's, on which was written: "I approve this work. C. M. D."

Smith escaped conviction in Detroit because he had been arrested before obtaining any money there and because the various facsimiles in his possession did not legally constitute forgery, since he had only exhibited and had not uttered them.

Some weeks later he turned up in New York City and found a score of victims. Then I caught him. One of the Seligman family had paid him $3,000, being one thousand for one hundred Associated Press papers, another thousand for a like number of United Press papers, and still another for a second hundred of the members of the Associated Press. I secured his indictment and he was tried, convicted, and sent to the penitentiary. His real name was Benjamin C. Smith; he belonged to a reputable family of Litchfield, Ill.

In the campaign for the relief of the legations at Peking in 1900, the organization won fresh laurels. Messrs. Collins, Kloeber, and Egan were sent to China. The Pacific cable had not been laid, and the messages were carried by Chinese runners from the army headquarters before Peking to Tientsin, and cabled thence, via Chefoo and Shanghai, the Indian Ocean, and the Red Sea, to London, and across the Atlantic Ocean to New York. Even following this tortuous line, they came as a rule a day ahead of the special telegrams to the London papers.

SIXTH DECADE

Forming a New Associated Press

MEANWHILE serious trouble developed for the Associated Press of Illinois. As early as January, 1898, the Chicago *Inter-Ocean*, having suffered a suspension of its news service for a violation of the by-laws of the organization, filed a bill in chancery to compel a restoration of its privileges as a member. There were hearings in the lower courts and the action of the Association was sustained, but on appeal to the Supreme Court of Illinois a decisive adverse decision was rendered. It was held that because of certain provisions of its charter, the Associated Press was so affected with a public duty that it must serve its news to any applicant. A compliance with this extraordinary judgment meant a destruction of the fundamental right of the members to unite for the collection, by their own agencies, of the news for their own exclusive use.

I resigned the position of general manager, and in common with certain members set out to organize a new association which should be free from the organic defects that had been disclosed. We sought the opinion of a number of the leading lawyers of the country, and finally incorporated a new Associated Press under the law of the State of New York. It took some months to perfect the details, and then in September, 1900, we began business. The Illinois Corporation was left in such condition that it ceased activity.

Mr. Frank B. Noyes was unanimously elected president of the new organization and from that time to this has been re-elected unanimously year by year. He is a man of sterling integrity, rare breadth of vision, and the highest sense of justice. I have felt myself singularly fortunate in my association with him. We have worked together as yoke-fellows without a trace of discord. I have found him at all times more than generous in our personal relation, and the contribution he has made to the success of the organization has been very great.

And as to the Board of Directors, both of the Illinois organization and the New York association, they have without exception worked earnestly, loyally, and without compensation for the upbuilding of the institution. No one could have been more fortunate than I in their companionship and in their effort to maintain the highest standard of excellence in the service.

In speaking of my associates in the work of the Associated Press, I find it impossible to do simple justice. Where everyone, associate officers, directors, and co-workers have so loyally worked to a common end, and where all have been so kind, so considerate, discrimination is impossible. It would take not one chapter, nor one volume, but several to give expression to the sense of gratitude I feel. Our relation has been one of undisturbed but growing affection throughout.

It is this New York corporation which for the last twenty-one years has been known as the Associated Press. As its name indicates, it is an organization of newspapers for the purpose of gathering news on joint account. It is purely mutual in its character, and in this respect is unique. The other news-supplying agencies of the world are proprietary concerns. It issues no stock, makes no profit, and declares no dividends. It does not sell any news to any one. It is a clearing-house for the interchange of news among its members only.

Each of the newspapers whose proprietors are members of the Association is obliged to give the representative of the Associated Press free access to its news as soon as received. Many times a day the Associated Press man calls at every newspaper office in the large cities and is given the latest local news. If it is sufficiently important, he instantly puts it upon the leased wires, and in a few seconds it is in the hands of hundreds of telegraph editors throughout the country.

For the purpose of administration the country is divided into four grand divisions, each controlled by a superintendent acting under the direction of the general manager. The Association leases over sixty thousand miles of telegraph wire, and expends over fifteen thousand dollars a day in its work. These leased wires, which are worked by its own operators, stretch from Halifax, by way of Boston, New York, Philadelphia, Baltimore, Washington, Pittsburg, Cleveland, Detroit, Chicago, St. Louis, Kansas City, Denver, and Salt Lake City, to San Francisco, San Diego, and Seattle; they radiate from New York through Albany, Syracuse, and Rochester to Buffalo; from Washington through the leading Southern cities to Atlanta; from Chicago south, by way of Indianapolis, Cincinnati, and Louisville, to Nashville, Atlanta, and New Orleans, as well as to Memphis, San Antonio, and the City of Mexico; and from Chicago north, by way of Milwaukee, to St. Paul and Duluth. They also extend from Philadelphia through the interior of Pennsylvania, and touch, by an extension from Kansas City, the interior cities of Nebraska and Iowa on the north, and Kansas and Oklahoma on the south. Thus every city of consequence is reached by the wire system of the Associated Press.

Three of these leased wires are operated between New York and Chicago at night and two by day. The volume of Associated Press report thus served daily to a morning newspaper in Philadelphia or Baltimore, through which cities the three night wires are extended, exceeds sixty thousand words, or forty ordinary columns. The telegraph operators are men of exceptional skill, and receive higher salaries than are paid by the telegraph or railway companies. To expedite their work, they use automatic sending-machines, which greatly exceed hand transmission in speed, and employ a system of abbreviations which can be sent with surprising rapidity. The receiving operators take the letters by sound and write them upon a typewriter, and since no one is able to manipulate a Morse key as swiftly as he can operate a typewriter, there is a constant effort to hasten the sending in order to keep pace with the ability of the receiver. The following example will illustrate the system of abbreviation. A message is sent thus:

    t scetus tdy dodd 5 pw f potus dz n xtd to t
    pips, ogt all pst cgsl xgn q sj is uxl.

And it is rendered thus by the receiving operator:

The Supreme Court of the United States to-day decided that the power of the President of the United States does not extend to the Philippines, on the ground that all past Congressional legislation on the subject is unconstitutional.

In the larger cities, where many copies of the messages are required, a sheet which has been immersed in wax is used in the typewriter. When written upon it forms a stencil, which is placed upon a rotary cyclograph operated by an electric motor, and as many as three hundred copies of the message may be reproduced in a minute. One of these is thrust into an envelope bearing the printed address of a newspaper and shot through a pneumatic tube to the desk of the waiting telegraph editor in the newspaper office. Even this almost instantaneous method of delivery is too slow, however, for news of a sensational character. A bulletin wire connects the Associated Press office with every evening newspaper in New York, and the bulletins are flashed over it by operators of the highest skill, in emergencies. When the result of a great race arrives, the receiving operator shouts the news through a megaphone, and every sending operator in the room flashes it over his circuit.

A storm is a serious thing, and there is hardly a day in the year which is free from a storm somewhere in the vast territory covered by these leased wires. The expedients then resorted to are often interesting. During the great blizzard of 1888, in which Senator Roscoe Conkling lost his life, all communication was cut off between New York and Boston, and messages were sent from New York by cable to London, thence back to Canso on the Nova Scotian coast, and from Canso to Boston. In 1902 every wire between Boston and Philadelphia went down, and then special messages were sent by train with the Associated Press telegrams. In the winter of 1905 the wires between New York and Utica were swept away along the Hudson River. Then messages were transmitted by way of Baltimore to Chicago, and back to Utica by way of Buffalo.

To meet the expense, each member is assessed a sum which is paid weekly in advance. In making up these assessments, an equitable system is followed, which provides that the heaviest tax shall fall upon the larger papers.

Annually the members gather in general convention in New York and elect a board of directors of fifteen members. By common consent, the members of this board are chosen from different parts of the country, so that each important division is represented. They are trained newspapermen who bring to the discharge of their duties an intimate knowledge of the business and a high sense of responsibility. The Board of Directors in turn elects a president, two vice-presidents, a secretary and general manager, an assistant secretary and assistant general manager, and a treasurer, and designate from their own number seven members to serve as an executive committee.

Wireless Telegraphy

Our first use of wireless transmission was in the case of the international yacht races off Sandy Hook. Stations were erected on Long Island and the coast of New Jersey, and a fast-going yacht, equipped with Marconi apparatus, followed the races. A running story, transmitted through the air to the coast, was instantly relayed by land wires to the main office of the Associated Press in New York, and thence distributed over the country. Such a report of a race cost over $25,000.

As the years have gone on this process has been so developed that during the World War and the succeeding Peace Conference we were able to transmit thousands of words daily for both morning and evening services. The method was not always reliable because of interference, but steadily improved and is destined to become of great value. It is now quite easy to send a message from the Eiffel Tower in Paris to a station in the United States. While in London, sitting talking with William Marconi in his office, we called up by telephone the master of his yacht, which was standing at sea, off the port of

Santander, Spain, several hundred miles distant, and talked with him with perfect freedom.

The Assassination of President McKinley

On the afternoon of September 6, 1901, worn out by a long period of exacting labour, I set out for Philadelphia, with the purpose of spending a few days at Atlantic City. When I reached the Broad Street station in the Quaker city I was startled by a number of policemen crying my name. I stepped up to one, who pointed to a boy with an urgent message for me. President McKinley had been shot at Buffalo, and my presence was required at our Philadelphia office at once. A message had been sent to me at Trenton, but my train had left the station precisely two minutes before the message arrived. Handing my baggage to a hotel porter, I jumped into a cab and dashed away to our office. I remained there until dawn of the following morning.

The opening pages of the story of the assassination were badly written, and I ordered a substitute prepared. An inexperienced reporter had stood beside President McKinley in the Music Hall at Buffalo when Czolgoz fired the fatal shot. He seized a neighbouring telephone and notified our Buffalo correspondent, and then pulled out the wires, in order to render the telephone a wreck, so that it was a full half hour before any additional details could be secured.

I ordered men and expert telegraph operators from Washington, Albany, New York, and Boston to hurry to Buffalo by the fastest trains. All that night the Buffalo office was pouring forth a hastily written but faithful and complete account of the tragedy, and by daybreak a relief force was on the ground. Day by day, through the long vigil while the President's life hung in the balance, each incident was truthfully and graphically reported. In the closing hours of the great tragedy false reports of the President's death were circulated for the purpose of influencing the stock market, and, to counteract them, Secretary Cortelyou wrote frequent signed statements, giving the facts to the Associated Press.

Prince Henry's Visit

In February, 1902, Prince Henry of Prussia arrived at New York, and on the evening of Washington's Birthday gave a small dinner on the *Hohenzollern*, the Kaiser's yacht. I was invited. The acquaintance thus begun grew to some degree of intimacy, not alone with him but with General von Plessen and Admiral von Tirpitz, who accompanied him. During the evening the Prince took me for a stroll over the boat and pointed out his brother's famous cartoon, "The Yellow Peril." Something, I do not know what, justified a compliment upon his English. He spoke with no trace of German accent. "Oh," he laughed, "everyone knows that I like the English language better than the German."

Prince Henry

A few days later a great newspaper dinner was given the Prince at the Waldorf Hotel. It was under the auspices of the New York *Staats Zeitung*. Whitelaw Reid presided. Someone moved that I send a message of greeting to the German Emperor. To my telegram I received the reply reproduced on page 242.

The Prince commissioned me to forward his cable messages to Europe. I received two daily during his journey over the country. I am betraying no confidence in saying that those to his Imperial brother were in German and exceedingly formal, while those to his wife, Princess Irene, were in English, most informal and affectionate.

The Martinique Disaster

On the night of May 2, 1902, a brief telegram from St. Thomas, Danish West Indies, reported that Mont Pelée, the volcano on the island of Martinique, was in eruption, and that the town of St. Pierre was enveloped in a fog and covered with ashes an inch deep. Cable communication was cut off. The following morning I set about securing the facts. We had two correspondents on the island, one at St. Pierre and the other at

Fort-de-France, nine miles away; but clearly neither of these could be reached.

Fortunately, investigation disclosed that an old friend, a talented newspaperman, was the United States consul at

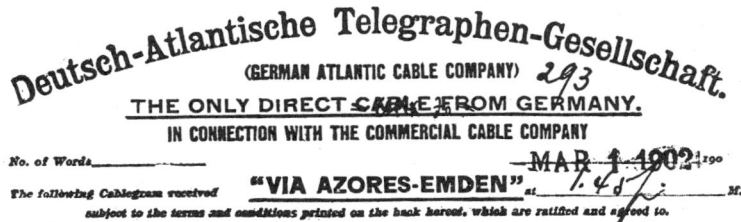

Facsimile of Kaiser's Cable

Guadeloupe, an island only twelve hours distant. I instantly appealed to the State Department at Washington to give him a leave of absence, and, when this was granted, I cabled him to charter a boat and go to St. Pierre at once, and secure and transmit an adequate report. The Associated Press men at St. Vincent, St. Thomas, Porto Rico, Barbados, Trinidad, and St. Lucia were instructed to hurry forward any information that might reach them, and to endeavour to get to Martinique by any available means. St. Thomas alone was able to respond with a short telegram, three days later, announcing the destruction of the Martinique sugar factories, which were only two miles distant from St. Pierre. The despatch also reported the loss of one hundred and fifty lives, and the existence of a panic at St. Pierre because of the condition of the volcano, which was now in full eruption and threatening everything on the island. Mr. Ayme, the consul at Guadeloupe, found difficulty in chartering a boat, but finally succeeded, and, after a thrilling and dangerous night run through a thick cloud of falling ashes and cinders, arrived before the ill-fated city. The appalling character of the catastrophe was then disclosed. Thirty thousand people, the population of the town, had been buried under a mass of hot ashes; one single human being had escaped. It was enough to make the stoutest heart grow faint.

But Ayme was a trained reporter, inured by long experience to trying scenes; and he set to work promptly to meet the responsibility which had been laid upon him. Our St. Pierre man had gone to his death on the common pyre, but Mr. Ivanes, the Associated Press correspondent at Fort-de-France, survived. With him Mr. Ayme joined effort, and, with great courage and at serious risk, they went over the blazing field and gathered the gruesome details of the disaster. Then Mr. Ayme wrote his story, returned to the cable-station at Guadeloupe, and sent it. It was a splendid piece of work, worthy of the younger Pliny, whose story of a like calamity at Pompeii has come down to us through two thousand years. It filled a page of the American newspapers on the morning of May 11th, and was telegraphed to Europe. It was the first adequate account given to the world.

Mr. Ayme returned to Martinique and spent three weeks in further investigation, leaving his post of duty only when the last shred of information had been obtained and transmitted. As a result of his terrible experience, his health was impaired, and, although he was given a prolonged leave of absence, he never recovered. It cost the Associated Press over $30,000 to report this event.

Extension of the Foreign Service of the Associated Press

Students of American history long ago observed that although we had established our political independence by the wars of 1776 and 1812, our literary and social dependence upon

England had never been fully broken. Our cousins overseas, in the persons of such recognized censors as Gifford of the *Quarterly Review*, had sneered at our novelists; Tom Moore had condemned our democratic institutions; and Charles Dickens had accused us of bad manners. We, on the other hand, had not been free from blame. We had taught our children a history of England which related little more of her than the fact that she had fought us in two wars, and we made no account of her splendid record in the development of the world's best civilization. All of these things made for unfriendly relations. And, all the while, we suffered London to dictate our opinion respecting every other nation. From its beginning the Associated Press had only one foreign agency, and that was located in the British metropolis. It was from a British news agency or through the English despatches that we derived all our European news. True, there were interesting letters from the continental capitals, but long before their arrival or publication the story of any important event had been told from London and had made its impress upon the American mind—an impress which it was not easy to correct. The fact that the British views were presented in the English language obviously made them easier of access and gave them wider currency in this country. Thus British opinion, in large measure, became our opinion.

With the Spanish War of 1898 our vision was suddenly widened. Then the ambassadors from the European continental nations at Washington began to urge that the time had come for the United States to look at their peoples through American eyes. M. Jules Cambon, the French ambassador, was particularly perturbed because all of the news respecting France came through London and took on a British *nuance*. It did not follow that such reports were inaccurate, but they were written to supply what the English people were presumed to want, and the London point of view, as Lowell said, is:

"Whut's good's all English; all thet isn't, ain't."

There was evidence of a strong desire on the part of European powers for pleasant relations with the United States; they were very anxious that the Associated Press should name its own competent correspondents, who should reside in the different continental capitals and should study each country as Americans. An unkind phrase respecting the United States in an altogether inconsequential German paper, when printed in the Associated Press despatches in this country, was likely to cause great friction. Although the character of the paper was unknown, it was assumed to voice German sentiment because it was a German paper. This led to a distinct protest on the part of our German-American newspapers against the character of that service, and an urgent demand that we establish a bureau at Berlin.

I explained to M. Cambon the reasons for the existing method. It had been our experience that if an Associated Press correspondent in any of the smaller cities of France should file a despatch for the Associated Press, it would be hung on a hook by a stupid clerk in the Government telegraph office. They would then send all the Government messages they had, and all the death messages, and all the commercial messages, and then they would take the Associated Press message from the hook and send it forward, but on its arrival in Paris it would suffer a like delay. The consequence was that it took us from six to seven hours to get a despatch through. On the other hand, we had found that we could obtain this news in Paris, send it by long-distance telephone to London, and there put it on the cable and forward it much more rapidly. To send a message from New York to Rome and secure a reply usually required twenty-four hours. I suggested that if the French Government could see its way clear to expedite our service, and if it would throw open all departments of the Government and give us the news, I should be very glad to establish a bureau in Paris and take all our news respecting France from Paris direct.

M. Cambon asked me to go abroad and take the matter up with his government, and after some delay and some discussion of the subject, I agreed to do so. I was able to reach the business in the autumn of 1902. The only preparation made was that Ambassador Cambon reported to the French Foreign

Office on the desirability of some change, and explained to them my wishes.

On my arrival in Paris I called on M. Delcassé, the Minister of Foreign Affairs. He received me cordially, was fully advised of the situation, and evinced much interest. He said that while it was a rather serious business, and one which he must take up with his confrères, particularly the Minister of Telegraphs, he sincerely favoured my views. He invited me to breakfast in the palace of the Ministry of Foreign Affairs. There I met two or three of the other ministers. I told them that our people must be absolutely free, that there must be no attempt to influence them. While, in order to be useful, the representative of the Associated Press accredited to any capital must be on friendly terms with the government at that capital, he must not be a servile agent of that government; we could not deny ourselves the right of free statement, and anything we might do must be done with the distinct understanding that the Government would not influence the character of the service as to its impartiality.

I found that there was likely to be a good deal of delay, and, after laying the matter before the French minister and telling him what I desired, and receiving an expression of his purpose to work it out as best he could, I left him.

My interview with M. Delcassé was in his private room in the palace set apart for the Department of Foreign Affairs. He called my attention to an old mahogany table at his side, which, he said, had served three times to affect the fate of the American Republic. On it was signed the convention which Benjamin Franklin and Silas Deane made with the French Government to secure funds for the United States in its struggling days. On it were also signed the Treaty of Peace following the War of 1812, and the Treaty of Peace with Spain in 1898.

I returned to New York, and a month later M. Delcassé presented his plan. The French officials would give the representative of the Associated Press all proper information. They would answer any questions that might be of interest to this country, and they would do all in their power to expedite the service. They issued three forms of telegraph blanks: one bearing across its face, in red ink, the words "Associated Press"; the second form, the words "Associated Press, *très pressé*"; and the third form, the words "Associated Press, *urgent.*" These they issued to us, to be used at our discretion and subject to a general order of the French Government, sent to all telegraph employees throughout France, which provided that when the first form was deposited in any French telegraph office, the operator should send forward all Government messages and then the Associated Press message should be transmitted immediately thereafter; if the second form, "Associated Press, *très pressé*," was used, the despatch should follow the Government message then on the wire and precede any other Government message; and if an "Associated Press, *urgent*" message should be presented, the operator should immediately stop the outgoing Government message and forward the press despatch immediately. This arrangement was put into force. After that our despatches from France, long and short, averaged about twenty-one minutes. We established an adequate bureau in Paris, and employed a large number of subordinate correspondents throughout the country, in some cases Frenchmen and in others Americans, and our service proved highly satisfactory. It was no more expensive, the rate from Paris direct being precisely the rate from London direct, so that we saved the transmission from Paris to London for which we had formerly paid. The office expenses were increased somewhat, but, in compensation, we reduced the office force in London.

I had suggested that Paris, and not London, was the natural point of concentration for our despatches from the Latin nations, and M. Delcassé, having that in mind, invited me to confer with the Italian and Spanish governments. I therefore went abroad again. The French Foreign Office was pleased with the experience they had had. They issued a formal letter of instructions to M. Barrére, French ambassador at the Quirinal, to take the matter up with the Italian Government, with a view to inducing that government to expedite our service from Italy to the French border, where the messages would be forwarded by the French administration and rushed on to New York. I went to Rome and, after paying calls on the American ambassador, saw M. Barrére, who had received his instructions, and who entered upon the work enthusiastically. He desired to secure the concession distinctly on behalf of the French Government; while he was glad to receive the coöperation of the American ambassador, he wished to make it his own special work. M. Barrére spoke English perfectly.

Audience of the Italian King

The American ambassador, Mr. Meyer, gave a luncheon in my honour, at which were present Signor Prinetti, the Italian Minister of Foreign Affairs, and M. Barrére. The subject was talked over in detail with Signor Prinetti and I was then commanded to an audience with the King. Going to the Quirinal, I entered a small anteroom at noon, where two aides were in waiting. His Majesty received me in an adjoining room. I found him dressed in the costume of an officer of the Italian army—dark-blue blouse and light-blue trousers with black stripes. He greeted me cordially, and asked me to be seated. He sat on a sofa, while I was given a chair, and we entered into a lively conversation. He said he knew the purpose of my visit, having been informed of it through Prinetti. He was glad that we were disposed to take up the matter of a service from Rome direct, assured me that he would do everything that could be done, and thought there would be no difficulty in meeting our wishes; I could rest assured of his loyal effort in the matter, and that it would be pursued without delay.

We talked at some length about Marconi, in whose work he displayed a deep interest, and of the relations between Italy and the United States. I suggested the difficult position in which an Associated Press representative would find himself in Rome because of the contest between the Vatican and the Quirinal. I found, however, that while officially affairs were strained, personal relations were not unkindly. Leo XIII was Pope. The King spoke most kindly of the Holy Father, and while, of course, they never met, there was no bitterness manifested on either side. I told him that ordinarily it would be necessary for me to appoint two representatives, one for the Vatican and one for the Quirinal, but that I had a man in mind whom I thought *persona grata* to both sides. I had talked of this man with Prinetti, who had expressed the highest confidence in him. The King said he thought it would be quite unnecessary to appoint two representatives if the Vatican were disposed to go half way; with one man there would be less danger of friction.

The King expressed his high appreciation of the work of the Association, and called attention to the fact that a number of his own ministers were newspapermen, and that his American ambassador at that time, Signor Mayor des Planches, was an old-time journalist in whom he had great confidence. He said, in speaking of the relations between the United States and Italy, that he trusted that they would always be cordial. The Italians felt that, through Columbus, they had given America to the world, and that they had a peculiar interest, therefore, in the United States. He also said that while Italy was spoken of as a kingdom, it was in fact a republic in disguise, having the same parliamentary freedom that existed in England and the United States. He said he was greatly pleased because a large number of the emigrants who went to the United States perfected themselves by their sojourn there, learned American methods, and then came back to Italy and applied these methods in their home life. He said that the percentage of Italians who emigrated to the United States and remained there was much smaller than was generally supposed. He added that it was the practice of many emigrants to go to the United States for work during the summer season, and then return to Italy and spend their surplus earnings in acquiring lands and bettering their condition. He expressed the hope that Italian subjects would be found to be good citizens of the United States. They were law-abiding and economical.

William H. Taft and Archbishop Ireland of St. Paul were housed at the Hotel Quirinal where I put up and we spent many delightful evenings together. Mr. Taft and I wandered about through the ruins of the Eternal City and lived over our studies of Roman history. Out of it all an abiding affectionate regard has grown year by year.

Audience of Pope Leo XIII

I also had audience of the Pope. It, too, was held at noon. I drove to the Vatican, and was received by a secretary. At every turn of the stairway were members of the Swiss Guard in their brilliant uniform. On my arrival at the residence floor a member of the Noble Guard greeted me and received my wraps. I was then taken through a long series of rooms until I arrived at the throne-room. There I met a French cardinal, who greeted me, and then I entered the anteroom of the papal reception-hall. A door was opened, and I was admitted to the presence of the Holy Father. The room was perhaps twenty feet by thirty. At one end, on a slightly raised dais, sat the Pope. The surroundings formed a striking picture. The venerable prelate was dressed in the cream-white garb of his office. His face was the colour of parchment, and not different from the tone of his vestments. A "dim, religious light" came in from the high window. On each side of him down the hall were ranged seats at a lower level.

As I entered, I bowed with formality, and in a faint voice I heard him call my name. He reached out his hand and asked me to approach. Grasping my hand, he requested me to sit at his side, though on a lower level. There was no one else in the room. He took my right hand in his and covered it with his left, and during the hour that I talked with him, he held it thus in an affectionate, parental way.

I said that I was afraid he could not comprehend all I had to say in bad French. To which he replied, "I am an Italian and speak French with an Italian accent, and if we speak very slowly we shall be able to understand each other."

He was most anxious that the United States should accredit an ambassador to his court. "I am told," he said, "that there are political difficulties about it, but I cannot see why there should be. Germany, which is a Protestant nation, sends an ambassador to my court as well as one to the Quirinal.

Russia, which is heretical and believes its own emperor the vicegerent of God, also sends one. Why cannot the United States? I should be very happy if I could close my long career by establishing relations with this young republic through their sending an ambassador to my court." Three or four times he referred to the subject with great earnestness. It seemed very near to his heart.

The Pope at the time had shown wonderful capacity in dealing with the Philippine question. He had been very prompt in his decisions, and I took the liberty of saying to him that he was almost an American in the energetic way in which he had dealt with the subject. He laughed and replied: "Yes, yes; but, after all, what is time to the Church? What is yesterday, or to-day, or to-morrow? The Church is eternal." Something was said about the Quirinal. I cannot tell what led to it, but I shall never forget the dramatic incident. He was leaning over his chair. "Yes, yes," he said, faintly; "I am nearly ninety-four years old. I am a prisoner, but I am a sovereign."

You cannot leave the presence of royalty until dismissed; you must receive your congé. As he was holding my hand and talking on in a kindly, gentle way, I saw no prospect of a dismissal. Finally I ventured to say, "I am afraid I am fatiguing you." He turned and said, "You will come and see me again?" "Unfortunately, your Holiness," I replied, "I must start for Paris at ten minutes to three to-day." "Yes, yes," he said; "I know you go to Paris to-day; that was the reason I fixed the audience at twelve o'clock. But you will come again? Come any time within ten years and I shall be glad to see you."

I called on Cardinal Rampolla, and had a long talk as to our representative, and I named the gentleman whom I had in mind. He said he had a very great regard for him, and that, while he thought his sympathies were with the Quirinal, he still thought he would be just in all questions pertaining to Roman news. I appointed the gentleman, Mr. Salvatore Cortesi, and during a quarter of a century's service he has proved very acceptable to both sides.

At a dinner Signor Prinetti had said that he had had a conference with his colleagues, and that he would be able to meet our wishes. Then he turned to me and said: "I have something which may interest you. Some time ago the Italian Government issued, in twenty-five or thirty parts, facsimiles of all the known reports and letters of Christopher Columbus—every known document bearing his handwriting and signature—and sent them to the royal libraries throughout Europe. I think we have one copy left, and I shall be very glad if you will permit me to present this one to you." I expressed my pleasure and gratitude.

Three or four days after this dinner I went to the hunt outside of Rome. On my return I learned that Prinetti had, while in audience of the King, suffered a stroke of apoplexy. I left my card at Signora Prinetti's and wrote a letter of condolence to his chief assistant. I received a reply expressing Signora Prinetti's appreciation and adding, "I think you will be interested to learn that the last official act of Signor Prinetti, before he was stricken, was to sign an order to deliver the copy of the Columbus books to our consul general in New York, to be forwarded to you."

Next day my business with the Italian Government was arranged, and after that our despatches came from Italy in less than half an hour. When the Pope died we received the bulletin announcing the fact from the Vatican, two miles distant from our office in Rome, in nine minutes, and retransmitted it to Paris, Berlin, and London, giving them the first news.

Dinner with the Kaiser

I went to Berlin, where I was "commanded" to an *Ordensfest*, and to dine with the Kaiser. It occurred on a Sunday. The *Ordensfest* was an annual reception given by the Imperial family to all persons who had been decorated during the preceding year. The most distinguished men of Germany were present to the number of several hundred. At noon, in the chapel of the Schloss in Berlin, all those entitled to admission assembled. I drove to the Schloss, presented my card, and mounted the stairs to the chapel. At the chapel door I was escorted by a court marshal to a seat, where I watched the company gather. There were generals and admirals and many distinguished men. Facing the pulpit was a space reserved for the Imperial family, three tiers of seats deep. After I had been sitting for some time Baron von Richthofen, of the Foreign Office, came up and said, "This is not the seat for you; you are misplaced. A seat has been reserved for you." Then he led me to a seat immediately behind the Imperial family.

When the chapel was filled the master of ceremonies, with his mace in hand, rapped, and the Imperial party entered. Everyone rose as the Emperor and the Empress appeared and passed to the seats reserved for them. Four pages carried the Empress's train. Prince Henry and Princess Irene, his wife; Prince Leopold and Princess Leopold; and Prince Eitel, the Emperor's second son, followed. The Emperor sat at the extreme end of a row, with the Empress at his side, and next to Prince Henry, Prince Leopold, and their wives. Behind them were the younger members of the Imperial family and the court attendants.

The form of service of the Lutheran faith began, and at the proper times the Emperor rose first, and all others followed his action. When he sat, everyone else followed. At the close of the service the Imperial party withdrew, and Baron von Muhlberg led me to the great White Hall, where a one-o'clock dinner was served. I was seated directly opposite the Kaiser. There were two long tables, one slightly raised on a platform, and in front of this another, at which I was seated. Herr Sydow, postmaster-general, sat on my right, and Doctor Becker, president of the Reichstag, on my left. There were about twenty at table, including the Imperial family. After those at the lower table had assembled there was a warning of some sort, and we all rose while the Imperial party, with the Emperor leading, entered.

They came in at the end of the hall and marched across and took their appointed places, everybody standing until the Emperor was seated. At the Emperor's left sat the Empress, and at his right, Prince Leopold. Farther along sat Prince Eitel and Prince Henry and Princess Irene. The Crown Prince was not present. The dinner proceeded without incident. When it had ended the Emperor rose and offered the health of his guests, and then with a martial air turned and marched out, the Imperial family following, while we at the lower table remained standing in our places. Then the Hofmarschall, gorgeously arrayed in the gold-braided costume of his office, came up and asked me to follow him. We went through a long series of halls and came to one where there were two doors with soldiers guarding them with crossed bayonets. As we approached, the guards raised their rifles, and we entered. I found myself in the presence of the Imperial family of Germany.

The Emperor stood at the farther side of the room, by a mantel, and standing about were the Empress, Prince Henry, Princess Irene, Prince Eitel, and Prince Leopold. Nobody else was in the room. I was presented to the Kaiser. He greeted me very cordially, and spoke in English of my mission to Berlin, and expressed his pleasure at the prospect that the people of the United States would be able to see Germany through American eyes. He said freely and at some length that he bore our people in affectionate regard, and assured me that he would give the necessary orders to put the Associated Press in a satisfactory position in Germany. Finally, turning to Prince Henry, he said: "Here is a gentleman whom you know." The Prince was standing by his side and greeted me, adding: "I want you to know my wife." He then presented me to Princess Irene. She was cordial, speaking of her English ancestors and the delight she had in meeting one who spoke her mother-tongue. Meanwhile, several hundred people had gathered in the hall outside, awaiting an audience. The Hofmarschall approached and said that the Empress was ready to receive me. She was very gracious and said: "I hope you will enjoy yourself; we want you to know you are welcome." General von Plessen, who had visited the United States with Prince Henry, entered the room and greeted me cordially. As Von Plessen began talking, a young fellow came up—a splendid, stalwart boy—and, clicking his heels together, said: "I am Eitel; and I want to thank you for the courtesies you extended to my Uncle Henry while he was in America. It was very kind of you, and we all appreciated it." I said it was a pleasure for which no American deserved thanks. He was delightfully diffident. "Do you like yachting?" he asked. "Have you seen the *Meteor?*" "Yes," I replied; "she is a fine boat." He answered: "I hope to have a sail in her. I am sorry that my brother, the Crown Prince, is not here. He has gone to Russia. He will be greatly grieved because he is not here. I know you return to Italy. How long will you be in Italy? My brother and I are going to Italy, and if you will do me the honour to call on me there I shall be pleased."

By this time the doors of the great hall opened, and the Emperor and the Empress went out among the waiting people. The Emperor walked up on one side of the hall and the Empress on the other, an improvised avenue being arranged for each. Baron von Richthofen presented me to a number of ambassadors. Prince Henry came up in a most informal way and said: "I know you will forgive me if I am not as attentive to you as I should like to be, because this is the one time in the year when everyone in Germany who has been decorated has the right to command our attention. But," he continued, "I hope you will enjoy yourself. We want to make you welcome. You will meet here many of the most distinguished men in Germany." The Hofmarschall signalled me to the presence of the Empress. Beside her was standing a little old man to whom she presented me. It was Menzel, the artist. He had just painted a picture of Frederick the Great, which he had dedicated to the people of the United States, and I congratulated him on the splendid work. Then I drifted to the other side of the hall as the Kaiser was coming up. He stopped and said: "I think you will find this an interesting ceremony. Every man who has been decorated within the year comes here, and we hold this reception. This man," he added, pointing to one obviously of the peasant class, "is a letter-carrier. He has been decorated. Back there is a locomotive-engine driver. A man may be decorated for courage or for skill. They all come here on this occasion."

The reception lasted until four o'clock, when the Imperial family withdrew.

I met Postmaster-General Sydow. We talked over the French plan for expediting our telegrams. I said I thought a simpler way could be adopted. We finally agreed upon a small red label bearing the word "America." Pasted on a despatch anywhere in Germany, it meant that the despatch must take first place on the wires.

I had now concluded arrangements of a most satisfactory character with the French, Italian, and German governments, and they all went into effect about the 1st of January, 1904.

A year later I was again invited to dinner by the German Emperor, and had an hour alone with him. He said he was greatly pleased with the better understanding which had developed between Germany and the United States, which he was good enough to attribute in large measure to the presentation of a just view of German events and German motives by the Associated Press. He freely declared his desire to cement the friendly relations existing between the two nations, not because of any immediate political consequences, but in the larger interests of the world's peace and progress. He made no secret of his impatience over the hypercritical, not to say censorious or malignant, tone of a number of journals of both countries, and said he believed that only harm could result from their utterances. His manner was wholly unrestrained, cordial, and democratic. He was greatly gratified at the reception accorded to his brother, Prince Henry, but hoped that no citizen of the United States would imagine that the visit of the Prince meant more than a sincere desire to foster good-fellowship between the two peoples.

He had a sense of humour which one could not fail to enjoy. He seemed like a boy who loved to "talk big," to rattle his sword and to swagger, but who, on the other hand, could "scuttle away" pretty rapidly when there was danger of real trouble. He boasted alike of having maintained the peace of Europe and of what he was to do in *Weltpolitik*.

We discussed the obvious friction between England and Germany. "Do you know," he said, "the first note of antagonism between Germany and England came from the English side? England's policy toward the continental powers has always been that of dividing and conquering. And they have always attached a moral side to every contest. In the days of Bonaparte he was, in their view, a very wicked man; although he was doing no more nor less than their own generals had done for centuries. After Waterloo, Alexander of Russia became the leading figure. Germany, Austria, Italy, and France, were all negligible because they were wrecked. Thereafter Russia, as the dominant power on the Continent of Europe, was the object of British hatred and continued so for years until, in the Crimean War of 1856, it was defeated. It was strange enough that a Christian nation like England should consistently support Turkey against Russia, but it did. When, in 1870, the German Empire became a strong nation, the first note of discord, as I have said, came from England. A book called the 'Battle of Dorking,' discussing a problematic invasion of England by Germany, was published and created a great sensation. It was the popular book of the day."

The Kaiser told me that his first two acts after ascending the throne were to stop duelling in the German army, and to insist upon greater comfort for the coal miners. He was amazed to find these acts made the subject of ridicule by the British newspapers.

"The trouble with England is 'mig'," said he. His eyes twinkled as I replied that I did not understand him. "It is 'mig'," he repeated. "Well," said I, "I know I am stupid, but I don't follow you." "It is 'mig,'" he said with increased emphasis. "M-I-G—'Made in Germany'—one very Solingen razor sold in the Strand of London! That is what hurts England! It is our competition!" And then he branched off into a discussion of the dignity of labour in Germany, as compared with England.

"The English technical schools are all gone. She has made too much money. She is drawing interest on her loans from almost every country, and is now happy in playing golf and cricket. In Germany, on the other hand, everyone works—even the agent of the great German electrical works in Tokio is the son of a German nobleman."

We talked of Russia and the Czar.

"Poor chap," he said, speaking of Nicholas. "I think he is likely to lose his throne. He takes too much counsel of the women of his household. Nick lives in daily terror of assassination. I invited him here to visit me and he accepted. I wanted him to come to Berlin or to Hamburg. He picked out Wiesbaden but he would not go there during the season. I sent Von Grumme, my personal aid, to see what could be done to make Nicholas's visit agreeable, and he reported that the question of personal security was uppermost in the Czar's mind. So, when we went to Wiesbaden, I drove all the inhabitants off the street, out of the doorways and out of the windows, off the roofs and out of the side streets, and lined the street through which we drove with troops. Poor little Wiesbaden! I would have ridden down the street on horseback, and every man, woman, and child would have greeted me cordially! But Nicholas and I rode down as if we were going to a funeral! And then, on his return to St. Petersburg, he wrote me a letter acknowledging my hospitality and closed it with the phrase that he 'was particularly pleased with the disposition of the troops'."

The Death of Pope Leo XIII

The illness and death of Pope Leo XIII in July, 1903, constituted an event which called for news-gathering ability of a high order. Preparation had been made long in advance. Conferences were held with the Italian officials and with the authorities at the Vatican, all looking to the establishment of relatious of such intimacy as to guarantee us the news. We had been notified by the Italian Minister of Telegraphs that, because of the strained relations existing between his government and the Papal Court, he should forbid the transmission of any telegrams announcing the Pope's death for two hours after the fatal moment, in order that Cardinal Rampolla might first notify the papal representatives in foreign countries. This was done as a gracious act of courtesy to the Church.

To meet the emergency, we arranged a code message to be sent by all cable-lines, which should be addressed, not to the

Associated Press, but to the general manager in person, and should read: "Number of missing bond——. (Signed) Montefiore." This bore on its face no reference to the death of the Pontiff, and would be transmitted. The blank was to be filled with the hour and moment of the Pope's death, reversed. That is, if he died at 2:53, the message would read:

Melstone, New York. Number of missing bond 352. (Signed) Montefiore.

The object of reversing the figures was, of course, to prevent a guess that it was a deception in order to convey the news. If the hour had been properly written, they might have suspected the purport of the message.

When, finally, the Pope died, although his bed was completely surrounded by burning candles, an attendant hurried from the room into an anteroom and called for a candle to pass before the lips of the dying man, to determine whether he still breathed. This was the signal for another attaché, who stepped to the telephone and announced to our correspondent, two miles away, that the Pope was dead. Unfortunately, the hour of his death was four minutes past four, so that whichever way it was written, whether directly or the reverse, it was 404.

Nevertheless, the figures were inserted in the blank in the bulletin which had been prepared, it was filed with the telegraph company, and it came through to New York in exactly nine minutes from the moment of death. It was relayed at Havre, and again at the terminal of the French Cable Company in New York, whence it came to our office on a short wire. The receiving operator there shouted the news to the entire operating-room of the Associated Press, and every man on every key on every circuit out of New York flashed the announcement that the Pope had died at four minutes past four; so that the fact was known in San Francisco within eleven minutes after its actual occurrence.

The Reuter, Havas, and Wolff agents located in our office in New York retransmitted the announcement to London, Paris, and Berlin, giving those cities their first news of the event. A comparison of the report of the London *Times* with that of any morning paper in the United States on the day following the death of the Pope would show that, both as to quantity and quality, our report was vastly superior. The London *Times* had a column and a half; the New York *Times* had a page of the graphic story of the scenes in and about the Vatican. The New York *Times* story was ours. This was so notable an event that it occasioned comment throughout the world.

During the illness of the Pope I ordered a number of the best men from our London, Paris, and Vienna offices to Rome to assist our resident men. The advantage of such an arrangement was that the London men were in close touch with Church dignitaries of England, while our representatives from France and Vienna had their immediate circle of acquaintances among the Church dignitaries of those countries. The result was that Mr. Cortesi, the chief of our Rome office, was perfectly familiar with the local surroundings and was on intimate terms with Doctors Lapponi and Mazzoni of the Vatican as well as with the other resident officials of the Church, and was always able to command attention from them. Besides, he had not only the advantage of their acquaintance. We were enabled day by day to present an extraordinary picture of the scenes at the Vatican, and day by day the bulletins upon the condition of the Holy Father were transmitted with amazing rapidity. The death-bed scenes at Buffalo, when President McKinley was lying ill at the Milburn House, were reported with no greater degree of promptness and no greater detail. The funeral scenes were also covered in a remarkably ample way and with astounding rapidity. Then came the conclave for the election of a new pope. It was to be secret, and every effort was made to prevent its proceedings from becoming public. A brick wall was constructed about the hall to prevent any one having access to it. But, to the amazement of everyone, the Associated Press had a daily report of all that happened. One of the members of the Noble Guard was an Associated Press man. Knowing the devotion of the average Italian for the dove, he took with him into the conclave chamber his pet dove, which was a homing pigeon trained to go to our office. But Cardinal Rampolla could not be deceived; he ordered the pigeon killed.

Other plans, however, were more successful. Laundry lists sent out with the soiled linen of a cardinal, and a physician's prescriptions sent to a pharmacy, proved to be code messages which were deciphered in our office. We were enabled not only to give a complete and accurate story of the happenings within the conclave chamber, but we announced the election of the new pope, which occurred about 11 A. M. in Rome, so promptly that, owing to the difference in time, it was printed in the morning papers of San Francisco of that day. We were also enabled to send the announcement back to Europe before it was received from Rome direct, and it was our message that was printed in all the European capitals. The Italian authorities did not interfere with these messages.

The Removal of the Russian Censorship on Foreign News

Satisfactory relations had been arranged between the Associated Press and France, Germany, and Italy, but obviously the place of chief interest was Russia. It had often been suggested that we station correspondents at St. Petersburg, but apparently the time was not ripe. It was the last country in which to try an experiment. Wisdom therefore dictated a delay until it could be determined how the agreement with other continental powers would work out. Moreover, it was important that the St. Petersburg bureau, in case one should be established, should be conducted by a correspondent of singular tact. With this possible course in view, I put in training for the post a gentleman from our Washington office in whom I had great confidence. He was a graphic writer and a man of wide information and rare discretion. He studied French until he was able to speak with reasonable freedom, and devoted himself to the study of Russian history.

The situation at the Russian capital was peculiar. Every conceivable obstacle was put in the way of the foreign journalist who attempted to telegraph news thence to any alien newspaper or agency. The business of news gathering was under ban in the Czar's empire. The doors of the ministers of state were closed; no public official would give audience to a correspondent. Even subordinate government employees did not dare to be seen in conversation with a member of the hated guild, and all telegrams were subject to a rigorous censorship. Count Cassini, the Russian ambassador at Washington, was friendly, and desired me to act. While I still had the matter under consideration, an agent of the Russian Government urged me to go at once to St. Petersburg. I sailed in December, 1903, and by arrangement met the Russian agent in London. To him I explained that we were ready to take our news of Russia direct from St. Petersburg, instead of receiving it through London, but, to do that, four things seemed essential: First, the Russian Government should accord us a press rate that would enable us to send news economically. Second, they should give us such precedence for our despatches as the French, Italian, and German governments had done. Third, they must open the doors of their various departments and give us the news. And, fourth, they must remove the censorship and enable us to send the news. If we should go there at all, we must go free to tell the truth. Obviously we could not tell the truth unless we could learn the truth and be free to send it.

The agent said that, acting under instructions, he would leave London immediately for St. Petersburg, in order to have a week there before my arrival, so as to lay the matter before the ministers in detail. Meanwhile, I went to Paris. At my suggestion, the French Foreign Office wrote to their ambassador at St. Petersburg, instructing him to use his good offices with the Russian Government, the ally of the French Government, in an attempt to secure for the Associated Press the service that was desired. They assured the Russian Government that they believed the best interests of the world and of Russia would be served by granting my request, which they regarded as very reasonable. I went to Berlin, and the German Foreign Office advised the German ambassador at St. Petersburg in the same manner. On my arrival in St. Petersburg, therefore, I had the friendly intercession of the ambassadors of both these governments, and the support of Count Cassini, as well as the influence of our own ambassador, Mr. McCormick.

An audience with Count Lamsdorff, the Russian Minister of Foreign Affairs, was arranged, and Mr. McCormick and I laid the subject before him. He was perfectly familiar with it, as he had received the report of the government agent and had also received favourable advices from Count Cassini. The minister assured me that he would do everything in his power to aid in the movement, because he felt that it was wise; but, unfortunately, the whole question of the censorship and of telegraphic transmission was in the hands of the Minister of the Interior, M. Plehve. Count Lamsdorff said that, the day before our call, he had transmitted their agent's report to Plehve, with an urgent letter advising the Russian Government to meet the wishes of the Associated Press. He told me that I could rely on his friendly offices, and I left him.

The reply of Count Lamsdorff, and later that of M. Plehve, disclosed the anomalous condition of the Russian Government. The ministers of state were independent of one another, each reporting to the Emperor, and frequently they were at odds among themselves.

Ambassador McCormick and I called on Minister Plehve. We found him most agreeable. I studied him with some care. A strong, forceful, but affable gentleman, he impressed me as a man charged with very heavy responsibilities, quite mindful of the fact, and fearful lest any change in existing conditions might be fraught with danger. He said, frankly, that he was not prepared to abolish the censorship. To his mind it was a very imprudent thing to do, but he said he would go as far as he could toward meeting our wishes. As to a press rate, unfortunately that was in the hands of the Minister of Finance, and he had no control of the subject; and as to expediting our despatches, in view of the entirely independent character of each minister, it would be beyond his power to stop a government message, or a message from any member of the Imperial family, in our favour. Beyond that he would give us as great speed as was in his power. He would be very glad, so far as his bureau was concerned, to give such directions as would enable our correspondent to secure all proper information.

As I have said, no newspaperman at that time could expect

to secure admission to any department of the Government. Indeed, a card would not be taken at the door if it were known to be that of a newspaperman. The consequence was that the correspondent would write his despatch and drive two or three miles to the office of the censor. The restrictions put upon foreign correspondents had been so great that they had virtually abandoned Russia; and when I arrived there, with the exception of our men who had preceded me, no foreign correspondent was sending daily telegrams from St. Petersburg. The thing was retroactive. Because the government would not permit despatches to go freely, no despatches were going. The censor's duties, therefore, had been so lightened that the government had added to his work the censorship of the drama, and the chances were that when the correspondent called he would have to run around to some theatre to find the censor; and he might be sure that between midnight and eight o'clock in the morning he could never see him, because a censor must sleep some time, and he would not allow anybody to disturb him between those hours, which for the American morning newspapers were the vital hours.

It happened that M. Lamscott, the censor of foreign despatches, was a very reasonable man. But he was a subordinate of a subordinate in the Ministry of the Interior. He was a conscientious, well-meaning person, disposed to do all that he could for us, and he personally was opposed to the censorship; but he could not pass a telegram that would be the subject of criticism by a minister or important subordinate in any department of the government, or by any member of the Imperial family. And since he was liable to be criticized for anything he might do, his department became a bureau of suppression rather than of censorship. He could take no chances. Certain rules had been adopted, and one of them provided that no mention whatever of a member of the Imperial family should appear in a despatch after the censor had passed upon it. If, by any chance, the correspondent succeeded in securing information and writing it in such fashion that it would pass the censorship, he drove two miles to the telegraph bureau and paid cash at commercial rates for his despatch. It then must wait till all government and commercial business had been cleared from the wires.

Under such a rule, it must be obvious that the business of sending despatches from Russia was impracticable. The mere matter of paying cash, which at first sight would not seem a great hardship, meant that, in the event of some great happening requiring a despatch of length, the correspondent must carry with him several hundred roubles. He could not trust a Russian servant with this, but must go in person. There were over two hundred holidays in Russia every year, when the banks were closed and cash was not obtainable. The obstacle presented by that fact, therefore, was a very serious one.

Such were the conditions. After my audience with M. Plehve, the case seemed nearly hopeless, and I was delaying my departure from Russia only until I should receive a definite statement that nothing could be done, when the following Sunday morning the American ambassador called me on the telephone and said that I was to be commanded to an audience with the Emperor. Ambassador McCormick thought it best to keep in touch with him, since I was liable to be summoned at any moment. During the day I received the command to an audience on Monday.

After seeing M. Plehve I had a talk with the censor. M. Lamscott spoke English perfectly. He said that if his opinion were asked respecting the censorship, he would be very glad to say that he disapproved of the whole thing; but he was not at liberty to volunteer his advice. I also, by suggestion of M. Plehve, had a conference with M. Dournovo, his chief subordinate, the Minister of Telegraphs. Dournovo was an ex-sailor, a hale, rough-and-ready type of man. He had spent some time in San Francisco while in command of a Russian vessel, spoke English perfectly, and proved a most progressive spirit. He was ready to do anything that he could, and assured me that by adopting a certain route via Libau he would be able to give our despatches the desired precedence. He said he would also issue orders to the Transsiberian lines, so that we could rest assured that our despatches would not take more than an hour from Port Arthur or Vladivostok to New York.

We were making progress. We had succeeded in securing rapidity of transmission, a satisfactory press rate, and an arrangement to make a charge account, so that it would not be necessary to pay cash. Meanwhile, successful efforts had been making for the appointment of an official in each ministerial department who would always receive our correspondent and aid him in his search for information if it fell within the jurisdiction of his department. General Kuropatkin, who at that time was Minister of War; Admiral Avelan, head of the Navy Department; and M. Pleske, the Minister of Finance, each appointed such a man. Finally, I was "commanded" to an audience of the Emperor.

A private audience of the Emperor of Russia in the Winter

Le Grand Maître des Cérémonies a l'honneur d'informer Son Excellence Mr. Robert McCormick, Ambassadeur des États-Unis d'Amérique, que Mr. Melville E. Stone, aura l'honneur d'être présenté à Sa Majesté l'Empereur le Lundi, 19 Janvier, à 3½ h. après midi, au Palais d'Hiver.

18 Janvier 1904

Arrivée au Palais par le Perron de S. M. l'Impératrice.

"Command" to audience of the Czar

Palace is an honour which must impress one. I was notified upon a slip accompanying the formal card of command what costume I was expected to wear—American evening dress, which, in the court language of Europe, is known as "gala" garb. At half-past three on the afternoon of February 1st I presented myself. A servant removed the ever-present overshoes and overcoat, and a curious functionary in red court livery, with long white stockings and a red tam-o'-shanter cap from which streamed a large white plume, indicated by pantomime that I was to follow him. We ascended a grand staircase and began an interminable march through a labyrinth of wide halls and corridors. A host of attendants in gaudy apparel, scattered along the way, rose as we approached and deferentially saluted. In one wide hall sat a company of guards who clapped silver helmets on their heads, rose, and presented arms as we passed.

I was shown into an anteroom, where the Grand Duke André awaited me. He introduced himself and chatted most agreeably about American affairs, until a door opened and I was ushered into the presence of His Imperial Majesty. The room was evidently a library. It contained well-filled bookshelves, a large work-table, and an American roll-top desk. Without ceremony and in the simplest fashion the Emperor fell to a consideration of the subject of my visit. He was dressed in the fatigue uniform of the Russian navy—braided white jacket and blue trousers. The interview lasted about an hour.

I represented to His Majesty the existing conditions, and told him of the difficulties which we encountered, and the desire on the part of his ambassador at Washington that Americans should see Russia with their own eyes, and that news should not take on an English colour by reason of our receiving it from London. I said that we felt a large sense of responsibility. Every despatch of the Associated Press was read by one half the population of the United States. I added that Russia and the United States were either to grow closer and closer or they were to grow apart, and we were anxious to do whatever we properly might to cement the cordial relations that had existed for a hundred years.

His Majesty replied: "I, too, feel my responsibility. Russia and the United States are young, developing countries, and there is not a point at which they should be at issue. I am most anxious that the cordial relations shall not only continue, but grow."

When assured, in response to an inquiry, that the Emperor desired me to speak frankly, I said: "We come here as friends, and it is my desire that our representatives here shall treat Russia as a friend; but it is the very essence of the proposed plan that we be free to tell the truth. We cannot be the mouthpiece of Russia, we cannot plead her cause, except in so far as telling the truth in a friendly spirit will do it."

"That is all we desire," His Majesty replied, "and all we could ask of you." He requested me to recount the specific things I had in mind.

I told the Emperor that the question of rate and speed of transmission had fortunately been settled by his ministers, and that the two questions I desired to present to him were those of an open door in all the departments, that we might secure the news, and the removal of the censorship.

"It seems to me, Your Majesty," I said, "that the censorship is not only valueless from your own point of view, but works a positive harm. A wall has been built up around the country, and the fact that no correspondent for a foreign paper can live and work here has resulted in a traffic in false Russian news that is most hurtful. To-day there are newspapermen in Vienna, Berlin, and London who make a living by peddling out the news of Russia, and it is usually false. If we were free to tell the truth in Russia, as we are in other countries, no self-respecting newspaper in the world would print a despatch from Vienna respecting the internal affairs of Russia, because the editor would know that, if the thing were true, it would come from Russia direct. All you do now is to drive a correspondent to send his despatches across the German border. I am able to write anything I choose in Russia, and send it by messenger to Wirballen, across the German border, and it will go from there without change. You are powerless to prevent my sending these despatches, and all you do is to anger the correspondent and make him an enemy, and delay his despatches, robbing the Russian telegraph lines of a revenue they should receive. So it occurs to me that the censorship is inefficient; that it is a censorship which does not censor, but annoys."

During the conversation, to illustrate the existing difficulties, I remarked that on the preceding Sunday we had received a cable message from our New York office to the effect that a very sensational despatch had been printed throughout the United States, purporting to come from Moscow, and alleging that, during the progress of certain army manœuvres under the direction of the Grand Duke Sergius [assassinated February 17, 1905], a large body of troops had been ordered to cross a bridge over the Moscow River, and by a blunder, another order had been given at the same time to blow up the bridge, and thus a thousand soldiers had been killed. This despatch came to us on Sunday evening, with the request that we find out whether it was true. There was no way to ascertain. Nobody could get any information from the War Department; nobody would be admitted to ask such a question; and I told the Emperor the chances were that, in the ordinary course of things, this would happen: three or four weeks later the false despatch would be sent back by post from the Russian Legation at Washington, and there would be a request made on the part of the Russian Government that it be denied, because there was not a word of truth in it; but the denial would go out a month or six weeks after the statement, and no newspaper would print it, because interest in the story had died out. Thus nobody would see the denial.

It happened in this case that we knew a man in St. Petersburg who had been in Moscow on the day mentioned, and when he saw the telegram he said at once: "I know all about that story. Two years ago the Grand Duke Sergius, at some manœuvres, did order some troops to cross a bridge, and a section of it was blown up and one man was killed." I said to His Majesty: "In this instance we were able to correct the falsehood; but it is most important that a correction of this sort should follow the falsehood at the earliest moment, while the thing is still warm in the public mind."

We talked of other things: of the negotiations pending at the time with Japan. He said over and over again that there must be no war, that he did not believe there would be one, and that he was going as far as self-respect would permit him in the way of meeting the Japanese in the matter of their differences. And of the internal affairs of Russia he spoke with great frankness. I suggested in a jocular way that there seemed to be some room for improvement in the Russian method of government.

He said in reply, frankly and with unmistakable sincerity: "You say there are some things which might be done better than they are; but you do not know our conditions. The problems presented to us are unlike those of any other government in the world. When I tell you that 126,000,000 of our people are illiterate, and that the great majority have only just emerged from barbarism, while of many even that could not be said, you can understand some of our difficulties. We have found in experience that if we take young men without fortune and put them in universities and graduate them, give them the higher education, but no means of applying their knowledge or of earning a livelihood, they become unhappy, discontented, and revolutionary.

"We consequently have adopted a plan which we think better. Every year we draw as many as possible into the army, not for war, because the world knows well that I desire peace, but for education. We require everyone in the army to learn at least to read and write, to have the rudiments of an education, before he can gain freedom from military duty. If he can attain this in three years, well and good; if not, he is compelled to remain for four or even five years. And it is our experience that when we have given him this elementary education and the discipline of army life we have done a great deal toward making him a good citizen.

"It is my desire to give Russia a constitution, and to create a government upon the British model. I am perfectly familiar with that. My mother, as you know, is an Englishwoman, my tutor was an English clergyman, and English is the language of my home life. There are many obstacles in my way. There is the illiteracy of the Russian people and the fact that the *intelligentsia* are so few. I do not know whether they will let me live to give them a constitution. My grandfather sought to give them one, and on the very day he attempted it he was assassinated."

I was then given my leave by His Majesty, who courteously suggested that he should see me at the court ball which was to take place that evening. Three or four hours later I attended the ball, and he came to me and reopened the conversation in the presence of the American ambassador, and was good enough to say to Mr. McCormick that he had had a very interesting afternoon.

Later in the evening Count Lamsdorff came up and expressed his gratification at the interview I had had with the Emperor. He said that the Emperor had told him of it, and Count Lamsdorff added: "I think it of great value to Russia, and I want to thank you for having told the truth to His Majesty, which he hears all too rarely."

While chatting with the Emperor at the ball I asked how I should transmit the memorandum referred to in the afternoon's interview, and he told me to send it through Baron de Freedericksz, Minister of the Palace.

The next day I prepared the memorandum for transmission, and then it occurred to me that it would be befitting the dignity of the Imperial office if it were neatly printed, and I set out to find a printer who could do it in English. I drove to the Crédit Lyonnais, and called on the manager, whom I knew, and asked him if there was a printing-office in St. Petersburg where English could be printed. He gave me a card to the manager of a very large establishment located in the outskirts of the city.

The manager was a kindly old German who spoke French. I told him what was wanted, and he said he would be delighted to do anything for an American: he had a son, a railway engineer, at Muskegon, Michigan. He said he had no compositors who understood English, but he had the Latin type, and, as the copy was typewritten, his printers could pick it out letter by letter and set it up, and then I could revise the proof and put it in shape. He asked me when it was needed. I replied that I must have it by noon of the following day. He said that would involve night work, but he would be very glad indeed to keep on a couple of printers to set it up.

As I was about to leave he glanced at the manuscript and said with a startled look: "This has not been censored."

"No," I replied, "it has not been censored."

"Then," he said, "it must be censored; there is a fine of five hundred roubles and three months in jail for setting one word that does not bear the censor's stamp. I should not dare, as much as I should like to accommodate you, to put myself in jeopardy. "But," he added, "you will have no trouble with it. It is now six o'clock. I will have the engineer stay and keep the lights burning, and have the two printers go out to dinner, and you can go and have it censored, in the meantime, very much more quickly than I can. Return here by eight o'clock, and we can work on it all night, if necessary."

I drove at once to M. Lamscott, he being the censor who had passed upon our despatches, and presented the case to him. His countenance fell at once.

"I hope you will believe that if it were in my power to help you, I would do so," he said; "but, unfortunately, my function is to censor foreign despatches only, and I have no power to censor job-work. That falls within an entirely different department, and my stamp would not be of any use to you whatever. But I may say to you, as a friend, that it is hopeless. If Minister Plehve, in whose department this falls, sought to have a document like this censored, it would take him a week to have it go through the red tape which would be necessary. And the very thing which makes you think that this should be easy to censor makes it the most difficult thing in the world, because no censor would dare to affix his stamp to a paper which is in the nature of a petition to the sovereign until it had passed step by step through all the gradations of office up to His Majesty himself, and he had signified a willingness to receive it. Then it would have to come back through all the gradations to the censor again; and it would be two or three weeks before you would get the document in shape to print it."

I laughed, and said a petition to remove the censorship required so much censoring that it was actually amusing.

He replied: "The only thing you can do is to write it."

So I took it to the American Embassy, had it engrossed, and transmitted it to the Emperor, and then waited for some word from him.

I received an invitation to the second ball, which the Emperor had assured me would be a much more agreeable function than the first, because, instead of thirty-three hundred people, there would be only six hundred present. This second ball was to occur a week later.

On Wednesday I transmitted the memorandum to His Majesty. On Thursday evening, at a reception, I encountered Minister Plehve. He said he knew of my audience with the Emperor and had seen the memorandum which I had left with him; and while he was desirous of doing everything in his power, I must remember that he was responsibile for the internal order of Russia, and he could not bring himself to believe that a step of this kind was wise. It was almost revolutionary in its character, and he wanted to know whether there could not be something in the nature of a compromise effected.

"All your other requests have been provided for," he said; "the only question that remains is the censorship, and I want to know if you would not be content with an arrangement by which I should appoint a bureau of censors at the central telegraph office and keep them on duty night and day, with instructions to give you the largest possible latitude. I can assure you there would be virtually nothing but a censorship in form so far as you are concerned."

I replied that I was sorry that I could not see my way clear to do the thing he asked. "I am not here, Your Excellency," I added, "to advise you as to your duties. That is a question which you must determine for yourself. Neither am I here to say that I think the suggestion you make an unwise one. I do not know. It may not be wise for you to remove the censorship. That is a question which I am not called on to discuss. I am here at the instance of the Russian Government, because it desired me to come. It desired us to look at Russia through our own eyes. Obviously we cannot do that unless we are absolutely free. Anything less than freedom in the matter would mean that we should be looking at Russia, not through our own eyes, but through your eyes. So, without the slightest feeling in the matter, if you do not see your way clear, I shall take myself out of Russia, and we shall go on as we have done for so many years—taking our Russian news from London."

"Oh, no," said he in a startled tone; "that must not be. I would not have you understand me as saying that your wishes will not be met. I believe His Majesty has given you assurances on the point, and of course it is in his hands, and he will do whatever he thinks best about it."

The Minister then suddenly saw, in another part of the room, a lady to whom he desired to speak, and we parted. Later in the evening he drew close to my side and asked in a whisper if I had heard the news.

"What news?" I asked. It was at a moment when the whole world was waiting breathless for Russia's last reply to Japan.

"The reply to Japan went forward to-night," he replied; "and I thought you might want to know it."

"Indeed," I said; "and when?"

"At seven o'clock."

He then quietly drew away, and I sought out our correspondent and communicated the fact to him. Going to the censor, he had his despatch censored and forwarded it. About an hour later, after twelve o'clock, the French minister said to me, "You know the news?"

I regarded Minister Plehve's information as confidential and asked: "What news?"

"I think you know very well, because Plehve told you," he answered.

"Yes," I said; "the answer has gone to Japan."

"No, not to Japan," he replied; "but to Alexieff, and it will not reach Baron Rosen, the Russian minister at Tokio, until Saturday or Monday."

I was naturally startled, because the despatch which had been sent to New York had reported that the answer had gone to Japan. Twelve o'clock had come and gone, there was no opportunity to secure a censored correction, and an inaccurate despatch was certain to be printed in all the American papers the following morning, and I was apparently powerless to prevent it.

Mr. Kurino, the Japanese minister, was anxious to know the news. I did not feel at liberty to communicate it to him, and he turned away, saying, "Well, I think this is a very unpleasant place for me, and I shall take my departure." So he and his wife left me to make their adieux to the hostess.

I also took my leave and drove at once to the telegraph office. Now, they did not censor private messages. I entered the telegraph bureau and wrote this despatch:

WALTER NEEF, 40 Evelyn Gardens, London:
Howard was slightly in error in his telegram to-night. The document has been telegraphed to the gentleman in charge in the East, and will reach its destination Saturday or Monday.

I signed my name and handed in the message, which was delivered promptly in London to Mr. Neef, the chief of our London office, who at once sent a correction to the United States, and the despatch appeared in proper form in the American papers.

Plehve was, I believe, a sincere man—one who felt that all the repressive measures he had adopted were necessary. He was not a reactionary in the fullest sense. He was a progressive man, but his methods were obviously wrong. He thought that "if the lines were loosed the horses would run away." I did not gain the impression that he was an intriguer or that he was sinister in his methods. He seemed direct and conscientious. He belonged to the number who believed that the greatest good must come to Russia by easy stages but by repressive measures. He did not believe in the press; he did not believe that the best interests of the people were to be served by education; he did believe in the Autocracy, with all that it implied. The impression left on my mind was that he was afraid the censorship would be abolished over his head, and he wanted terms less dangerous from his point of view.

I received a telegram asking me to go to Berlin and dine at the American ambassador's house, the Kaiser to be present. This was to occur on the night of the 11th of February, and through the good offices of our ambassador to Russia (I having said I should remain in St. Petersburg to await His Majesty's pleasure) I asked leave to go to Berlin, and it was granted.

On my return I was in a dilemma. The war with Japan was on. I had given my word to the Emperor that I would await his pleasure, but I was aware that his mind and heart were full of the disasters that had befallen the Russian arms in the East, and that he probably had had no time to give thought to my mission. There was a fair prospect of waiting indefinitely and without result. Before going to Russia I had been warned by a number of friends, in sympathetic tones, that my visit would be a failure; that it was well enough to go to St. Petersburg in order to learn the conditions; that the journey would probably be worth the trouble involved; but that any effort to remove the censorship on foreign despatches would be sheer waste of time.

William T. Stead had gone to Russia a year before on the same mission, and had had the advantage of the personal friendship of Plehve. Stead was known as the most active pro-Russian journalist in the world. He had had a personal audience of the Czar at his country place in Livadia, and had signally failed. I felt, therefore, that these prophecies of evil were likely to be fulfilled, and I determined to leave as soon as I could do so with propriety.

I asked Ambassador McCormick if he would call on Count Lamsdorff and say frankly to him that I knew how occupied the attention of all the officials was, and I thought it perhaps an inopportune time to pursue the matter, and would, therefore, if agreeable, take my leave. Mr. McCormick called at the Foreign Office that afternoon on some official business, and, before leaving, told Count Lamsdorff of my predicament, and asked his advice.

Count Lamsdorff replied in a tone of surprise: "The thing is done."

"I do not follow you," said Ambassador McCormick.

"Mr. Stone left a memorandum of his wishes with His Majesty, did he not?" said Count Lamsdorff. "Well, the Emperor wrote 'Approved' on the corner of the memorandum, and all will be done. There may be a slight delay incident to working out the details, but it will be done."

"Would it not be well," asked Mr. McCormick, "for Mr. Stone to call on Minister Plehve and talk the matter over with him as to the details?"

President Roosevelt

Prince William of Sweden

"There is nothing to say," said Count Lamsdorff; "it is finished. Mr. Stone has no occasion to see Plehve or any one else. It will all be done as speedily as possible."

Mr. McCormick reported this conversation to me, and I determined to depart, at once leaving the matter entirely in the hands of the authorities. I wrote, and despatched by hand, letters thanking Count Lamsdorff and Minister Plehve for their courtesy and for what they had done, and indicating my purpose to leave by the Vienna express on the following Thursday. Count Lamsdorff made a parting call, and Plehve sent his card. I left St. Petersburg on Thursday evening.

On my arrival in Vienna I received the following from Mr. Thompson, chief of our St. Petersburg office:

I know you will be gratified to learn that on my return to the office from the station after bidding you adieu, and before your feet left the soil of St. Petersburg, we were served with notice that the censorship was abolished so far as we were concerned. But Count Lamsdorff feels that it is a mistake, and that we shall be charged with having made a bargain, and any kindly thing we may say of Russia will be misconstrued. He thinks it would be much wiser if the censorship were abolished as to all foreign correspondents and bureaus, and desires your influence to that end.

I wired back at once that I fully agreed with Count Lamsdorff's views, and certainly hoped that it would be abolished as to the correspondents of the English, French, and German press at once; and forty-eight hours after the restriction was removed from the Associated Press, it was removed from everybody.

After my departure from St. Petersburg, not only our correspondents, but all foreign correspondents, were as free to write and send matter from any part of Russia, except in the territory covered by the Russo-Japanese War, as from any other country in the world. We found ourselves able to present a daily picture of life in Russia that was most interesting and edifying, and even in the war district the Russian authorities gave the largest possible latitude to our correspondents. They turned over to us in St. Petersburg, daily, without mutilation, the official reports made to the Emperor and to the War Department, and the world was astonished by the frank character of the despatches coming from Russia. Ninety per cent. of the real news concerning the war came in bulletin first from St. Petersburg, and later in detail from the field; and there was no attempt on the part of the Government to influence the despatches, or even to minimize their disasters, when talking officially to our correspondents, who made daily visits to the War, Navy, Foreign, and Interior offices, and were given the news with as much freedom as in Washington.

Until Port Arthur was invested, we found that we were able to receive despatches with extraordinary speed. On one occasion a despatch sent from New York to Port Arthur requiring a reply occupied for transmission and reply two hours and forty-five minutes; and on the occasion of the birth of the son of the Emperor at Peterhof, twenty-eight miles from St. Petersburg, we received the despatch announcing the fact in exactly forty-three minutes after its occurrence.

The foreign governments were as well pleased as I was with the improved intercommunication. Royal decorations rolled in upon me in rapid fashion. I was made an officer of the Legion of Honour, a commendatore of Italy, and something or other of Russia, Germany, Sweden, Japan, and Belgium.

The Russo-Japanese War

There were numerous occasions, during the progress of the Boer War and of contests in Venezuela, in which brilliant exhibitions of courage and enterprise were presented, but it was in the Russo-Japanese struggle of 1904 that the service reached a very high level of excellence.

Long before the troubles between Russia and Japan had reached a critical stage, I ordered Mr. Egan, then of our New York office, a gentleman of wide experience and rare ability, to Tokio to establish an independent bureau. I went to St. Petersburg, and was there when diplomatic relations with Japan were broken off and the war begun. I engaged a number of Russian correspondents, who set out at once for the Far East.

One of them, Mr. Kravchenko, was received in private audience by the Czar before his departure. I cabled directions to my assistant at New York, and he sent a corps of men to Tokio to act under Mr. Egan's orders.

We were enabled to place correspondents at every point of possible interest, and their telegrams were transmitted much more rapidly and safely than if sent by the long lines through the Indian Ocean and the Red Sea. The great newspapers of London and New York promptly engaged the ablest special correspondents available and sent them to the front. Among these were a number of war reporters of long experience and international fame. It soon became apparent, however, that no special service could successfully compete with the Associated Press alliance. For months the special men were held in a courteous imprisonment at Tokio, while the Associated Press men at the Russian headquarters and at points of vantage in China and Korea were forwarding daily stories of surpassing interest at each step in the contest. In the end, nearly all the special men were ordered home, and the work of reporting the war was left to the press agencies.

A number of our American and English representatives were welcomed at Russian headquarters. Among these were Mr. Middleton, one-time chief of the Associated Press bureau at Paris, who died of disease at Mukden. He was buried with military honours, but, later, at my request, Viceroy Alexieff sent the remains through the lines, and a second burial took place at Chefoo.

Mr. Kravchenko waited three nights and three days on the bluffs about Port Arthur for the sea fight which Admiral Makaroff was certain to have with Admiral Togo. He was rewarded by a sight of the tragic destruction of the *Petropavlovsk*, which he described in a telegram so graphic that, by common consent, it was held to be the best specimen of war reporting during the conflict.

Mr. Popoff, a young Russian known by his *nom de guerre* of "Kiriloff," was wounded at the battle of Liao-yang. He had completed on the battle-field a well-written pen-picture of the Japanese attack upon Stakelberg's corps when a shot pierced his lung. He had ridden to a battery on the firing line and found that, out of sixty gunners, forty were killed or wounded. The officers had eaten nothing for twenty-four hours, and Popoff shared with them such provisions as he had. "Prudence urged me to leave the spot, but I was fascinated," he wrote. And here the message ended. A Russian officer, who sent the telegram forward, added: "Kiriloff was shot through the right lung while standing by our battery, and fell back, suffering intense agony. He insisted upon being placed on a horse, so that he could get to Liao-yang and file his despatch. It took him five hours and a half to cover the five miles to the telegraph station. When he reached there he was so exhausted and weak from loss of blood that we got him into the hospital, although against his protest. He asked me to complete his message for him. I am a soldier, and no writer; but I will say that after the awful fight to-day we were still holding our position. Japanese bodies bestrew all the heights. Their losses must have run into tens of thousands. We have lost five thousand thus far."

Mr. Hagerty, from the Chicago office of the Associated Press, served at Chefoo. He was at the nearest cable station to Port Arthur. He organized a corps of Chinese junkmen, who ran the blockade and reported to him. There was sharp competition with a number of special correspondents of London newspapers, and he put in service every available dock-labourer in the port. On the arrival of a boat, day or night, he was notified by his native assistants, and thus enabled to report every story that came out of the beleaguered city. Two Associated Press men in Port Arthur sent messsages to him whenever possible.

Mr. Richmond Smith was detailed to accompany the besieging Japanese army. He was not permitted to report daily, but was given every facility for observing the movements, and finally was permitted to take a despatch-boat to Chefoo, whence he transmitted a telegram of over five thousand words, which was the first authentic report from a newspaper eye-witness covering the operations.

He was told by the Japanese authorities that he might send

from Chefoo his story of all that happened from the beginning until October 29th, inclusive. A boat, the *Genbu Maru*, was at his disposal for the journey, and was lying in the adjacent harbour of Shaoping-tao. Smith at once set out. He rode to the Japanese press headquarters, had his message censored, and then went forward to the port. He arrived at Shaoping-tao about ten o'clock at night, and found his boat at anchor in the roadstead. He had been ordered to report to the naval officer in command of the harbour. He went aboard the commander's ship, and was astounded when that official politely but firmly notified him that in no circumstances could he or his despatch-boat leave before daybreak. This was indeed a blow, because Smith had private information that the Japanese had given all the other correspondents like permission to send messages; and these correspondents had set out for the telegraph station at Yinkow, each believing himself specially favoured. Smith was heartbroken. The commander took pity on him, and showed him his instructions, which stated definitely that the *Genbu Maru* might sail after the fall of Port Arthur and not before. "These instructions can be changed only by an appeal to the rear-admiral at Shaoping-tao and the admiral of the fleet," he said.

This meant a delay of several days. The commander would not insist upon the letter of his instructions, as he could see from Smith's message that it was properly censored, and he would allow the ship to go at daylight. But this concession meant nothing. The other correspondents would be at Yinkow, and Smith would be beaten. Then, in a dramatic attitude, he took his precious telegram and held it over the blazing fire in the cabin, and said that if he could not sail until daybreak he would burn his message, and the important objects which the Japanese War and Navy departments had sought to attain would never be accomplished. This was too much, and the officer relented. He agreed that the *Genbu Maru* might go out to the guard-ship, and if the officer in command there would assume the responsibility of passing it, it might sail on to Chefoo. Fortunately, that commander shut his eyes, and Smith went his way. It turned out later that the extreme caution exercised was due to the fact that the roadstead was full of mines, which were invisible at night and might have destroyed a boat at any moment. Smith reached his destination in safety, but, as it turned out, his rivals were delayed, so that his message was printed in New York and London four days ahead of those sent from Yinkow. It was no mean tribute to the Associated Press and its representative that the Japanese authorities read his telegram, approved it, and then sent him alone to Chefoo, accepting his word of honour that he would not change it, or disclose to any one the disposition of their troops or their plan of campaign.

At Tokio, very early in his service, Mr. Egan established a relation with the government which was easily more intimate than that of any other journalist. His high sense of honour, his administrative ability, and his tact were appreciated, and soon won for him the confidence and esteem of the Japanese authorities. He was given the official reports from the generals in the field several hours ahead of any other correspondent, and his wishes in regard to the treatment accorded to Associated Press men at the front were respected in a remarkable manner. At St. Petersburg our correspondent was given copies of the official telegrams by direct command of the Czar, and we were able to present a daily pen-picture of the Russian activities which won high praise from every intelligent observer.

The Qualities Needed in a War Correspondent

In reporting a war, the most important question naturally arises over the selection of correspondents. The number of men qualified by nature and education for such a task is very limited. Your war correspondent must be physically capable of withstanding the hardships of the field. He must also be as courageous as any soldier. Indeed, his lot is an even harder one, because he must put himself in places of the greatest danger without the patriotic fervour, the touch of the comrade's elbow, or the possession of a rifle, all of which are large factors in making up a trooper's bravery. He must be capable of describing accurately and graphically what he sees. He must have as large a perspective as the commanding general, if he seeks to tell the whole story of the battle.

But he may have all of these primal requisites and still prove a failure. He must be temperamentally a diplomat and capable of ingratiating himself into the sympathetic and helpful friendship of those with whom he comes in contact. He may be an ideal representative at the headquarters of an American general, but wholly incapable of serving satisfactorily with a foreign army. He must, of course, be able to speak the language of the army to which he is assigned.

Above all, the war correspondent must possess in marked degree that familiarity with events and affairs which will command the confidence of those in power about him. His influence often extends beyond his primary mission of reporting, and strays into the field of international diplomacy. For instance, during the Boxer Rebellion in China, one of the Associated Press correspondents was sought out and consulted by the commander of one power represented in the allied expedition as to his proper attitude toward the military representative of another power whose actions were causing grave concern in that delicate hour.

When a battle has been fought, and the correspondent, at great hazard, has written his story, then his troubles have only fairly begun. He must "pass the censor." This may be easy or it may be most difficult. Much depends upon the character and intelligence of the censor.

Next, the messages must be transmitted. The correspondent must be "first at the wire," or his work may all come to naught. Here, again, he must exercise tact; otherwise a petty telegraph official, who is often a very monarch in his field, may spoil everything. And all along the long line—for the telegram is retransmitted half a dozen times before it reaches America—the cable officials must be friendly and painstaking and intelligent, or the news will fail to reach its destination promptly and in the form in which it was sent. Delays in transmission are inevitable, and it speaks volumes for the efficiency of modern telegraphy that they are so infrequent.

Foreign operators handle and transmit these messages, often in bad chirography, in a language which they do not understand, and seldom make a serious mistake.

In the World War no nation seemed to have had the faintest idea of the merit of real neutrality on the part of this country. Their theory was that, "He who is not for me is against me." Some extraordinary things arose from this condition. An Associated Press man, trained for years to impartiality, was not acceptable to France or Russia if he had been in Germany or Austria. And there was like objection in Germany to one who had been in Great Britain or another of the allied countries. They did not see how any newspaperman could be worth considering unless he were willing vigorously to do battle for them.

But our troubles do not end with the receipt of the message; for with all the care that has been observed by correspondents and telegraph officials, it does not often reach us in shape to go at once to the press. There is no "padding," but, for the sake of speed, the correspondents omit unnecessary words, such as "and" and "the," and these are filled in at our receiving offices. The telegram is very carefully written out to convey the correspondent's precise meaning. In these receiving offices are all the war maps, and libraries filled with books and documents that may prove of value in deciphering a message. Lists of foreign officials and warships and army organizations, spelled correctly and sent to us by mail, are on file. There are complete sets of all directories of every important city in the world. But, more valuable than all else, there are carefully indexed scrap-books containing every cable message received by the Associated Press during the last twenty-seven years. These serve to illuminate every new event with the antecedent and the collateral history.

The Portsmouth Conference*

In his autobiography—page 586—Colonel Roosevelt, speaking of the Peace Conference at Portsmouth, New Hampshire, thus refers to the Emperor of Germany:

**Saturday Evening Post,* January 30, 1915.

During the course of the negotiations I tried to enlist the aid of the government of one nation, which was friendly to Japan, in helping to bring about peace. I got no aid from either. I did, however, receive aid from the Emperor of Germany.

Behind this lies a singularly dramatic story: The Conference for the settlement of the Russo-Japanese War assembled early in August, 1905. Something like a fortnight before the opening Mr. Martin Egan, of the Tokio bureau of the Associated Press, had sent me a memorandum of the Japanese claims. It contained fifteen clauses.

The Japanese Government was represented by Baron Jutaro Komura, as chief commissioner, a Harvard graduate of the class of 1878, who had served his country as minister at Washington in 1898 and then gone to St. Petersburg as minister in 1900. His associate commissioner was Baron Kogoro Takahira, who had represented Japan in the United States in several capacities—first, as secretary of legation at Washington in 1881; next as consul-general at New York in 1891, and finally as minister to Washington in 1900, which post he still held at the opening of the Portsmouth Conference.

Besides these gentlemen there was an unofficial commissioner for Japan who had been in the United States throughout the war as personal representative of Prince Ito. This was Baron Kentaro Kaneko, who had taken his degree from the Harvard Law School.

The Russian Government was represented by Count Sergius Witte, who at the moment was unquestionably the most distinguished statesman of his country, a man of remarkable capacity, who had risen from an humble origin to a post of commanding influence in the Czar's government. Associated with him was Baron Roman Rosen, who had been Russian minister at Washington for a number of years, and had then been transferred to Tokio, where he was serving as minister at the opening of the Russo-Japanese contest.

All of these commissioners were personal friends of mine, and after their arrival in this country I had frequent interviews with them. The conditions imposed by the Japanese were fairly well understood by both sides and were naturally the subject of consideration between us.

At the outset, or within a day or two after his arrival in New York, Witte told me in a most emphatic way that he had no sympathy whatever with President Roosevelt's efforts to secure peace. At the moment he believed the time to be most inopportune. He was convinced that the Japanese had passed the high-water mark and had reached a point where they had neither the men nor the money with which to continue the conflict.

He firmly believed that if the Emperor of Russia had refused to accept the Roosevelt invitation, and had gone on fighting, the tide would have turned and Russia would have won. As to any proposition for the payment of an indemnity, Russia would never pay a penny. It was well understood that the Japanese proposed to claim eight hundred million dollars; but Witte said that if such a demand were made a condition of peace there would be no peace.

"Why should we pay an indemnity?" he asked. "The Japanese have never invaded Russia. No Japanese has ever set foot on Russian soil. The contest has been fought out on Chinese soil and no claim for indemnity has ever been recognized, nor can one ever be recognized, unless the victorious party to a war has actually invaded the enemy's territory."

The Conference went into session almost at once, and most of the points at issue were met, discussed, and settled in due course; but finally the commissioners came to a deadlock on the question of indemnity.

On Friday, August 25th, an *impasse* having been reached, Witte and Rosen received peremptory orders from their sovereign to quit the conference on the following Tuesday. Whereupon they packed up their belongings and made ready to leave at a moment's notice.

At that time I was living at the Lotos Club, in Fifth Avenue, in the city of New York; and at an early hour on the following Sunday morning I received a telephone message from Baron Kaneko, who asked whether he might see me on an important matter—he thought, perhaps, that I was able to influence the

Russian commissioners, and so on. He was living at the Leonori, an apartment house on the corner of Madison Avenue and Sixty-third Street.

As the Lotos Club was a rather public place for a conference, I told him I would go to his apartment; and I went there shortly before noon. We entered at once on a consideration of the critical situation at Portsmouth. He asked me whether I thought the Russian Government would pay any indemnity. He was impressed with the idea that Witte and Rosen were bluffing, and that Russia would pay something if by doing so she would save her face.

He had a number of suggestions along this line, and asked whether I thought the Russians would give compensation under some other guise, or whether there was not some form that could be adopted to satisfy the Russian *amour propre*.

"For example," he said, "Russia might pay for the care of Russian prisoners in Japan or for the return of some part of the South Manchurian Railroad line."

I told him I was positive that the Russian refusal to pay money was final and that Russia could not be moved from its determination in this regard. He suggested that Witte had already said he was willing to pay as much as the United States paid for Alaska.

To this I replied that the amount paid for Alaska was something like seven million dollars, and that the payment of such a sum on a claim of eight hundred million was so ridiculously small that Japan could not afford to take it.

"Moreover," I added, "you have settled every question except that of money, and it now becomes important for Japan to consider whether she can afford to go on fighting over a mere matter of indemnity."

Baron Kaneko was quick to say that Japan recognized that point, and added: "We shall never be placed in the attitude of fighting for mere money. But the situation is very serious; the conference is at a standstill, and day after to-morrow the Russian commissioners will break up the conference. I fully recognize the force of what you say; but now, if we take the ground that we will not go on with the war merely to enforce the payment of indemnity, there is really no alternative except to waive all claim on Russia for our tremendous losses.

"But suppose we waive this point," he went on; "our immediate necessity is to hold the conference together. Witte and Rosen are about to quit. I take it they have no sympathy with the conference anyhow, and are quite ready and glad to sieze on the authority given them to end our negotiations."

"There is one man who can intervene and save the situation," I replied.

"Whom do you mean?" Kaneko asked.

"The German Emperor."

"But," said he, "you know he is not our friend. You cannot have forgotten the cartoon of the 'Yellow Peril' which he drew."

"That is all very true," I replied, "but he is more anxious for peace at this hour than to emphasize any sentimental views he may have concerning the 'Yellow Peril.' He is a close friend of the Emperor of Russia, and I have no doubt he would be glad, if he were appealed to, and if he were advised that Japan was prepared to abandon her claim for indemnity, to intercede with the Czar to prolong the conference and reach a settlement."

By this time we had gone to luncheon, and Baron Kaneko asked how the German Emperor could be reached. I replied that it was not a difficult matter and that I should be glad to arrange it. He asked me to do so.

Baron Speck von Sternberg, the German ambassador, was not in America at the time, and in his absence Baron von dem Bussche-Haddenhausen, counsellor and first secretary of the Embassy, was acting as chargé. The latter was spending the summer at Lenox and I proceeded at once to get in touch with him. Leaving the luncheon table at the Leonori, I stepped to the telephone and asked long distance to connect me with Baron von dem Bussche.

There was some delay about the connection, however, and as I had another engagement I left word to have the call transferred to me at the Lotos Club. I then took my leave, Baron Kaneko agreeing that he would remain at his apartment and await word from me. A little later, at the Lotos Club, I received word that Baron von dem Bussche was at the other end of the telephone wire. I told him I wanted to talk to him about a very important diplomatic matter and asked how soon he could come to New York.

He replied that he could reach the city by five o'clock that afternoon; he realized that it must be a matter of considerable importance and asked no questions, but agreed to come to the Lotos Club at the earliest possible moment. I suggested that he bring with him his diplomatic code book.

I then telephoned Baron Kaneko and asked him to come to the club, which he did. I told him of Von Bussche's coming and said I had now gone as far as I could without notifying President Roosevelt about what we had in mind. He acquiesced, and I called up Oyster Bay and asked the President whether I might go out at once and talk with him about a very important matter connected with the Portsmouth Conference. He replied that he would be very glad to have me come, and soon after I was at the President's house on Sagamore Hill.

I told Mr. Roosevelt all that had happened, and he expressed himself highly gratified at the course matters had taken. I then suggested that he write a message to the Kaiser, and he started to prepare one. At first he dictated and I wrote, but when I questioned the form of his message, he suggested that he do the writing and I the dictating. The following is the message that resulted:

August 27, 1905.

Mr Bussche: Please cable His Majesty the Emperor from me as follows:

Theodore Roosevelt.

Your Majesty: Peace can be obtained on the following terms: Russia to pay no indemnity whatever, and to receive back the north half of Sakhalin, for which it is to pay Japan whatever amount a mixed commission may determine. This is my proposition, to which the Japanese have assented reluctantly and only under strong pressure from me. The plan is for each of the contending parties to name an equal number of members of the commission, and for them to name the odd member. The Japanese assert that Witte has in principle agreed that Russia should pay something to get back the north half of Sakhalin, and, indeed, he intimated to me that they might buy it back at a reasonable figure, something on the scale of that for which Alaska was sold to the United States.

These terms, which strike me as extremely moderate, I have not presented in this form to the Emperor of Russia. I feel that you have more influence with him than I or any one else can have. As the situation is exceedingly strained and the relations between the plenipotentiaries critical to a degree, immediate action is necessary. Can you not take the initiative by presenting these terms at once to him? Your success in the matter will make the entire civilized world your debtor. This proposition virtually relegates all the unsettled issues of the war to the arbitration of a mixed commission as outlined above; and I am unable to see how Russia can refuse your request if in your wisdom you see fit to make it.

THEODORE ROOSEVELT.

The second sentence of the letter was inserted, after deliberation, as a diplomatic phrase to avoid saying that the offer came from the Japanese.

At the President's suggestion I took this message, which was in his own handwriting, to one of his secretaries, Mr. Barnes, who was on duty at a hotel in Oyster Bay, and Mr. Barnes made copies of it for the President's file and for me. I then hurried back to New York, and about five o'clock was joined by Kaneko and Bussche at the Lotos Club.

It then occurred to me that there was one feature of the subject which had not been provided for: Baron Kaneko was, as I have said, an unofficial commissioner, and it dawned on me that I must assure myself of his authority before, by any act of mine, I committed either the President of the United States or the German Emperor to his assurance that the Japanese Government would waive its claim for indemnity.

I frankly told him of my dilemma and said that I could not go further without definite evidence of his authority. He recognized the propriety of my suggestion and asked me to telephone Baron Komura, at Portsmouth, and receive his personal assurance on the subject. I felt that though this was but a matter of form it was essential; and I accordingly put in a long-distance call for Baron Komura.

To save time Baron Bussche had gone into another room at the club and was converting as rapidly as he could the Roosevelt message into code. For a time we had no response to our call for Portsmouth; and while we were waiting I called up President Roosevelt to tell him of what I had done. He expressed his hearty approval of the precaution.

Hour after hour passed without a word from Komura. Bussche at length finished coding the message and was impatient to transmit it to Berlin. He finally decided to cable it, with an explanation of the circumstances.

Late that night, despairing of reaching Komura by telephone, I telegraphed one of our correspondents at Portsmouth and, in a guarded message asked him to wire me concerning Baron Kaneko's authority. The reply came at length; and to say the least it gave me pause, for it was to the effect that Baron Takahira had informed the correspondent that Kaneko was in no way authorized to speak for the commission. Naturally I was dumfounded at this turn of affairs; and though I could not believe that Baron Kaneko had deliberately tricked us, I made haste to report the news to President Roosevelt.

My news was as much of a surprise to the President as it had been to me. It was difficult for us to reconcile matters. For days we had both been receiving Baron Kaneko as though he were fully empowered to speak for his government, and we were loath to believe that such was not the case; but in the face of the message from Takahira what were we to believe? Finally, it was decided that the President should send a frank statement of what we had done to Baron Komura and see whether he could not shed some light on the matter. This message was the following:

Aug. 28th, 1905, Oyster Bay, N. Y.

MY DEAR BARON KOMURA: I have had as you know a number of interviews with Baron Kaneko since your arrival in this country. These have always been held at his request and in the assumption that he was acting for you, this having been my understanding of what you said in our conversation when you were out here at my house, and when the matter of keeping me informed of what was being done at Portsmouth arose.

Moreover, he has frequently transmitted to me copies of your telegrams evidently written to be shown to me—for instance such telegrams of yours were inclosed in his notes sent to me yesterday and the day before yesterday, August twenty-sixth and twenty-seventh. I have therefore assumed that I could safely accept whatever he told me as being warranted by his understanding with you. To my astonishment a telegram was received by the Associated Press from Portsmouth last night purporting to contain statements from Minister Takahira to the effect that Baron Kaneko was not authorized to see me and containing at least by implication an expression of surprise that I should have treated him as having any such authorization.

The Manager of the Associated Press refused to allow this despatch to go out, and I take it for granted that it was false and that Mr. Takahira had given utterance to no such expression. But in view of its receipt I retraced a cable I had prepared to send His Majesty the German Emperor if Baron Kaneko approved, this cable having been prepared by me after consultation with Mr. Stone, who had himself seen Baron Bussche of the German Embassy and who understood it was along the line you desired. [Here was inserted the cablegram as given above.]

At the end Baron Bussche stated to the Kaiser that if the Czar could be persuaded to come to these terms I should at once publicly give him the credit for what had been accomplished and try in every way to show that whatever of credit might attach to bringing the negotiation to a successful conclusion should come to him in the most public and emphatic manner. This was added at my suggestion, for I need not tell you my dear Baron that my sole purpose has been to try to bring about peace and I am absolutely indifferent as to anything that is said about me in connection with the matter.

But of course under these circumstances I shall not send the cable unless I am definitely assured by you that this cable has your approval. Moreover in view of the statement credited to Minister Takahira, I do not feel that Baron Kaneko should communicate with me any longer unless I am assured by you that it is your desire that he should do so and that he speaks with authorization from you.

Sincerely yours
THEODORE ROOSEVELT.

Monday was a day of great activity and great anxiety in many places and in many ways. In Tokio the Elder Statesmen,

Lord Northcliffe

President Taft

against great obstacles, but with high courage and infinite wisdom, were moving straight on in their effort to secure an honourable peace. They were fully advised of the situation at Portsmouth. They knew that, on the preceding Wednesday, Komura had made his last despairing effort to enforce the demand for indemnity. He had reduced the claim from eight hundred million to six hundred million dollars, but had made no impression; and, instead, had noted that the Russian commissioners were ready and anxious to seize on any demand for tribute as an excuse to end the whole business and go on with the conflict. At home they were confronted with a populace burning with patriotism, glorying in their unexampled triumph, and fully convinced of the ability of their nation to cope with any measure of resistance on the part of their enemy. At the moment, Marquis Ito proved to be the controlling force and touched the highest level of his extraordinary career. Under his commanding influence Japan refused to make monetary compensation a *sine qua non* in her negotiations. She braved the danger of a revolting war spirit, accepted the burden of her immense war debt, and instructed her plenipotentiaries in America to sign a treaty of peace on the terms already agreed to.

In Russia the situation was no less complicated. There, too, was a war party confident and insistent. After the series of disasters that culminated at Mukden, Kuropatkin had been relieved as General-in-Chief of the Manchurian Army and Linevitch had taken his place. The new commander had a great record as a warrior; he had been first lieutenant to the great Skobeleff and shared in his glory. During the half year that had followed his appointment he had received a hundred thousand fresh troops and had fully reorganized his army. Now he was anxious to flesh his sword, and had no sort of doubt of his ability to wipe out his country's disgrace. With his associate officers he telegraphed the Czar in terms almost disrespectful. He said:

I have the honour to inform Your Majesty that all my comrades and myself, after fully discussing the arguments for peace and the respective positions of the opposing armies, unanimously and resolutely voted for the continuation of the war until such time as the Almighty shall crown the efforts of our brave troops with success. It is no time to talk of peace after the battles of Mukden and of Tsushima.

The Czar himself, but a few days before, had issued a manifesto declaring that he would consent to no dishonourable peace. Yet there were countervailing influences that must be reckoned with; threatening revolutionary movements were observable in his European domains, and the rank and file of his Manchurian forces were not so enthusiastic for war as were his generals.

It was at this juncture that the German Emperor did his most effective work. Before the peace commissioners had assembled at Portsmouth he had held an advisory conference with the Czar on the Russian royal yacht in the Baltic Sea. Now, with Bussche's telegram before him, he sought once more to calm the troubled waters. There were telegrams flying back and forth between Berlin and St. Petersburg; and, as a result on this fateful Monday, Witte and Rosen received a forty-word cable from their Imperial master which held them in leash until the final purpose of the Japanese should be disclosed.

In New York and Oyster Bay there was a day of impatient waiting. Early in the morning we learned that our failure to get word from Komura by telephone was due to a heavy storm, which had put the wires out of commission. Later I learned that the disturbing message which quoted Takahira as repudiating Kaneko was due to the fact that for prudential reasons my own telegram of inquiry had been almost cryptic. I had been so brief and had disclosed so little and asked so much that it was not understood; and a worse than non-committal reply had resulted.

I made another visit to Roosevelt; and after discussing the situation he and I agreed that I should announce through the Associated Press that evening that the Japanese had determined to waive their claim for indemnity—this with a view to committing them irrevocably to the pledge that Kaneko had given Bussche and myself.

This despatch was sent out, and of course reached Portsmouth instantly. As it was read to Komura and Takahira, they declined to say anything. Witte and Rosen thought it a ruse and went on with their preparations to quit the place the next day. Their plans were well laid. If, as they expected, there should be any further pressing for indemnity on Tuesday, Witte was to leave the conference room at 11.50 A.M., and in a casual way call to one of his secretaries the following Russian command, "*Pochlite sa moymy rousskymy papyrossamy*" ("Send for my Russian cigarettes").

This was a signal; the secretary told off for the task was to step to a private telephone connecting with their headquarters at the Wentworth Hotel, in Portsmouth, repeat the words to a member of the mission standing at the other end, and a single code word, already agreed on, should be instantly cabled to St. Petersburg. On receipt of this word in the Russian capital the signal was to be flashed to General Linevitch, and a battle of the centuries was to begin. A million men were to participate.

Such was the plan and such the expectation on Monday night.

On Tuesday morning the London *Times* and the London *Telegraph* led off in their despatches from Portsmouth with the comments of their respective correspondents. These were George W. Smalley, of the *Times*, and Dr. E. J. Dillon, of the *Telegraph*.

They spent their wrath in ridicule and denunciation of the Associated Press, which had assumed to know all things and had asserted that the Japanese were about to withdraw their claim for indemnity. Such a thing was inconceivable. There would be further negotiations, said they, and Heaven alone knew what would result.

On Tuesday morning Roosevelt received a message from Komura assuring him that Kaneko was a quite responsible gentleman, and that we had made no mistake in receiving and in dealing with him. With this we awaited the result from the naval-stores room at Kittery Point, five miles from Portsmouth, with intense interest.

Up there it was a situation that, in point of dramatic interest, has rarely been equalled. The Conference met. The utmost secrecy respecting the proceedings prevailed. Then the fateful hour of eleven-fifty arrived. And Witte came from the room—but not to ask for his Russian cigarettes. Instead, with flushed face and snapping eyes, he uttered, not the expected five Russian words, but two—"*Gospoda, mir.*" ("Gentlemen, peace.")

When the Conference gathered, Satoh, the Japanese secretary, calmly rose and announced that, obedient to instructions from their government, the claim for any indemnity was withdrawn; Japan would not fight for mere money, and peace was possible on the terms already accepted and agreed on by the Russian commissioners.

The Case of Lagerkranz

It was about the 10th of July, 1907. Baron Lagerkranz, Swedish minister to America, called on me in the afternoon at the Lotos Club. He introduced himself and said he had been instructed by his government to see me. His mission was a peculiar one. Prince William, the second son of King Oscar, had come to America aboard the battleship *Fyglia* to attend the Jamestown Exposition. That was now over, and under his instructions Baron Lagerkranz asked me if I would be good enough to arrange a week of social entertainment for the Prince at Newport. This request was, of course, a command and I told him I would do what I could. The next day I went to Newport and called upon Mrs. Stuyvesant Fish who was the acknowledged leader of the Four Hundred. She was more than pleased to take the matter in hand, and a programme for the week's entertainment was easily adjusted. Mrs. Fish was to give an initial luncheon and a final dinner, and the interval between the two functions was to be filled up by events and entertainments galore.

All went well and closed with a final dinner given by His Royal Highness aboard his ship. Then he came to New York and fell into my hands for further attention. He was anxious to visit Coney Island. I had a small yacht under charter and was a member of the Atlantic Yacht Club at Sea Gate, immediately adjoining Coney Island. I took him with Baron Lagerkranz and wife, and two gentlemen to the Yacht Club. We dined there and then made a tour of Coney Island. He expressed a desire to see Chinatown. I telephoned to police authorities of New York for some detectives to meet us on our arrival at the city and we at once returned. We went to Chinatown and began at once a tour of inspection. We visited the shops, the theatres, and wound up at an opium den. I sent for "Chuck" Connors, the famous "Mayor of Chinatown." He was a little, impudent, slangy Irishman, scarcely above five feet. He was the original of Edward Townsend's "Chimmie Fadden." Prince William clearly stood six feet three inches in his stockings. When I introduced them Connors looked up at the tall scion of Swedish royalty and with a twinkle in his eye said: "Well, princes do come high in Sweden, don't they?"

As we stood there we were startled by the appearance of a Salvation Army trio singing religious hymns and beating their tambourines outside the opium den. Madame Lagerkranz, whom I was escorting, turned and said she could not stand the disgusting and fetid atmosphere and desired me to take her out to the Salvation Army people and the fresh air. We all went out and found an elderly man, a young man, and a woman perhaps of forty years of age. They continued their service for a moment or two and then the young woman with an exclamation threw herself on Madame Lagerkranz and with the deepest emotion the two embraced each other. Each called the other by their first name, and it was obvious that they were old acquaintances. There was an arrangement for a further meeting but no explanation and we took our departure. As we went home Baron Lagerkranz whispered he would tell me all in the morning.

The next day he came and this was his story: "Our father left my brother and myself the largest steel factory in Sweden. My brother was a very religious man of a formal type, a Lutheran. I was not a professing Christian. One day two Salvation Army lassies came to the office of which I was immediately in charge and sought an audience. They told me they had undertaken to found a rescue home for unfortunate women in

Stockholm and that they were three or four thousand kronen in debt for the enterprise. They asked modestly if my brother and I would willingly make a contribution. The opportunity was one that I enjoyed. I told them I would see what I could do and asked them to return the following day. That night, with a malicious pleasure, I presented the matter to my sanctimonious brother and suggested that if he was willing we should between us wipe out the total debt. He had no alternative and of course, consented. The amount, as you see, was not a large one and the whole thing was rather in the nature of a joke as far as I was concerned.

"Some time elapsed and then I received another call from these two ladies. They said that General Booth, the distinguished commander-in-chief of the Salvation Army, was about to visit Stockholm and they wondered if I would be willing to entertain him as a guest at my house. I told them that my wife had charge of such matters and they telephoned her and were assured that Baroness Lagerkranz would be happy to play hostess to so celebrated a personage."

General Booth arrived for a week's stay. In a few days Baron Lagerkranz and his wife were both converted and joined the Salvation Army. Giving up temporarily activities in the steel works they went out as lieutenants of the Commander-in-Chief and established the Salvation Army throughout Asia.

"It was in India that the young woman whom we met in Chinatown last night was my wife's assistant in the work. We had not seen her for years, and you can well imagine the surprise and delight in again encountering her."

Baron Lagerkranz continued his activities in the Salvation Army for seven years and then returned to Stockholm and the steel works. The King tendered him the post of ambassador to England but he asked to be excused on the ground that he had been known in London as a Salvation Army man and had dined with King Edward at Buckingham Palace in the costume of an officer of General Booth's army. King Oscar readily saw the embarrassment and then offered him the post of minister to Washington. This he accepted, and thus and therefore I met him.

SEVENTH DECADE

Genesis of the World War

ONE needs but to trace the history of the Near East from the Treaty of San Stefano, concluded on March 3, 1878, after Russia's victory over the Sultan, which was nullified by the Treaty of Berlin of June, 1878, down through to the crisis of 1908, when Austria boldly annexed Bosnia and Herzegovina in violation of the Berlin Treaty, to see that in some sense all the events led up to the great World War of 1914. Servia had been looking forward to the acquisition of Bosnia and Herzegovina, which was largely Slav, and which would give Servia a port on the Adriatic. When the two provinces were thus taken over by Austria, intense bitterness developed at Belgrade, and it finally culminated in the assassination of the Grand Duke at Serajevo in 1914, the savage ultimatum, and the great cataclysm.

Things were going well in the United States in 1908. We had weathered the financial panic. It had really done the country good. It had made it obvious that the wild orgies of so-called "High Finance" must end, and the necessity for a central bank of discount had become evident. The Associated Press was sailing along on an even keel. The foreign agencies which I had set up had demonstrated their efficiency.

The directors then suggested that I take a journey around the world to see if anything more could be done with profit. It took me a good while to get ready. My wife and my daughter went over ahead of me, as they wished to go up the Nile once more. I had a number of things to do. I had a delightful visit from William Ferrero, the great Italian historian. He was accompanied by his wife, who was the daughter of an old-time acquaintance of mine, Doctor Lombroso of Turin. We trotted about New York to luncheons, dinners, and theatres as three children out of school.

Early in April Mark Twain and I accompanied our friend Henry H. Rogers to attend the formal opening of the Virginia Railway, which Mr. Rogers had built wholly with his own means. This was one of many happy outings we had together. I had no business relations with Mr. Rogers, but enjoyed his company greatly as a friend. I believe him to have been a high-souled, honest gentleman and one of infinite humour. A few weeks after I delivered an address to the Pulitzer School of Journalism at Columbia University, and in June another in Detroit on the occasion of the anniversary of the founding of the first daily newspaper in that city.

The Presidential campaign of the year was not an exciting one. Mr. Taft was nominated at the Republican National Convention in Chicago. There was an attempt to stampede the organization for Roosevelt, although he had three times definitely said he would not be a candidate. Mr. Bryan was nominated without opposition at Denver.

Taft did not want to be President. He much preferred a judicial office. Roosevelt twice offered him a seat on the Supreme bench, but for personal reasons which he felt bound him in honour he twice declined the tender. He found the duties at the White House irksome and was really happy when, four years later, he failed of reëlection.

From the viewpoint of the pothouse politician, whether in Congress or out of it, he was the greatest blunderer on the rolling globe. He would go out to Columbus, Ohio, to make a speech opening a State campaign and roundly denounce the bosses on whom Republican success was dependent. He would go to Boston and eulogize Senator Aldrich for the aid he had given in securing legislation and the next day would give out a statement defending the accused Secretary Ballinger. This, said the political trickster, was "spilling the beans" in most woeful fashion. And so it was for the moment. But in the long run the American people like a manly man, one who will tell the truth as he is given to see the truth, and Taft outlived in fame the foxy fool who carped at him. His quality was that of President Cleveland, who saw beyond the immediate consequences in dealing with public questions and sturdily went his way to the undying respect of his fellow-citizens.

Discovery of the North Pole

Suddenly, on September 1, 1909, Dr. Frederick Cook turned up at Copenhagen with the announcement that he had been at the North Pole. A few days later I received this telegram from Admiral Peary:

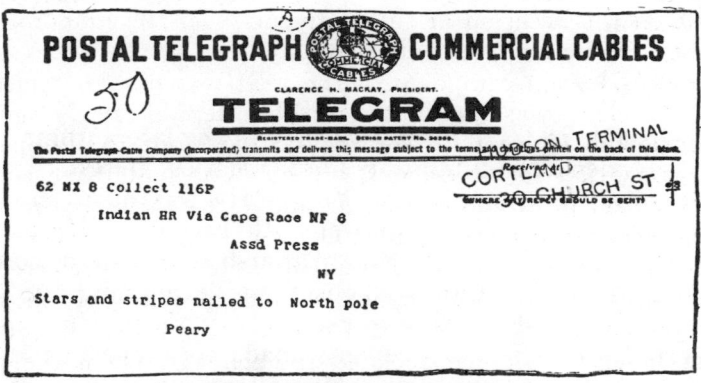

Admiral Peary's Telegram

I knew both of these candidates for immortal fame. I had some suspicion respecting Cook. He had not convinced me of the truth of his claim that he had climbed Mt. McKinley in Alaska some time before. I had no doubt of Peary's veracity, but the telegram was so startling that I feared it might not be genuine. Before using it, I wired back to Indian Harbour, Labrador, to have it verified and called attention to Cook's claim. Then I received the following:

Indian Harbor via Cape May N. J. Sept. 6.
 MELVILLE E. STONE,
  Associated Press New York.
 Regret unable despatch details. My despatch Stars and Stripes nail d to North Pole authoritative and correct. Cook's story should

not be taken too seriously. The two Eskimos who accompanied him say he went no distance North and not out of sight of land. Other members of the tribe corroborate their story.

PEARY.

Of course this was a personal message in reply to mine and perhaps it should not have been made public. It was, however, and, I am sorry to say, aroused criticism of the Admiral. I asked him a number of times if it was not fair for me to announce that his message was not a voluntary attack on Cook, but he was quite indifferent to anything Cook's friends might say of him.

An English Panic

I was able to leave for my journey in the late autumn. Before my departure Admiral Lord Charles Beresford spent some time with me in New York. He was quite sure that Germany was preparing for war with England. He told me German agents had been going through the Eastern Counties of England listing the farmhouses and examining the coast line for favourable landing spots.

Lord Northcliffe was over in Canada speaking on the same theme. "The Englishman's Home" was the popular play on the London stage. I laughed at Beresford, but at the same time I received a letter from a friend who had just been travelling in England. He said:

We had a delightful trip abroad and met many interesting people. The astonishing thing, however, is the English fear of a German invasion. In the most enlightened circles—indeed, among the most eminent men—the invasion is spoken of as something that will eventually occur. A spark would cause an explosion there.

Before I sailed the Pilgrim Society of New York gave a dinner in honour of the British admirals, Seymour and Hamilton, who happened to be here. They asked me to speak. I derided the hysteria of my English friends. I saw no reason for alarm. Moberly Bell, the long-time editor of the London

Times, sat beside me and followed me as a speaker. He disagreed with me and portrayed the danger in exceedingly plain terms.

Beresford hurried back to London before I was able to get away.

My friends insisted upon giving me a send-off. It took the form of a parting dinner at the Lotos Club on October 3rd, and was a notable event. The company was large, the addresses brilliant, and the spirit most gratifying. I was presented with a handsome bronze plaque commemorative of the occasion.

I sailed on October 5th.

I spent a few days in London, lunched with the Whitelaw Reids at Dorchester House, and hurried away to Paris. There I received this letter:

London, 3rd November, 1909.
DEAR MR. MELVILLE STONE:

I have been trying to find you, and am delighted to hear that you have come over.

I am in the middle of a tremendous fight, but will win.

Let me know when you come over to London, dine with me, and meet some of your friends. There are very few people who could do more to stop the coming war through Great Britain's unpreparedness. As I told you before, war will put back the progress of humanity one hundred years. The English-speaking nations can prevent war.

Yours sincerely,
CHARLES BERESFORD.

And I had a note from Moreton Frewen who wanted to talk of bimetallism as a panacea for the world's unrest.

Days in Paris

These invitations did not tempt me. My friend James Hazen Hyde had plans for me in Paris, and these for the moment were more interesting. I wanted to feel the pulse of France rather than to share with what seemed to me the neurosis of Britain.

Mr. Hyde's contributions to an *entente* between our republic and France were of incalculable value. If you were fortunate enough to be invited to his house, you were sure to meet every Frenchman worth while sooner or later. At his table I met Millerand, who at this writing is President of France. There were but the three of us at luncheon. Millerand was Minister of War. He was anxious to send half a dozen young army engineers over to the United States to work for a while in our great factories to learn our methods, particularly of bridge building. I saw no possible objection and promised to aid him. So, later, the young fellows came over and were welcomed in our establishments and gained valuable experience.

While I was in Paris in 1909 Mr. Hyde gave two remarkable dinners for my benefit. One was a literary dinner at which he had over a dozen members of the French Institute. The other was a political dinner at which he gathered an equal number of the leading publicists of France. That year he was President of the Société des Gens de Lettres, and I was their guest of honour at a banquet at Margueray's. There were over a hundred of the authors and artists of Paris participating.

I saw no signs of fear of the Germans among my French friends. Of course they did not like their Teutonic neighbours. They never had liked them. And the crape still hung over the Statue of Strasburg on the Place de la Concorde. There was still hope that the score left in 1870 would be settled. But that seemed to be all.

The German Situation

Then I set out for Berlin. I wanted to see the Kaiser. When I arrived he was out of town, but he sent me word that on a certain evening he would return for an hour at the Potsdam railway station and would be glad to see me. He was to go somewhere in South Germany to shoot wild boar, but would stop over for a brief talk. He was very frank and I cannot believe that he had any idea of the forthcoming war. He still regretted the friction with England. The logical alliance, he said, was one including England, Germany, and the United

States against the Latin countries and the Roman Church. And this relation to the Roman Church meant much to the Kaiser as it had to his grandfather and Bismarck throughout their lives. It had come down to them through four centuries from the Hussite contest, the Thirty Years' War, the attempt at peace by the Westphalian Treaty, and the never-ending struggle between Protestant and Catholic. I laughingly said: "Here is an interesting situation. Austria is without a direct heir to her throne, Bavaria is without a direct heir to her throne, Württemberg is without a direct heir to her throne, and Baden is without a direct heir to the Grand Duchy, and you have almost enough heirs to fill every one of the positions." "No, not Austria," said he. "I want no more Catholic influence in the German Empire. There are now 129 members of the Reichstag who owe no allegiance to the Imperial Government but whose whole devotion is to the Vatican."

The Kaiser arranged for me to see Bethmann-Hollweg, who had been appointed Chancellor of the empire a few months before, supplanting Von Bülow. I spent the next evening with the Chancellor. He was as candid as his Imperial master.

The situation in Germany seemed to be:

1. The Kaiser had not perceptibly changed. Before my first meeting with him, back in 1902, Von Bülow had said: "You will find His Majesty interesting. There are a good many contradictions in his make-up. He is at once an eighteenth-century autocrat and an up-to-date, twentieth-century democrat."

And so I had found him. He was for ever rattling his sword and running away from a fight. He would say, as he did on July 4, 1900, at the launching of the battleship *Wittelsbach*, that "Neither upon the water nor upon the land, in faraway countries, must decisions be reached or events happen without the consent of Germany and the German Emperor," and in the next breath would assure you that his mission in life was to maintain peace among the nations.

I think we can see now how the militant spirit developed. William II was the child of his grandfather rather than of his father. The life of "Unser Fritz" was so short as to be of little avail in determining the character of his son. In his closing years the old Emperor gave the care of both external and internal politics to Bismarck, and devoted himself to his army. The young grandson was educated in this atmosphere. When he was called to the throne, the Empire was still an experiment. The South German Catholic states hated Prussia and its king, and there had grown up in Prussia what does not develop in a truly Catholic country, Socialism; there was real fear of the Pan-Slavic power on the east; and of the burning desire for revenge in France. It was but natural that the young emperor with these elements of menace before him should foster the military force of his nation, for police purposes within, as well as for protection from his dangerous neighbours. He was a Frankenstein, creating a monster, which was destined to destroy him.

2. As to the German people. I could see no evidence that any of them had any thought of an invasion of England. Not that they liked the English or any of the other nations. They were sorely disappointed at the outcome of the Morocco business and they did not feel that they had a "place in the sun." They were always violating what the young college student calls rule 5—never to take oneself too seriously. Their besetting sin, as Prince Hohenlohe once told Dr. Andrew D. White, was envy. After 1870 Bismarck had steadfastly opposed any attempt at colonial expansion, because he was engaged in unifying the empire. It was not long after that they awoke to find that other nations had been busy and all available colonial territories of value had been preëmpted. Wherefore their grief, their jealousy, and their hatred of their neighbours. But this discontent had not, in my judgment, been translated into any purpose to attack England. On the contrary, they felt that they could and would defeat almost any other nation if they could be assured that Britain would keep hands off. This, I am sure, was always their attitude. My observations in Berlin confirmed my judgment that Beresford and Northcliffe were needlessly alarmed.

Then I went to Rome. Mr. Cortesi, chief of the Associated Press service in Italy, gave me a dinner at which were gathered a number of conspicuous gentlemen. Among them was Von

Jagow, who later became German Minister of Foreign Affairs. At that time he was First Secretary of the German Embassy in Rome. I talked with him and was still further confirmed in my view.

Visiting Asia

I set out for the East. My wife and my daughter met me at Cairo and we left for India on January 5th. Among the passengers on the boat to Bombay was an intelligent German. It was obvious that he and the Englishmen aboard did not like each other. And so it fell out that he and I became acquainted. Yankee like, I plied him with questions. "Yes," he said in reply to my inquiry, "I live in India six months of every year. My business calls me there. I am in the aniline dye industry. We do a fine trade in India and make large profits from it."

I expressed some surprise and said that as aniline dyes were of English discovery and development, and as India was akin to a British colony, I should have thought it a difficult field of operations for Germans.

"Not so," he said. "Practically our only competition is from two other German factories on the Rhine and one Swiss concern at Basle. You are quite right in saying that aniline dyes as a substitute for vegetable dyes were of English origin. The invention of Sir William Perkin gave the Greenford Green Works a monopoly. But they limited their output to red and mauve dyes. We Germans widened the field by making dyes of all colours. The people of India liked yellow and green as well as red. The English would not furnish them. We did, and we secured the trade."

At a hotel in India it was noted that all of the table china, except the egg cups, were of English or French make. The Germans, in their ceaselesss hunt for commerce, had learned that the Indian hen laid a smaller egg than the European hen and they had made a small egg cup and found a sale for their product. This sort of commercial penetration was going on everywhere: Germany was growing rich and her people were content with her government.

At Bombay we encountered Douglas Robinson and his wife (sister of President Roosevelt). We took our way leisurely across the country, halting at Agra, Delhi, Cawnpore, Benares, and the other points of interest, and reached Calcutta in about a month. Here we ran across Sir Thomas Lipton, and here I was entertained by the Earl of Minto, at the time Viceroy. We moved on down to Madras and over to Colombo. After making a tour of Ceylon, we took a boat for the China Coast. We stopped a day at Penang to see Kang Yu Wei, the famous associate of Yuan Shih-kai as a revolutionist. A few days at Hong Kong and Canton and Shanghai, and we reached Japan early in March. We met a good many old friends and made a number of new ones. We were the guests of the American ambassador, Mr. Thomas J. O'Brien, of Grand Rapids, Michigan. With him I was commanded to an audience of the Emperor. I addressed about one hundred members of the Friends of America Society, composed of young men who had been educated in the United States, and I spoke to the Japanese Peace Society at Count Okuma's. I was called home to attend the annual meeting of the Associated Press, and sailed from Yokohama to San Francisco. My wife and my daughter went to Pekin and thence by the Transsiberian railway to Moscow, and back to our old home in Switzerland.

On May 11, 1911, I addressed a small company of people on my experiences and observations in Asia. Very much to my surprise much of what I said on this occasion was used as an article in the *National Geographic Magazine*. It was copied in some of the papers in Japan and created a sensation. As I had noted a dozen years before that practically all of Africa had been occupied by the European nations, in like fashion I found an extraordinary invasion in Asia. Nearly two thirds of the area of the Asiatic continent was under the control of European nations. And I found great injustice to the natives of India and China and Japan, for which the white race was responsible. All this seemed to me very menacing and I said so. There was a demand on the part of the European residents in Japan that I retract my statements. I not only declined but had more to say on the subject, and there the debate came to a close.

In 1911 the Ohio Wesleyan University conferred a degree of Doctor of Laws upon me *in absentia*.

Selecting an Associate

In 1912, at no small personal sacrifice, Mr. Frederick Roy Martin retired from the editorship of the *Providence Journal* and came to me as assistant general manager of the Associated Press. There then began a companionship and affection that have grown steadily to this hour. I cannot imagine that I could have made a better selection. Not alone by reason of his intellectual qualification, breadth of information, and executive ability, but by what was indispensable in a great coöperative organization, patience and a genial temperament, he was eminently fitted for the post.

Frederick Roy Martin

Little or nothing beyond the usual routine happened during 1913 or the early months of the succeeding year.

The World War

I think it was Joseph McCullough, the talented editor of the St. Louis *Globe-Democrat*, who said that the secret of real newspaper work was to know where something was to break loose and to have a man on the spot. If it be so, I must confess that I missed it at the beginning of the great World War. As I have said, for several years before the outbreak in 1914, while many others, and those whose judgment was clearly better than mine, were warning us of trouble, I did not believe them. I would have none of it.

Even when in June, 1914, there was a serious financial crisis in Vienna, I did not see its significance, and when the assassination of the Austrian Grand Duke at Serajevo was announced, harking back to the murder of Alexander and Draga, it seemed to me that Servia was about to receive a well-merited rebuke. The savage change of kingship in Servia from the Obrenovitch line to the Karageorgevitch line by assassination had led me to feel that it was quite possible that Servia was culpable in the Serajevo business. The ultimatum of Austria seemed rather the case of a stalwart man striking a small boy, but, after all, the small boy seemed a pretty bad boy. And as to Belgium, we were likewise indifferent. We had never had intimate relations with Belgium. We did not like the stories we had read of the licentious character of King Leopold, and we had been shocked by the tales of atrocities in the rubber fields of the Congo. Also, while we were thrilled by the moving speech of Sir Edward Grey and recognized it as a tocsin call to chivalry, we could not forget that, after all, Antwerp was a pistol pointed straight at the heart of Britain, and that Britain had and must have a strategic interest in the Belgian invasion by Germany. It was only another European imbroglio in which we had doubtful concern.

As the months went on, we began making munitions for the Entente powers. Out of this a few people were making large profits. This did not mean much for the great body of our citizens. Far more important was the fact that there was a lively demand for our farm products. Britain and France needed food which we could supply and from which we could profit largely in the supplying. We were a long way from the battle-field, we were living a life of ease, we did not want war.

Some of the more unselfish of us had a feeling that in the great conflict which was raging perhaps we could do more for humanity by maintaining an attitude of neutrality, so that in the end we might be accepted as an arbiter by the warring nations.

Lack of Preparedness

This was in the summer and fall of 1914. In November we elected a new national Congress. President Wilson felt, as the months went on, that we were certain to drift into the war but also that any president having the proper sense of his responsibility must be very slow about plunging his country into such a struggle.

I was with President McKinley in the early days of April, 1898, when the bellicose Americans were demanding war with Spain, and when his close friends, including Vice-President Hobart, Senators Hanna, Spooner, Aldrich, Frye, Fairbanks, and others, were watching the situation to see if they could muster strength enough in the Senate to sustain a veto in case a war resolution should be prematurely passed. McKinley was in great distress, but he sturdily refused to be forced even by a pugnacious Congress until he had exhausted all diplomatic agencies to secure peace.

On several occasions President Wilson asked me if I thought that Congress, which under the Constitution had the power to declare war, would declare war. I was forced to say it would not and I am sure now that it would not have done so.

As late as May 5, 1916, the New York *Tribune* tested the question. The following special telegram appeared in its issue on the morning of May 6th:

Washington, May 5. Congress, the sole war-making power of the Government, is overwhelmingly opposed to going to war with Germany, on the record of the submarine controversy in the last fifteen months. Congress believes that the severance of diplomatic relations with Germany would not be justified by the circumstances of the dispute, it being generally realized that a diplomatic break would lead to war eventually.

"The sentiment in Congress was disclosed by a poll of the opinions of the Senators and Representatives. To each Legislator was put the following question:

"Do you believe that up to this time Germany has given the United States sufficient provocation to go to war?

"Only one Senator—Williams of Mississippi—and three Representatives—Dale of Vermont, Greene of Massachusetts, and Platt of New York—answered in the affirmative."*

The question was asked of 81 Senators and 318 Representatives.

A month later the Republican National Convention for the

---
*New York *Tribune*, May 6, 1916, page 2, column 4.

nomination of a Presidential candidate met in Chicago and declared in its platform that:

"We believe in maintaining a strict and honest neutrality between the belligerents in the great war of Europe."

Governor Hughes was nominated on this platform. In a letter to James Bryce Theodore Roosevelt said there was a feeling that Hughes was nominated by the pro-German influence in the Republican Party.

So you see our going into the war or staying out of it was not at all an issue in the campaign. There was a good deal of talk about 100-per-cent. Americanism and the protection of our rights, but from first to last neither party was disposed to declare for war, and none of the candidates in the campaign speeches declared for our participation in the conflict.

So we went on to the Presidential election of 1916. There were opposing and clamorous forces. The outcome was clearly doubtful. And the situation was complicated by the manner of our Presidential election. In the early days of the Republic the date of our Presidential election was fixed for an early day in November and the inauguration of the Chief Magistrate for an early day of the succeeding March. This was necessary because at the time the means of communication were so limited that a lapse of four months was requisite to determine the result of the balloting. George Washington's inauguration was postponed several weeks because even this four months was insufficient. Later we passed to party rule, and then nominations for Presidential candidates were made by conventions which met in the springtime. So it came about that now we have a period of suspense of eight months every four years. And if there be a change of parties the retiring incumbent is practically estopped from adopting any new and definite policy lest he embarrass his successor, while the incoming Chief Executive is powerless to enforce a policy until he is inaugurated.

In 1916 the party conventions were held in June and July, and the usual period of waiting and of doubt as to the result began. It may be true that Mr. Wilson was reëlected because he had "kept us out of war." If so, his "keeping us out of war" met the approval of the voters.

The campaign was a difficult one to report. The first thing, as in every Presidential contest, was to have some words with the candidates. Mr. Wilson had learned the ropes in 1912, so it was unnecessary to see him. Governor Hughes was a "new hand at the bellows." I made an appointment and he came to New York for a meeting at the Hotel Astor. I introduced him to the mysteries of "advance matter"; and told him how impossible it was to secure any newspaper publicity from a "tail-end" tour—meaning a journey over the country with speeches in halls and from the platforms of railway cars. Of all the performances this is about the most illusory and profitless. It is pretty nearly true that no Presidential candidate who has ever engaged in it has won.

Judge Douglas tried it in 1860 and was defeated by Mr. Lincoln, who stayed at his home in Springfield. Andrew Johnson "swung around the circle" and came within one of being impeached. Horace Greeley galloped over the Middle West in 1872, while Grant, his opponent, stayed in the White House and carried the election. Blaine failed in the same way in 1884. Taft's journey to the Pacific Coast in 1909 did not help him.

Perhaps the most striking illustration was the struggle of 1896. Bryan, a brilliant orator, stumped the country, speaking to enormous crowds. The Associated Press men who travelled with him were greatly impressed, and told me of the millions who gathered to welcome the itinerant, the wild enthusiasm displayed, and the certainty of his ultimate victory. I replied that they failed to take into account the human curiosity involved, that nine out of ten in the great crowds greeting Bryan would have been equally excited by a visit of a circus, and that McKinley, who was making one speech a week from his cottage porch at Canton, was really reaching the public mind as Bryan was not by the practice he had adopted. And so it proved.

I told Governor Hughes what was sure to happen with his "touch-and-go" talking. He would arrive at a town in the evening, make a hasty speech, and move on. The reporters would make a hurried report to be handed to a telegraph operator at the next stopping place. The operator would probably be an incompetent. The report would necessarily be greatly abbreviated in order to secure transmission. On its receipt by a newspaper in the rush hour it would be again "cut down," so that when Hughes read the story as it appeared in print he would probably be unable to recognize it as his own speech. On the other hand, if he would give me half a dozen well-prepared addresses a week in advance, so that I could mail them to our newspapers throughout the country, they would be put in type during the leisure hours in the newspaper offices and on the day of their delivery would be released by two or three words of telegraph. I told him how President Roosevelt had managed things, how he had given me his messages to Congress on some occasions six weeks in advance, so that they were released and printed in Tokio and St. Petersburg on the morning after delivery.

But my advice was not accepted. The managers sent Governor Hughes on his journey. Things turned out as I knew they would, President Wilson made a speech a week at Long Branch and gave it out in advance, and when the campaign was over the Republicans felt that the Associated Press had not given them their fair share of publicity.

When Election Day came we had our hands full. We had made great preparations and were really alone in the business of consolidating the vote of the country to determine the result. Early in the evening and long before the polls had closed in the Far West the Democratic papers of the East conceded Hughes's election. Of course it was not our business to announce anybody's election until we knew what the count would disclose. Then began the clamour. Message after message came asking if I was owned by the Democrats, and why on earth I did not accept the admissions of the Wilson papers and announce Hughes's election. Hour after hour passed and the outcome appeared more and more doubtful. At one time it was thought the State of Minnesota was a determining factor. The suspense was great. It was not until Friday that we finished counting the votes and found that Wilson had carried California and therefore had won.

There had been such a shifting of party lines that nothing save a most careful count could be used as a basis for any declaration in respect of the matter. On former occasions, when party lines were sharply drawn, I had been able to announce the result at seven or eight o'clock in the evening, so that even the papers in London, with a difference of five hours in time against them, advised their readers of the name of the victorious candidate.

Within a month after his inauguration and the assemblage of a new Congress having a different mind, in 1917, we were in the war at Wilson's urgency. We were not well prepared as to an army or as to munitions. We were prepared in that which was of far greater worth—the public mind. The mind of Germany had been made up in an hour, at Potsdam, on the 5th of July, 1914, because it was the mind of one man—the German Emperor. With us, the national mind was the mind of one hundred and ten millions of people. And in 1917, when President Wilson said the word which called us to battle, we were ready, and we challenged the admiration of the world by our unity of purpose and consequent energy and efficiency.

Other nations were as little prepared as we were. The King of Italy sent for Mr. Cortesi, chief of our Italian service, early in November, 1914, and talked with him very freely about the situation. He emphasized the difficult position of Italy between the Central Empires which had been her allies for thirty-two years, and the powers of the Triple Entente toward which she was inclined, for reasons which everyone knew. He said that the war took Italy by surprise, as it did all other countries. He thought the complaint of people that the Italians were not prepared was unjustified as her fleet was in the fittest condition, and as to the army, he said that no army in any country on the eve of a war did not lack a thousand things, while Italy "lacked a thousand and two hundred, but hastened to get ready in all directions" and at the moment of the conversation had 650,000 men under colours in perfect condition and this number could be doubled in the shortest time. The King said that he did not believe it possible for Italy to keep out of the war and that her neutrality should be understood as a preparation for joining in the conflict. He gave Mr. Cortesi the impression that Italy would go to war against Germany in the following spring, as she did. He said that Italy wanted a restoration of the Trentino and Trieste, but not Dalmatia because that had almost entirely become inhabited by people of Slav nationality and its possession would be difficult to defend; it would be a source of constant struggle with the Balkan States and with Russia. Italy, however, he said, aspired to all the many islands in the Adriatic so as to have complete command of that sea. He said there was an understanding between Rumania and Italy by which Rumania was to join the Entente forces and Italy follow.

He told a number of amusing incidents respecting the Italian censorship. As was known, he was a passionate sportsman and on one occasion, hunting in a forest, had been so fortunate as to kill a very rare bird called the "Knight of Italy." Knowing that a bird collector in Naples had been for years vainly trying to obtain a specimen of the bird, he rushed to the nearest village and sent the collector the following wire:

In the forests near the hunting lodge of San Rossore, have killed Knight of Italy.

The telegram went on its way but was soon stopped by the authorities, and the police set out to find the scene of the murder and to capture the supposed assassin. The forest was carefully searched, and a description of the sender of the message given by the telegraph clerk resulted in the arrest of several suspected people. The mystery was finally cleared up when one of the officials suggested that they interrogate the bird collector at Naples respecting the matter, and thus the truth was discovered.

The situation in England was little better. Fortunately Haldane, as War Minister, had created a body of militia, the Territorials, and these constituted a nucleus which made it possible to rush relief to France.

France was likewise in trouble. We had come to look upon her as an emotional nation, splendid in a charge upon the battle-field, but not likely to stand fire for a long period. We were mistaken. She showed remarkable endurance from first to last of the war. There has never been a more thrilling or decisive struggle than the Battle of the Marne. The steadfast defence of Paris evoked world-wide amazement and applause.

And even Germany was not prepared. Her army was all right, but her diplomacy all wrong. She thought England on the verge of civil war over the Irish question, France decadent, and Russia still incapacitated from the war with Japan. She made no account of the High Court of Public Opinion of the world, which, in the end, was to decide the business.

Reporting the War

Before the war it was easy to report the world's happenings. We had developed a system which gave reasonable assurance that practically every event of great moment should come promptly into the knowledge of every civilized community. Then the war came. In a night all of the processes of civilization, so carefully established and conserved, went down. Certain agencies which for more than half a century had been devoted coöperating associates became enemies by governmental order and were prohibited from any commerce with each other. It was evident that this war was to be unlike any former contest. It was not to be a struggle between praetorian armies but between nations in arms. The battle line extended from the North Sea to the Swiss border. There were to be no dramatic cavalry charges, no opportunity for thrilling reportorial descriptions. Long-distance gunnery furnished little opportunity for word pictures. Take it altogether, however, we did fairly well.

Our first difficulty was with the censorship established in England. Army censors as a rule are unwise in that their aim is inordinately to suppress all information. They lose sight of the great value of discrimination and of permitting the public mind which is back of them to know enough of the situation to enable them to sympathize with the military endeavour.

A number of the British censors were half-pay retired colonels and some of the things they did, while annoying, were amusing. For instance, when war was declared on Austria, a stupid censor refused to allow the information to come to the Associated Press, but released it for publication to one New York newspaper. There was an investigation, and he calmly said that he knew the Associated Press was a great organization and that he felt he could not take the responsibility of permitting the message to go to it, but he thought it would do no harm to let it go to an individual paper in the United States. Again, when the Battle of Jutland was fought and a victory won by the British, a censor refused to permit the Admiralty story to come out on the ground that he had been notified that he must not allow any dispatch to go out indicating the location of any British warship. Once more, when Premier Asquith made an important speech, the censors refused to allow it to come to the Associated Press because, as Mr. Asquith himself said, "I suppose they thought I was disloyal to the British cause." All this led to many complications, but in time adjustments were effected.

When Mr. Arthur Balfour came to the United States in May, 1917, after we were in the war, I saw him and called his attention to our experiences with the British censors and he agreed that it was all wrong and that he would seek to remedy it. He was not able to do all that he desired and it was far into 1918 before the administration of the British censorship was intelligent.

René Viviani and Marshal Joffre came over as a commission from France. I had a delightful visit with the dear old Marshal. Later, when I was in Paris, I saw him with some frequency, and the other day I received a letter from Mr. Roberts, chief of our office in France, in which he said that Marshal Joffre wanted to send me a photograph of himself. At his request Roberts selected one and the Marshal inscribed it and sent it to me. He is a great character, and his victory at the outbreak of the war in the Battle of the Marne has immortalized him.

The Case of Cardinal Mercier

There was the case of Cardinal Mercier, Archbishop of Malines, in Belgium. He was in no small sense one of those who won the great World War. For it was not, after all, the armies or navies that did the thing. It was the public opinion of the world. Public opinion made armies and navies possible. And who did more than Cardinal Mercier to create that controlling public opinion?

Cardinal Mercier

The ruthless invasion of Belgium filled the world with horror. Bethmann-Hollweg, whom I knew as a kind-hearted creature, was forced, speaking for his Imperial master, to make abject apology, admitting the infamy, but pleading necessity. It called to mind the phrase in the Fifth Book of "Paradise Lost," where Satan in trying to justify his entry to the Garden of Eden, was quoted:

> Thus spake the fiend, and with necessity
> The tyrant's plea, excused his devilish deed.

In that hour there was one man in Belgium who gave to chance the keeping of his life, and bravely spoke the truth. It was the Primate of Malines. His Christmas pastoral of 1914 rang out over the world, a challenge of civilization to savagery.

Von Bissing, the German Commander in Belgium, was furious, and was ready to resort to extreme measures. The Cardinal was subjected to offensive espionage, was forbidden to make his usual round of pastoral visits, and there were rumours of much worse things. Then, in the ordinary course, and as a part of the daily routine, I sent some messages to our correspondents, instructing them to watch the case. These telegrams came to the attention of the authorities in Berlin and they promptly directed Von Bissing to keep "hands off." The Cardinal, when he visited this country, hailed me as his "saviour," and betrayed a sense of gratitude out of all proportion to the service I was conscious of having rendered.

Case of the Lusitania

In April, 1915, my son Herbert had occasion to go to Europe, and particularly to Germany, on business. He determined to sail on the *Lusitania*. Before going, he went to Washington and secured from Count Bernstorff, the German ambassador, a number of letters to important men in Berlin. Bernstorff knew that he was going on the *Lusitania*. My son was the more ready to ask this favour of the German ambassador because he knew that in a large measure Bernstorff owed his position to me. Bernstorff's predecessor, Speck von Sternberg, was an intimate personal friend of mine. He developed an inflammation upon his cheek which some of us feared was cancerous. One day, when I was in Berlin, talking with the Kaiser, I asked about Sternberg's health and the Emperor said that he had had the case examined by court physicians, who had pronounced it a harmless thing. "But," said the Kaiser, "Sternberg is forced to wear a very offensive white plaster on his cheek and he cannot easily attend social functions. I think I shall have to place him on the retired list for this reason. Of course, we shall have to have as his successor an ambassador with an American wife." And then he laughed and called attention to the fact that the French ambassador to the United States had an American wife. The Belgian minister had an American wife and George Bakhmeteff was slated for the Russian Embassy and he had an American wife. "What would you think of Count Bernstorff?" he continued, "he has an American wife." I replied that I had known Bernstorff for a number of years as secretary of the German Embassy in London, and thought very highly of him. "Then I shall appoint him," said the Kaiser, and within a few days he did so.

Therefore when Bernstorff came to this country we at once became friends. And he knew my son and his family.

On the morning of May 1st our whole family went down to the boat to see my son depart. Marconi joined us. We had noted the advertisement of caution in the morning papers, and in common with everyone else we laughed about it. I had said that unless some such ship as the *Lusitania* was torpedoed, the U-boat threat of Germany would become ridiculous. But to sink a boat like the *Lusitania* was so barbarous an act as to be unthinkable. Such was our feeling when the *Lusitania* left her dock.

I know that a number of interesting but wholly untruthful tales about this business have been told. They have been invented by publicity seekers who were not over-scrupulous about their facts. For instance, the claim that a code message devised from the "New York World Almanac," and indicating the prospective sailing of the *Lusitania*, was sent by wireless to the German authorities was a pure invention. And the statement of William Roscoe Thayer, in his Life of Theodore Roosevelt (p. 409) seems to me equally lacking in verity. He says:

> Bernstorff, we know now, planned the sinking and gave the German Government notice by wireless just where the submarines could best destroy the *Lusitania* on that Friday afternoon.

On reading this statement, I wrote to Thayer, telling him of my peculiar interest in the matter and asking for his authority. He replied in a curt note that a Government secret service man, whose identity he could not disclose, was his informant. I thought he could at least have said that, in the light of the fact that my son was a Harvard graduate, he would make some effort to give me the proof of his assertion. But he did not. Presumably because he could not.

On Friday, May 7th, I was at the Hotel Vanderbilt, taking luncheon with a friend. Suddenly I heard a boy paging me. He said I was wanted at the telephone, the Associated Press was calling me. My secretary then told me that the *Lusitania* had been torpedoed. I hastened to my office and learned the sad truth. Late that night it became evident that my son was among the lost.

As I was wondering whether Bernstorff could have been so much a savage as to let my son go on the *Lusitania*, knowing that the boat was to be a target, I was called on the telephone by a Chicago friend, Mr. William G. Beale, law partner of Robert Lincoln. He said that he felt he should tell me that on the memorable Friday afternoon he and Mrs. Beale, en route from the Virginia Hot Springs, were sitting in a parlour car. After the stop at North Philadelphia, Bernstorff came in with blanched face and apparently terrified. He said the afternoon paper which he had just bought announced the sinking of the

Lusitania. "Believe me," said Beale, "he could not simulate the surprise or grief which he betrayed." I have never had anything to do with Bernstorff since, but in common justice, from the evidence before me, I accept as true his statement to Hayden Talbot:

"Do you think—had I known it—I should have allowed three of the best friends I had in America to take passage on the *Lusitania?*"
As he spoke tears came into his eyes and his voice shook.
"I not only let them go. I gave them friendly letters of introduction to certain gentlemen in London. Those three men were Mr. Vanderbilt, Charles Klein, the playwright, an Englishman, and the young son of Melville Stone, head of the Associated Press. No one will suggest that any man could be such a monster as deliberately to send three human beings, his friends, to their graves!"

I learned from survivors that my son went to his death as I should have expected him to do. Before he sailed I had given him a note of introduction to Madame Depage, the wife of the eminent Belgian surgeon, who was to be a fellow-passenger. When the torpedo struck the boat Herbert put on a life belt and hunted out Madame Depage. She was a frail little woman and asked if my son would permit her to be attached to him when they went into the water. Before it could be done a certain Doctor Houghton, who knew them both, said he was strong and a good swimmer and had better look after the poor lady. And so it was agreed. Then Herbert saw an unfortunate woman, obviously from the steerage, with no life belt. He took off his own, put it on her, and went to his death unprotected and without a tremor.

Herbert Stone was born in Chicago in May, 1871. He received his preparatory education at Château de Lancy, Geneva, Switzerland, and subsequently entered Harvard University, graduating in 1894. He started the publishing business of Stone & Kimball in 1894, while still at Harvard, He was the founder of the *Chap Book*, a semi-monthly literary magazine which created some interest and had a host of imitators. He owned and edited *The House Beautiful*. He sold his interest in the publications in 1897.

My second son, Melville E. Stone, Jr., was also a Harvard man. He won distinction as president of the famous Hasty Pudding Club. He graduated in 1897. After some association with his brother in the publishing business he became editor of the *Metropolitan Magazine*, a service in which he was distinctly successful. He was forced to retire from this office as he was attacked by tuberculosis. With my wife and daughter, he journeyed to northern Italy, Switzerland, the Adirondacks, and Arizona to recover his health. When the war came on he was in Pasadena, California, and was most active in urging America's participation. His contribution was too great for his enfeebled condition, and he passed away in January, 1917.

Herbert Stuart Stone

Melville E. Stone, Jr.

Doctor Depage's Hospital

I have spoken of Madame Depage. Let me tell you of her husband.

Gaston Calmette, the famous editor of the Paris *Figaro*, who was killed by Madame Caillaux, was a friend with whom I spent many delightful hours on my visits to Paris years ago. After his fashion he was a successful journalist. One day he printed what purported to be a circumstantial telegraphic story of the massacre of many citizens of New York by savage Indians who invaded Broadway. It was not at all a whimsical hoax, to be exposed and laughed over the next day; it was an imposition upon his readers.

I upbraided him for it. "Nonsense," he replied, "you are too serious with your ideas of accuracy. There are, among the readers of *Figaro*, thousands of the demi-monde, to whom this story is more interesting and pleasing than any of the commonplaces you call news."

There was a world congress of physicians and surgeons at Washington and Gaston's brother, Doctor Calmette, came over and called on me. He introduced an eminent Belgian physician, one Doctor Depage, who presided over the congress.

Years went by and early in 1915 the wife of this Doctor Depage came to America to collect funds for the Belgian Red Cross, of which her husband was acting as chief. She came to me, and I was able to advise her to some purpose. As I have said, she sailed for home on the *Lusitania*. When the boat was torpedoed she was among those drowned.

The work that Doctor Depage did in the great war was very notable. But he was always embarrassed by the inadequate means at his command. He had learned, when in this country, how much further we had advanced in our surgical methods than had Europe. There had never been, either in France or Belgium, such a hospital or such a school for the training of nurses as we had. He longed to found such an institution in Brussels in memory of his dead wife, and of Edith Cavell, who had been one of his nurses. He came back to New York and to me in 1920, to see what could be done. He thought he would need approximately three million dollars and hoped for one million from us, another from England, and the third million from France and Belgium.

I told him frankly how, after the end of the fighting, our generous emotions had suffered a sudden collapse, and of the difficulties I felt he was sure to encounter. I suggested that before attempting any nation-wide "drive" for funds it would be well to submit the matter to the Rockefeller Foundation and the Red Cross Society. If they would give the enterprise their approval and make contributions, however small, it would greatly aid his undertaking.

To this end, I gave a small dinner in his honour, inviting several surgeons and other friends to meet him. Among the guests was Dr. George Vincent, whose father and mine had been fellow Methodist ministers in Illinois. Depage's plan was presented and Doctor Vincent, on behalf of the Rockefeller Foundation, of which he was president, agreed to make an investigation with a view to a possible contribution.

President Wilson

The Hero of the Battle of the Marne

Then I heard no more of the business for a year. Doctor Depage had gone home and I confess that his needs had almost passed from my mind. Suddenly he reappeared and with tears in his eyes told of the wonderful result of our little dinner. Vincent had kept his word, they had sent investigators to Belgium, and now they had notified him that the Foundation would give two and a half million dollars toward a great enterprise, including a municipal hospital and the medical laboratories of the University of Brussels. This was much more than the good Doctor Depage had thought at all possible and aided in surprising measure to the realization of his ideals. All and more than he hoped for had in a way come to pass. He was overwhelmed with gratitude.

In the early summer of 1915 I was the recipient of an honorary degree of Master of Arts from Yale University.

America in the War

On April 6, 1917, the new Congress at Washington adopted a resolution declaring that a state of war existed with the German Government and authorizing the President to employ the entire resources of the Government to carry on the war and to bring the conflict to a successful termination. Three weeks later the annual meeting of the Associated Press assembled in New York and unanimously adopted by a rising vote a resolution:

That as loyal citizens of the United States, we hereby pledge our hearty support of the effort of the executives of the Government to carry out effectively the mandate of the nation as expressed in the war resolution adopted by Congress.

Two or three days later I went to Washington and accompanied Mr. Noyes to the White House, when he notified President Wilson of the action of the Associated Press. Growing out of our experience with the foreign censorship, we suggested to the President that the newspapers of the United States were deeply interested in the war and quite as anxious as any branch of the Government for our success, and that it seemed to us that it would be wise to establish by law a censorship, but it would also be well to include in the governing board of the censorship a competent journalist. This because the army and the navy, out of their general impulse to suppress everything, would be likely to excise matter which would really be valuable to stimulate the national morale. The President agreed with us.

Of course, the appointment of Mr. George Creel as a representative of the American press surprised us. He was not recognized as a leading journalist by the great body of newspapermen in the country, although he later assured me that Mr. Hearst had offered him some fabulous salary to enter his service. A great many complications resulted from the appointment of Creel. On the 3rd of July, 1917, he gave out a story of two battles between our first transport fleet under Admiral Gleaves and German submarines. The statement said the attack by the submarines "was made in force, although the night made impossible any exact count of the U-boats gathered for what they deemed a slaughter."

Since U-boats are blind when submerged it was necessary that they travel alone, lest they collide and injure each other. They do not attack "in force." But this fact was no deterrent for Creel.

When this account of the "two battles" reached England and was read at Admiral Sims's station, we received a despatch which read as follows:

July 5, 1917. London. Thursday confidential following Americas naval base *passed for publication USA only* quote private attitude official circles here that Daniels story made out of whole cloth there no submarine attack whatever no torpedoes seen no gunfire from destroyers stop our destroyers dropped explosive charge as precaution but no submarine or wreckage seen stop explained destroyers frequently fire at logs or anything which might prove periscope stop officials therefore decline permit aftermath story from this end. A. P.

It will be seen on its face that this telegram would seem to be intended for publication in the United States, but the fact is that the words "passed for publication in the United States only" were stamped on the despatch by the English censor and should not have been transmitted by cable. Out of the misunderstanding the despatch, which was really intended to be confidential, was given to the American press and Secretary Daniels was notified of it. He was greatly excited and over the long-distance telephone asked me to kill the message. In obedience to the policy laid down by the annual meeting and our general desire, I did send out a notice to kill, but it was too late; it had already been published in a good many newspapers.

A few days later I went to Washington and saw Secretary Daniels. He said that as we were friends of many years' standing, we would have no quarrel over the matter, but that Gleaves would never forgive me. I said I was sorry but it could not be helped.

Then two or three weeks after Mayor Mitchel of New York gave a large dinner to one of the numerous foreign missions that came to New York that year. In the anteroom the guests assembled to have their cocktails. Suddenly I felt someone take me by the arm, and looking about, found it was Admiral Gleaves. In a very cheery way he said: "Mr. Stone, is there any reason why you and I can't have a cocktail together?" I accepted his invitation. And then he told me that he wanted to have a talk with me, to which I replied that I was equally anxious to talk with him. He invited me out to his ship in the Hudson River to lunch with him and I accepted. On the appointed day he was called to Washington and the luncheon was off. A day or two after I met him in the Metropolitan Club and he repeated the invitation for a cocktail and I again joined him. We made another appointment for luncheon, and one Sunday he came. To my utter amazement he opened the conversation by saying: "Mr. Stone, I owe you a debt that I never can repay. I mean for denying that silly story given out from Washington respecting two fierce battles with submarines. I am a plain common sailor and not given to that kind of statement. I do not know any better than you whether there was a submarine anywhere near us or not. Of course, the order to all our boats was that if anything like a periscope appeared to fire at it, and that was done. The officers on the individual boats thought they saw evidences of one or more periscopes and, as they ought to do, took a shot at them. With the denial which the Associated Press sent out, I can now show my face among my fellow naval officers, as I could not otherwise have done."

So far as Admiral Gleaves was concerned, the bloody chasm seemed to have been very easily bridged. Not long after my niece happened to be in New York and stopping at a little private hotel on 32nd Street. I asked her to luncheon with me at Sherry's and went to the hotel to call for her. While waiting for her to descend from her room Admiral Gleaves dashed out of the dining room and said his wife was anxious to meet me; she was stopping at the hotel. I went into the dining room and was presented, and she said she had been very anxious to meet me in order to thank me for the denial of the silly 4th of July story. From that day to this Admiral Gleaves and I have been warmer friends than we ever were before, which is saying a good deal.

A curious side-incident developed. President Wilson took great offence at the matter and announced that he would never speak to me again, to which I replied that I would strive to exist as best I could nevertheless. As a matter of fact, for nearly two years I never saw the President or spoke to him.

During the progress of the Peace Conference in Paris Colonel House and I frequently went out for a ride in the suburbs of the city. On one occasion he said that the President would like to know if I would accept an invitation to lunch with him, his other guest being the British Prime Minister, Mr. Lloyd George. He said that he had assured the President that the Prime Minister and I were on good terms and he thought it would be agreeable. He wanted to know what I had to say. I replied that the President had said he would never speak to me, I thought he must have forgotten. However, if he should invite me, it would be like a command from a sovereign and I would be bound to accept. House reported this to the President, who said yes, in a fit of anger he had undoubtedly said that, but he would like to forget it. So I received the invitation.

The luncheon was in what was known as the Paris White House. Besides Lloyd George and myself the others present were Mrs. Wilson and Colonel House. At the table the President said grace and was most felicitous as a host. He told a number of amusing stories and then had something to say about the Scotch-Irish, remarking that he was of Scotch-Irish descent, that his father was a clergyman, and turning to me said that Mr. Stone was also of Scotch-Irish ancestry and the son of a minister. I said that it was quite true and that in my infancy I had taken great care to select the right kind of an ancestry, so that every drop of blood in my veins was either English, Irish, or Scotch, and that I had taken equal pains to see that there was no Welsh, this being directed at Lloyd George. The Prime Minister turned with a laugh and said, "Well, Taffy was a Welshman, wasn't he!" Later, when I was at 10 Downing Street in London with Lloyd George, I asked if he was at all surprised that the President should say grace at such a luncheon. I said that my father, being a minister, always "asked a blessing" at every meal, but that President Wilson was not a minister. "Did it occur to you," I asked, "that it is rather unusual?" "Yes," he replied, "but I thought it was done for your benefit."

The Memorable Year 1918

After all, the year 1918 was perhaps the most important in my life. It certainly was an exceedingly busy one.

I went out to St. Louis to address the Chamber of Commerce. It was the 23d of March. A committee met me at the railway station in the early morning and after breakfast took me for a ride about the city. About noon I suggested that I should call at our local office. Arriving there I found I was badly needed. An amazing cable message had been received from France. It announced that a heavy siege gun had been bombarding Paris throughout the forenoon. The shells had been fired a distance of seventy-two miles at intervals of fifteen minutes, beginning shortly after five o'clock. It order to reach the city it was estimated that each shell must mount at least twenty miles in the air. The cablegram was sent from Paris at eleven o'clock Paris time.

The story was so improbable that it gave much concern to our New York office and I must decide whether we should assume responsibility for it. To add to the complication, the gunnery men of the Government at Washington denounced the tale as absurd. Here was a dilemma. Of course, if the thing were untrue, the consequences would be most serious. We should never hear the last of it.

I took the telegram into a private room for meditation. I knew Mr. Roberts, the chief of our Paris bureau, was not a man who would lose his head. And he had waited five hours after the firing began before sending the cable. Finally, there was a French censor who would not permit a canard to be sent. I said we would "stand pat."

That evening the president of the club chaffed me about my claim for accuracy for the Associated Press, and asked what I had to say of the impossible story from Paris which had appeared in the evening papers. "Well," I replied, "back in New York I have a friend, the Rev. Dr. Minot J. Savage, Unitarian, who holds with a Cape Cod farmer that the religious faith of the Evangelical Christian is 'believin' in a thing that you know ain't so.' Such is my position. I believe this story 'that I know ain't so,' because the Associated Press says it."

A few days later the Indiana members of the Associated Press held a meeting and by a rising vote adopted a most gratifying greeting, which was transmitted by telegraph. On April 18th I went to Pittsburg and with Herbert Hoover and Stephane Lauzanne, editor of the *Matin* of Paris, addressed a large company on the occasion of the anniversary of the founding of the Pittsburg Press Club.

A Fine Funeral

I had served as general manager for twenty-five years, my seventieth birthday was approaching, and for some time I had recognized that in obedience to the natural law I would soon have to drop out of the activities of my vocation. It became important to determine who should succeed me as general manager of the Associated Press. I had chosen in Mr. Martin, a gentleman in whom I had full confidence. For twenty-five years I had had unchallenged authority to employ, discipline, and dismiss every member of the Associated Press staff. I believed that I had built up a personnel that was capable of continuing the work after my retirement. If I had not done so my work would have been in large measure a failure. But this was not all. It was not sufficient that I should be satisfied with the fitness of the gentlemen whom I had employed to conduct the work after my disappearance; it was equally important that the Board of Directors and the members of the Associated Press and the public should be convinced. I asked a private meeting of the directors and told them very frankly my feeling. The spirit manifested by the directors was as affectionate as any one could wish. They reluctantly accepted my view and it was arranged that I should go to Europe, ostensibly in connection with the Associated Press work, but really for the purpose of giving my associates in the executive department an opportunity to demonstrate their capacity.

Then the Board of Directors held a secret meeting to which I was not invited. The annual meeting of the organization was approaching. It was usual, at the annual meeting, to have either a dinner or a luncheon. Much to my surprise I was not consulted about the luncheon, as to who should speak or what the programme should be, but was told by my friends on the board that they would arrange the matter. Then on the 23d of April the luncheon came off and proved to be a function in my honour. The Board of Directors, at their secret session, had adopted the following resolutions:

WHEREAS, MELVILLE E. STONE, on the 3rd of March, 1918, completed a period of twenty-five years as General Manager of the Associated Press; first leading with unflagging courage and determination in the battle which freed the telegraphic news service of the Nation from control and exploitation by selfish private interests, and with wise enthusiasm and clear vision labouring for the firm establishment of the coöperative principle in ownership and management; then with extraordinary resourcefulness and constructive genius planning and directing the development of a world-wide system of news-gathering and distribution—always with unswerving devotion to the highest ideals of the newspaper profession and the best standards of American citizenship;

RESOLVED: That a suitable volume be compiled, to set forth in permanent form the record of the service of Melville E. Stone, his life and activities as a loyal and public-spirited American citizen; his contributions by voice and pen to the advancement of the cause of liberty and of freedom of speech and of the press as furthered by a clean, responsible, efficient, and courageous American journalism; and more particularly his work for and in the Associated Press, to whose character, growth, and achievements he has contributed so much of fidelity, industry, and inspiration.

RESOLVED: That upon the occasion of the Annual Meeting of The Associated Press in April, 1918, a copy of this volume be delivered to each member of the Association, and that a special copy, suitably bound and inscribed, be presented to Mr. Stone, with due expression of the admiration, gratitude, and affection of his colleagues.

A beautiful copy *de luxe* of the volume in question, which was entitled "M. E. S., His Book. A Tribute and a Souvenir of the 'A. P.' 1893–1918," with twenty-five one-thousand-dollar Liberty Bonds interleaved, was presented to me. Fifteen hundred other copies had been printed for distribution among the members of the organization. The work contained several flattering encomiums, and perhaps I may gratify my vanity by reproducing certain of them from men with whom I had been most intimately associated. The following was from my old-time partner, who had served with great sacrifice, devotion, and ability as the president of the Associated Press of Illinois, and was the real father of the self-governing news-gathering organization:

MY DEAR MEL:

For fifty years we have known each other, and for more than forty years we have been intimately associated. Out of the memories of the years I give you this day the greetings of affectionate friendship.

Someone has said that the great things of life often lie with their little ends toward us. It was a little thing that nearly forty-two years ago you asked me to join you in the then little adventure of the *Daily News*. But it was a great thing that twenty-five years ago, as a direct consequence of our earlier association, you and I, and the friends who are now gone, joined in the great adventure of the Associated Press.

And how little a thing it was—that four-page, five-column *Daily News*, "published somewhere on Fifth Avenue behind a tree," as a condescending five-cent contemporary observed—that brought us together forty-two years ago, and how great a thing, world-wide in its activities and its consequence, has been born out of the convictions and the labours of the later years— labours in which you and I have been privileged to have a part with the good men and true of those early days and those who remain unto this present.

Victor F. Lawson

You have now rounded out a quarter of a century in the service of the Associated Press. I congratulate you, and the Associated Press. When you were called to this service—and I say "called" advisedly—the import and large consequence of the high calling already foreshadowed themselves to your and our recognition. You came to the work in a day of stress when, in very truth, the independence of the American press was challenged by a selfish commercialism. How well you bore your part through all those years of anxious conflict, and how faithfully and wisely you contributed in these and later days to those constructive labours upon which has been reared the structure of the American coöperative news service, is in a very large measure the history of the Associated Press.

But not alone to us of the newspaper calling have you given the loyalty and strength of your years, but in a very real sense, and in a measure that only we who share with you the like responsibility for the maintenance of the wellsprings of public information and right action pure and untainted by sinister influences can fully appreciate, your life has been truly devoted to the public good. In a word, in all these years you have been the right man in the right place, a place of high service and of corresponding honour. And so I congratulate you on both your opportunity and your success. And I congratulate the Associated Press not only on what has been accomplished in all these years under your directing hand, but also that the past is but an earnest of the future as you bring to each day's service the gathering resources—the added experience and the ripened judgment—of the years, each better than the last. May the years that remain be many, as many for you and for us, as the all-ruling love that is better to us each than can be our own desires shall permit.

And so, as these things of the past crowd upon the memory, shall we not say—you and I, partner—that along with the chastening sorrows of life—mysteries which it is not given us now to understand—have come to us both the generous rewards of service, and that unto us the lines have indeed fallen in pleasant places. And at the last—whether it come soon or late—for you and for us and for all we love, may it be light at eventide.

Yours in the fellowship of the years.

VICTOR F. LAWSON.

Chicago, Feb. 4, 1918.

The contribution of Mr. Frank B. Noyes, who has been president of the Associated Press of New York from its incorporation in 1900 was as follows:

> Too often we wait until a man has passed away before we say the things that are always in our hearts concerning him, and so the opportunity of recording, even haltingly, as I must, the regard and deep affection for Melville E. Stone that the long years of close association have brought to me is peculiarly welcome, as the present year of his service to the cause he has laboured for finds him serving as greatly as the first.

Frank B. Noyes

> . . . .
>
> When, in 1893, Western newspapermen, headed by Victor F. Lawson, resolved to make their fight for a press service that should belong to its newspaper members and be controlled by them and by them alone; that should be coöperative and non-profit-making, they turned to Melville E. Stone, not then engaged in active newspaper work, and laid on him the heavy burden of leading in this battle for a principle.
>
> In all the world, in my belief, there was no man so fitted for this great duty as the man then selected.
>
> It is not my function to tell the epic story of the giant conflict between the organization then formed, founded on the belief that

the safety of the press and of the people required that the news service of the American newspapers should be controlled by the newspapers, and that other organization, then dominant, which had for its purpose only the making of profits. That struggle ended in the complete triumph of the coöperative principle, with the Associated Press admittedly the greatest news-gathering and distributing organization in the world. Nor am I to tell you of his insistent fight through years for the principle of Property Right in News—for the right of the news gatherer to the fruit of his labour. The records of these endeavours and many others are written elsewhere in this volume.

My acquaintance with Stone began in 1893, some time before the Associated Press, of which he was General Manager, began actually to function. Early in 1894 I became a director and member of the Executive Committee of the organization, and from that day to this have been in intimate touch with him, either in the Illinois organization or in the present New York organization that was formed later.

First let me speak of his immense services to the newspapers of this country, regardless of whether or not they are represented in the membership of the Associated Press. Melville E. Stone came into the fight for a news service that would be unsubservient to private interests, with a full sympathy for its object and an absolute belief that such a service was vital to an honourable American press.

He was extraordinarily equipped for the part he was to play, both in the war with the opposition and in the constructive work of establishing, maintaining, and constantly developing a great world-wide news service. He was a tactician of the highest order, fertile of resource, ready to meet any emergency, perceiving unerringly the weak spot in the enemy line and deadly in his blows on that line, though in this war the blow took the form of persuasion of the enemy and the victory that of a new recruit to the cause of an unfettered press.

I would not be just to Stone nor to others if I gave the impression that he fought alone. Those of us who were comrades in that struggle know and appreciate the mighty part taken by Victor F. Lawson, who staked his all that right as he saw it should triumph. These two men worked untiringly for the great end they sought, backed by the most loyal following that men ever had.

It is one thing, however, to win a fight for a principle and altogether another thing to put that principle into working practice. And this is where Stone's genius came into full play. His range of knowledge; his acquaintance with men of all stations of life and of all countries;

his understanding of conditions throughout the world and his ability to call into instant service his knowledge; this acquaintance and this understanding are simply marvellous. Under his direction the news arms of the Associated Press have year by year reached out until now the whole globe contributes to its daily story of world happenings.

The men engaged in this work throughout the world have become saturated with his high ideals for the service, his determination that it should be truthful, should be impartial, should not be tainted with bias or propaganda.

The Boards of Directors of both the Illinois and the New York organizations have been made up of strong men, but I have never found in all the changing membership anything but steadfast devotion to the highest ideals, and this I attribute to the standards set in the early days by both Stone and Lawson.

I am sure that every man still living who has served on these Boards will bear me out when I assert that every one of us is wiser and more hopeful of human nature by reason of our association with this work and these men and has come to understand the spirit of fairness and unselfishness that has guided the Boards' activities.

I would not be understood as indicating that there have been no differences of opinion—no meeting of the Board has ever been held, I think, without such differences—but the differences have been as to *what was the right thing to do* and not such as breed distrust as to motives.

In this respect I can speak with intimate knowledge of Stone's characteristics. For eighteen years I have served as President of the organization formed in 1900, and during those eighteen years Stone has been General Manager in charge of the news service. During this time we have differed widely on a thousand questions, but always the difference has been one of judgment, never of a nature that left in my mind misgivings as to his intention to do the right thing as he saw the right, and I only hope that he has the same feeling concerning me.

Our working relationship during these years has been a very wonderful thing to me. His patience and tolerance of an abruptly differing view and his unreserved acceptance of a decision by the Board of Directors adverse to his own point of view mark a mind disciplined to an amazing degree, when the masterful nature of the man is considered, and an underlying kindness and charity of spirit that come to few of us.

In his social relationship Stone has great charm. With an enormous fund of information is also a marked ability to give out that information. His wit is very keen and he is one of the best conversationalists and *raconteurs* of our time. While not an orator he is a most interesting speaker and is one of the best after-dinner talkers I ever heard.

I suppose that every man who amounts to anything has enemies, and he has a select assortment; but it seems to me that more people throughout the world regard Stone as a friend than any one else that I know of.

It seems to me almost a law of nature that with him an acquaintance should be a friend.

As one of those whose relationship is more than of an "acquaintance friend" it is difficult for me to speak. During the long years we have worked together there has grown up what has been to me, and I hope and think to him, a very tender and beautiful friendship. We have been together in days of trial and days of triumph, in days of heavy sorrow and those of radiant gladness, and throughout I have found him true. This friendship has been a precious thing in my life.

.   .   .   .

And this is why I prize this opportunity of placing my little laurel wreath on the living brow of the great man whose monument is the Associated Press of to-day and of having the unwonted pleasure of wearing my heart on my sleeve for the dear friend of so many years.

Mr. Frederic B. Jennings, who had been General Counsel of the Associated Press from 1900, wrote as follows:

The completion of a quarter of a century of successful effort is a notable event in the life of any man. When that effort has resulted in such achievements as those accomplished by Melville E. Stone, it is natural that his friends should desire to mark the occasion by some testimonial of their esteem and affection. I consider it a privilege to be permitted to join in that testimonial.

I met Mr. Stone for the first time in April, 1900, when he and certain publishers consulted me in regard to the organization of the Associated Press. The questions involved were important, and their determination not free from doubt. The publishers desired to form a coöperative organization, which could be conducted for the mutual benefit and protection of its members, free from obligation to others not admitted to membership.

Mr. Stone was chiefly interested in the adequacy, accuracy, and integrity of the news service, and believed that in the public interest a news association should be under coöperative control and not subject to the domination of any one newspaper or group of newspapers.

After careful consideration it was decided to organize an association under the Membership Corporations Law of New York, and the Associated Press was accordingly incorporated in May, 1900. In its organization and the preparation of the plan for its development Mr. Stone's great experience and thorough knowledge of the news business, his clarity and breadth of vision, his intelligent appreciation of the difficulties to be avoided and of the objects to be realized, his sound judgment, and, above all, the fact that he enjoyed the confidence of the publishers generally, whose enlistment as members was essential, were invaluable, and without his assistance the formation of the Association would have been impossible.

Its successful career, which has continued for seventeen years and abundantly justified its organization, is largely due to the wise and resourceful management of Melville E. Stone. The confidence of its members in the Association, the reliance of the public upon its news, the high morale of its employees, the breadth of its activities, its world-wide arrangements for the collection of news, and its great success, are chiefly the result of his efforts.

One of his notable achievements is the recent adjudication by the courts that a news agency or a newspaper, which, by the expenditure of money and effort, has gathered the news, has a *property right* in it which is not lost by publication and can be protected by injunction.

Mr. Stone for a long time had felt strong conviction upon this subject, and when the appropriation of our news by the International News Service during the war became so frequent and extensive as seriously to injure the Association, he urged that a suit be brought to enjoin it. This was done, and, upon a decision rendered by the U. S. Circuit Court of Appeals sustaining our contentions, an injunction was obtained fully protecting our rights.

Thus, Mr. Stone's opinion, long and earnestly maintained, has become the settled law, and all honest news agencies and newspapers are largely indebted to him for the establishment of this principle, as applicable to news, so vital to the protection of their rights. It may well be doubted whether this decision would thus have been obtained had it not been for his clear and positive views upon the subject and his pertinacity in maintaining them. If his twenty-five years of devoted service to the news profession had produced no other result than this, they would not have been spent in vain. But this has been only an episode in his busy and useful life.

He has built up an organization for the collection and dissemination of news which, I suppose, has no equal anywhere in the world. He has placed it upon the sure foundation of fairness, accuracy, and reliability, upon which he has always insisted. Thus he has improved not only the quality of the news service, but also the character of the employees who are engaged in it.

He has successfully served for twenty-five years two such critical masters as the Press and the Public, and still retains their confidence and esteem. Perhaps no greater tribute than this could be paid to the impartiality and success of his management.

But this is not all. He has made few, if any, enemies, and his friends are legion. As he looks back upon this period of his life, one of his greatest sources of satisfaction must be that he has gained the confidence and respect of all, and the regard and affection of his many friends.

I have had somewhat close and frequent association with him during the last seventeen years, and my relation with him has been one of the most delightful and cherished experiences of my life. During that time I have come to have the highest opinion of his intellectual ability, and the warmest esteem and affection for him. In my professional experience of more than forty years I have never had a more considerate, intelligent, helpful, and satisfactory client than he.

His apprehension is so quick and keen, his mind so active and resourceful, his judgment so sane and fair, that it has always been a great advantage and pleasure to work with him.

But, after all, impressed as I have been by his remarkable intellectual powers, I have been quite as much affected by his qualities of heart, his good fellowship, his human sympathy, his sincerity, his kindly consideration for others, his toleration, his great fairness and lack of resentment even under the strongest provocation. These are the qualities which have so endeared him to his friends, all of whom will agree with me when I express the earnest hope that he may continue to serve the Press and all mankind, and to honour and delight us with his friendship for very many years to come.

And at the luncheon Mr. Adolph Ochs said, among other things:

I am impelled to say a few words to express what I regard as an obligation of the members of the Associated Press to Melville E.

Stone, who has served them for twenty-five years with a fidelity that had no reservations and with ability that can best be characterized as genius.

The Associated Press to-day is one of the monumental achievements of the age. We little appreciate its potentiality, its importance as a factor in our civilization, its superb organization, its honesty, integrity, and practice of the highest standards in news gathering. We accept now as a matter of course that enlightened public opinion regards the reports of the Associated Press as reliable, trustworthy, and scrupulously honest, fair, and impartial. That this is so is due in a large measure to the integrity, genius, ability, and self-sacrifice of Melville E. Stone.

As to its accuracy and legal limitations I need only refer to the fact that libel suits have cost the Associated Press a negligible sum. In fact, there never has been a substantial sum realized in a libel suit against the Associated Press, and altogether, not a half-dozen suits these past twenty-five years. "Libel suit judgments have cost the Associated Press in the last twenty-five years less than the expenditure for lead pencils in the same period."

Adolph S. Ochs

Indulge me a few minutes to say a word concerning the Associated Press—itself. There is a popular superstition that the Associated Press is a monopoly. Yes, it is in the sense that a family monopolizes its personal possessions and its coördination; that is, if it coördinates. I wish to remind you that the Associated Press is, in fact, a family, a club, for it is incorporated as a social club under the State laws of New York. The primary purpose of a social club is to bring into association congenial persons. It is their personality that constitutes all that makes the club congenial. To force an objectionable member into such a club impairs its purpose. So with the Associated Press. It consists of kindred interests united for mutual advantage where each and every one contributes voluntary personal service. Each giving a part of himself to make a thing greater collectively than they can create individually. It is a service that cannot be imposed by law, even though the Associated Press is impressed with a public interest. Governmental supervision can extend only to good conduct so that the power created is not to be misused. It cannot be successfully contended that in law or morals it should be under

à Monsieur Melville Stone
en hommage d'amitié
G Clemenceau

Georges Clemenceau

Marshal Foch

government control and made to conform to the requirements of a common carrier, for that cannot be done except by the exercise of the powers of a master over a slave; that is if personal service is to be exacted, and otherwise there cannot be an Associated Press such as now exists.

The success of the Associated Press is Melville E. Stone's success. The Association is stamped all over with Stone's handiwork, his thought, his ideals, his abilities, and his sense of public service. It is his monument, and may it ever endure on the foundation that he built so masterly and with so much sagacity and self-sacrifice. I emphasize the much-abused word "self-sacrifice," for in the case of Melville E. Stone and his relation to the Associated Press it is applicable in its true significance. He might have been a captain of industry, a banker of great repute, an important member of a president's cabinet or an ambassador extraordinary and minister plenipotentiary at one of the chief courts in Europe. And who knows but that had he been the latter, this world's calamity might have been averted. I am not indulging in a flight of imagination. I also know that a great publisher offered him a substantial fortune to undertake the management of his affairs, and this was one of many similar seductive offers. But they offered Melville E. Stone no temptation. He was wedded to his idol—the Associated Press—for he worships it, dreams of it, and it occupies all his thoughts during his waking hours. He cherishes it, he nourishes it, he suffers for it and truly spiritualizes it. His work for the Associated Press is to him congenial employment, and in it he realizes every good man's highest ambition—public service He gives the cause the best that is in him; in fact, gives himself wholly. His personality inspires the whole organization from top to bottom. There is no man in the service of the Associated Press who has not been impressed with the management's demand for honesty, impartiality, and thoroughness.

Never did a man occupy a more trying position than Mr. Stone created for himself when he inaugurated and put into operation for several hundred newspapers representing every shade of public opinion a news service that was to be comprehensive, intelligent, enterprising, and scrupulously fair and impartial—to be universally so recognized and esteemed. It all appears simple enough now that organization has been perfected and the newspapers and the public have faith. But it was a stupendous undertaking, and it needed a man of courage and preëminent ability, and, above all, perseverance and the faculty of dealing with men of most diverse and suspicious temperaments. Had I the time, and you the patience, I could recite innumerable instances in the history of the Associated Press where its reputation and its very existence rested on the integrity of Melville E. Stone.

With these words of flattery ringing in my ears I set sail on June 15th. I had felt that I never wished to see France again, the France that I had often visited and to which I was devoted. To see it in its ruined and devastated state could give no pleasure. Now, however, had come a day when I had a real call to go. Not out of curiosity, nor as a mere sightseer. But to do service. And so, and therefore, I went.

I sailed from New York on a French steamer, bound for Bordeaux. The weather was mild, the sea calm, and the voyage an agreeable one. There were some interesting episodes. We had a thousand soldiers aboard, and approximately an equal number of Red Cross and Y. M. C. A. men. The soldiers under very proper orders from the War Department were forbidden to show themselves on deck, for the good reason that if the ship were known to carry soldiers, it became a transport and therefore fair game for a submarine. But the Red Cross and Y. M. C. A. men were constantly promenading the decks in khaki, and it was inconceivable that a man behind a periscope could observe the small red cross or triangle on one's uniform which, otherwise, was precisely like the garb of a soldier. One class of men would endanger the safety of the boat quite as much as the other. But the ways of our war conduct were always in some fashion past finding out.

Creel Committee

The boat was crowded and many people were forced to "double up." A Chicago friend of mine had as a "bunkie" a Baptist Doctor of Divinity from Laurel, Mississippi. He was a strange being. He wore an ordinary dark civilian suit of clothes with a black slouch hat plus several other things: namely, puttees over his mufti trousers, and low shoes. And between the puttees and shoes exposed bare ankles, proving that he eschewed socks. His room-mate, my Chicago friend, told me that he slept nightly in these clothes. Day by day, hour by hour, and almost minute by minute he stood by the gunwale peering into the offing for a periscope. He was undeniably nervous. One day he confided to me that he carried three days' rations in the right-hand pocket of his sack coat, and a "jiffy life preserver," whatever that might be, in the left-hand pocket.

I could not resist the impulse to chaff him. As with anxious eyes he was scanning the horizon, when I had a sympathetic audience, I called out:

"Doctor, you are a minister of the Gospel, and are afraid of death."

"N-no," he stammered.

"You are a Baptist and afraid of water."

"N-no," he haltingly replied.

"You sleep in your clothes, because as a Southerner you must die with your boots on."

Again he demurred, and spat out a liberal allowance of tobacco.

Then I related what the French call a *petite histoire* which seemed apt:

Once upon a time there lived on a high mountain in Virginia a distinguished astronomer. One evening a farmer called, his boots covered with red clay and he chewing plug tobacco earnestly. The savant undertook an elemental lesson in his field. He pointed out the various constellations and indicated their size and importance. Finally he pointed to a little star and told his open-eyed visitor that it was Orion, so many million times larger than the moon, the earth, or the sun, and perhaps the centre of the celestial universe and mayhap the seat of the throne of God. "Do you mean to say that that little star which I can hardly see is all that?" asked the farmer. And when the astronomer acquiesced, the quite practical Virginian spat out some tobacco and declared himself: "Well," said he, "all I've got to say is, it has a darned poor way of showing itself."

My ministerial friend told me he was going to France for Creel's Committee on Public Information "just to look around and report." He did not expect to stay long and it was the first time he had been abroad. I saw him once in Paris. The Boches were bombing the city. He did not like it. He had done all the "looking around" he cared to, and hurried home to "report."

On the boat was a worthy Pittsburg woman on the same errand. She frankly confessed that Creel, wanting a Congressional appropriation, was giving some friends of congressmen opportunities to visit Europe at Government expense. Putting two and two together, I remembered that Pat Harrison, one of the most influential members of the House of Representatives, served the district in which my timorous Baptist divine lived. Wherefore, without doubt, his joy ride.

Although we took all precaution, running without lights at night and zig-zagging, indeed, there was little or no danger, because the French Line had been immune from attack throughout the war. There was much speculation as to the reason for this exemption. The best explanation was that the Germans found these boats about their only means of communication with the outside world. They freely sent letters to friends in Switzerland. There the substance of these epistles was rewritten into new letters from the Swiss friends and forwarded as their own. As we had among our passengers the Swiss minister to Washington, a thoroughly worthy gentleman, some fun-loving fellows proposed a resolution of thanks to him instead of to the company, for providing us a safe journey, a suggestion which he did not fully enjoy.

The ride up the Garonne from the seacoast to Bordeaux was a thrilling one as it gave us our first real idea of the vast war work the American had done in France. Mile upon mile of vast storehouses and factories, with thousands of American locomotives and railway cars, a great army of Yankee workmen, and many of our newly constructed freighters greeted and startled us.

When we reached our dock and went ashore we found gangs of German prisoners at work everywhere.

Then we set out for Paris. The metropolis was shrouded in gloom day and night. All of the old-time jollity was gone.

I called on my old friend Clemenceau, saw Marshal Joffre, and early in July spent a couple of days with General Pershing at Chaumont. I was stricken with the prevailing influenza and was interned for some days. Then I went to London.

Greetings Abroad

Much to my surprise, on July 25th a dinner in my honour was given by the British press at the Ritz Hotel in London. The committee in charge included Lords Burnham, Northcliffe, Riddle, and other distinguished journalists, and the company gathered comprised substantially all of the leading newspapermen of the British metropolis. Addresses were made by Lord Burnham, who presided, Lord Riddle, Sam Blythe, and Admiral Sims. It was a compliment of which any one might well be proud.

The British Newspaper Conference.
Chairman, The Right Hon. Lord Burnham.

Dinner to Welcome
Mr. Melville E. Stone
of
The Associated Press of America,
at the
Ritz Hotel, Piccadilly, W.
Thursday, 25th July, 1918.
at 6-45 for 7 p.m.

Dinner of the British Press

A few days later I went with Lord Chancellor F. E. Smith to luncheon at Gray's Inn. I had been in the historic hall years before with Lord Coleridge, but this occasion was much more interesting. When we came to the cigars "F. E." took me to the library where there were something like a half-dozen big-wigs who wanted to know something about my struggle on behalf of property in news, a subject then before our courts on my initiative. I explained to them in detail my views and there was no dissent from the conclusions I drew. They said that undoubtedly if the same case was presented to the British courts, they would grant an injunction.

Then on August 2nd Mr. Arthur Balfour asked me to luncheon, his other guests being Prime Minister Lloyd George and the War Minister Lord Milner. We discussed the censorship again with interest and I found them thoroughly sympathetic with my point of view.

The following day at Manchester a large company of editors and newspaper proprietors from the provinces and from Scotland and Ireland assembled at the Midland Hotel for a luncheon in my honour. It was a very notable occasion. The presiding officer was Mr. John R. Scott of the Manchester *Guardian*, and among the speakers were his father, C. P. Scott, the Lord Mayor of Manchester, and Mr. Phillips of the *Yorkshire Post*. I was particularly gratified at the presence of an old-time friend, Sir Edward Russell of the Liverpool *Daily Post*, who had come over to propose my health and speak some kindly words. He and I had been acquainted for many years. He had visited me in the United States and I had seen him in his lair at Liverpool. He was then well-nigh eighty years old.

Three days later General Smuts and I had luncheon with Lloyd George at 10 Downing Street. It was an occasion full of interest. There was a frank consideration of every question that was uppermost at the moment.

Then I went back to France and on to Switzerland. At Berne I spent an afternoon with Doctor Muehlon, the one-time manager of the Krupp works, who was so outspoken in denunciation of Germany's misconduct.

On September 13th the press of Italy honoured me with a luncheon at the Villa Borghese in Rome. Andrea Torre, president of the Press Association, made the speech of welcome in the name of the entire Italian press. Premier Orlando was with the army at the front, but sent a message of a most appreciative character. Nitti, who at the moment was Minister of the Treasury, followed in most flattering terms.

Mr. Gallenga, whose father in former days had been a famous correspondent of the London *Times*, had now risen to the post of Minister of Propaganda. He motored me down to his home in Perugia, where on the following Sunday I addressed two or three thousand people in the theatre, Gallenga interpreting for me. The next day we went to Padua, where I had a short visit with General Diaz, then commanding the Italian army.

Back to Paris; a luncheon with Lord Derby, the British ambassador; a short visit with the Prince of Wales; and a luncheon in state by the Paris press, presided over by Mr. Naléche, editor of the *Journal dès Débats*. There were many notables at the luncheon, including Minister Pichon and André Tardieu.

Then on October 22d I sailed from Bordeaux for New York.

On November 16th I was given a home-coming dinner by my friends at the Lotos Club.

Our directors felt that I should go back again to give the staff a longer opportunity and also because the Armistice had come, the war was over, and President Wilson was going over to attend the Peace Conference. I sailed again on December 5th and followed the President into Paris by one day.

I shall not undertake to tell the story of the Peace Conference. That has been done by many and in many ways. The best book on the subject, one free from bias, accurate, and complete, has been written by a member of the Associated Press staff, Mr. Charles T. Thompson. It is entitled "The Peace Conference Day by Day."

I shall content myself with a few observations which seem to me pertinent.

It is as well to bear in mind that the Armistice was only a truce and not at all a definite close of the war. Yet, after the exhausting struggle of more than four years, it was hailed in all of the Entente countries as the end of the contest. There was as little fight left in the Allied armies as in Germany. And this was as well understood in Berlin as in London or Paris.

Second, the Armistice was based on President Wilson's Fourteen Points and his subsequent proclamations, all of which were susceptible of varying interpretations. There was a very practical fifteenth point which was neither presented to the Germans nor accepted by them. That was a plain declaration that Germany had wantonly imposed upon the world a horribly wicked war, had been defeated, and ought in all justice to pay the penalty for the crime. The sixty millions of people in Germany were the culprits. But they were unrepentant. Nor were they conscious that they had lost the war. They were hoping, and not without cause, that a split would develop in the ranks of their enemies. None of the Allied governments had accepted the Fourteen Points with real whole-heartedness. Their acquiescence had been really forced from them because the United States held a commanding place in the business. All this meant that the Armistice signed on the 11th of November had left a Pandora's box to be dealt with.

Wilson expected to attack at once the problems presented —Lloyd George and Clemenceau were cautious. In order to maintain the morale of their people in the hours of stress they had held out the promise of an indemnity, impossibly large, from the Germans, when the contest should end. Wilson's plans did not contemplate this. And there were secret commitments that had seemed necessary to hold the Entente together in the days of trial. Wherefore, although Clemenceau and Lloyd George had fixed December 17th for the opening of the Peace Conference, and the American Delegation had been appointed and had hurried over to meet the convenience of their French and English allies, there was a rather uncivil delay so that our oversea friends could find out precisely in which quarter sat the wind. Wilson had just been defeated in the American Congressional election, a fact which was significant.

England was in the throes of a general election and the French had not even named their delegates. President Wilson and his associates were left "waitin' at the church" for over a month. A round of royal entertainments was arranged to fill in the days. There was a reception at the American Embassy in Paris attended by a large number of French notables; a state dinner at the Elysée Palace, given by President Poincaré in honour of the King of Italy and his son, to which the American President was invited; the conferring of a doctor's degree upon Wilson at the Sorbonne; a spectacular visit to King George in London; a presentation of the "Freedom of the City" at Manchester; and a whirlwind tour to Rome to visit King Victor Emmanuel and to call on Pope Benedict. During all these days the President made it clear that he was appealing to the people of Europe over the heads of their governmental officers, precisely as he had, during the progress of the war, endeavoured to appeal to the German populace against their constituted authorities. He gave a notable interview outlining his views to the London *Times*—the only interview he gave to any one while in Europe. He spoke to great crowds in England and in Italy. At Manchester he took issue squarely with the old-time European devotion to a balance of power. There was unmistakably a growing divergence of views between him and Clemenceau.

It was another of those speaking tours to which I have alluded.

All of this seemed to me a blunder. Wilson was hailed by the populace as a veritable Messiah, but they understood little of his idealistic utterances. Those who heard him in Italy did not even understand the English language, in which he spoke. Behind it all remained the fact that so far as any of the governments were concerned the officials alone could be vocal in any peace conference. The mob could cheer, even though they did not understand, but they could have no real share in solving the terrible problems presented.

Few of those in authority in any European state were at one with President Wilson in his views. They interpreted his declaration for "self-determination" to suit themselves. In order to learn their precise desires, the staff of the Associated Press went among their representatives and we telegraphed to the American papers an extraordinary revelation of their greedy demands. It covered several columns and illustrated how little a part generosity was playing in their attitude.

Certain of the demands were grotesque. For instance,

Venizelos, the Greek statesman, asked for a strip of territory along the littoral of European Turkey out to the Black Sea, and another down the coast of Asia Minor to and including the villayet of Smyrna. And he wanted to extend a like strip up the eastern shore of the Adriatic to include about one half of Albania. All this because there was a small Greek colony in Smyrna, and ancient Thrace and Albania had at one time belonged to Greece. It was an outrageous claim; it shut off Bulgaria and Asia Minor from access to the Mediterranean. As well might he have asked to include Alexandria and practically every seaport town in the Levant. They all had Greek colonies for the reason that the Greeks were the adventurers of the sea in the olden days and planted their colonies almost everywhere. I suggested to Venizelos that under his contention he was fairly entitled to the west side of Sixth Avenue in New York where there were any number of Greek restaurants and obviously a Greek colony. Yet in the end the Greek claim was allowed.

Poor France! She hardly knew how to extricate herself from the difficulty in which she was plunged. After all, the worst offence of the Germans was not the slaughtering of something like ten millions of the very flower of the civilized nations in battle, nor the killing of women and children by submarine or aeroplane. The dead, at least, were at peace. The worst offence of the Germans was that they left us a world in which the living could hardly live. France and Belgium were ravaged and torn beyond description. It was not strange that Clemenceau and his fellow publicists looked in absolute terror upon the future. It was only human for them to seek a mandate in Syria and for control of southern Russia that they might secure the resources of that territory. In their situation it was but natural for them to ask unreasonable things. They wanted to pool the cost of the war as from August, 1914, with the idea that they had been fighting America's war for three years and that it was only fair that we should pay our proportion of the cost. Of course this could not be done and it was a mistake to propose it. Turning from this they next suggested that the whole cost of the war from the beginning should be paid in proportion to the number of lives sacrificed. That is, that among the Allied nations the one which contributed the largest number of lives should pay the least in money, and the nation having contributed the smallest number of lives should pay the largest share. This was equally inadmissible, because in both cases it meant the imposing of the chief financial burden of the war on the United States.

And France was not at all sure of the military situation which, although she had consented to the Armistice, was still menacing. At the close of the year, on New Year's eve, Mr. Hyde and I went for a talk with Foch. In an inoffensive address at a public gathering in Paris a few months before the German collapse, I told the audience that we had come to a new fashion of speech, so that initials such as "G. H. Q." and "A. E. F." were perfectly well understood and much briefer than the extended appellations. "There are three such letters, 'U. S.A.', to be seen everywhere in France to-day," I continued. "I suppose to you they mean 'United States of America.' To us they mean 'Unconditional Surrender Always'." This jocular utterance was picked and made much of by the press of Paris. And so in talking with Marshal Foch I ventured to say that I thought perhaps the Armistice was a mistake. "Oh, no," he replied, "I am a father, and so long as there was the life of one of our soldiers to be saved, I could not refuse to cease hostilities." One of the affectionate phrases in use about this kindly old soul was that "Foch was a miser about his men." He never wanted to part with one of them. I suggested that if he had fought on for ten days, he would have bagged the whole German army and won the greatest victory of all history. This did not interest him.

Through all the weary weeks of the Conference President Wilson was the only participant who was assured of a definite tenure of office. It therefore became necessary for Lloyd George, Clemenceau, and all the other confrères to keep a close eye on their constituents back home, and instead of viewing the problems with international mind they were much like the American congressman whose sole aim is to care for the people of his district. Wilson was not "bamboozled," as Mr. Keynes put it. He was all the time looking at a world as it ought to be, while his associates, the European premiers, were looking at the world as it was. Of course, in a case of such magnitude some compromises were necessary, but as a whole the American President won a victory from his point of view. The important question is whether, with human nature as it existed, the realization of his hopes was possible.

It may well be assumed that the Conference went much too far into the details of territorial allotment and new national boundaries. The attempt to carry the principles of self-determination to a finality could not in every case be wise for the reason that ethnic solidarity and economic association were often not coincident. And it is quite doubtful whether ethnic unities were of first importance. Indeed, it might be that such coherence would really prove a menace to the world's peace. Someone has said the immediate cause of the great war was the destruction of the Tower of Babel on the Plain of Shinar and the consequent division of the world into peoples who could never understand each other. Madame de Staël once wrote very philosophically that "the patriotism of nations ought to be selfish." So self-determination might encourage widespread chauvinism, might mean the creation of national races, national languages, national interests, with international jealousies, envies, and hatreds. It was one of the Kaiser's pet theories that the enforcement of the German language upon his people tended to solidify his empire. He refused to permit the use of the word "telephone" and coined the word "*Fernspracher*" as a substitute. The United States, taught tolerance by the hourly contact of people of different races, languages, and religions, was suggested as an object lesson, as was Switzerland where people of German, French, and Italian origin live in perfect harmony. What was needed was that the world should be made a melting pot.

Another complication was the vexed question of super sovereignty. We of the United States had at our birth wrested from the ruler the right to declare war and placed that power in the keeping of the representatives of the people—the Congress. This provision we had embodied in our organic law, the Constitution. It was a principle which none of our peacemaking commissioners would dare to violate. In this respect we were not on even terms with the representatives of our Allied nations. The declaration of war with them was a prerogative of the sovereign. It was wrestled with for months and finally left in the equivocal phrase of the famous Article Ten.

An organization had been set up in the United States with a policy which, had it been adopted at Paris, might have proved more successful. It was "The League for the Enforcement of Peace." The method it proposed provided, as a basic step, for the establishment of a high court to frame a body of agreed international law and to hear and decide certain contests between nations. Of course this would have involved in some measure the principle of super-sovereignty, because a court having no power to enforce its decrees would have been valueless, but it would probably have been less difficult to secure general consent for such an exercise of force than for the Paris plan. It cannot be denied that it would also have involved the principle of a "balance of power," but of a sort that might have been approved.

Such a document would have been very simple, easily understood, and would have left a great number of comparatively trivial issues to the adjudication of a tribunal qualified to act.

The Peace Treaty was practically settled in the middle of April and I returned to America to attend the annual meeting of the Associated Press, and was once more and for the twenty-sixth time elected general manager.

From time to time I saw Clemenceau. He impressed me as much the brightest mind at the peace table. I doubt if any other man could have brought France through the great stress of the war. He knew his people. Behind his brusque exterior there was a kindly, considerate soul that endeared him to the mass of his countrymen. He lived in a shabby old house in the little Rue Franklin, the last place in Paris for the abode of a French premier. I doubt if there was another residence in his immediate neighbourhood. The street was choked with grocers' shops, tobacconists, and every other sort of tumble-down rookery. He had a delightful sense of humour.

While I was in Rome Mr. Galenga had given a dinner in my honour, at which he assembled a number of members of the

Italian Cabinet. They were greatly disturbed over the military outlook. Their army had suffered the great defeat of Caporetto; their commanding general had been supplanted by Diaz, in whom they had limited confidence; the Austrians who confronted them on the Piave were much their superior in numbers and in munitions; Lombardy and Piedmont were ablaze with the fires of socialism. With the collapse of Russia large bodies of Austrian troops had been withdrawn from the eastern front and pitted against the Italians. If the enemy should reopen their attack there was grave danger that Italy would be driven out of the war. They were most anxious for aid from the Allies. They thought there would be less danger if the Stars and Stripes could be shown on their battle-front. There was a good deal of justice in their view. They had at the moment more Italians on the French front than all of the Allied troops on the Italian front. They had only one regiment of American troops in Italy and three fourths of this regiment were at Padua, many miles from the trenches. Secretary Baker was in France at the time, and as I was about to return to Paris, they implored me to present their perilous situation to him. I did so, but of course the Secretary replied that he could not properly interfere with the military operations. Then General Diaz went up to see Clemenceau about the business. He told him the fighting qualities of the Austrians had been much underrated, that they were veritable lions, and that they outnumbered the Italian army and had more guns. The French premier was forced to refer him to Foch. There were many reasons why Foch could not meet the wishes of the Italians, and Diaz returned to his command greatly disheartened. A few days later Foch took some 5,000 Austrians as prisoners on the French front. Then Clemenceau sent a telegram practically in these words:

My dear Diaz:
 We have taken as prisoners 5,000 of your lions. What shall we do with them? Affectionately—
                                                            The Tiger.

During my absence, on December 23, 1918, Mr. Justice Pitney, speaking for the Supreme Court of the United States, rendered a decision of a very momentous character. I must relate the story of the case here and now.

In 1875, when we founded the Chicago *Daily News*, we had as co-tenants in the office of publication a morning newspaper conducted on peculiar lines. It was called the Chicago *Courier*. It had no reporters, no correspondents, no alliance with any news-gathering organization. The other morning papers went to press shortly after midnight and could be purchased at, say, 3 A. M. The *Courier's* practice was to buy copies of these papers, glean from them all the news of the day, put it in type hurriedly, and issue about daybreak. This meant that the paper had all the news, it was never beaten on anything, and its expenses for gathering its information were practically nothing.

Not long after Major O. J. Smith came to Chicago from Terre Haute, Indiana, with an enterprise of much the same character. He founded the American Press Association. It also bought the morning papers in the early morning, gleaned their news, put it in type, made stereotype plates and shipped them to neighbouring cities, where they were incorporated in small dailies, which were sold in competition with the Chicago journals from which the news had been taken.

It was a day when the custom of reprinting matter from newspapers without permission in this fashion was well-nigh universal. To me it seemed all wrong, and I began an investigation to see if there was no legal remedy. I found little to encourage me. From time to time I set a trap and exposed a news thief as in the case of the *Post and Mail*.* But these cases, while they amused the public, did not afford relief.

When reading Isaac Disraeli's "Calamities and Quarrels of Authors," I came across a chapter on the "History of Literary Property" which impressed me greatly. It was a revelation. "Is it wonderful," he asked, "that even successful authors are indigent? They are heirs to fortune, but by a strange singularity they are disinherited at their birth; for, on the publication of their works, these cease to be their own property."

I read the illuminating chapter on the "History of Property"

---
*See page 63.

in Henry Sumner Maine's "Ancient Law." I read all the existent books on copyright, and I re-read my Blackstone. Definitions were obviously a matter of evolution. At first property was, of course, corporeal, as coal, a physical thing, having length, breadth, and thickness. Under the Roman law, when a man wrote a thing on, for instance, a sheepskin, the title to the thing was in the man who owned the sheepskin. How could it be otherwise? The sheepskin was the only corporeal contribution, and to be property anything must be corporeal. The ideas of the writer were incorporeal and clearly, therefore, not property.

In England there came a time when the ideas of the writer seemed to have value. But again it was not the author of the ideas who was recognized as entitled to any reward. It was his assignee, the publisher, who produced the corporeal book or pamphlet who had the property, as property was understood, and who therefore was deserving of protection at law. Wherefore the absurd recompense to Milton and every other author of his day and the profiteering of the publishers. It was not until 1709, in the reign of Queen Anne of England, that any one seemed to have the slightest interest in the work of the author. Even this interest was not great. Because the printers quarrelled with the publishers, claiming their lawful share in the plunder, attention was directed to the prevailing injustice. Then the first copyright act was passed. All along the theory was that occupancy, possession, was the distinguishing mark of property, and it was quite logical to say that with publication, unless through the saving grace of some statute, occupancy or possession must cease and that thereafter there was abandonment of all right of monopoly. The statute of Queen Anne gave the author, after compliance with certain preliminaries, monopoly of his book after publication, for fourteen years, and later this term of monopoly was considerably extended. Yet all the time there was no fair conception of the real meaning of the word "property" nor of the just right to protection of the man who contributed the ideas of the publication, which constituted the "property," after all.

The invention of the electric telegraph and the consequent

development of news gathering created a new problem. It had been held, following the accepted theory underlying copyright law, that, unless a book or painting was registered, publication was equivalent to abandonment of the author's rights, so that thereafter any one was privileged to produce an article at will. It was clear that for a news dispatch, which must be published immediately upon receipt by a newspaper, this sort of protection from piracy constituted no protection at all. And it was to this obviously unforeseen situation, as far as all statutory copyright measures were concerned, that I addressed myself.

I have said that in 1880, after Mr. Charles Stewart Parnell, the Irish leader, returned to Ireland, he sent me several important cable messages for publication in the Chicago *Daily News*. I was anxious to guard my right of property in them. Under the law, in order to copyright them, it was necessary to print the title and deposit it with the fee with the librarian of Congress at Washington before publication, and to deposit two copies of the printed article with the same official after publication. As the only way to meet these requirements a subterfuge was, with the approval of the librarian of Congress, resorted to. Upon the receipt of a Parnell message, the title was telegraphed to my Washington correspondent. He "printed" it on a sheet of paper with a typewriter, enclosed this with the fee in an envelope, and slipped it under the door of the librarian's residence. This was accounted a compliance with the statute. But it only served to convince me that the law was never intended to apply to this sort of literature.

Then I dreamed a dream. There was a defect in the law which should, and perhaps might, be remedied. There were equities involved, and I had learned in the days when I studied law that there was no wrong which the arm of the chancellor was not long enough to reach. I knew of the "tasteless" lawyers and their point of view. Precedent, as found in the books, with them was all-controlling. But, mayhap, there were others who could see beyond the books into the final authority of justice, and it was worth while to find out.

I talked freely of my belief that there was some way to protect news from piracy, and early in 1883 I received the following note from the then general manager of the Associated Press:

> **The New-York Associated Press:**
>
> No. 195 BROADWAY.
>
> Representing the New-York Journal of Commerce, Herald, Tribune, Times, Express, Sun, and The World. Acting also for the Reuter Telegram Company, and all the leading Journals throughout the Union and the British Provinces.
>
> P. O. Box 3363.   New York, March 27, 1883
>
> I am anxious and curious to know how you are progressing with your plan to test ownership in news. It is growing more and more important.
>
> Yours truly,
> William Henry Smith
>
> M. E. Stone, Esq.

Every lawyer turned to the statutory protection for literary composition as furnishing a solution. Without any faith in the effort, I thought it well enough to seek from Congress such an amendment to the law as would meet the emergency. So it happened that at the meeting of the Western Associated Press, held at Detroit, October 17, 1883, the following committee was appointed, on my motion, to take up the matter at Washington: Henry Watterson, A. C. Hesing, I. F. Mack, Albert Roberts, and J. G. Siebeneck. Of the matter Mr. Watterson says in his Autobiography, Volume 2, page 104:

I was sent by the Associated Press to Washington on a fool's errand—that is, to get an act of Congress extending copyright to the news of the Association—and, remaining the entire season, my business to meet the official great and to make myself acceptable, I came into a certain intimacy with the Administration circle, having long had friendly relations with the President. In all my life I have never passed so delightful and useless a winter.

Very early in the action I found that my mission involved a serious and vexed question—nothing less than the creation of a new property —and I proceeded warily. Through my uncle, Stanley Matthews, I interested the members of the Supreme Court. The Attorney General, a great lawyer and an old Philadelphia friend, was at my call and elbow. The Joint Library Committee of Congress, to which the measure must go, was with me. Yet somehow the scheme lagged.

I could not account for this. One evening at a dinner Mr. Blaine enlightened me. We sat together at table and suddenly he turned and said: "How are you getting on with your bill?" And my reply being rather halting, he continued, "You won't get a vote in either House," and he proceeded very humorously to improvise the average member's argument against it as a dangerous power, a perquisite to the great newspapers and an imposition upon the little ones. To my mind this was something more than the post-prandial levity it was meant to be.

Not long after a learned but dissolute old lawyer said to me, "You need no act of Congress to protect your news service. There are at least two, and I think four or five, English rulings that cover this case. Let me show them to you." He did so and I went no further with the business, quite agreeing with Mr. Blaine, and nothing further came of it. To a recent date the Associated Press has relied on these decisions under the common law of England. Curiously enough, quite a number of newspapers in whose actual service I was engaged opened fire upon me and roundly abused me.

That the mission of this committee was unavailing did not surprise me. It confirmed my suspicion that I was travelling the wrong road. Relief must be sought from the arm of the Chancellor. This was obviously no easy task. It meant a successful revolution in all of the accepted theories of the law so far as literary property was concerned. It meant new and wider definitions of the words "property" and "publication," and it meant forward-looking men of no mean order both upon the bench and at the bar. I was somewhat surprised that Watterson's committee never reported to the Association.

Fortunately I found as a fellow resident at the Virginia Hotel in Chicago, where I lived during a winter season, precisely such a forward-looking man as I was seeking, in the person of Judge Grosscup, then presiding in the United States Circuit Court for the Eighth Circuit. He listened to me and was interested. He saw with me eye to eye, and frankly stated so. No one else did. And as I had other things pressing for attention, I waited.

Some time after I encountered Judge Grosscup on a railway

train, and he asked me to restate my case for the protection of news against piracy. And this was my putting of it:

First, that to keep pace with the progress of the world there must be a revised definition of the word "property" so that it should cease to cover simply "movables" and "immovables," and should include everything having an exchangeable value. This would take it out of the narrow place it had theretofore occupied in legal parlance, and should connote incorporeal rights. Second, there should also be a revised definition of the word "publication." I took the ground that the printing of a news telegram in the columns of a newspaper which was sold for one cent a copy should not, and did not, constitute such a publication as would mean abandonment to the public for republication. One was justly entitled to buy the newspaper, to read it, to enjoy or regulate his conduct by the information thus obtained, but it was manifestly unfair that he should be permitted to use the telegrams in competition with one who had paid his money and exercised his ingenuity to obtain them. The publication in this case was a limited one, and the legal doctrine of *animus domini*—intent of the owner—should apply.

The Judge had a case in his court involving the principle, and soon after rendered a decision evidently sustaining my contention. The case went to the United States Supreme Court, and the decision was confirmed. Yet so universal was the piracy of news telegrams, and so confirmed were the "tasteless" lawyers, that I could still get no encouragement in any quarter.

Meanwhile, in all of the conferences for the establishment of international copyright, the question of protection for news had arisen, and such protection had been refused. The Berne Convention of September, 1886, expressly excluded from copyright protection "news matter or current topics [*foits divers*]." [Bowker, page 319.] The Berlin Convention of 1908 expressly denied protection to "news of the day or press information on current topics." [Bowker, page 318.] The Pan-American Conference and Convention at Buenos Aires in 1910 decided that even credit was not required for "news and miscellaneous items published merely for general information." [Bowker, page 337.]

Finally, on the evening of November 12, 1916, I invited Judge Grosscup, Frederick W. Lehman of St. Louis, and Frederic B. Jennings, General Counsel of the Associated Press, to dine with Mr. Frank B. Noyes, our president, and I delivered to them my lecture on "Property in News." Then I presented the matter to the Board of Directors of the Associated Press and rather out of courtesy to me than because of any faith in my endeavour, they authorized me to go ahead and voted to pay any expense involved.

While Mr. Jennings, our general consul, was by no means confident of the success of the enterprise, he entered zealously into the work as was his custom with all his cases, and a conclusive brief was prepared. Mr. Jennings, who for the twenty years that I knew him until his death, was not only a wise counsellor, but a devoted friend. He argued at the first hearing in the United States District Court and from the presiding judge we were given a satisfactory decision. Then it went to the United States Circuit Court of Appeals, and Judge Grosscup made the argument. The court not only affirmed the decision below, but added distinct strength to our contention. Finally, before the Supreme Court of the United States, Frederick W. Lehman made the argument, and then there was a most decisive victory.

Thus thirty-six years after I had settled the equities in my own mind was the law finally revolutionized.

During the summer certain questions arose respecting our relation with some of the foreign agencies and it was thought best that I should return to Europe. I sailed late in November and spent a couple of months on the other side. Then in April, 1919, by a unanimous vote of the Board of Directors, I was relieved from the office of general manager; Mr. Martin was chosen to that office; and a new office, that of counsellor, was created for me.

The Associated Press of To-day

The Associated Press has grown in strength and character with the years. From the 63 members in 1893 it has reached out until to-day there are nearly 1,300 members. From the annual expenditures of about $500,000 in the beginning it has widened its activities until its annual budget is now nearly $6,000,000. Each of the 1,300 members is either a partial or sole owner of a daily newspaper. These members have no common aim or partisanship of any sort. They are as varied in their advocacy of political, religious, or economic principles as it is possible for human beings to be. And this, they believe, is the best guarantee that the news they receive and print ,is and must be accurate, impartial, and honest. Often they personally dislike certain of their fellow-members. They are at one on one thing alone, and that is that their news service shall never be tainted. There is no master hand of any governmental censorship, but there is a most exacting and jealous control of a highly sensitive body of intelligent editors with varying views upon every discussible subject, each one of whom has his voice and vote in the management of the institution. There is no pretence that the Associated Press is perfect, but it is believed to furnish the best-known method for giving to the American public an impartial service of news.

The four-years' struggle with the old United Press was waged over this principle. Victor F. Lawson of the Chicago *Daily News*, Charles W. Knapp of the St. Louis *Republic*, Frederick Driscoll of the St. Paul *Pioneer Press*, Frank B. Noyes of the Washington *Evening Star*, and those associated with them in that contest, deserve the lasting gratitude of the American people for having established, at a vast cost of time, labour, and money, a method of news gathering and distribution free from a chance of contamination.

The Associated Press is several times greater in magnitude and in the importance of its work than any other like institution in the world. It furnishes more than one half of the news the American newspapers print, and its despatches appear in journals having an aggregate issue of over 20,000,000 copies a day. If the recognized formula of three readers for each copy be accepted, it is evident that its telegrams are read by more than one half of the people of the nation. How wide is the influence exercised by this service in a land where readers demand the facts only and form their own judgment, none may estimate. The Association certainly plays a most important part in our national life. Yet, if one may judge from inquiries that come to the general office, it is little understood either by editors or readers.

The world at large is divided, for the purpose of news gathering, among four great agencies. The Reuter Telegram Company, Ltd., of London, gathers and distributes news in Great Britain and all her colonies, China, Japan, and Egypt. The Continental Telegraphen Gesellschaft of Berlin, popularly known as the Wolff Agency, performs a like office in the Teutonic, Slav, and Scandinavian countries; and the Agence Havas of Paris operates in the Latin nations. The field of the Associated Press includes the United States, the Hawaiian Islands, the Philippines, and Central America, as well as the islands of the Caribbean Sea. Each of these agencies has a representative in the offices of the others. Thus the Associated Press bureau in London adjoins the Reuter offices. The telegrams to the Reuter company are written on manifold sheets by the telegraph and cable companies, and copies are served simultaneously to the Associated Press bureau, the Wolff representative, the Havas men, and the Reuter people. A like arrangement obtains in Paris, Berlin, and New York, so that in each of these cities the whole panorama of the day's happenings passes under the eyes of representatives of each of the four agencies.

But the scheme is much more elaborate than this arrangement would indicate. Operating as tributary to the great agencies are a host of minor agencies—virtually one such smaller agency for each of the nations of importance. Thus in Italy the Stefani Agency, with headquarters in Rome, gathers and distributes the news of Italy. It is the official agency, and to it the authorities give exclusively all governmental information. It is controlled by Italians, but a large minority of its shares are owned by the Agence Havas of Paris, and it operates in close alliance with the latter organization.

Thus, if a fire should break out in Milan, the *Secolo*, the leading newspaper of that city, would instantly telegraph a report of it to the Stefani Agency at Rome. Thence it would be telegraphed to all of the other Italian papers, and copies of the *Secolo's* message would also be handed to the representatives, in the Stefani headquarters, of the Reuter, Wolff, Havas, and the Associated Press agencies.

In like fashion, if a fire should happen in Chicago, the Associated Press would receive its report, transmit it to the American papers, and furnish copies to the representatives of the foreign agencies stationed in the New York office of the Associated Press.

Of the minor agencies the most important are the Fabri Agency of Madrid, the Norsky Agency of Christiania, the Swiss Agency of Berne, and the Svensky Agency of Stockholm.

But the Associated Press is not content to depend wholly upon these official agencies. It maintains its own bureaus in all the important capitals, and reports the more prominent events by its own men, who are Americans and familiar with American newspaper methods. These foreign representatives are drawn from the ablest men in the service, and the offices they fill are obviously of great responsibility. They must be qualified by long training in the journalistic profession, by familiarity with a number of languages, and by a presence and a bearing which will enable them to mingle with men of the highest station in the countries to which they are accredited.

Thus, with its alliances with the great foreign agencies covering every point of the habitable globe, with its own city, with special commissioners to report events of great moment, with the correspondents and reporters of virtually all of the newspapers of the world laid under contribution, and with official recognition in a number of countries, the Associated Press is able to comb the earth for every happening of interest, and to present it to the newspaper reader with almost incredible speed.

Within the limits of the United States the task was a comparatively easy one. Here men of the required character were obtainable. It was necessary to select them with care and to drill them to promptness, scrupulous accuracy, impartiality, and a graphic style. So widespread is American education that it was soon discovered that the best men could usually be found in the villages and the smaller cities. They were more sincere, better informed, and less "bumptious" than the journalistic Garçons so frequently employed on the metropolitan press.

Presidential Years

"Presidential years" are always trying ones for the management. In 1896 the friends of Speaker Reed were incensed because we were unable to see that a majority of the delegates to the Republican National Convention were Reed men. Not that I think they really believed this; but everything is accounted fair in the game of politics, and they thought it would help their cause if the Associated Press would announce each delegation, on its selection, as for Reed. They appealed to me; but of course I could not misstate the facts, and they took great umbrage. The St. Louis Convention, when it assembled, verified our declarations, for Mr. Reed's vote was insignificant.

The national nominating conventions are our first care. Preparations begin months before they assemble. Rooms are engaged at all the leading hotels, so that Associated Press men may be in touch with every delegation. The plans of the convention hall are examined, and arrangements are made for operating-room and seats. The wires of the Association are carried into the building, and a work-room is usually located beneath the platform of the presiding officer. A private passage is cut, connecting this work-room with the reporters' chairs, which are placed directly in front of the stand occupied by speakers, and enclosed by a rail to prevent interference from the surging masses certain to congregate in the neighbourhood.

A week before the Convention opens a number of Associated Press men are on the ground to report the assembling of the delegates, to sound them as to their plans and preferences, and to indicate the trend of the gathering in their despatches as well as they may. The National Committee holds its meetings in advance of the Convention, decides upon a roll of members, and names a presiding officer. All this is significant, and is often equivalent to a determination of the party candidates.

Of the Convention itself, the Associated Press makes two distinct reports. A reporter sits in the hall and dictates to an operator, who sends out bulletins. These follow the events instantly, are necessarily very brief, and are often used by the newspapers to post on bulletin-boards. There is also a graphic running story of the proceedings. This is written by three men, seated together, each writing for ten minutes and then resting twenty. The copy is hastily edited by a fourth man, so that it may harmonize. This report is usually printed by afternoon papers. Finally, there is an elaborated report, which is printed by the large metropolitan dailies. A corps of expert stenographers, who take turns in the work, are employed. As a delegate rises in any part of the hall, one of these stenographers dashes to his side and reports his utterances. He then rushes to the work-room and dictates his notes to a rapid typewriter, while another stenographer replaces him on the convention floor. The nominating speeches are usually furnished by their authors weeks in advance, and are in type in the newspaper offices awaiting their delivery and release.

The men who report these conventions are drawn from all the principal offices of the Associated Press. Coming from different parts of the country, they are personally acquainted with a large majority of the delegates. There is a close division of labour—certain men are assigned to write bulletins; others to do descriptive work; still others to prepare introductory summaries; a number to watch and report the proceedings of secret committees; and a force of "scouts" are kept in close touch with the party leaders, and learn of projects the instant that they begin to mature. Out of it all comes a service which puts the newspaper reader of the country in instant and constant possession of every developing fact and gives him a pen-picture of every scene. Indeed, he has a better grasp of the situation than if he were present in the convention hall.

When the candidates are named and the platforms adopted the campaign opens, and for several months the Associated Press faces steadily increasing responsibilities. The greatest care is observed to maintain an attitude of strict impartiality, and yet to miss no fact of interest. If a candidate, or one of the great party leaders, names a "stumping journey," stenographers and descriptive writers must accompany him. As I have said, while Governor Hughes was "on tour," it was his practice to speak hurriedly from the rear platform of his train, and instantly to leave for the next appointment. While he was speaking the Associated Press stenographer was taking notes. When the train started, these notes were dictated to a typewriter, and at the next stopping-point were handed over to a waiting local Associated Press man, who put the speech on the telegraph wires. In the general offices records are kept of the number of words sent out, so that at the end of the campaign the volume of Republican and Democratic speeches reported is expected to balance.

Finally, the work of Election Day is mapped out in advance with scrupulous care, and each correspondent in the country has definite instructions as to the part he is to play. On Election Day brief bulletins on the condition of the weather in every part of the nation, and on the character of the voting, are furnished to the afternoon papers. The moment the polls close, the counting begins. Associated Press men everywhere are gathering precinct returns and hurrying them to county headquarters, where they are hastily added, and the totals for the county on Presidential electors are wired to the state headquarters of the Association The forces of men at these general offices are augmented by the employment of expert accountants and adding-machines from the local banks, and the labour is so subdivided that some years the result of the contest is announced by eight o'clock in the evening, and at midnight a return, virtually accurate, of the majority in every state presented to the newspapers.

Our Critics

If I were not what Mr. Gladstone once called "an old parliamentary hand," if I had not given and taken the buffets of aggressive American journalism for many years, and if Heaven had not blessed me with a certain measure of the saving grace of humour, I think I should have been sent to an early grave by the unreasonable and unfair attacks made upon my administration of the Associated Press news service. In the exciting Presidential campaign of 1896, Senator Jones, the Democratic national chairman, openly charged me with favouring the Republicans; while Mr. Hanna, his opponent, was at the point of breaking a long-time personal friendship because he regarded me as distinctly "pro-Bryan." The truth is, both men had lost their balance; neither was capable of a judicial view; each wanted, not an impartial service, but one that would only help his side. Fortunately, the candidates preserved a better poise than their lieutenants. At the close of the campaign both Bryan and McKinley wrote me that they were impressed with the impartiality that we had observed.

During a congressional inquiry a number of trade-unionists appeared and testified for days in denunciation of the Associated Press, because they conceived it to be unfriendly to their cause. Later, but with equal injustice, the secretary of the Citizens' Industrial Association was pelting me with letters charging our association with favouring organized labour.

When we reported the death of Pope Leo XIII in a manner befitting his exalted station, a number of Methodist newspapers gravely asserted that I was a Catholic, or controlled by Vatican influences, although, as a matter of fact, my father was a Methodist clergyman and my mother, as I have said, was the grandniece of a coadjutor of John Wesley. On the other hand, when the Associated Press reported the Marquise des Monstier's renunciation of the Catholic faith, certain Catholic newspapers flew into a rage and asserted that I was an anti-Catholic bigot.

The more frequent criticisms, however, result from want of knowledge of the true mission of the organization. Many persons, unfamiliar with newspaper methods, mistake special telegrams for Associated Press service, and hold us to an undeserved responsibility. Many others, having "axes to grind," and quite willing to pay for the grinding, find it difficult to believe that not only does the association do no grinding, but by the very nature of its methods such grinding is made impossible. The man who would pay the Associated Press for "booming" his project would be throwing his money away. Any man in the service of the association, from the general manager to the humblest employee, who should attempt to "boom" a project would be instantly discovered, disgraced, and dismissed.

Such is the process by which the Associated Press is writing history. Now it is an exhaustive review of the causes leading up to a war; again it is a scene painted in high lights to illumine the march of the world's progress. Here it is the first announcement of the negotiation of a treaty; there it is a thrilling interview with a refugee from Port Arthur, depicting all the horrors of a desperate and sanguinary campaign.

It seems hardly necessary to say that in all this work the Associated Press is writing the real and enduring history of the world, and is not chronicling the trivial episodes, the scandals, or the chit chat. And the searchlight that it throws upon the world's happenings has a substantial moral value. The mere collection and distribution of news has an ethical worth. No great and lasting wrong can be inflicted upon the sons of men anywhere so long as this fierce blaze of publicity is beating upon the scene. For, in the end, the world must know; and when the world knows, justice must be done. The most absolute and irresponsible authority must finally yield to the demands of a great public sentiment.

The assertion, often made, that the Associated Press is a monopoly rests upon the fact that its news service is available to a limited number only. There could be no pretense that it controls the information at the point of origin, or that it has any advantages or exclusive rights in respect to the manner of transmitting its news to those who publish it. At the point of origin, the news, in order that it be news at all, must be of such moment that everyone may have it if he chooses. None of the events reported by the Associated Press is a secret at the point of origin. The destruction of the *Maine* in Havana harbour, and the eruption that overwhelmed Saint Pierre, were known by everybody in Havana and Martinique, and the rates paid to cable companies for transmission to New York, or to the telegraph companies for the distribution of the news throughout the United States, are such as are open to any one. Any other association may gather, transmit, and distribute the news on equal terms. But A———, who is a member of the Associated Press, may receive and publish its news, while B———, who is not a member, may not. Does this make a monopoly? If so, it is unlike any other monopoly. It is the essence of the charge against other alleged monopolies that they are able to control the output of certain products or to ship it over quasi-public routes of transportation at rates not open to their competitors, or that by reason of some unfair advantage which they enjoy they are able unduly to advance prices to the consumer. None of these objections lies against the Associated Press. What, then, is the allegation? It is this: that by reason of the magnitude of its business it is able to deliver news to its members cheaper than a rival is able to, and that it will not admit to its membership everyone who applies.

The Supreme Court of Illinois, after mature deliberation, decided that news was a commodity of such high public need that any one dealing in it was charged with a public duty to furnish it to any other one demanding it and ready to pay the price. The Supreme Court of Missouri, in an equally well-considered opinion, held in effect that news gathering was a personal service, and to say that a public duty to serve everyone attached to the business was to say that any one—a lawyer, for instance—was obligated to give any information of which he was possessed to whomsoever might demand it.

Rivals of the Associated Press do exist, and do profess to furnish their members an equally valuable service. They have the same opportunity for securing the news at the points of origin, and are accorded precisely the same cable and telegraph tolls for its transmission. Their revenues are smaller, to be sure, and therefore their ability to cover the field is more restricted, their service less complete, and, naturally, since there are fewer to pay the bills, the cost to each is greater. But who, on reflection, can say that these facts constitute the Associated Press as unlawful monopoly?

The Associated Press is not perfect. Far from it! All of the frailties of human nature attach to it. Inerrancy is not possible in this blundering world of ours. But neither is the

Associated Press corrupt. It lives in the open. Its news service is published in millions of words every month. It wears its heart upon its sleeve. There are no secrets about it. There is no mystery concerning it. It is striving to tell the truth about the world's important happenings. It goes out into the world and with its many correspondents is atouch with things wherever human activities have play. It brings to you, by the processes of electricity, by telegraph and telephone, by cable and by wireless, everything of moment that goes to make up the history of the world, and you may read and profit by this information in a newspaper costing you two cents a copy. It is a propagandist of no opinion or activity however worthy. It rests down on the theory that in a self-governing nation the people must needs be capable of forming their own opinions, and it strives to give you the facts without the least hint that the thing done is right or wrong. It is:

> Not a ladder from earth to heaven,
> Not an altar of any creed,
> But a simple service simply given
> To our own kind in our common need.

Since the annual meeting of the Associated Press in April, 1918, I have been leading a post-epitaph life. There have been things to do, but in the main my duty has been to keep aloof from the management of the daily service, and thus to demonstrate that my associates were competent to do the work. And how they have succeeded! Nothing now gratifies me so much as the consciousness that the men with whom I have worked through all the years—officers, directors, and fellow-employees—still bear me in affectionate regard. They are all mindful that the standards set up in our co-service must be observed and are proud to contribute their share to that end.

THE END

PN 4874 .S7 A3 1970